LAW AND GLOBALIZATION

This book is an unprecedented attempt to
global movement for social justice. Case stu...
leading scholars from both the global South and the global ...
combine empirical research on the ground with innovative sociolegal theory
to shed new light on a wide array of topics. Among the issues examined are the
role of law and politics in the World Social Forum; the struggle of the anti-
sweatshop movement for the protection of international labour rights; and the
challenge to neoliberal globalization and liberal human rights raised by grassroots movements in India and indigenous peoples around the world. These
and other cases, the editors argue, signal the emergence of a subaltern cosmopolitan law and politics that calls for new social and legal theories capable of
capturing the potential and tensions of counter-hegemonic globalization.

BOAVENTURA DE SOUSA SANTOS is Professor of Sociology at the University
of Coimbra, Portugal; he is also a Distinguished Legal Scholar at the
University of Wisconsin-Madison Law School.

CÉSAR A. RODRÍGUEZ-GARAVITO is Assistant Professor of Law and
Sociology at the University of the Andes, Colombia, and Fellow of the
Institute for Legal Studies, University of Wisconsin, Madison.

Cambridge Studies in Law and Society aims to publish the best scholarly work on legal discourse and practice in its social and institutional contexts, combining theoretical insights and empirical research.

The fields that it covers are studies of law in action; the sociology of law; the anthropology of law; cultural studies of law, including the role of legal discourses in social formations; law and economics; law and politics; and studies of governance. The books consider all forms of legal discourse across societies, rather than being limited to lawyers' discourses alone.

The series editors come from a range of disciplines: academic law; socio-legal studies; sociology; and anthropology. All have been actively involved in teaching and writing about law in context.

Series Editors

Chris Arup
Victoria University, Melbourne
Martin Chanock
La Trobe University, Melbourne
Pat O'Malley
Carleton University, Ottawa
Sally Engle Merry
Wellesley College, Massachusetts
Susan Silbey
Massachusetts Institute of Technology

Books in the Series

The Politics of Truth and Reconciliation in South Africa
Legitimizing the Post-Apartheid State
Richard A. Wilson
0 521 80219 9 hardback
0 521 00194 3 paperback

Modernism and the Grounds of Law
Peter Fitzpatrick
0 521 80222 9 hardback
0 521 00253 2 paperback

Unemployment and Government
Genealogies of the Social
William Walters

The Paradox of Inclusion
Joel F. Handler
0 521 83370 1 hardback
0 521 54153 0 paperback

Law, Anthropology and the Constitution of the Social
Making Persons and Things
Edited by Alain Pottage and Martha Mundy
0 521 83178 4 hardback
0 521 53945 5 paperback

Judicial Review and Bureaucratic Impact
International and Interdisciplinary Perspectives
Edited by Marc Hertogh and Simon Halliday
0 521 83918 1 hardback
0 521 54786 5 paperback

Immigrants at the Margins
Law, Race, and Exclusion in Southern Europe
Kitty Calavita
0 521 84663 3 hardback
0 521 60912 7 paperback

Lawyers and Regulation
The Politics of the Administrative Process
Patrick Schmidt
0 521 84465 7 hardback

Law and Globalization from Below
Towards a Cosmopolitan Legality
Edited by Boaventura de Sousa Santos and César A. Rodríguez-Garavito
0 521 84540 8 hardback
0 521 60735 3 paperback

LAW AND GLOBALIZATION FROM BELOW

Towards a Cosmopolitan Legality

Edited by

Boaventura de Sousa Santos
University of Coimbra and University of Wisconsin-Madison

and

César A. Rodríguez-Garavito
University of the Andes and University of Wisconsin-Madison

CAMBRIDGE
UNIVERSITY PRESS

CAMBRIDGE UNIVERSITY PRESS
Cambridge, New York, Melbourne, Madrid, Cape Town, Singapore, São Paulo

CAMBRIDGE UNIVERSITY PRESS
The Edinburgh Building, Cambridge, CB2 2RU, UK

PUBLISHED IN THE UNITED STATES OF AMERICA BY CAMBRIDGE UNIVERSITY PRESS,
NEW YORK

www.cambridge.org
Information on this title: www.cambridge.org/9780521607353

First published 2005

Printed in the United Kingdom at the University Press, Cambridge

Typeface Goudy 11/13 pt.   3B2 *Advent* 8.07f [PND]

A catalogue record for this book is available from the British Library

ISBN-13 978-0-521-84540-3 hardback
ISBN-10 0-521-84540-8 hardback
ISBN-13 978-0-521-60735-3 paperback
ISBN-10 0-521-60735-3 paperback

Contents

Notes on the contributors

Fran Ansley is Distinguished Professor of Law at the University of Tennessee in Knoxville. Her goals are to study processes of globalization through local lenses in both the North and South, and to collaborate with grassroots groups in ways that move toward action in the world. Her work on globalization has appeared in numerous US law reviews and she has contributed chapters to *Laboring Below the Line*; *Women Working the NAFTA Food Chain*; *Neither Separate Nor Equal*; and *Hard Labor*.

Luis Carlos Arenas earned a JD from the National University of Colombia and an LLM from the University of Wisconsin-Madison. He worked for several years as a researcher and human rights activist at the Latin American Institute for Alternative Legal Services (ILSA). He is the Executive Director of the Wisconsin Coordinating Council on Nicaragua (WCCN), a non-profit, membership-supported organization based in Madison, Wisconsin, promoting social and economic justice in Nicaragua through alternative models of development and activism.

João Arriscado Nunes is Associate Professor of Sociology at the School of Economics, and researcher at the Center for Social Studies of the University of Coimbra, Portugal. His research interests include the social studies of science, political sociology, sociology of culture, globalization, and social theory. He is co-editor of *Reinventing Democracy: Grassroots Movements in Portugal* (special issue of *South European Society and Politics*, 2004), and *Enteados de Galileu? A Semiperiferia no Sistema Mundial da Ciência* (Afrontamento, 2001).

Susana Costa is a sociologist and a researcher at the Center for Social Studies of the University of Coimbra, Portugal. Her research interests include social studies of science, with a focus on the sociology of law and science and forensic medicine. She is the author of *A Justiça no Laboratório* (Coimbra, 2003), an ethnography of DNA profiling in criminal investigation in Portugal.

Peter P. Houtzager is a Fellow at the Institute of Development Studies, University of Sussex. He has taught at Stanford and St. Mary College in the United States. His work on the institutional roots of collective action has appeared in *Theory and Society*; *Comparative Studies in Society and History*; and the *Journal of Development Studies*. He is co-editor of *Changing Paths: International Development and the New Politics of Inclusion* (University of Michigan Press, 2003).

Heinz Klug is Professor of Law at the University of Wisconsin Law School and Honorary Senior Research Fellow at the Witwatersrand. He is Director of the Global Legal Studies Initiative at Wisconsin and formerly taught law at the University of the Witwatersrand. He served on the secretariat and was a staff member of the African National Congress Land Commission. He is the author of *Constituting Democracy: Law, Globalism and South Africa's Political Reconstruction* (Cambridge University Press, 2000).

Jane E. Larson is Voss-Bascom Professor of Law at the University of Wisconsin-Madison. She is the author of many articles on law and informality, as well as works addressing sexual regulation and its history. She is co-author of *Hard Bargains: The Politics of Sex* (Oxford University Press, 1998).

Marisa Matias is a sociologist and a researcher at the Center for Social Studies of the University of Coimbra, Portugal. Her research interests include the sociology of environment and public health, social studies of science, and public policy and participation. She has published on environmental conflicts and scientific controversies in Portugal and in Europe, especially in relation to waste management policies.

Marjorie Mbilinyi is a founding member of the Tanzania Gender Networking Programme (TGNP) and head of its Activism, Lobbying and Advocacy programme. She is a former Professor of Education at the University of Dar es Salaam, and is currently an activist and gender specialist, focusing on macro policy, agrarian and participatory democracy issues. She is co-editor of *Activist Voices* and *Against Neo-Liberalism* and *Food is Politics* (Institute of Development Studies, University of Dar es Salaam, 2002).

Chandrika Parmar is Adjunct Professor at the Mudra Institute for Communication in Ahmedabad, India. She was Associate Director of Programmes at the Centre for the Study of Developing Societies in Delhi. Her research interests center on the sociology of violence, cultures of knowledge, disasters, popular culture, and futures. She has published several articles on constitutional law and democracy, biotechnology, and environmental values. She is currently finishing a monograph on partition and a book on disasters.

José Manuel Pureza is Professor of International Relations and researcher at the Center for Social Studies at the University of Coimbra, Portugal. He has published numerous scholarly articles and book chapters on international law and human rights. He is the author of *Fogo sobre os media! Conhecimento, Informação e Crítica em Conflitos Armados* (Afrontamento, 2003), and *Património Comum da Humanidade: Rumo a um Direito Internacional da Solidariedade?* (Afrontamento, 1998).

Balakrishnan Rajagopal is the Ford International Assistant Professor of Law and Development and Director of the Program on Human Rights and Justice at the Massachusetts Institute of Technology. He served with the United Nations in Cambodia for many years as a human rights lawyer and has been a legal and human rights advisor to international and non-governmental organizations. He has published articles in leading law journals and is the author of

International Law from Below: Development, Social Movements, and Third World Resistance (Cambridge University Press, 2003).

César A. Rodríguez-Garavito is Assistant Professor of Law and Sociology at the University of the Andes (Colombia), and a Fellow at the Institute for Legal Studies, University of Wisconsin-Madison. He is a founding member of the Center for Law, Justice and Society (DJS), and editor of the journal *Beyond Law*, published by the Latin American Institute for Alternative Legal Services (ILSA). He has published scholarly articles and book chapters on law and society, political sociology, labor, development, and globalization. He is the author of *Globalization, Governance and Labor Rights* (ILSA, 2005), and co-editor of *Law and Society in Latin America* (ILSA, 2003) and *The New Latin American Left* (Norma, 2004).

Mary Rusimbi is a founding member and Executive Director of the Tanzania Gender Networking Programme (TGNP). She is an activist, adult educator, and gender specialist, focusing on macro policy issues, women's rights, and gender budget analysis. She is co-editor of *Activist Voices* and author of several articles in the same book and in *Against Neo-Liberalism* (TGNP and E&D Ltd, 2003).

Boaventura de Sousa Santos is Professor of Sociology at the School of Economics, University of Coimbra (Portugal), and Distinguished Legal Scholar at the University of Wisconsin-Madison Law School. He has published widely on globalization, sociology of law and the state, and epistemology. His books include *Toward a New Common Sense: Law, Science and Politics in the Paradigmatic Transition* (Routledge, 1995) and *Toward a New Legal Common Sense: Law, Globalization, and Emancipation* (Butterworths, 2002). He is the editor of *Democratizing Democracy: Beyond the Liberal Democratic Canon* and *Another Production is Possible: Beyond the Capitalist Canon* (Verso, 2005).

Ronen Shamir is Associate Professor of Sociology at Tel-Aviv University, Israel. He has published articles on the legal profession, legal history, legal pluralism, and corporate social responsibility and globalization, in leading sociolegal journals, including *Law and Society Review*; *Law and Social Inquiry*; and *Social and Legal Studies.* He is the author of *The Colonies of Law: Colonialism, Zionism and Law in Early Mandate Palestine* (Cambridge University Press, 2000) and *Managing Legal Uncertainty: Elite Lawyers in the New Deal* (Duke University Press, 1995).

Shiv Visvanathan is Professor at the Dhirubhai Ambani Institute of Information and Communication Technology in Ahmedabad, India. He is a former Senior Fellow at the Centre for the Study of Developing Societies, Delhi. His research interests center on cultures of knowledge, sociology and philosophy of science, history of technology, social movements, globalization, culture, and the politics of environmentalism. His books include *Organizing for Science* (Oxford University Press, 1985) and *Carnival for Science* (Oxford University Press, 1997).

CHAPTER 1

LAW, POLITICS, AND THE SUBALTERN IN COUNTER-HEGEMONIC GLOBALIZATION

Boaventura de Sousa Santos and *César A. Rodríguez-Garavito*

1.1 INTRODUCTION

This book arose from our puzzlement at the paradoxical state of socio-legal knowledge on globalization. The beginning of the new millennium has witnessed a groundswell of proposals for the transformation or replacement of the national and international legal institutions underpinning hegemonic, neoliberal globalization. Put forth by variegated counter-hegemonic movements and organizations and articulated through transnational networks, these proposals challenge our sociological and legal imagination and belie the fatalistic ideology that "there is no alternative" to neoliberal institutions.

The initiatives are as diverse as the organizations and networks advocating them, as the case studies in this book lay bare. Impoverished women in Tanzania as well as marginalized communities and progressive parties in Brazil mobilize to change and democratize the national and international regulatory frameworks that effectively exclude them from key political arenas such as the process of allocating public budgets (see Rusimbi and Mbilinyi's and Santos' chapters on participatory budgeting). NGOs, unions, consumers, workers, and other actors in the global North and South organize to challenge the market-friendly regulation of labor conditions, corporate accountability, intellectual property rights, and the environment which fuels the spread of sweatshops in the Americas, the African AIDS pandemic, and environmental degradation in Europe (see Rodríguez-Garavito's, Shamir's, Klug's, and Arriscado, Matias, and Costa's chapters).

Progressive activist-researchers, people of faith, and members of marginalized communities in the US – the "inner Third World" of laid-off industrial workers, migrants, and informal laborers – come together to collectively conceive cosmopolitan identities and legal rules in opposition to the exclusionary ideologies and laws of immigration (see Ansley's and Larson's chapters). Social movements involving some of the most marginalized classes in the global South – landless peasants, subsistence farmers, and indigenous peoples – strategically mobilize national courts and transnational advocacy networks (TANs) to assert their rights to the land, their culture, and the environment (see Houtzager's, Rajagopal's, Visvanathan and Parmar's, and Rodríguez-Garavito and Arenas' chapters). Articulated through now well-established regional and global mechanisms such as the World Social Forum (see Santos' chapter), these and myriad other initiatives have shown not only that "another world is possible," but have spurred an unprecedented effervescence of debate and experimentation in bottom-up legal reform and new international legal regimes (see Pureza's chapter).

Against the background of such fervent experimentation and institutional creativity at the grassroots level, the paradox lies in that theories and empirical studies on law and globalization have multiplied apace while missing almost entirely this most intellectually challenging and politically compelling aspect of globalization. Indeed, the existing literature draws on a rather conventional account of globalization and global legal transformations as top-down processes of diffusion of economic and legal models from the global North to the global South. Thus, the literature overwhelmingly focuses on the globalization of legal fields involving the most visible, hegemonic actors (whose visibility is thereby further enhanced) such as transnational corporations (TNCs) and Northern states. The result is a wide array of studies on such topics as the global spread of corporation-made *lex mercatoria* (Dezalay and Garth 1996; McBarnett 2002; Teubner 1997), the expansion of the interstate human rights regime and international law at large (Brysk 2002; Falk 1998; Falk, Ruiz, and Walker 2002; Likosky 2002), the exacerbation of legal pluralism brought about by the globalization of production and new communication technologies (Snyder 2002), and the export and import of rule of law and judicial reform programs (Carothers 1998; Dezalay and Garth 2002a; Rodríguez-Garavito 2001; Santos 2002).

Therefore, law and society studies have largely failed to register the growing grassroots contestation of the spread of neoliberal institutions and the formulation of alternative legal frameworks by TANs and the populations most harmed by hegemonic globalization. Thus, despite a strong tradition of studies on the use of law by domestic social movements (Handler 1978; McCann 1994; Scheingold 1974) and a growing literature on transnational social movements (Evans 2000; Keck and Sikkink 1998; Tarrow 2001), the role of law in counter-hegemonic globalization and the challenges that the latter poses to legal theory and practice have yet to be tackled.[1]

Aware that the diagnosis of the insufficiencies of this approach was shared by numerous social scientists and legal scholars based in or deeply involved with the South (either the global South or the "inner South" in the core countries), who have themselves been participants in the global justice movement, in 2000 we decided to launch a collaborative research network (CRN) on law and counter-hegemonic globalization. The CRN was meant to serve as a meeting and discussion space for scholars and scholars/activists from around the world engaged in critical sociolegal research and legal advocacy across borders. Emphasizing the participation of researchers and activists from the global South, it brought together a core group of participants (including several of the contributors to this volume) in meetings in Miami (2000), Budapest (2001), and Oxford (2001).[2] The group rapidly expanded as we took the project to the sites of our own work in Latin America, Africa, Europe, and the US. It thus became a broad, loose circle that partially overlapped with other networks of sociolegal research and transnational advocacy in which the CRN members were involved.

The effort to bridge the divides between South and North and between academic work and political engagement made the process of producing this book an exceptionally challenging and stimulating transnational endeavor. Further conversations and debates among contributors to this volume took place in such venues as the World Social Forum in Porto Alegre (2003, 2005) and Mumbai (2004), the Latin American Conference on Justice and Society organized by the Latin American Institute for Alternative Legal Services (ILSA) in Bogotá (2003), the International Conference on Law and Justice at the University of Coimbra (2003), and the Conference on Global Democracy

---

[1] Some exceptions that confirm the rule are studies on law and "globalization from below" such as Falk (1998), Rajagopal (2003), and Santos (1995, 2002).

[2] The Law and Society Association sponsored the Miami and Budapest meetings. The Oxford meeting took place by invitation from the Centre for Socio-Legal Studies. We are grateful to both for financial and logistical support that made the take-off of the CRN possible.

and the Search for Justice at the University of Sheffield (2003). Moreover, several of the case studies were written in the field as the authors worked closely with the movements, state agencies, and NGOs they analyze in their chapters. Thus, like the movements themselves, the contributors combined local engagement with transnational dialogue.

While the complications associated with this type of enterprise – from language barriers to the hectic pace of grassroots activism – made the editorial process all the more difficult, they also give this book its distinctive character. Indeed, in our view, the specific contribution of this volume and the common thread running through all its chapters lies in the particular, bottom-up perspective on law and globalization that it advances and empirically illustrates. This perspective has both an analytic and a political dimension. From an analytic viewpoint, it entails the detailed empirical study of legal orders as they operate on the ground. This includes not only the official law of courts and legislatures but also the myriad legal rules created and enforced by such disparate social actors as civil society organizations, corporations, and marginalized communities. This staple analytic strategy of sociolegal research tends to exhaust the meaning of the "bottom-up" approach in the US law and society tradition (see, for instance, Munger 1998). When applied to global social and legal processes, this research strategy calls for the type of approach that Marcus (1995) has dubbed "multi-sited ethnography": a combination of qualitative methods applied to the study of different locales that aims to examine the operation of global sociolegal processes shaping events in such sites.

To our mind, the bottom-up perspective illustrated by the case studies in this book also has a distinctly political dimension that goes hand in hand with its analytic counterpart. As we explain in more detail below, the purpose driving the analysis is to expose the potential and the limitations of law-centered strategies for the advancement of counter-hegemonic political struggles in the context of globalization. This entails amplifying the voice of those who have been victimized by neoliberal globalization, be they indigenous peoples, landless peasants, impoverished women, squatter settlers, sweatshop workers, or undocumented immigrants. Including those at the bottom, therefore, is a key part of our bottom-up approach. This is indeed how this approach is overwhelmingly understood in the global South, as the longstanding "alternative law" movement in Latin America (ILSA 1986; Lourdes Souza 2001; Santos 1991) and "social action litigation" in India (Baxi 1987) bear witness.

In the remainder of this introductory chapter, we further characterize this approach in three steps. First, in order to locate this book in the context of the literature on law and globalization, we look more closely into the dominant sociolegal approaches and inquire into the reasons why they have rendered invisible grassroots resistance to neoliberal institutions and initiatives for alternative legal forms. Secondly, we elaborate on the tenets of our bottom-up approach to law and globalization, which we call subaltern cosmopolitan legality. We argue that subaltern cosmopolitan legality is a mode of sociolegal theory and practice suitable to comprehend and further the mode of political thought and action embodied by counter-hegemonic globalization. Finally, we explain the selection of topics and the organization of the book. Throughout the chapter, we describe, as we go along, the case studies contained in the remainder of the book and point to the ways in which, in our view, they illustrate subaltern cosmopolitan legality in action.

1.2 BETWEEN GLOBAL GOVERNANCE AND GLOBAL HEGEMONY: THE INVISIBILITY OF COUNTER-HEGEMONY IN SOCIOLEGAL STUDIES

Two lines of research stand out among the growing number of empirically grounded studies of law in globalization. On the one hand, a copious literature on "global governance" has developed which inquires into the transformation of law in the face of eroding state power and the decentralization of economic activities across borders. Concerned with social engineering and institutional design, this approach focuses on non-state-centered forms of regulation allegedly capable of best governing the global economy. On the other hand, a post-law-and-development generation of students of international legal transplants has unveiled the power struggles and alliances between and within legal elites in the North and the South through which the hegemony of transnational capital and Northern states is reproduced. Contrary to the emphasis of the governance approach on successful institutional designs, hegemony theorists focus on the structural reasons that explain the *failure* of ostensibly progressive global legal designs (e.g. the export of the rule of law and human rights) and the reproduction of the legal elites who promote them.

These approaches can be seen as reverberations of time-honored traditions in sociolegal scholarship. The governance perspective echoes the US legal realists' and social pragmatists' concern with social engineering that inspired the first generation of law and development scholars and practitioners in the 1960s. However, as argued below, governance scholars have considerably moderated (if not abandoned) the reformist and oppositional political agenda that inspired their predecessors. Hegemony scholars, in turn, draw on a rich tradition of critical social theory of law – from Marx to Bourdieu and Foucault – to show the contribution of law to the resilience and pervasiveness of domination within and across borders. Nevertheless, as explained later on, in emphasizing the moment of hegemony they sideline the moment of counter-hegemony, which at least since Gramsci has been at the core of critical social theory.

In what follows we briefly examine these seemingly opposite approaches to set up the background against which we advance our own approach in the next section. We argue that, despite their radically different goals and theoretical roots, they share a top-down view of law, globalization, and politics that explains their failure to capture the dynamics of bottom-up resistance and legal innovation taking place around the world. We further argue that they produce the invisibility of counter-hegemonic politics and legality in different ways: while, in the governance paradigm, organized bottom-up resistance becomes irrelevant, in the global hegemony literature resistance is ineffectual at best and counterproductive at worst as it tends to further reproduce hegemony.

1.2.1 From regulation to governance: the irrelevance of counter-hegemony

A vast literature has developed over the last few years that theorizes and empirically studies novel forms of governing the economy that rely on collaboration among non-state actors (firms, civic organizations, NGOs, unions, and so on) rather than on top-down state regulation. The variety of labels under which social scientists and legal scholars have pursued this approach is indicative of both its ascendancy and its diversity: "responsive regulation" (Ayres and Braithwaite 1992), "post-regulatory law" (Teubner 1986), "soft law" (Snyder 1994; Trubek and Mosher 2003), "democratic experimentalism" (Dorf and Sabel 1998; Unger 1998), "collaborative governance" (Freeman 1997), "outsourced regulation" (O'Rourke 2003), or simply "governance" (MacNeil, Sargent, and Swan 2000; Nye and Donahue 2000).

Differences in labeling and content notwithstanding, these studies broadly share a diagnosis and a proposal for the solution of the regulatory dilemmas posed by globalization. According to the diagnosis, the "regulatory fracture" of the global economy stems from the divergence between law and current economic processes. Such divergence results from the different scales at which global economic activities and national states' regulations operate, and from the difficulties that national states face in applying their top-down regulatory logic to industries whose highly globalized system of production is based on a combination of market and network organizational logic.

From this viewpoint, the solution lies neither in the state nor in the market, but rather in a third type of organizational form – collaborative networks involving firms and secondary associations. By following a reflexive logic that fosters continuous dialogue and innovation, networks, it is argued, have the potential to overcome the regulatory dilemmas that markets (which follow the logic of exchange) and states (which follow the logic of command) cannot solve on their own.

Drawing to different degrees on pragmatist social theory, governance scholars have applied this insight to the analysis of institutions in a variety of fields and scales. Some examples are participatory school boards at the local level (Liebman and Sabel 2003), decentralized environmental regulation (Karkkainen 2002), mechanisms of regional regulatory coordination involving non-state actors (Zeitlin and Trubek 2003), and corporate codes of conduct to regulate labor conditions in global factories (Fung, O'Rourke, and Sabel 2001).

The governance approach to law and society rests on four theoretical claims derived from its pragmatist roots. First, interests are discursively formed rather than derived from actors' locations in the social field (Sabel 1994:139). Actors' definition of interests, goals, and means takes place during their engagement in the deliberative processes characteristic of pragmatist institutions of governance (participatory councils, developmental associations, and so on) (Dorf and Sabel 1998:285). Secondly, gains in economic and political efficiency result from the use of local knowledge. Thus, decentralizing and democratizing institutions are needed to devolve decision-making authority to the local scale and to involve all the relevant "stakeholders." Thirdly, asymmetries of power among societal actors are not so profound as to impede the type of horizontal collaboration envisaged by pragmatist governance (Dorf and Sabel 1998:410). The bargaining disadvantages of the have-nots are not insurmountable, politics is an uncertain and open-ended game, and the results of deliberation are not predetermined by differences in resources among participants. Therefore, against "liberal legalism," sociolegal scholars contributing to this approach reject structuralist conceptions of power as well as "populist views" of law and society that draw a stark contrast between powerful actors (e.g. corporations) and powerless "victims" (e.g. unions, the poor, etc.) (Simon 2003:5). Fourthly, in line with its conception of interests and power, this approach explicitly shies away from any discussion of the preconditions – namely, redistribution of resources to counter power asymmetries among "stakeholders" – that would be necessary for collaborative governance to work. Given that the limits of "interests, values or institutions . . . can always become the starting point of their redefinition" (Sabel 1994:158) through deliberative processes, the conditions for the success of governance are contingent upon the particularities of each social context.

This is not the place to undertake a detailed critical analysis of the governance approach as applied to the regulation of the global economy.[3] In light of the specific purpose of this chapter, our chief concern is with the contributions and failures of the approach with regard to the task of studying and valuing the potential of experiences in counter-hegemonic legality of the type documented in this book. In this sense, contributors to the governance debate within legal academia must be given credit for having steered discussions away from the obsession of legal doctrine with ever more sophisticated criteria for separating law and politics. Indeed, they have cogently reconceived "legal analysis as institutional imagination" (Unger 1996:25), thus reconnecting legal and sociolegal scholarship with the political debates of our time, including those on globalization.

However, the kind of political action envisaged by the governance approach is a far cry from that of counter-hegemonic globalization. Given its conception of power and its focus on problem solving, the governance approach tends to bracket deep power asymmetries among actors (for instance, those between capital and labor in global code of conduct systems) and to view the public sphere as a rather depoliticized arena of collaboration among generic "stakeholders" (see Rodríguez-Garavito 2005). In contrast to critical theories of law that view contentious collective action by the excluded as a political requisite for the attainment of meaningful legal transformations, "the Pragmatist . . . relies on 'bootstrapping' – the bracketing of self-interest and distributive claims in order to focus attention on common interests and values," thus explicitly rejecting the "victim's perspective"

---

[3] See Rodríguez-Garavito (2005) and Chapter 2 by Santos.

(Simon 2003:26) that is central to subaltern cosmopolitan politics and legality.

As a result, the governance perspective's telling call for participatory exercises in institutional imagination lacks a theory of political agency suited to the task. By default or by design, those doing the imagining are the elites or members of the middle-class with the economic and cultural capital to count as "stakeholders." Either way, the process is a top-down one in which those at the bottom are either incorporated only once the institutional blueprint has been fully laid out or are not incorporated at all. The post hoc inclusion of the excluded is illustrated by Unger's otherwise powerful theory of democratic experimentalism: "if social alliances need institutional innovations to be sustained, institutional innovations do not require preexisting social alliances. All they demand are party-political agents and institutional programs, having those class or group alliances as a project – as a project rather than as a premise" (1996:137). The exclusion of those at the bottom from governance schemes is candidly acknowledged by Simon: "pragmatist initiatives are likely to by-pass the most desperate and the most deviant. Pragmatism supposes a measure of mutual accountability and engagement that may not be attractive to or possible for everyone" (2003:23).

As it turns out, in the context of neoliberal globalization, the most desperate and marginalized – those living in poverty and excluded from the benefits of social citizenship due to class, gender, racial, or ethnic oppression – account for the immense majority of the world population. The challenge of institutional imagination, therefore, cannot be met but by privileging the excluded as actors and beneficiaries of new forms of global politics and legality. This is the strategy of counter-hegemonic globalization and its legal counterpart, subaltern cosmopolitan legality.

1.2.2 Global hegemony and the law: the futility of resistance

With theoretical tools and practical goals that stand in stark contrast with those of the governance literature, sociolegal analysts of the role of law in hegemonic globalization have made a provocative contribution to the debate. The merits of this approach are twofold. First, by combining the insights of neo-institutional and reflexive sociology, scholars in this tradition have dug into the origins of global legal designs (from international arbitration to the rule of law and judicial reform) that provide neoliberal globalization with political and scientific legitimacy. This genealogical expedition has unearthed the hierarchies, power struggles, and tactical moves through which hegemonic institutions are produced and reproduced, and through which non-elite actors are systematically excluded.

Secondly, analysts of global hegemony have made a methodological contribution by following across borders the actors of the processes of exportation and importation of legal models. The results are empirically grounded accounts of the complex transnational mechanisms whereby elite lawyers and economists in the North and the South, NGOs, US foundations, state officials, and transnational economic elites have interacted to spread "new legal orthodoxies" around the world – from the ideologies of monetarism and law and economics to human rights and judicial reform projects in Latin America (Dezalay and Garth 2002a) to global commercial arbitration (Dezalay and Garth 1996).

For the present purposes, what is particularly relevant about this line of work are its epistemological tenets and its conception of hegemony, which stand in explicit contrast with those of subaltern cosmopolitan legality. Studies of global legal hegemony aim at a "more realist understanding of the production of the new international economic and political order" (Dezalay and Garth 2002b:315). Such a realist perspective is explicitly built on a twofold critique of approaches such as ours that seek to expose and underscore the potential of counter-hegemonic forms of political and legal action. On the one hand, it draws a sharp (and, as we will see, problematic) distinction between description and prescription and confines proper scholarship to the former. On the other hand, it is keen on highlighting the links between hegemonic and counter-hegemonic actors – for instance, between philanthropic foundations in the North and human rights organizations in the South – as well as tensions and contradictions within transnational activist coalitions. From this viewpoint, such links and tensions reveal that, far from "happily coexisting in this effort to work together to produce new and emancipatory global norms" (Dezalay and Garth 2002b:318), NGOs and other actors of counter-hegemonic globalization are part and parcel of the elites benefiting from neoliberal globalization and thus contribute to the construction of new global orthodoxies through programs to export US legal institutions and expertise.

We offer a response to these criticisms in laying out the epistemological and political tenets of subaltern cosmopolitan legality in the next section. For the purposes of this section, a brief discussion of the limitations and tensions of the hegemony approach is in order.

First, despite its call for realist descriptions, the reality grasped with its analytical lenses is a highly partial one. Since its entry point of choice into global legal processes is the world of transnational elites, the description it offers is as revealing as it is limited. Missing from this top-down picture are the myriad local, non-English-speaking actors – from grassroots organizations to community leaders – who, albeit oftentimes working in alliance with transnational NGOs and progressive elites, mobilize popular resistance to neoliberal legality while remaining as local as ever. From Bolivian peasants resisting the privatization of water services to indigenous peoples around the world resisting corporate biopiracy, these subaltern actors are a critical part of processes whereby global legal rules are defined, as the current contestation over the regulation of water provision and property rights on traditional knowledge bear witness (Rajagopal 2003).

Secondly, the analysis misses differences among sectors of the elites that are as real as the links among them. Conflating international human rights lawyers risking their lives on the job with transnational corporate lawyers making a fortune attains analytical bite at the cost of descriptive oversimplification. While lawyers and activists participating in TANs benefit from transnational connections and support, they advance agendas that stand in explicit contrast with those of hegemonic actors. As several of the chapters in this book show, this makes for a radically different type of legal practice and political engagement than those of corporate consultants. Witness, for instance, the hardships of grassroots legal advocacy against patriarchal neoliberal institutions in Tanzania described in Rusimbi and Mbilinyi's chapter, or the perils of straddling the line between legality and illegality in Houtzager's chapter on the landless peasants' movement in Brazil. This does not mean that counter-hegemonic coalitions are devoid of tensions, or that subaltern legal strategies are always productive. Indeed, several chapters explore these tensions and limitations (see, for instance, Shamir's contribution on corporate cooptation of some NGOs, and Rajagopal's chapter on the limits of law in counter-hegemonic globalization). Such tensions, however, do not obliterate the distinction between hegemonic and counter-hegemonic globalization, which is clear to practitioners in either camp. Therefore, in addition to a description of global structural constraints and the workings of hegemonic legal discourses and practices, we need an analysis of spaces for and strategies of counter-hegemony.

Thirdly, this partial picture, far from being a non-prescriptive description, has a normative connotation. Collapsing highly diverse actors and organizations into a generic category of elites and very different agendas into a catch-all category of global orthodoxies yields a politically demobilizing picture of law and globalization. If hegemonic structures and discourses are so pervasive as to absorb and dilute counter-hegemonic strategies (which renders the latter undistinguishable from what they oppose), we are left with a deterministic image of globalization in which there is virtually no space for resistance and change. Resistance goes on happening and alternatives continue to arise nonetheless. To take some examples from the following chapters, corporate dominance of the global regulation of intellectual property rights and labor have not prevented activists, human rights lawyers, workers, and marginalized communities in South Africa and the Americas from successfully pushing for new legal frameworks allowing the production of affordable antiretroviral drugs for AIDS patients and fighting sweatshop conditions in global factories (see Klug's and Rodríguez-Garavito's chapters). The fact that these counter-hegemonic coalitions aim to substitute such solidaristic, cosmopolitan legal frameworks for the existing corporate-friendly laws means that they indeed seek to establish a new legal hegemony (in the Gramscian sense of a new common sense) or "global legal orthodoxy." But it hardly needs explaining that the effects of this new hegemony on the lives and livelihoods of the marginalized majorities of the world would be radically different from those of currently dominant regulations.

In sum, in addition to hegemony theories that explain why global legal structures are as they are, we need sociolegal approaches capable of telling why and how they change. This entails turning our analytic gaze to plural forms of resistance and embryonic legal alternatives arising from the bottom the world over. This is the goal of subaltern cosmopolitan legality, to which we now turn.

1.3 SUBALTERN COSMOPOLITAN LEGALITY

In critically engaging with sociolegal research on globalization in the previous section, we touched upon the core elements of subaltern cosmopolitan legality, the perspective that informed the dialogue leading to this volume. In this section we gather together and elaborate on those elements to lay out the claims of our approach.[4] We speak of

---

[4] For a detailed discussion of the concept of subaltern cosmopolitan legality, which served as a common reference point in the dialogue among contributors to this volume, see Santos (2002:Chapter 9).

subaltern cosmopolitan legality as a perspective or an approach rather than as a theory for several reasons. To our mind, the plurality of efforts at counter-hegemonic globalization cannot be encompassed by an overarching theory. Rather, the scholarly task consists in providing analytical clarity and translation devices to make such efforts mutually intelligible. Further, the potential contribution of our approach lies in its distinctive bottom-up perspective as explained above, rather than in a set of fixed substantive claims. Finally, the chapters in this volume – which are inspired by different theoretical perspectives and tackle diverse topics – cannot be subsumed in a rigid general framework. Still, since they originated from a collaborative research project that explicitly engaged with subaltern cosmopolitan legality, a further characterization of this approach is in order to lay bare some of the traits that we believe are shared by the case studies in this volume. We undertake this task by first looking into the meaning and viewpoint of subaltern cosmopolitan legality and then spelling out its epistemological tenets and analytical instruments.

1.3.1 The subaltern, the cosmopolitan, and the legal

Cosmopolitan projects have a long and ambiguous history anchored in Western modernity. In opposition to global designs aimed to manage the world – from colonial Christianity in the sixteenth century to nineteenth-century imperialism to contemporary neoliberal/military globalization – cosmopolitanism has vindicated the basic moral claim that "neither nationality nor state boundaries, as such, have moral standing with respect to questions of justice" (Satz 1999:67). Thus, cosmopolitanism – be it in the form of the Enlightenment's human rights doctrines, anti-colonialism, or contemporary transnational social movements – entails counter-hegemonic projects seeking to subvert interstate hierarchies and borders (Santos 1995:263). As Mignolo has put it, cosmopolitanism "is a set of projects toward planetary conviviality" (2002:157). Such convivial sociability focuses on conversations among places whereby people in disparate geographic and cultural locations understand and welcome their differences while striving to pursue joint endeavors (Appiah 2003; Santos 2002:460).

More often than not, however, cosmopolitan political and legal projects have been as Western- or Northern-centric and exclusionary as the global designs they oppose. For instance, human rights institutions and doctrines, with their Western roots and liberal bent, have oftentimes been blind to non-Western conceptions of human dignity and collective rights that hold out the prospect for an expanded, cosmopolitan conception of rights (Mutua 1996; Rajagopal 2003). This is the case, for instance, of indigenous peoples' oppositional understanding of property rights as collective entitlements subordinated to the imperative of environmental and cultural preservation (see Rodríguez-Garavito and Arenas' chapter).

Instead of discarding cosmopolitanism as just one more variety of global hegemony, we propose to revise the concept by shifting the focus of attention to those who currently need it. Who needs cosmopolitanism? The answer is straightforward: whoever is a victim of local intolerance and discrimination needs cross-border tolerance and support; whoever lives in misery in a world of wealth needs cosmopolitan solidarity; whoever is a non- or second-class citizen of a country or the world needs an alternative conception of national and global citizenship. In short, the large majority of the world's populace, excluded from top-down cosmopolitan projects, needs a different type of cosmopolitanism. Subaltern cosmopolitanism, with its emphasis on social inclusion, is therefore of an oppositional variety (Santos 2002:460).

Providing the intellectual and experiential foundations of this oppositional stance is a shift of perspective from which global processes are analyzed and evaluated. Post-colonial scholars have variously theorized this move as a shift to a view from the experience of the victims, in the terms proposed by Dussel (1998); a new perspective from the exterior of Western modernity, in the terms of Mignolo (2002); or a view from the reality of coloniality of power, in Quijano's (2000). In our own terms, we conceive this change of perspective as one that shifts from the North to the South, with the South expressing not a geographical location but all forms of subordination (economic exploitation; gender, racial, and ethic oppression; and so on) associated with neoliberal globalization. The South, in short, denotes the forms of suffering caused by global capitalism. In this sense, the South is unevenly spread throughout the world, including the North and the West (Santos 1995:507). In inquiring into globalization from the point of view of the lived experiences of the South, therefore, subaltern cosmopolitanism takes the perspective of what Dussel (1998) has aptly called "the community of the victims."

The victims in this transnational community of suffering, however, are not passive, nor is the separation between the South and the North a static one. The perspective of subaltern cosmopolitan studies of globalization aims to empirically document experiences of resistance, assess their potential to subvert hegemonic institutions and ideologies, and learn from their capacity to offer alternatives to the latter.

In the specific realm of legal knowledge and practice, subaltern cosmopolitanism translates into the bottom-up approach to the study of law in globalization described above. In line with its analytical focus on detailed case studies of counter-hegemonic legal forms and its goal of furthering the potential of the latter, subaltern cosmopolitanism calls for a conception of the legal field suitable for reconnecting law and politics and reimagining legal institutions from below. This involves several tasks that stand in contrast to those privileged by existing approaches to the study of law in globalization. First, it entails inquiring into the combination of legal and illegal (as well as non-legal) strategies through which transnational and local movements advance their causes. Rallies, strikes, consumer boycotts, civil disobedience, and other forms of (oftentimes illegal) direct action are part and parcel of counter-hegemonic movements that simultaneously pursue institutional avenues such as litigation and lobbying. This is clear, for instance, in Larson's chapter on squatter settlements (*colonias*) in Texas, where marginalized immigrant communities have imaginatively straddled the border between legality and illegality and challenged the state to conceive a hybrid approach to regulation that implies a gradual enforcement of the law suited to their realities and housing needs. Another eloquent example of the relation between legal, illegal, and non-legal strategies is the combination of land occupation and litigation by the landless peasants' movement (MST) in Brazil analyzed in Houtzager's chapter, which goes a long way to explaining the success and endurance of the movement in the face of stiff resistance from large landowners. Similarly, the participatory budgeting process of Porto Alegre (Brazil), which has become an icon of progressive institutional reform, remains an informal arrangement not codified by state law. As discussed in Santos' chapter on the matter, this non-legal character, together with continuous political support, helps explain the success and flexibility of this mechanism of participatory democracy.

Secondly, with regard to the long-standing sociolegal debate on the politics of rights (Rosenberg 1991; Scheingold 1974), subaltern cosmopolitan legality seeks to expand the legal canon beyond individual rights and focuses on the importance of political mobilization for the success of rights-centered strategies. The emphasis on the expansion of the range of rights does not mean the abandonment of individual rights. Indeed, individual rights are a central part of subaltern cosmopolitan legality in the current context of unilateral militarism at the global scale and repressive neoliberalism (with its attendant trends toward coercive control of marginalized populations) at the national and local scales (Wacquant 2004). However, experiments in subaltern cosmopolitan legality also seek to articulate new notions of rights that go beyond the liberal ideal of individual autonomy, and incorporate solidaristic understandings of entitlements grounded on alternative forms of legal knowledge. This is evident, for instance, in the multifarious grassroots struggles for the collective rights to the commons, culture, land, and traditional knowledge in India that Visvanathan and Parmar study in their chapter.

Further, regardless of the type of rights in question, subaltern cosmopolitan legality highlights the centrality of sustained political mobilization for the success of grassroots legal strategies. Given the deep power asymmetries between hegemonic and counter-hegemonic actors, only through collective action can the latter muster the type of countervailing power necessary to bring about sustained legal change. Thus, contrary to the depoliticized view of law of the governance approach, subaltern cosmopolitan legality views law and rights as elements of struggles that need to be politicized before they are legalized. This relation between politics and law is at work, for instance, in the political movement for affordable antiretroviral drugs in South Africa which eventually was taken to the national courts (see Klug's chapter), as well as in the national and transnational movement against the construction of the Narmada dam in India, which only at a later phase and after much debate within the movement was brought before the Indian Supreme Court (see Rajagopal's chapter).

Thirdly, subaltern cosmopolitan legality operates by definition across scales. Social movements and TANs embodying this approach pragmatically resort to political and legal tools at every scale. Also, by mobilizing state and non-state legal orders, they exploit the opportunities offered by an increasingly plural legal landscape. For instance, Arriscado, Matias and Costa's chapter discusses the combination of local, national, and regional legal strategies through which Portuguese communities have sought to protect their right to a clean environment by creatively exploiting the tensions between Portuguese laws and European directives and regulations. Also, in the struggle against exploitative conditions at the Kukdong factory in Mexico studied in Rodríguez-Garavito's chapter, members of the transnational anti-sweatshop coalition simultaneously mobilized local courts, threatened to bring the case before the NAFTA panel on labor rights, and targeted, on a global scale, the image of the brands for which the factory produced collegiate apparel.

1.3.2 The epistemology of subaltern cosmopolitan legality: the sociology of emergence

For all their accomplishments, the experiences analyzed in this book are admittedly fragile. Going against entrenched and powerful interests, ideologies, and institutions that are hegemonic precisely because they are seen as commonsensical, experiments in counter-hegemonic uses of law are in constant danger of cooptation and obliteration. Contrary to what the criticisms of theorists of global legal hegemony would suggest, actors and analysts of subaltern cosmopolitan legality are only too aware of these tensions.

With full consciousness of such limitations – and precisely because of them – theorists and practitioners of subaltern cosmopolitan legality take it upon themselves to interpret these embryonic experiences in a prospective spirit that can be called the sociology of emergence (Santos 2002:465; 2004). This entails interpreting in an expansive way the initiatives, movements, and organizations that resist neoliberal globalization and offer alternatives to it. The traits of the struggles are amplified so as to render visible and credible the potential that lies implicit or remains embryonic in the experiences under examination. This symbolic blow-up seeks to expose and underscore the signals, clues, or traces of future possibilities embedded in nascent or marginalized legal practices or knowledge. The contribution of this approach is to allow us to identify emerging qualities and entities at a moment in which they can be easily discarded (and are indeed discarded by hegemonic actors and mainstream social science) as idealistic, hopeless, insignificant, or past-oriented.

The sociology of emergence, as with all critical theories, is rooted in an enriched conception of reality and realism. The point of departure of critical theory is the statement that reality cannot be reduced to what exists. From this point of view, a realist analysis is one that offers, together with an exploration of what is real and what is necessary, a prospective account of what is possible. The sociology of emergence thus avoids the discrediting of budding options brought about by structuralist conceptions of global legal hegemony as well as by the disenchanted and celebratory views of hyper-deconstructive postmodern legal analysis.

In starting "from where we are" – i.e. from the available options, no matter how incipient they may be – subaltern cosmopolitan legality follows the path of counter-hegemonic struggles first theorized by Gramsci (1971). As in Gramsci, counter-hegemonic politics and legality aim to erode the ideology and coercive institutions that sustain and naturalize the hegemony of dominant classes and groups (1971:12). This vital deconstructive task is illustrated by the trenchant critique of regulations and discourses of corporate social responsibility offered by Shamir in his chapter, as well as in Visvanathan and Parmar's critique of dominant understandings of economic development and constitutional rights in India. Counter-hegemonic politics and subaltern cosmopolitan legality, however, go beyond this deconstructive phase. Indeed, they ultimately seek to offer new understandings and practices capable of replacing the dominant ones and thus of offering a new common sense (Hunt 1993). Driving the undocumented immigrants' struggles analyzed in Ansley's chapter, for instance, is not only a critique of xenophobic views of immigration in the US, but also a nascent conception and institutional framework of global citizenship. Similarly, behind the rise of international legal regimes of crimes against humanity and the common heritage of humankind studied by Pureza in his chapter lies a radically reconceived, solidaristic understanding of international relations and international law. Finally, behind the experience of participatory budgeting in Tanzania and Brazil documented by Mbilinyi, Rusimbi, and Santos is both a critique of dominant conceptions of low-intensity, representative democracy and an ambitious proposal for the radicalization of political and economic democracy.

1.4 TOPICS AND ORGANIZATION OF THE BOOK

Out of the immense variety of movements and experiences in counter-hegemonic globalization, we chose to focus on three thematic areas in which the confrontation between hegemonic and counter-hegemonic actors over the content and the scale of law is particularly acute: (1) the construction of a global economy of solidarity; (2) the struggle to reform the international human rights regime in a cosmopolitan, bottom-up, and multicultural direction; and (3) the radicalization of democratic politics through new forms of participatory democracy.

We close this introductory chapter by briefly presenting these topics and the case studies on each of them.

1.4.1 Law and the construction of a global economy of solidarity

Over the last few years, legal scholars, activists, government representatives, and other actors have been debating innovative ways of regulating the global economy based on principles of solidarity and environmental sustainability rather than profit maximization. Among the signs of the emergence of a "solidarity economy" and a cosmopolitan economic law are myriad proposals to protect labor rights in the face of changing economic conditions associated with globalization – from initiatives to include social clauses in free trade agreements to experiments in monitoring the implementation of corporate codes of conduct concerning labor in factories producing for TNCs – the rise of a system of "fair trade" supported by legal agreements between corporations in the North and governments and local producers in the South, the inclusion of effective clauses for the protection of the environment in trade agreements, initiatives aimed at eroding the exclusionary economic and social regulations that prevent unskilled workers from gaining the status of legal immigrants, and recent legal challenges by states in the South (e.g. South Africa, Brazil, and India) against global intellectual property rights systems that deprive most of the world's population of access to basic medicines.

The chapters in the first part of the book tackle several of these issues. Based on an examination of the World Social Forum (WSF) as the most prominent site of articulation of proposals for a global economy of solidarity, Boaventura de Sousa Santos contrasts the counterhegemonic legality embodied by the WSF (subaltern cosmopolitan legality) with that of neoliberal globalization ("global governance"). César A. Rodríguez-Garavito analyzes the struggle over international labor rights pitting TNCs against cross-border anti-sweatshop coalitions. Focusing on the Americas, he illustrates such a struggle with a case study of the campaign for the unionization of workers at Kukdong, a global apparel factory in Mexico. The chapter by Ronen Shamir also examines the issue of the regulation of TNCs, but looks more broadly into the construction of the field of "corporate social responsibility." By carefully dissecting social responsibility discourse and practice, he offers a critical view of strategies aimed to create corporate-friendly regimes of voluntary regulation. Heinz Klug analyzes the clash between the neoliberal intellectual property rights regime (as embodied by the

WTO's TRIPS agreement) and the right to affordable medicines. He illustrates the legal and political issues involved in this struggle with a vivid account of the effort by South African social movements and the state to guarantee access to antiretroviral medicines to the victims of the pandemic in that country. Moving from the global South to the "inner South" in the North, Jane Larson looks into the gray zone, between legality and illegality, that new migrants in the US have exploited to build informal housing settlements as an economic survival strategy. Based on her work in such *colonias* in Texas, she offers a proposal for a regulatory strategy that imaginatively protects the migrants' right to housing. In closing this part of the volume, Fran Ansley examines grassroots efforts to put in contact the global South and the North's inner South. She offers first-hand accounts of worker exchanges between the US and Mexico, anti-NAFTA activism, and solidarity campaigns for migrants' right to a driver's license in Tennessee which aptly illustrate both the potential and the difficulties and tensions of subaltern coalitions seeking to establish solidaristic legal frameworks and forms of economic exchange.

1.4.2 Transnational social movements and the reconstruction of human rights

Albeit a quintessential cosmopolitan legal and political project, the construction of an international system of human rights has been weakened by its aforementioned Western- and state-centric biases. Thus, while acknowledging the importance of the existing international legal framework for the protection of civil, political, socioeconomic, and collective rights, the global movement for social justice has challenged some of its substantive and procedural tenets. The indigenous movement has called for a multicultural reconstruction of human rights so as to counter the liberal and individualist bias of the latter and incorporate alternative understandings of rights based on collective entitlements and the inclusion of nature as a subject of rights. Grassroots movements and civil society organizations have contested the traditional status of the state as the sole actor in processes of construction and enforcement of international human rights regimes. The international feminist movement has effectively denounced the patriarchal character of the human rights tradition and pushed forward new legal instruments and conceptions of rights embodying gender justice. Other organizations and movements have continued to challenge the separation between "generations" of human rights and strived to articulate struggles for civil and political rights, on the one hand, with efforts to protect socioeconomic and collective rights, on the other. These and other pressures largely account for the ongoing reconfiguration of human rights in the direction of gender, ethnic, racial, and economic justice.

The chapters in the second part of the volume document several such challenges in different parts of the world. Balakrishnan Rajagopal analyzes the role of law in the well-known national and transnational movement to protect the rights of families affected by the Indian government's plan to construct dams along the Narmada River. Focusing on the role of the Indian Supreme Court, he offers a rich assessment of the potential and the limits of law and human rights for the Narmada Valley struggle and for transnational social movements writ large. Peter Houtzager addresses very similar questions in his study of the way in which the Brazilian movement of the landless (MST) has combined land occupation with the mobilization of local courts and international political pressure to challenge property rights systems that keep most of the land in Brazil in the hands of a small elite. Through a comparative analysis of cases in which the MST has asked Brazilian courts to regularize its possession of occupied lands, he discusses the gradual shift that the movement has promoted in the state's conception and institutions of property rights. Continuing with Latin America, César A. Rodríguez-Garavito and Luis Carlos Arenas offer a case study of the prominent struggle of the U'Wa people in Colombia against oil drilling in their ancestral land. Vindicating collective rights to territory, nature, and cultural difference, the U'wa, in alliance with transnational indigenous rights and environmentalist organizations, have combined direct action and legal strategies to fend off oil exploration, thus illustrating the powerful challenge raised by indigenous people around the world to TNCs, governments, and conventional human rights conceptions and instruments. Finally, José Manuel Pureza takes the discussion of human rights to the global scale by inquiring into the counter-hegemonic potential of two nascent international legal institutions: the International Criminal Court and the common heritage of humankind regime. By carefully examining their origins and characteristics, he argues that, while the former embodies a "defensive" type of counter-hegemonic international legal framework, the latter stands as an instance of "oppositional" international law holding out the promise of a profound reconstruction of the tenets of international law and human rights.

1.4.3 Law and participatory democracy: between the local and the global

At the same time that liberal democracy has spread around the world, the global justice movement has forcefully argued that national and transnational institutions suffer from a deficit of democracy. Thus, liberal democracy and law have become less and less credible in both the North and the South. The twin crises of representation and participation are the most visible symptoms of such a deficit of credibility and legitimacy. In the face of this, two clusters of practices are emerging that aim to radicalize democracy at the local, national, and global scales. On the one hand, TANs have launched campaigns and drafted alternative charters to democratize international institutions, from the WTO and the World Bank to the proposed Free Trade Area of the Americas. On the other hand, communities and governments in different parts of the world are undertaking democratic experiments and initiatives – from participatory budgeting to participatory environmental policy – based on legal frameworks and models of democracy in which the tension between capitalism and democracy is reborn as a positive energy behind new, more inclusive, and more just social contracts. Albeit generally taking place at the local level, these initiatives have quickly spread throughout the world and thus constitute a dynamic source of counter-hegemonic politics and law.

The contributions to the third part of the volume focus on the latter type of initiative by discussing case studies of local experiments in participatory democracy and law-making that illustrate similar efforts going on in different parts of the globe. Mary Rusimbi and Marjorie Mbilinyi offer a detailed account of their work in a fascinating experience in participatory democracy – "gender budgeting" in Tanzania. Gender budgeting, promoted by the Tanzanian feminist movement, has not only reclaimed for the citizenry the decision-making power on economic decisions normally reserved for global and national techno-elites, but has also infused budget allocation and legislation with gender justice. Attesting to the global spread of counter-hegemonic local initiatives, Boaventura de Sousa Santos studies another experience in participatory budgeting – the pioneering initiative of the Workers' Party in Porto Alegre (Brazil) to involve the citizenry in the process of budget allocation. Based on an analysis of the political and legal details of the system, he discusses the factors that account for its success, as well as the tensions and contradictions within it. Moving to the opposite corner of the world, Shiv Visvanathan and Chandrika

Parmar take us into an experiment in democratic interpretation and practice of law through an examination of the way in which Indian social movements have articulated progressive understandings of the Directive Principles of State Policy of the Indian constitution. The conception and practice of rights thus emerging from the bottom up, the authors show, stand in stark contrast with those of state authorities and the country's elites. Finally, João Arriscado Nunes, Marisa Matias, and Susana Costa study the struggle over environmental law in Portugal. Grounding their analysis on a case study of a high-profile dispute over waste management, they contrast the limited democratic potential of the dominant understanding of "community consultation" in environmental law with the democratic process of grassroots participation, legal mobilization, and production of "expert knowledge" employed by the affected community to contest the government's decision to dump hazardous industrial waste in its territory.

References

Appiah, K. Anthony. 2003. "Citizens of the World." Pp. 189–232 in *Globalizing Rights*, edited by Matthew Gibney. Oxford: Oxford University Press.

Ayres, Ian, and John Braithwaite. 1992. *Responsive Regulation: Transcending the Deregulation Debate*. New York: Oxford University Press.

Baxi, Upendra. 1987. "Taking Human Suffering Seriously: Social Action Litigation Before the Supreme Court of India." In *The Role of the Judiciary in Plural Societies*, edited by Neelan Tiruchelvan and Radica Coomaraswamy. New York: St. Martin's Press.

Brysk, Alison (Ed.). 2002. *Globalization and Human Rights*. Berkeley: University of California Press.

Carothers, Thomas. 1998. "The Rule of Law Revival." *Foreign Affairs* 77:95–106.

Dezalay, Yves, and Bryant Garth. 1996. *Dealing in Virtue: International Commercial Arbitration and the Construction of the Transnational Legal Order*. Chicago: University of Chicago Press.

2002a. *The Internationalization of Palace Wars: Lawyers, Economists, and the Contest to Transform Latin American States*. Chicago: University of Chicago Press.

2002b. "Legitimating the New Legal Orthodoxy." Pp. 306–334 in *Global Prescriptions: The Production, Exportation, and Importation of a New Legal Orthodoxy*, edited by Yves Dezalay and Bryant Garth. Ann Arbor: University of Michigan Press.

Dorf, Michael, and Charles Sabel. 1998. "A Constitution of Democratic Experimentalism." *Columbia Law Review* 98:267–473.

Dussel, Enrique. 1998. *Ética de la Liberación en la Edad de la Globalización y la Exclusión*. Madrid-Mexico: Trotta-UAM.

Evans, Peter. 2000. "Fighting Marginalization with Transnational Networks: Counter-Hegemonic Globalization." *Contemporary Sociology* 29:230–241.

Falk, Richard. 1998. *Law in an Emerging Global Village: A Post-Westphalian Perspective*. New York: Transnational Publishers.

Falk, Richard, Lester Ruiz, and R. B. J. Walker (Eds.). 2002. *Reframing the International: Law, Culture, Politics*. New York: Routledge.

Freeman, Jody. 1997. "Collaborative Governance in the Administrative State." *UCLA Law Review* 45:1–98.

Fung, Archon, Dara O'Rourke, and Charles Sabel. 2001. *Can We Put an End to Sweatshops?* Boston: Beacon Press.

Gramsci, Antonio. 1971. *Selections from the Prison Notebooks of Antonio Gramsci*. New York: International Publishers.

Handler, Joel. 1978. *Social Movements and the Legal System: A Theory of Law Reform and Social Change*. New York: Academic Press.

Hunt, Alan. 1993. *Explorations in Law and Society: Toward a Constitutive Theory of Law*. New York: Routledge.

ILSA (Ed.). 1986. *Los Abogados y la Democracia en América Latina*. Bogotá: ILSA.

Karkkainen, Bradley. 2002. "Environmental Lawyering in the Age of Collaboration." *Wisconsin Law Review* 2002:555–574.

Keck, Margaret, and Kathryn Sikkink. 1998. *Activists Beyond Borders: Advocacy Networks in International Politics*. Ithaca: Cornell University Press.

Liebman, James, and Charles Sabel. 2003. "A Public Laboratory Dewey Barely Imagined: The Emerging Model of School Governance and Legal Reform." *NYU Journal of Law and Social Change* 28:183–305.

Likosky, Michael (Ed.). 2002. *Transnational Legal Processes: Globalisation and Power Disparities*. London: Butterworths.

Lourdes Souza, Maria de. 2001. *El Uso Alternativo del Derecho*. Bogotá: ILSA.

MacNeil, Michael, Neil Sargent, and Peter Swan (Eds.). 2000. *Law, Regulation, and Governance*. Don Mills, Ontario: Oxford University Press.

Marcus, George. 1995. "Ethnography in/of the World System: The Emergence of Multi-Sited Ethnography." *Annual Review of Anthropology* 24:95–117.

McBarnett, Doreen. 2002. "Transnational Transactions: Legal Work, Cross-Border Commerce and Global Regulation." Pp. 98–113 in *Transnational Legal Processes*, edited by Michael Likosky. London: Butterworths.

McCann, Michael. 1994. *Rights at Work: Pay Equity Reform and the Politics of Legal Mobilization*. Chicago: University of Chicago Press.

Mignolo, Walter. 2002. "The Many Faces of Cosmo-Polis: Border Thinking and Critical Cosmopolitanism." Pp. 157–188 in *Cosmopolitanism*, edited by Carol Breckeridge, Sheldon Pollock, Homi Bhabha, and Dipesh Chakrabarty. Durham: Duke University Press.

Munger, Frank. 1998. "Mapping Law and Society" Pp. 21–88 in *Crossing Boundaries: Traditions and Transformations in Law and Society Research*, edited by A. Sarat, M. Constable, D. Engle, V. Hans, and S. Lawrence. Chicago: Northwestern University Press.

Mutua, Makau wa. 1996. "The Ideology of Human Rights." *Virginia Journal of International Law* 36:589.

Nye, Joseph, and John Donahue (Eds.). 2000. *Governance in a Globalizing World*. Washington, DC: Brookings Institution.

O'Rourke, Dara. 2003. "Outsourcing Regulation: Analyzing Non-Governmental Systems of Labor Standards Monitoring." *Policy Studies Journal* 31:1–29.

Quijano, Aníbal. 2000. "Colonialidad del Poder y Clasificación Social." *Journal of World-Systems Research* 6:342–386.

Rajagopal, Balakrishnan. 2003. *International Law from Below: Development, Social Movements and Third World Resistance*. Cambridge: Cambridge University Press.

Rodríguez-Garavito, César A. 2001. "Globalization, Judicial Reform and the Rule of Law in Latin America: The Return of Law and Development." *Beyond Law* 7:13–42.

    2005. "Global Governance, Cross-Border Organizing, and Labor Rights: Codes of Conduct and Anti-Sweatshop Struggles in Global Apparel Factories in Mexico and Guatemala." *Politics & Society* 33(2).

Rosenberg, Gerald. 1991. *The Hollow Hope: Can Courts Bring About Social Change?* Chicago: University of Chicago Press.

Sabel, Charles. 1994. "Learning by Monitoring: The Institutions of Economic Development." Pp. 137–165 in *The Handbook of Economic Sociology*, edited by Neil Smelser and Richard Swedberg. Princeton: Princeton University Press.

Santos, Boaventura de Sousa. 1991. *Estado, Derecho y Luchas Sociales*. Bogotá: ILSA.

    1995. *Toward a New Common Sense: Law, Science and Politics in the Paradigmatic Transition*. New York: Routledge.

    2002. *Toward a New Legal Common Sense*. London: Butterworths.

    2004. "A Critique of Lazy Reason: Against the Waste of Experience." In *The Modern World-System in the Longue Durée*, edited by Immanuel Wallerstein. New York: Free Press.

Satz, Debra. 1999. "Equality of What Among Whom? Thoughts on Cosmopolitanism, Statism, and Nationalism." Pp. 67–85 in *Global Justice*, edited by Ian Shapiro and Lea Brilmayer. New York: NYU Press.

Scheingold, Stuart. 1974. *The Politics of Rights: Lawyers, Public Policy, and Political Change*. New Haven: Yale University Press.

Simon, William. 2003. "Solving Problems v. Claiming Rights: The Pragmatist Challenge to Legal Liberalism." Paper presented at the Conference on

"Regulation, Governance, and Law in the 21st Century: Towards a New Legal Process?" University of Wisconsin, Madison, October 1, 2003.

Snyder, Francis. 1994. "Soft Law and Institutional Practice in the European Community." Pp. 197–227 in *The Construction of Europe*, edited by S. Martin. Boston: Kluwer.

2002. "Governing Globalisation." Pp. 65–97 in *Transnational Legal Processes: Globalisation and Power Disparities*, edited by Michael Likosky. London: Butterworths.

Tarrow, Sidney. 2001. "Transnational Politics: Contention and Institutions in International Politics." *Annual Review of Political Science* 4:1–20.

Teubner, Gunther. 1986. "After Legal Instrumentalism? Strategic Models of Post-Regulatory Law." Pp. 299–326 in *Dilemmas of Law in the Welfare State*, edited by Gunther Teubner. Berlin: De Gruyter.

(Ed.). 1997. *Global Law Without a State*. Aldershot: Dartmouth.

Trubek, David, and James Mosher. 2003. "New Governance, Employment Policy, and the European Social Model." Pp. 33–58 in *Governing Work and Welfare in a New Economy*, edited by Jonathan Zeitlin and David Trubek. New York and Oxford: Oxford University Press.

Unger, Roberto. 1996. *What Should Legal Analysis Become?* London: Verso.

1998. *Democracy Realized: The Progressive Alternative*. London: Verso.

Wacquant, Loïc. 2004. *Deadly Symbiosis: Race and the Rise of Neoliberal Penality*. London: Polity Press.

Zeitlin, Jonathan, and David Trubek (Eds.). 2003. *Governing Work and Welfare in a New Economy: European and American Experiments*. New York and Oxford: Oxford University Press.

PART ONE

LAW AND THE CONSTRUCTION OF
A GLOBAL ECONOMY OF SOLIDARITY

CHAPTER 2

BEYOND NEOLIBERAL GOVERNANCE: THE WORLD SOCIAL FORUM AS SUBALTERN COSMOPOLITAN POLITICS AND LEGALITY

*Boaventura de Sousa Santos**

2.1 INTRODUCTION

Elsewhere, I have argued that there are two forms of globalization: neoliberal globalization and what I call counter-hegemonic globalization, which has been challenging the former for some time (Santos 2002: Chapters 5, 9). Counter-hegemonic globalization I define as the vast set of networks, initiatives, organizations, and movements that fight against the economic, social, and political outcomes of hegemonic globalization, challenge the conceptions of world development underlying the latter, and propose alternative conceptions.

Counter-hegemonic globalization is focused on the struggles against social exclusion. Since social exclusion is always the product of unequal power relations, counter-hegemonic globalization is animated by a redistributive ethos in its broadest sense, involving redistribution of material, social, political, cultural, and symbolic resources. In this sense, redistribution is based both on the principle of equality and on the principle of recognition of difference. At stake is the struggle for equal exchanges and authority (rather than power) relations. Because unequal exchanges and power relations are crystallized in politics and

* I thank Celeste Benson, Arturo Escobar, Marc Galanter, Candido Grzybowszki, Joel Handler, Antonio Martins, Paula Meneses, Moema Miranda, Walter Mignolo, Nelson Maldonado-Torres, Cesar Rodríguez-Garavito, Jorge Romano, Pedro Santana, Jai Sen, Ronen Shamir, David Sugarman, Teivo Teivonan, Virginia Vargas, Peter Waterman, Francisco Whitaker, Lucie White, and Bill Whitford for their comments on an earlier version of this chapter. My very special thanks to Maria Irene Ramalho, who prepared the English language version.

law, counter-hegemonic globalization unfolds as political and legal struggles guided by the idea that hegemonic legal and political structures and practices can be challenged by alternative principles of law and politics. These alternative principles and the struggles for them I have called subaltern cosmopolitan politics and legality (Santos 2002). They comprise a vast social field of confrontational politics and law in which I distinguish two basic processes of counter-hegemonic globalization: global collective action through transnational networking of local/national/global linkages; and local or national struggles, whose success prompts reproduction in other locales or networking with parallel struggles elsewhere. In this chapter I deal with the first process by analyzing the politics and legality embodied by the World Social Forum (WSF) and contrasting it with neoliberal politics and legality. To this end, I divide the chapter into three sections. First, I focus on some of the legal innovations under neoliberal globalization, specifically on governance as an alleged mode of post-state social regulation. Then, I analyze the WSF as an expression of counter-hegemonic globalization within which a subaltern cosmopolitan politics and legality is being forged. Finally, I draw an explicit contrast between these forms of hegemonic and counter-hegemonic politics and legality.

Before proceeding, given the narrow view of law and politics dominant in legal scholarship, it is necessary to clarify the conception of law and politics that I use throughout the chapter. Underlying neoliberal globalization and counter-hegemonic globalization are different conceptions of legality and of politics of legality. Both, however, demand a radical expansion of the conventional understanding of legality and the politics of legality. To my mind, four conceptual expansions are needed to capture the politics of legality under globalization. The first concerns the breadth of legal actions, struggles, or disputes. Under conditions of conflicting globalizations, collective legal practices combine political mobilization with legal mobilization, and the latter may involve legal as well as illegal and non-legal actions. The second expansion concerns scale. The politics of legality needs to be conceptualized at three different scales – the local, the national, and the global. In most cases, all the scales involved interpenetrate each other. Power struggles over the relevant scale of law are today fought in the context of the growing prevalence of the global scale. The third expansion concerns legal knowledge and legal expertise. The politics of law involves a variety of legal knowledges and expertise among which the professional legal knowledge is only one component. In an increasingly fragmented and transcalar legal field, rival legal knowledges (local or national v. transnational; professional v. lay; old legal doctrine v. emergent conceptions) often collide in a context of increasing dominance of neoliberal economic knowledge. Finally, the fourth aspect of an expansive conception of the politics of law concerns the temporal dimension. This conceptual expansion is twofold. Modern state law is subjected to the time frame of state action (e.g. that of the judicial process, the electoral cycle, the legislative process, and bureaucracy). However, legal mobilization often involves contrasting time frames. On the one hand, we find the instantaneous time of financial capital (for which the long term is the next ten minutes). On the other hand, we find the *longue durée* of capitalism and colonialism, or even the longest duration (glacial time) of the ecological deterioration or exhaustion of natural resources (e.g. in legal conflicts involving indigenous peoples fighting against oil companies operating in their territories; see Rodríguez-Garavito and Arenas' chapter in this volume). Radically different conceptions of time are often present in legal struggles and the conflicts are fought in a context in which the dominant time frame seems to get closer and closer to the instantaneous time of financial capital. The second dimension concerns the contrast between the linear time presiding over the Western logic of development – based on a unilinear conception of development, according to which different pasts converge in a single future – and a pluralistic conception of time based on the idea that there are alternative development paths, and that therefore different pasts underlie different presents and may lead to different futures.

With such a reconceptualization in mind, it becomes possible to analyze the contours of the role of politics and the law in hegemonic and counter-hegemonic globalization. To this task I now turn.

2.2 GOVERNANCE AS NEOLIBERAL LEGALITY

From the beginning of recorded time until 1975, the British Library catalogue registered forty-seven titles with the word "governance." Since then this term has exploded in all the disciplines of the social sciences. This sudden and overwhelming presence has only one parallel, in the same period, in the term "globalization." This convergent trajectory is no coincidence. As I will try to show, since the mid-1990s, governance has become the political matrix of neoliberal globalization. I call it a matrix because it is both an embedding or grounding structure and a generative environment for an interconnected network of prag-matic ideas and cooperative patterns of behavior, shared by a group of selected actors and their interests, a self-activated network to deal with chaos in a context in which both outside-generated top-down norma-tive order and autonomous bottom-up non-pre-selected participatory ordering are unavailable or, if available, undesirable. Crucial to this matrix is the idea that it sees itself as cooperatively self-generated and, therefore, as inclusive as it can possibly be. As with any other matrix, it is, in fact, based on a principle of selection, and, thus, on the binary inclusion/exclusion. However, in this case, the excluded, rather than being present as excluded, are utterly absent. Governance is therefore a matrix that combines horizontality and verticality in a new way: both are self-generated, the former as all-existing, the latter as non-existing. It operates through a false dialectic of governance and disgovernance, one in which the second term, rather than disconfirming governance by confronting it, ratifies it by lacking either object or agency.

Jessop (1998) calls this ideological and political phenomenon the "governance paradigm." Paradigm is probably too strong a concept to characterize this phenomenon, particularly if we take it in Kuhn's (1970) original formulation of paradigms as universally recognized scientific achievements that for a time provide model problems and solutions to a community of practitioners. Because different concep-tions of governance abound, located differently in the political spectrum,[1] I prefer to use a weaker and narrower term – the governance matrix. Both a governance matrix and a governance crowd are there-fore discernible. An elusive ideology and by and large an untested practice function as a vague call that manages to mobilize social scientists, policy-makers, and lawyers from different intellectual back-grounds and political loyalties.

I distinguish the governance matrix from the governance crowd because, however vague, the matrix is less heterogeneous than the groups that claim it. We are at a stage of the development of the concept of governance very similar to that of globalization in the mid-1990s, when the social practices had not allowed one fully to discern the cleavages and contradictions being engendered by the processes of globalization themselves. In the following I will try to answer three questions: (1) How and why has governance come

---

[1] Since Chapter 1 discusses the concept and the literature on governance, I will not dwell further on them here.

about? (2) What is its political meaning? (3) Are there other stories of governance?

2.2.1 The genealogy of governance

In order to understand the emergence of the governance matrix we have to go back to the early 1970s, the student movement, and the crisis of legitimacy it gave rise to. As Offe (1985) and Habermas (1982) have shown, the crisis derived from the radical questioning of both the social and the democratic content of the social contract that underlay social democratic states since the end of the Second World War. For the student movement, soon to be joined by the feminist and the ecological movements, the apparently inclusive social contract was indeed exclusionary. It completely excluded large social groups (minorities, immigrants) and important social issues (such as cultural diversity and environment), and included other groups by subordinating them to disempowering forms of inclusion – as was the case, most notably, of women. On the other hand, all this had been possible because democracy had failed to fulfill its promise of building free and equal societies. The ideas of popular sovereignty and popular participation had been hijacked by elitist forms of democratic rule with the complicity of the two social actors historically charged with the task of deepening democracy and bringing about social emancipation: the working-class parties and the labor unions. It was a crisis of legitimacy because it was a crisis of government by consent. It dominated the political contestation in the North in the first half of the 1970s (Monedero 2003).

The turning point occurred in 1975 when the Trilateral Commission published its report on the crisis of democracy authored by Crozier, Huntington, and Watanuki (1975). According to them, there was indeed a crisis of democracy but not because there was too little democracy, but because there was too much democracy. Democracies were in crisis because they were overloaded with rights and claims, because the social contract rather than being exclusionary was too inclusive, precisely due to the pressures brought upon it by the historical social actors decried by the students (the working-class parties and the labor unions). The crisis of government by consent was thereby transformed into a crisis of government *tout court*, and the crisis of legitimacy became a crisis of governability.

The nature of political contestation was thereby profoundly changed. The focus shifted from the incapacity of the state to do justice to the new social movements and their demands to the need to contain and control society's claims on the state. Soon the diagnostic of the crisis as a crisis of governability became dominant, and so did the political therapy proposed by the Trilateral Commission: from the central state to devolution/decentralization; from the political to the technical; from popular participation to the expert system; from the public to the private; from the state to the market (Crozier *et al.* 1975).The subsequent decade saw the construction of a new social and political regime based on these ideas, a regime soon to be imposed globally under the name of Washington Consensus. It was a decade of profound political and ideological transformations that paved the way for the rise of the all-encompassing solution to the crisis of governability: the market rule.

While the crisis of legitimacy perspective saw the solution in state transformation and enhanced popular participation through autonomous new social movements, the crisis of governability stance saw the solution in the shrinking of the state (through the latter's withdrawal from the economic sphere and social services), and in the taming of popular participation (through policies constraining popular participation, based on an individualistic conception of civil society dominated by business organizations). The latter, whose belonging to civil society had been made problematic by the increasing autonomy of republican civil society vis-à-vis the market, were smuggled into civil society by a process of double identification, as both market agents and social actors.

By 1986, it was evident that all the other recommendations of the Trilateral Commission were to be accepted as "natural," once three ground rules were put in place: privatization, marketization, and liberalization. These three ground rules became the three pillars of neoliberalism and neoliberal globalization. The following decade (1986–1996) was the high time of neoliberalism: withdrawal of the state from the social sector and economic regulation; market rule as both economic and social regulation; proliferation of civil society organizations, aggregated under the general designation of "third sector," whose goal is to fulfill the human needs that the market cannot fulfill and the state is no longer in a condition to fulfill (Santos 2002: 439–495; Santos and Jenson 2000). It is also the period in which the failures of the market, as the major principle of social regulation, become evident. The dramatic increase in income and wealth polarization, and its devastating effect on the reproduction of the livelihoods of large bodies of populations, the generalized rise of corruption, the perverse effects of the mix of market rule and non-redistributive democracy leading to the implosion of some states and inter-ethnic civil wars – all these facts became too pervasive to be discarded as anomalous deviations. It was at this juncture that governance emerged as a new political and social matrix.

The last thirty years can thus be summarized in this sequence of concepts: from legitimacy to governability; from governability to governance. To put it in Hegelian terms, we can think of governance as being the synthesis that supersedes both the thesis (legitimacy) and the antithesis (governability). Governance seeks, indeed, to combine the demand for participation and inclusion called for by the legitimacy reading of the social crisis with the demand for autonomy and self-regulation called for by the governability reading. However, it is a false synthesis, since it operates entirely within the governability framework. Rather than resuscitating the legitimacy quest of the 1970s, it seeks to reconstruct governability in such a way as to turn it into an alternative conception of legitimacy.

2.2.2 The political meaning of neoliberal governance

In order to identify the political meaning of neoliberal governance we must pay attention not only to what it says but also to what it silences. The most important silences in the governance matrix are: social transformation, popular participation, social contract, social justice, power relations, and social conflict. These were the concepts with which the legitimacy crisis was formulated in the 1970s. They were also the concepts that grounded modern critical theory. By silencing them and offering no positive alternative to them, governance signals the defeat of critical theory in both social and political affairs. Indeed, the alternatives offered by governance to the silenced concepts are all of them negative in the sense that they define themselves by opposition to the legitimacy concepts: rather than social transformation, problem-solving; rather than popular participation, selected-in stakeholders' participation; rather than social contract, self-regulation; rather than social justice, positive sum games and compensatory policies; rather than power relations, coordination and partnership; rather than social conflict, social cohesion and stability of flows.

These alternative concepts are not unequivocally negative. Indeed, some of them echo some of the aspirational features of deep democracy. They are negative in so far as they are used in opposition to the other silenced concepts, rather than as complementary parts of the same political constellation. Thereby, rather than being at the service of a project of social inclusion and social redistribution, they are at the service of social exclusion and economic polarization.

At the core of the legitimacy crisis was the idea of popular sovereignty and popular participation, which grounded the basic equation of enabling social transformation: there is no benefit without participation; there is no participation without benefit. This equation was based on the following premises: the right to determine benefit is vested in those who participate; the condition for such self-determination is the self-determination of participation. The governance matrix deals with this equation in a complex way. It accepts the equation on the condition of replacing self-determined participation with participation based on a principle of selection according to which some actors, interests, or voices are selected in while others are selected out. Participation may be autonomous but not the criteria by which participants are chosen. Those who are selected in may benefit, but always at the cost of those who are selected out. The equation is thereby deradicalized and instrumentalized. If the principle of selection is questioned and the selected out enter the picture, they may be conceded some benefits, but on the condition of not participating. If the nature or range of the benefits is questioned by the selected-in participants, these may be granted the possibility of continuing participating but on the condition of not insisting in the self-determination of their benefits. In extreme cases, the benefit will be said to reside in participation per se.

Applying the sociology of absences (see Santos and Rodríguez-Garavito's chapter in this volume) to governance, two non-existing actors can be detected: the state and the excluded. They are made non-existent in different ways. The state per se is not absent, but rather the principle of sovereignty and the power of coercion that goes with it. The state is therefore a legitimate partner of governance, provided that it participates in a non-state capacity, ideally on an equal footing with other partners. But this is only part of the story. The movement from legitimacy to governability was brought about by the incapacitation of the state as a social regulator. But the state was not deprived of its role as meta-regulator, that is, as the entity responsible for creating the space for legitimate non-state regulators. Needless to say, this is a very different type of state intervention when compared with the one that presided over the social democratic contract. In the latter case, the state selected two very well-defined social actors (capital and labor) and brought them to the negotiating table, which was controlled by the state, and sought to reach agreements that could be verified and enforced through state coercion if necessary. The political formation being thereby generated was one of institutionalized conflicts rather than of stable flows; of peaceful coexistence rather than of common goals.

The excluded are made nonexistent in a very different way. They cannot be simply kept outside as they were in the social contract and the welfare state because, contrary to the latter, the governance matrix does not accept the binary inside/outside. Whatever is outside is not conceived as a source of an enabling power that can turn exclusion into inclusion. Inclusion and exclusion are thereby depoliticized. They are technical dimensions of coordination. In the absence of a sovereign command, exclusion only exists as the dilemma of exclusion: how to get power to fight for inclusion in the governance circle if all the power there is derives from belonging to the governance circle.

Critical theorists of law, myself included, have written that the modern juridification of social life – that is, the conception of social transformation as struggle for rights regulated by liberal democracy and the rule of law – has meant the receding of politics as the protection of more and more social interests became a function of technically minded legal experts rather than of political mobilization and political leverage (Santos 1995, 2002). In a retrospective comparison, the juridical paradigm appears as much more political than the governance matrix. Critical theorists have argued that the depoliticization brought about by law was a highly political option. The same is true of governance.

The conception of governance as neoliberal governance may be disputed because, after all, the ideological and technical conceptual apparatus of governance is at odds with the one that underlies market rule. Instead of competition, coordination and partnership; instead of creative destruction, social problems; instead of profitability, social cohesion; instead of unintended consequences, consequences to be dealt with as if they were intended; instead of market, civil society. In sum, the governance matrix has emerged to correct market failures impelled by a social rather than an economic logic. The high period of neoliberalism saw indeed the exponential growth of civil society organizations, and NGOs, many of them with the purpose of offering some relief to populations caught by the phasing out of the safety nets once provided by the welfare state and unable to buy welfare in the market.

The resurgence of civil society in the 1980s and 1990s is a complex phenomenon non-susceptible of monocausal explanation. I distinguish three different processes. The first process is comprised by the civil society organizations (CSOs) that emerged in Central and Eastern Europe to reclaim an autonomous non-state public sphere from where to fight against the authoritarian state socialist regimes. They were very influential in the period of democratic transition that followed the demise of the socialist regimes. A similar type of civil society emerged in many Latin American countries during the period of democratic transition that followed the demise of the military dictatorships that had ruled from the mid-1960s or mid-1970s to the mid-1990s. While in Central and Eastern Europe CSOs questioned both the political and the economic regime, in Latin America the CSOs questioned the authoritarian political regime but, in general, not the economic model being put in place concomitantly with democracy, i.e. neoliberalism. When the democratic transitions were completed, most of these CSOs disappeared, turned into political parties or consultancy or lobbying firms, or reconstructed themselves so as to fit the third type of CSOs mentioned below.

The second process is the most closely related to the governability crisis and consists of CSOs that questioned neither the political regime (liberal democracy) nor the economic model (neoliberal capitalism) but rather saw themselves as solidarity organizations fulfilling the human needs of victims of economic restructuring, dispossession, discrimination, environmental degradation, warfare, massive violations of human rights, and so on. They are the bulk of the third sector or the NGOs field. Their focus is on the private, not on the public; on the social, not on the political; on the micro, not on the macro (liberal democracy, neoliberal capitalism).

Finally, there is a third process underlying the resurgence of civil society. It comprises the CSOs, many of them originating in new social movements, both in the South and in the North, that fight against neoliberal globalization. Although many of them provide services similar to those of the CSOs of the second type, they frame their actions in a broader concept of political activism. They question the hegemonic model of democracy and advocate participatory grassroots democracy. They refuse the idea that there is no alternative to neoliberal globalization, consider themselves anti-capitalistic, and advocate alternative economies, alternative models of development, or alternatives to development. Although most of them are locally based, they network with similar organizations in other locales and with global organizations. These local/global linkages and networking constitute counter-hegemonic globalization.

The landscape of CSOs is thus very rich and diverse. The different processes that accounted for the resurgence of CSOs in the 1980s and 1990s led to two main types of civil society. The first one is the liberal civil society, constituted by the CSOs of the first kind described above. The second type is the subaltern, counter-hegemonic civil society, consisting of the social movements and CSOs that keep in unstable balance the macro and the micro, the public and the private, the social and the political, by focusing on the deeper causes of the human suffering they seek to minimize. They are involved in the creation of subaltern non-state public spheres at the local, national, and global scale.

This cleavage between two major types of civil society explains the centrality of the principle of selection in the governance matrix. The selected-in civil society is the liberal civil society because only its organizations share the values that underlie self-regulated coordination and partnership. Problem solving and social cohesion are best achieved when politics or ideology does not interfere with the construction of common goals and common interests. Only open-ended, fragmented, pragmatic conceptions of interests and benefits can be made intelligible to and have an impact on the market, the most flexible and indeterminate institution of all, thereby helping the markets to flourish unimpeded by their all too evident failures.

In light of this, neoliberal governance operates what De Angelis calls "Polanyi's inversion" (2003:23). While Polanyi argued that the economy is embedded in society, the governance matrix is premised upon the need to embed society in the economy. As the UN global compact states, "the rationale is that a commitment to corporate citizenship should begin with the organization itself by embedding universal principles and values into the strategic business vision, organizational cultural and daily operations" (UN 2000:3).

In other words, the "universal values" are good for business and on this premise lies the voluntary character of the compact (see Shamir's chapter in this volume). There is no possibility of such values or principles endangering the profitability that grounds the flourishing of economic organizations – as was the case, for instance, with taxation when it was first imposed. Because it was imposed, the public policy of taxation ended up selecting the businesses that could survive under taxation. On the contrary, in the governance matrix it is up to businesses to select the values and principles they can live with. Even when, under pressure from activists pursuing negative publicity campaigns, businesses agree to abide by basic codes of conduct, they do so based on economic (rather than social) calculations.

In light of this, I would suggest that governance is a genetically modified form of law and government that seeks to make itself resistant to two dangerous plagues: on one side, bottom-up, potentially chaotic pressures; on the other side, unpredictable changes in the rules of the game of capital accumulation brought about by state or inter-state regulation.

2.2.3 Social struggles within the governance frame

The historical relationship between democracy and capitalism is non-linear, if for no other reason because in the last two hundred years different models of democracy (Macpherson 1966, 1977; Held 1987) as well as different models of capitalism have been in place (Boyer 1986; Boyer and Drache 1996; Santos 2001). Throughout the twentieth century the tension between democracy and capitalism in the global North centered around the question of social redistribution. This was one of the core questions underlying the crisis of legitimacy in the 1970s. The conversion of the crisis of legitimacy into the crisis of governability was the capitalist response to the pressures for wider and deeper social redistribution. Neoliberalism neutralized or strongly weakened the democratic mechanisms of social redistribution: social and economic rights and the welfare state. Deprived of its redistributive potential, democracy became fully compatible with capitalism, and to such an extent that they became the twin concepts presiding over the new global model of social and political affairs, being imposed worldwide by neoliberal globalization, structural adjustment policies and, lately, by neocolonial warfare as well.

Thirty years later, the question of redistribution is more serious than ever. The rates of exploitation have reached such high levels in some sectors of production and some regions of the world that, together with the mechanisms used to obtain them, they suggest that we are entering a new period of primitive capital accumulation. Moreover, the unexploited or unexploitable populations are in an even more dramatic situation as the conditions of reproduction of their livelihoods have deteriorated due to economic restructuring and environmental degradation. They have been declared discardable populations. Finally, the triadic recipe of privatization, marketization and liberalization has eroded the state-sponsored commons and transformed it into a new generation of enclosures. A new form of indirect rule has emerged in which powerful economic actors hold an immense amount of unaccountable power of control over the basic livelihoods of people, be they water, energy, seeds, security, or health.

Social redistribution is the most serious issue confronting us at the beginning of the twenty-first century. But it is not the only one. Since the 1980s, the issue of social redistribution has been compounded by the issue of the recognition of difference. Today we live in societies tremendously unequal, but equality is not the only value we cherish. We also cherish difference, equal difference, an aspiration which was not prominently present in the conception of the crisis of legitimacy of the 1970s.

The litmus test for governance is therefore the extent to which it can confront both the question of social redistribution and the question of the recognition of difference. In light of what I said above, I do not see any potential for meaningful social redistribution being generated in the governance matrix. Governance may better address the question of recognition of difference than the question of social redistribution, but even here the structural limitations of governance will surface.

This does not mean that governance arrangements will not bring some benefits to the more disadvantaged groups within the circle of partnership. Such benefits may even spill over to the excluded. But this does not entail any potential for enabling popular participation or for social redistribution as a matter of right. In other words, what is beneficial does not determine, by itself, what is emancipatory. If the population of the homeless is growing exponentially, it is a good thing that homeowners allow them to take shelter in the porches of their houses. It is better than nothing. But, because of its voluntary character, redistribution is achieved under the logic of philanthropy. That is, it does not occur in an enabling way, in recognition of both the right to the benefit and the right to reclaim the effectiveness of the economic right in an autonomous, participatory way.

It may be argued that, under certain circumstances, the voluntary character of compliance is more virtual than real, given the pressures exerted upon the governance circle, often times from the outside. In this case, different social processes may be at work and they must be distinguished. In order to illustrate this I refer very briefly to two examples of outside pressure brought about by the state. I take the first example from César Rodríguez-Garavito's (2005) study on the operation of codes of conduct in apparel sweatshops in Guatemala. In the process of negotiation of the Central America Free Trade Agreement (CAFTA), the Guatemalan state was pressured by the US government to be more active in the repression of human rights violations in the workplace. Risking being excluded from CAFTA, the Guatemalan state, in turn, put pressure on the apparel brand (Liz Claiborne) and its supplier factory to comply with the former's code of conduct, which eventually allowed for the unionization of workers at the factory. In the second case, as analyzed by Heinz Klug in his chapter in this volume, the South African state, pressured by a strong social movement calling for free or affordable antiretroviral medicines for HIV/AIDS patients, successfully pressures the pharmaceutical companies to withdraw their suit against compulsory licensing and the production of generics and to lower the prices of their brand products.

It is important to note that in both cases the state, which had ejected itself from social regulation, intervenes supposedly from the outside, using its sovereign prerogative, if not formally at least informally, to put pressure on the governance circle and obtain a given outcome, considered politically important. But while in the Guatemalan case the state intervenes under pressure from above and the benefited workers are not called upon to participate in the deliberation over the benefits, in the South African case the state is pressured from below and yields to the pressure of the social movement. Indeed, the state joins forces with the social movement for that particular purpose. In the first case, if the benefits are taken away from the workers, they will be as powerless as before to reclaim them. In the second case, the state action contributes to empower the social movement, to enhance its leverage in social contestation in a particular case and possibly in other future cases, eventually even against the state. In sum, these two cases show that the state is the present–absent structure of the governance matrix – a fact that is best revealed in conditions of institutional stress – which means that the governance matrix operates inside the "self-outsidedness" of the state. The cases also show that, notwithstanding the unfavorable conditions of the present, the enabling struggle for the right to social redistribution – the right to have rights, in Arendt's formulation (1968:177) – may have some success, not because of governance, but in spite of governance.

Before concluding the examination of the governance matrix, it is important to stress that, while I question the self-characterization of governance as "post-state," it is not my purpose to defend a return to the old forms of state-centered regulation – which in any case were always relatively underdeveloped in the US (at least when compared with the European forms of regulation). My purpose is rather to advance a new form of regulation that, without dispensing with the energy of civil society (both in its liberal and counter-hegemonic forms) attributes to the national state or to supranational democratic political institutions the strategic role of defining the inequalities of power within the governance circle as political problems to be dealt with in political terms. To this type of legality and governance I now turn.

2.2.4 Are there other stories of governance?

In this section I have so far dealt with neoliberal governance. It may appear to be "the only game in town." But it is not. As argued above, in recent years neoliberal globalization, albeit still the dominant form of globalization, has been confronted with another form – counter-hegemonic globalization. In the last ten years, and most clearly since the Seattle protests at the 1999 WTO meeting, another form of global-ization has been emerging by force of the social movements and civil society organizations that, through local/global linkages, are conduct-ing a global struggle against all the forms of oppression brought about or intensified by neoliberal globalization. In the next section I will elaborate on the political conditions for the emergence of a subaltern cosmopolitan legality as derived from the practices of the social move-ments and NGOs coming together at the WSF. I argue that, in the womb of this alternative counter-hegemonic globalization, another governance matrix is being generated, an insurgent counter-hegemonic governance. It entails articulation and coordination among an immense variety of social movements and civil society organizations with the purpose of combining strategies and tactics, defining agendas, and planning and carrying out collective actions.

Strikingly, the main features of the neoliberal governance matrix are also present in the insurgent governance matrix: voluntary participa-tion, horizontality, autonomy, coordination, partnership, self-regulation, etc. Different historical trajectories have led to this surprising conver-gence. On the side of neoliberal governance, the driving impulse has been the rejection of state centralism and state coercion and the formulation of a new model of social regulation based on the interests and voluntary participation of the stakeholders. On the side of counter-hegemonic governance, as shown in the next section, the originating impulse has been the rejection of the working class parties and labor unions as the privileged historical agents and modes of organization of progressive social transformation and the formulation of a new model of social emancipation based on the recognition of the plurality of eman-cipatory agency and social transformative goals.

Even more striking is the fact that counter-hegemonic governance faces some of the challenges and dilemmas that confront neoliberal governance. For instance, in both cases a principle of selection is at work. In the case of counter-hegemonic governance, the most excluded social groups, those that would conceivably benefit most from a successful struggle against neoliberal globalization, do not participate and are unlikely to see their interests and aspirations taken into account. The negative utopia that aggregates all the movements and NGOs – the refusal of the idea that there is no alternative to the current capitalist global disorder – coexists with the different and even contradictory interests, strategies, and agendas that divide them. The struggle to expand the circle of counter-hegemonic governance goes on, and some of the movements and NGOs that participate in it are the same ones that struggle for the expansion of the circle of neoliberal governance.

Will neoliberal governance and counter-hegemonic governance ever meet in a dialectical synthesis of global governance? As I argue below, this is very improbable. Are they going to influence each other? This is possible and, indeed, it is already occurring, as the examination of the WSF in the next section will lay bare.

2.3 THE WORLD SOCIAL FORUM AS A SUBALTERN COSMOPOLITAN POLITICS AND LEGALITY OF THE GLOBAL SOUTH

2.3.1 The WSF as subaltern cosmopolitan politics and legality

The WSF represents one of the most sustainable manifestations of an emergent subaltern, counter-hegemonic global civil society. In its broadest definition, the WSF is the set of initiatives of transnational exchange among social movements and NGOs, articulating local, national, or global social struggles conducted (in accordance with the Porto Alegre Charter of Principles) against all the forms of oppression brought about or made possible by neoliberal globalization.

In practice, the WSF is the set of forums (global, regional thematic, and local) that are organized according to the Charter of Principles. The WSF is not confined to the five meetings that have taken place in Porto Alegre (Brazil) in 2001, 2002, 2003, and 2005, and in Mumbai (India) in 2004. It also includes all the other forums that have been meeting parallel to the WSF: the several editions of thematic forums such as the Forum of Local Authorities, the World Parliamentary

Forum, the World Education Forum, the World Forum of Judges, the World Trade Unions Forum, the World Water Forum, the World Choral Forum, the World Junior Forum, and the Forum of Sexual Diversity. It includes also all the forums that have taken place on their initiative for the past few years – national, regional, and thematic forums. These are too numerous to list fully. Among the regional ones are the several editions of the Pan-Amazonic Forum, the European Social Forum, the Africa Social Forum, and the Social Forum of the Americas. Among the thematic forums, special mention should be made of the first thematic forum, held in Argentina in September 2002, on the Crisis of Neoliberalism in Argentina and the Challenges for the Global Movement, and the Forum on Democracy, Human Rights, War and Drug Trade held in Cartagena (Colombia) in June 2003. Also, the national or international meetings of movements or organizations to prepare the aforementioned forums must also be included in the WSF. Finally, even though the Charter of Principles prevents the WSF from organizing collective actions in its own name, regional and global actions carried out by the networks of movements and organizations that are part of the WSF must be considered part of the WSF process, as long as they abide by the Charter of Principles. For instance, actions agreed upon by the assembly of the Global Network of Social Movements, which meets parallel to the WSF, are part of the WSF process. In the assembly that took place during the third WSF, the decision was taken to convene a global march against the war and for peace on February 15, 2003. The same happened during the fourth WSF, the date set for the rally being this time March 20, 2004, the first anniversary of the invasion of Iraq. Although they are not carried out formally in the name of the WSF, these collective actions must be considered part of the WSF process.[2]

The WSF is a new political phenomenon. It is not an event, nor is it a mere succession of events, although it does try to dramatize the formal meetings it promotes. It is not a scholarly conference, although the contributions of many scholars converge into it. It is not a party or an international of parties, although militants and activists of many parties

---

[2] The inclusion of these actions in the WSF process is not uncontroversial. The International Council of the WSF includes organizations whose representatives deny any organic relation between the WSF and the actions decided by the Global Network of Social Movements, or any other network of movements or organizations. According to them, the comprehensiveness and inclusiveness of the WSF can only be preserved if no specific collective action can be said to represent the WSF as a whole.

all over the world take part in it. It is not an NGO or a confederation of NGOs, even though its conception and organization owe a great deal to NGOs. It is not a social movement, even though many participants designate it as the movement of movements. Although it presents itself as an agent of social change, the WSF rejects the concept of a privileged historical subject, that is, it confers no priority on any specific social actor in this process of social change. It holds no clearly defined ideology, in determining either what it rejects or what it asserts.

The social struggles that find expression in the WSF do not adequately fit either avenue of social change sanctioned by Western modernity: reform and revolution. Aside from the consensus on nonviolence, its modes of struggle are extremely diverse and appear spread out in a continuum between the poles of legality/institutionality and direct action/insurgency. Even the concept of nonviolence is open to widely disparate interpretations. Finally, the WSF is not structured according to any of the models of modern political organization, be they democratic centralism, representative democracy, or participatory democracy. Nobody represents it or is allowed to speak in its name, let alone make decisions, even though it sees itself as a forum that facilitates the decisions of the movements and organizations that take part in it.[3]

In what follows, I begin by stating what the political novelty of the WSF is. I then proceed to analyze the problems and tensions that this novelty creates particularly in what concerns political strategy and political action, and their relation to institutional action and law.

2.3.2 The political novelty of the World Social Forum
The political innovations of the WSF can be formulated in the following way:

2.3.2.1 A new critical utopia
The WSF entails the reemergence of a critical utopia, that is to say, the radical critique of present-day reality and the aspiration to a better society. It has arisen as an alternative to the dominance of the conservative utopia of neoliberalism –the utopian belief in the unregulated market as the source of economic and social well-being and the standard by which all other alternatives are to be measured (or, rather,

---

[3] For a better understanding of the political character and goals of the WSF, see Sen, Anand, Escobar, and Waterman (2004). See also the Charter of Principles (http://www.forumsocialmundial.org.br).

discarded). As all conservative utopias, neoliberalism distinguishes itself from critical utopias by the fact that it identifies itself with present-day reality, so that its utopian dimension is the radicalization or complete fulfillment of the present (Hinkelammert 2002:278).

The utopian dimension of the WSF consists in affirming the possibility of a counter-hegemonic globalization. Thus, the utopia of the WSF asserts itself more in negative terms (the definition of what it critiques) than in positive terms (the definition of that to which it aspires). As the first critical utopia of the twenty-first century, the WSF aims to break with the tradition of the critical utopias of Western modernity, many of which turned into conservative utopias. The openness of the utopian dimension of the WSF is rooted in its attempt to escape this perversion. For the WSF, the claim of alternatives is plural. The affirmation of alternatives goes hand in hand with the affirmation that there are alternatives to the alternatives.

Moreover, the utopia of the WSF is a radically democratic one. The WSF's focus on the processes of intercourse among the movements (rather than on an assessment of the movements' political agendas) is the main reason for its internal cohesion. It helps to maximize what unites and minimize what divides. This utopian design, which is clear in the WSF's Charter of Principles, is aimed at promoting consensuses beyond the ideological and political cleavages among the participating movements and organizations.

2.3.2.2 A very broad conception of power and oppression

Neoliberal globalization did not limit itself to submitting ever more interactions to the market, nor to raising the workers' exploitation rate by transforming the labor force into a global resource while preventing the emergence of a global labor market. Neoliberal globalization showed that exploitation is linked with many other forms of oppression that affect women, ethnic minorities, indigenous peoples, peasants, the unemployed, workers of the informal sector, legal and illegal immigrants, ghetto subclasses, gays and lesbians, and children and the young. All these forms of power create exclusion. One cannot ascribe to any one of them, in abstract, nor to the practices that resist them, any priority as to the claim that "another world is possible." Political priorities are always situated and conjunctural. They depend on the concrete conditions of each country at a given historical moment. To respond to such conditions and their fluctuations, the movements and organizations must give priority to the articulations among them. This ultimately explains the organizational novelty of a WSF with no leaders, its rejection of hierarchies, and its emphasis on networks made possible by the internet.[4]

2.3.2.3 Equivalence between the principles of equality and of recognition of difference

We live in societies that are obscenely unequal, and yet equality is lacking as an emancipatory ideal. Equality, understood as the equivalence among the same, ends up excluding what is different. Herein lies the grounding of the aforementioned political and organizational novelty, as well as the grounding of the WSF's option for participatory democracy as ruling principle of social emancipation, to the detriment of closed models such as that of state socialism.

2.3.2.4 Privileging rebellion and nonconformity to the detriment of revolution

There is no unique theory to guide the movements strategically, because the aim is not so much to seize power but rather to change the many faces of power as they present themselves in the institutions and sociabilities. Furthermore, even those for whom seizing power is a priority are divided as to the strategy. Some within the WSF prefer drastic breaks to bring about a new order (revolution), while others prefer gradual changes by means of an engagement and dialogue with the enemy (reform). At this level, the novelty consists in the celebration of diversity and pluralism, experimentalism, and radical democracy as well.

2.3.3 The issue of strategy and political action

Given its political novelties, the translation of the WSF's utopia into strategic planning and political action cannot but be difficult. This task is marked by the historical trajectory of the political left throughout the twentieth century. The reality of the divergences is often a ghostly one, in which disagreements about concrete political options get mixed up with disagreements about codes and languages in which such options are articulated.

The WSF has managed so far to overcome political divergences. Contrary to what happened in the thinking and practice of the left in Western capitalist modernity, the WSF has created a style and an atmosphere of inclusion of and respect for disagreements that made it very difficult for the different political factions to self-exclude

---

[4] On this subject, see Waterman (2003a, 2003b) and Escobar (2003).

themselves at the start under the excuse that they were being excluded. A decisive contribution to this was the WSF's "minimalist" program stated in its Charter of Principles: emphatic assertion of respect for diversity; access hardly conditioned (only movements or groups that advocate violence are excluded); no voting or deliberations at the Forum as such; no representative entity to speak for the Forum.

All this has contributed to making the WSF's power of attraction greater than its capacity to repel. Even the movements that are most severely critical of the WSF, such as the anarchists, have not been absent. There is definitely something new in the air, something that is chaotic, messy, ambiguous, and indefinite enough to deserve the benefit of the doubt or be susceptible to manipulation. Few would want to miss this train, particularly at a time in history when trains had ceased to run. For all these reasons, the desire to highlight what the movements and organizations have in common has prevailed upon the desire to underscore what separates them. The manifestation of tensions or cleavages has been relatively tenuous and, above all, has not resulted in mutual exclusions. It remains to be seen for how long this will to convergence and this chaotic sharing of differences will last.

Neither the kinds of cleavages nor the way the movements relate to them are randomly distributed inside the WSF. On the contrary, they reflect a meta-cleavage between Western and non-Western political cultures. Up to a point, this meta-cleavage also exists between the North and the South. Thus, given the strong presence of movements and organizations of the North Atlantic and white Latin America, it is no wonder that the most salient cleavages reflect the political culture and historical trajectory of the left in this part of the world. This means, on the one hand, that many movements and organizations from Africa, Asia, the indigenous and black Americas, and the Europe of immigrants do not recognize themselves in these cleavages; on the other hand, that alternative cleavages that these movements and organizations might want to make explicit are perhaps being concealed or minimized by the prevailing ones.

Bearing this caveat in mind, let us examine briefly the main manifest cleavages. Taken together, they represent the horizon within which the possibilities and limitations of subaltern cosmopolitan legality unfold.

2.3.3.1 Reform or revolution

This cleavage carries the weight of the tradition of the Western left. It is the cleavage between those who think that another world is possible through the gradual transformation of the unjust world in which we live – through legal reform and mechanisms of representative democracy – and those who believe that the world we live in is fundamentally a capitalist one that will never tolerate reforms that put it in question, and that it must therefore be overthrown and replaced by a socialist world. This is also regarded as a cleavage between moderates and radicals. Either field comprises a wide variety of positions. For instance, among revolutionaries, there is a clear cleavage between the old left aspiring to a variety of state socialism, the radically anti-statist anarchists, and some newer left rather ambivalent about the role of the state in a socialist society. Although they amount to a very minor proportion of the WSF, the anarchists are among the fiercest critics of reformism, which they claim controls the WSF's leadership.

This cleavage reverberates, albeit not linearly, in strategic options and options for legal and political action. As to legal action, the reformists are more willing to include legal and judicial mobilization in their political struggles, provided that political mobilization defines the framework for legal mobilization and not the opposite, while the revolutionaries are highly suspicious of law, even of bottom-up informal law or international human rights. In their view, there is a deep (strategic but also ideological) fault line between political mobilization and legal mobilization that makes the articulation between the two virtually impossible. Legal action tends to individualize the conflicts, to prioritize legal professional knowledge, to take away from the movements the rhythm of the struggle, to inflate small reversible achievements into major irreversible victories – in sum, it tends to have a demobilizing effect. Concerning more specific political choices, one of the most salient is the strategic choice between reforming and engaging the institutions of neoliberal globalization (the WTO and the international financial institutions), and confronting them and fighting for their elimination or replacement.

What is new about the WSF as a political entity is that the majority of the movements and organizations that participate in it do not recognize themselves in these cleavages and refuse to take part in them. There is great resistance to rigidly assuming a stance and even greater to labeling it according to the classificatory orthodoxies of the past. The majority of movements and organizations have political experiences in which moments of confrontation alternate or combine with moments of dialogue and engagement, in which long-range visions of social change cohabit with the tactical possibilities of the political and social conjuncture in which the struggles take place, in which radical denunciations of capitalism do not paralyze the energy for small changes when the big changes are not possible, in which resorting to courts is now considered useful and now detrimental.

Above all, for many movements and organizations, the cleavage reform/revolution is Western- or Northern-centric, and is more useful for understanding the past of the left than its future. Indeed, many movements and organizations do not recognize themselves, for the same reasons, in the dichotomy between left and right.

Precisely because for many movements and organizations the priority is not to seize power but rather to change the power relations in oppression's many faces, the political tasks, however radical, must be carried out here and now, in the society in which we live. Gramsci's (1971) concept of hegemony is useful to understand the movements' political actions. What is necessary is to create alternative, counter-hegemonic visions, capable of sustaining the daily practices and sociabilities of citizens and social groups. The work of the movements' leaderships is of course important, but it is not conceived of as the work of an enlightened vanguard that breaks the path for the masses, ever the victims of mystification and false consciousness. On the contrary, as Subcomandante Marcos has suggested, it behooves the leaderships to "walk with those who go more slowly." It is not a question of either revolution or reform. It is, for some, a question of rebellion and transgression; for others, a question of revolution in a non-Leninist sense, one about civilizational change occurring over a long period of time.

2.3.3.2 Socialism or social emancipation

This cleavage is related to the previous one but there is no perfect overlap between the two. Regardless of the position taken vis-à-vis the previous cleavage, or the refusal to take a position, the movements and organizations diverge as to the political definition of the other possible world. For some, socialism is still an adequate designation, however abundant and disparate the conceptions of socialism may be. For the majority, however, socialism carries in itself the idea of a closed model of a future society, and must, therefore, be rejected. They prefer other, less politically charged designations, suggesting openness and a constant search for alternatives. For example, social emancipation as the aspiration to a society in which the different power relations are replaced by relations of shared authority. This is an inclusive designation focusing more on processes than on final stages of social change.

Those framing their struggles in terms of social emancipation tend to have a more positive view of subaltern cosmopolitan legality based on the historical record of successful legal and judicial struggles that became known as landmarks of social emancipation.

But many movements of the South think that no general labels need be attached to the goals of the struggles. Labels run the risk of taking off from the practices that originated them, acquiring a life of their own, and giving rise to perverse results. As a matter of fact, according to some, the concept of socialism is Western-centric and Northern-centric, while the concept of emancipation is equally a prey of the Western bias to create false universalisms. Hence many do not recognize themselves in either term of this dichotomy, and are wary of proposing an alternative one.

2.3.3.3 The state as an enemy or as a potential ally

This is also a cleavage in which movements of the North recognize themselves more easily than movements of the South. On the one hand, there are those who think that the state – although an important arena of struggle in the past – for the past twenty-five years has been transnationalized and turned into an agent of neoliberal globalization. Either the state has become irrelevant or is today what it has always been – the expression of capitalism's general interests. The privileged target of counter-hegemonic struggles must, therefore, be the state – or, at a minimum, such struggles must be fought with total autonomy vis-à-vis the state. On the other hand, there are those who think that the state is a social relation and, as such, is contradictory and continues to be an important arena of struggle. Neoliberal globalization did not rob the state of its centrality; rather it reoriented it better to serve the interests of global capital. Deregulation is a social regulation like any other, hence a political field where one must act if there are conditions for acting.

The majority of the movements, even those that acknowledge the existence of a cleavage in this regard, refuse to take a rigid and principled position on this issue. Their experiences of struggle show that the state, while sometimes the enemy, can often be a precious ally in the struggle against transnational impositions. In these circumstances, the privileged stance with the WSF is, again, pragmatism. If in some situations confrontation is in order, in others collaboration is rather advised. In others still a combination of both is appropriate. What is highlighted in the discussions on this issue within the WSF is that, at every moment or in every struggle, the movement or organization in question be clear and transparent regarding the reasons for the adopted option, so as to safeguard the autonomy of the action.

Here also the cleavage prolongs itself in the ways in which legal mobilization can or cannot be part of counter-hegemonic struggles. The pragmatic position vis-à-vis the state tends to go together with a more positive view about the progressive potential of legal and judicial action. While never considering the state as an unconditional ally, this stance is open to the possibility that in specific cases the institutionalization of arrangements embodying the convergence of state action with counter-hegemonic movements can be beneficial for the latter.

2.3.3.4 National or global struggles

This is the most evenly distributed cleavage among the movements and organizations that comprise the WSF. On one side, there are the movements that, while participating in the WSF, believe that the latter is no more than a meeting point and a cultural event, since the struggles that are truly important for the welfare of marginalized populations are fought at the national level against the state or the dominant national civil society. For instance, according to a report on the WSF prepared by the Movement for National Democracy in the Philippines that privileges the national scale:

> the World Social Forum still floats somewhere above, seeing and trying yet really unable to address actual conditions of poverty and powerlessness brought about by Imperialist globalization in many countries. Unless it finds definite ways of translating or even transcending its "globalness" into more practical interventions that address these conditions, it just might remain a huge but empty forum that is more a cultural affair than anything else ... [N]ational struggles against globalization are and should provide the anchor to any anti-globalization initiative at the international level
> (Gobrin-Morante 2002: 19)

On the other side, there are the movements according to which the state is now transnationalized and thus is no longer the privileged center of political decision-making. This decentering of the state also brought about the decentering of the civil society, which is subjected today to many processes of cultural and social globalization. Furthermore, in some situations, the object of the struggle (be it a decision of the WTO, a World Bank policy, or a TNC's decision to explore for oil in indigenous territory) is outside the national space and includes a plurality of countries simultaneously. This is why the scale of the struggle, from this viewpoint, must be increasingly global, a fact that highlights the relevance of the WSF.

According to the large majority of the movements, this is again a cleavage that does not do justice to the concrete needs of concrete struggles. What is new about contemporary societies is that the scales of sociability – the local, the national, and the global – are increasingly interconnected. In the most remote village of the Amazon or India the effects of hegemonic globalization and the ways in which the national state engages with it are clearly felt. This applies also to counter-hegemonic struggles. For movements participating in the WSF, although every political or social struggle privileges a particular scale, its success lies in the combination of different scales. The decision on which scale to privilege is a political one that is made on a case-by-case basis.

The impact of this cleavage on the politics of legality is shown in the relative weight given to international law, international human rights, and transnational legal advocacy in framing political actions. Whenever the movements or NGOs regard legal mobilization as an integral part of political mobilization, they tend to resort to legal strategies at different scales. Such "transcalar" character is part and parcel of subaltern cosmopolitan legality – the type of legal mobilization that, by targeting the global in the local and the local in the global, advances counter-hegemonic globalization (Santos, 2002:468).

2.3.3.5 Direct or institutional action

This is the cleavage with the most direct impact on the politics of legality. It is clearly linked to the above-mentioned cleavages concerning reform/revolution and the role of the state. It is also a cleavage with a long tradition in the Western left. Those for whom this cleavage continues to have a great deal of importance are the same that slight the newness of neoliberal globalization in the historical process of capitalist domination.

On the one side, there are movements that believe that legal struggles, based on dialogue and engagement with state institutions or international agencies, are ineffectual because the political and legal system of the state and the institutions of capitalism are impervious to any legal or institutional measures capable of really improving the living conditions of the popular classes. Institutional struggles call for the intermediation of parties, and parties tend to put those struggles at the service of their party interests and constituencies. The success of an institutional struggle has, therefore, a very high price – the price of cooptation, denaturalization, and banalization. But even in the rare case in which an institutional struggle leads to legal measures that correspond to the movements' objectives, it is almost certain that the concrete application of such measures will end up being subjected to the legal-bureaucratic logic of the state, thereby frustrating the movements' expectations. This is why only direct action, mass protest, and strikes will yield the success of the struggles. The popular classes have no weapon but external pressure on the system. If they venture into it, they are defeated from the start.

In contrast, the supporters of institutional struggles assume that the "system" is contradictory, a political and social relation where it is possible to fight and where failure is not the only possible outcome. In modernity, the state and specifically state law was the center of this system. In the course of the twentieth century the popular classes conquered important institutional and legal spaces, of which the welfare system is a clear example. The fact that the welfare system is now in crisis, and the "opening" that it offered the popular classes is now being closed up, does not mean that the process is irreversible. Indeed, from this point of view, it may be reversed if the movements and organizations continue to struggle inside the institutions and the legal system.

In general, the stronger movements and organizations are those that more frequently privilege institutional struggles, whereas the less strong are those that more frequently privilege direct action. This cleavage is much more lively among movements and organizations of the North than of the South. The large majority of the movements, however, refuse to take sides in this cleavage. According to them, the concrete legal and political conditions must dictate the kind of struggle to be privileged. Conditions may actually recommend the sequential or simultaneous use of the two kinds of struggle. Historically, direct action was at the genesis of progressive institutional changes, and it was always necessary to combat the cooptation or even subversion of such changes through direct action.

In spite of the differences, all the movements and NGOs tend to agree that legal mobilization demands a double investment that most movements and NGOs cannot afford. One the one side, the choice of the most adequate legal forum oftentimes demands prohibitive legal and financial resources. On the other, the kind of legal activism called for – in which a high level of legal expertise must combine with a progressive political stance providing the stimulus to seek beyond conventional legal interpretation and adjudication – is rarely found. This explains why the stronger movements or NGOs, which often have a legal department of their own, tend to have a more positive view of legal, institutional action.

2.3.3.6 *The principle of equality or the principle of respect for difference*

As noted above, one of the novelties of the WSF is the fact that the large majority of its movements and organizations believe that social emancipation must be grounded on two principles – the principle of equality and the principle of respect for difference. The struggle for either of them must be articulated with the other, for the fulfillment of either is a condition of the fulfillment of the other. Nonetheless, there is a cleavage among the movements and even, sometimes, inside the same movement on whether priority should be given to one of these principles, and in that case to which one. Among those that answer the first question in the affirmative, the cleavage is between those that give priority to the principle of equality (for equality alone may create real opportunities for the recognition of difference) and those that give priority to the principle of the recognition of difference, for without such recognition equality conceals the exclusions and marginalities on which it lies, thus becoming doubly oppressive (for what it conceals and for what it shows).

This cleavage occurs among and within movements. It cuts across, among others, the workers', the feminist, the indigenous, and the black movements. For instance, whereas the workers' movement has privileged the principle of equality to the detriment of the principle of the recognition of difference, the feminist movement has, in general, privileged the latter in detriment to the former. But the most widespread position – most forcefully advanced by the indigenous movement – is that both principles have priority, and that no principle should be privileged in the abstract. According to this view, concrete political conditions will dictate to each movement which one of the principles is to be privileged in a given concrete struggle. Any struggle conceived under the aegis of one of these two principles must be organized so as to open space for the other principle.

In the feminist movement of the WSF, this position is now dominant. Virginia Vargas (s/d) puts this position in the following terms:

> At the World Social Forum, feminists have begun ... nourishing processes that integrate gender justice with economic justice, while recovering

cultural subversion and subjectivity as a longer term strategy for transformation. This confronts two broad expressions of injustice: socio-economic injustice, rooted in societal political and economic structures, and cultural and symbolic injustice, rooted in societal patterns of representation, interpretation and communication. Both injustices affect women, along with many other racial, ethnic, sexual and geographical dimensions.

Vargas asks for new feminisms constituting a heterogeneous and expansive panorama, generating polycentric fields of action that spread over a range of civil society organizations and are not constrained to women's affairs, although women undoubtedly maintain them in many ways. And she concludes: "Our presence in the WSF, asking these very questions, is also an expression of this change."

The dynamic coexistence of the principle of equality and the principle of recognition of difference carries enormous weight in defining the position of the politics of legality in subaltern cosmopolitan struggles. The crisis of both demo-liberal and demo-socialist reformism had its most direct impact on the principle of equality, which indeed had provided the rationale for the progressive reformist struggles of the twentieth century (Santos 2002:441). The crisis did not affect the principle of recognition of difference in the same way and it can even be said that, simultaneously with the deepening of the crisis of the principle of equality, important victories were obtained as regards the social validation of the principle of recognition of difference, as shown most notably both by the feminist movements from the 1970s onwards and by the indigenous movements from the 1980s onwards. These victories injected a new credibility into the politics of legality both in the North and in the South, a credibility likely to spill over into other areas of political struggle.

2.3.3.7 Trans-conflictuality
Many of the tensions and cleavages mentioned above are not specific to the WSF. They in fact belong to the historical legacy of the social forces that for the past two hundred years have struggled against the status quo for a better society. The specificity of the WSF resides in the fact that all these cleavages coexist in its bosom without upsetting its aggregating power. To my mind, three factors contribute to this. First, the different cleavages are important in different ways for the different movements and organizations, and none of them is present in the practices or discourses of all the movements and organizations. Thus, all of them, at the same time that they tend toward factionalism,

liberate the potential for consensus. That is to say, all the movements and organizations have room for action and discourse in which to agree with all the other movements or organizations, whatever the cleavages among them. Secondly, there has so far been no tactical or strategic demand that would intensify the cleavages by radicalizing positions. On the contrary, cleavages have been fairly low intensity. For the movements and organizations in general, what unites has been more important than what divides. Thirdly, even when cleavages are acknowledged, the different movements and organizations distribute themselves amongst them in a nonlinear way. If a given movement opposes another in a given cleavage, it may well be on the same side in another cleavage. Thus, the different strategic alliances or common actions featured by each movement tend to have different partners. In this way are precluded the accumulation and strengthening of divergences that could result from the alignment of the movements in multiple cleavages. On the contrary, the cleavages end up neutralizing one another. In such trans-conflictuality, to my mind, lies the WSF's aggregating power.

2.4 THE POLITICS OF LEGALITY IN A CONTEXT OF CONFLICTING GLOBALIZATIONS

I have described the WSF as a critical realist utopia. At this point it should be asked what kind of relation of law and politics (what I call politics of legality) is congruent with this utopia and what political strategies it has been giving rise to. Does it comprise a legal utopia? How does it compare to neoliberal governance, the privileged legal form of hegemonic globalization?

I have argued elsewhere that the transformation, in the nineteenth century, of the modern idea of progress into the idea of infinite and ever expanding repetition of bourgeois society entrusted both modern science (and, specifically, the social sciences) and law with the task of discovering and guaranteeing the regularities of social life and social transformation that made possible "normal change" (Santos 2002:71–82). Law, in the meantime reduced to state law, was available both as an instrument to fulfill the imperatives of social regulation and as a pre-understanding of the scientific knowledge of society still to be developed.

This unlimited availability of the law of the state for social engineering was at the roots of its conversion into a utopia of its own – a legal utopia. This legal utopia was the engine behind normal change – the idea that, through a dialectics of amelioration and repetition, social change was a continuous process proceeding through gradual transformations sanctioned by the state law, itself changing continuously and gradually.

This pattern of normal change is based on the following presuppositions. First, no matter how diverse its application from state to state, the pattern of normal change is the transnational political logic of the inter-state system. Secondly, the national steering mechanisms developed and deployed by the state are available and are efficacious throughout the national territory, whose boundaries are also guaranteed by the state. Thirdly, the financial capacity of the state to implement all of its strategies depends above all on the sustainability of economic growth, and hence on the success of the accumulation strategies. Fourthly, human aspirations and the well-being of the people can be fulfilled or guaranteed by mass-produced services and products designed according to a commodity form, even if not distributed by commodity markets. Fifthly, the risks and dangers that the state is asked to protect its citizens from occur rarely, and are predominantly small-scale or medium-scale.

This legal utopia is undergoing a deep (final?) crisis that started in the early 1970s and continues today (Santos 2002:71–82, 447–458). It is in the shadow (if not in the ruins) of this legal utopia and its crisis that both neoliberal governance and subaltern cosmopolitan legality must be understood. They represent two contrasting interpretations of the conditions deriving from the crisis of modern legal utopia and, consequently, offer two contrasting prospective readings of our time. Neoliberal governance sees the crisis of the legal utopia not as a problem but as a solution. According to the governance matrix, modern legal utopia is part and parcel of a command-and-control bureaucratic rule, centered on the state and the judiciary, which, besides being authoritarian, rigid, and non-participatory, is ridden by inefficiencies and haunted by the enactment/enforcement gap (Simon 2003). The above-mentioned features of governance are thus designed to offer the solution to the problems created by modern legal utopia, not by its crisis.

For subaltern cosmopolitan legality, modern legal utopia was a false solution to the very real problem of managing the tensions between democracy and capitalism. On one side, democratic struggles for inclusion in the social contract, which resulted in expanding rights, some measure of social redistribution, and the growth of non-mercantile interactions among citizens, were made possible by the welfare state. On the other side, profit-driven capitalism viewed social redistribution as a form of expropriation. The modern legal utopia never managed to solve the contradiction between redistributive democracy and capitalism, but kept it within manageable boundaries, thus laying the foundation for the consensus politics that ruled the core countries from the second post-war period to the end of the 1960s. The crisis of the legal utopia has worsened the problem of social distribution. Paradoxically, it has done so in such a way that the contradictions between democracy and capitalism seem to have vanished. Deprived of its redistributive potential, democracy is today globally promoted by the same agencies that promote capitalism around the world. The tension has dissolved in complementarity.

This, however, is only part of the story. The other part is a deep disjuncture between political regime and social regime, which I have described as the rise of social fascism (Santos 2002:453). It is a new socio-political constellation characterized by the confinement of democracy to an ever more narrowly defined political field that coexists (rather than interferes) with forms of sociability, in which the more powerful non-state actors assume veto power over the life and well-being of less powerful or powerless ones. It is a highly unstable political constellation, reproduced in the core countries by a hitherto efficacious transformation of consensus politics into resignation politics, and in the peripheral countries by the imposition of structural adjustment policies often coupled with the collaboration of corrupt local elites. Social fascism on a global scale is the problem that subaltern cosmopolitan legality sees itself confronted with. There is no point in trying to revive the modern legal utopia nor in inventing a new legal utopia. The solution lies in a critical realist utopia whose pragmatic unfolding may involve legal mobilization as part of broader political mobilization.

In order to be successfully mobilized in a counter-hegemonic context, law must undergo a deep process of revision. At stake is, first of all, the inquiry into the possibility of the counter-hegemonic use of a hegemonic tool such as law. Secondly, the inquiry is into non-hegemonic traditions of law and legality and the possibility of its mobilization in counter-hegemonic struggles. As I argued at the outset, this unthinking of law involves an expansion of the conception of the politics of legality. The legal struggles conducted by the movements and NGOs combined in the WSF bear witness to the need for such an expansion. I emphasized the internal diversity of the WSF by focusing on the main cleavages among the movements, which should suffice to caution us against the idea that a new paradigm is emerging. What can be said is that in spite of all differences they share the quest for the fourfold expansion of the politics of legality mentioned in the introductory section of this chapter.

First, subaltern cosmopolitan legality is never formulated as a legal strategy but rather as a political strategy that comprises legal components. Moreover the struggles do not focus exclusively on the principle of equality (social redistribution), as was the case of modern legal utopia, but rather on a complex and dynamic balance between the principle of equality and the principle of recognition of difference.

Secondly, whenever law is resorted to, it is not necessarily the nation-state law; it may be the local unofficial law, as well as international or transnational law. Herein lies the transcalar nature of legal mobilization. The difference of subaltern cosmopolitan legality vis-à-vis modern legal utopia is evident as the latter focused exclusively on official state law.

Thirdly, legal knowledges susceptible of being mobilized in subaltern cosmopolitan legal struggles are very diverse. Only rarely do the struggles rely exclusively on state-certified professional legal knowledge. Indigenous people, urban squatter settlers, over-exploited workers in sweatshops, landless peasants and peasants trying to secure traditional land tenure against market-led tenure regimes, discriminated women, minorities, religious groups and lower castes, migrants, workers in the informal economy, environmentalists, and peace activists – all of them act under the assumption that law is a strange substance made of different ingredients and in different doses to be carried in different vessels and used (or discarded) in different ways along the road toward a more just society.

Fourthly, the priority of political mobilization over legal mobilization and the diversity of political tools resorted to are congruent with a conception of social struggle whose time frame is much more complex than the one that presided over legal mobilization under the aegis of modern legal utopia. On the one hand, the social groups involved in counter-hegemonic struggles refuse to be seen as residual, inferior, ignorant, unproductive, or local. On the other hand, they refuse to forget the long duration of capitalism and colonialism as a factor explaining both their grievances and their resistance.

In sum, the WSF's utopia is in the antipodes of the legal utopia that is at the core of modern capitalist societies. But, aware of the danger of throwing out the baby with the bath water, counter-hegemonic globalization struggles cannot afford not to use any non-violent means available to them against capitalist modernity, including those invented by capitalist modernity to betray its promises of freedom, equality, and non-discrimination. Herein lies a transmodern conception of law.

References

Angelis, Massimo de. 2003. "Neoliberal Governance, Reproduction and Accumulation." *The Commoner* 7:1–27.

Arendt, Hannah. 1968 (1951). *The Origins of Totalitarianism.* New York: Harcourt Brace Jovanovich.

Boyer, Robert. 1986. *Capitalismes fin de siècle.* Paris: Maspero.

Boyer, Robert, and Daniel Drache (Eds.). 1996. *States Against Markets: The Limits of Globalization.* New York: Routledge.

Castells, Manuel. 1996. *The Rise of the Network Society.* Cambridge: Blackwell.

Crozier, Michel, Samuel Huntington and Joji Watanuki. 1975. *The Crisis of Democracy: Report on the Governability of Democracies to the Trilateral Commission.* New York: New York University Press.

Escobar, Arturo. 2003. *Other Worlds Are (Already) Possible: Cyber-Internationalism and Post-Capitalist Cultures.* Paper presented at the Cyberspace Panel, Life After Capitalism Programme, 3rd World Social Forum, Porto Alegre, January 23–28.

Gobrin-Morante, C. 2002. "The World Social Forum Fights Imperialist Globalization." In *We, the Peoples of the World Social Forum*, edited by L. Nisula and K. Sehm-Patomäki. Network Institute for Global Democratization. Discussion Paper 2/2002, 19–21.

Gramsci, Antonio. 1971. *Selections from the Prison Notebooks of Antonio Gramsci.* New York: International Publishers.

Habermas, Jurgen. 1982. *Theorie des Kommunikativen Handelns.* Frankfurt: Suhrkamp.

Held, David. 1987. *Models of Democracy.* Cambridge: Polity Press.

Hinkelammert, Franz. 2002. *Crítica de la razón utópica.* Bilbao Desclée de Brouwer.

Jessop, Bob. 1998. "The Rise of Governance and the Risks of Failure: The Case of Economic Development." *International Social Science Journal* 155:29–45.

Kuhn, Thomas. 1970. *The Structure of Scientific Revolutions.* Chicago: University of Chicago Press

Macpherson, C. B. 1966. *The Real World of Democracy.* Oxford: Clarendon.
1977. *The Life and Times of Liberal Democracy.* Oxford: Oxford University Press.

Monedero, Juan Carlos. 2003. *La Trampa de la Gobernanza: Nuevas Formas de Participacion Politica*. Mexico City: Cámara de Diputados.

Offe, Claus. 1985. *Disorganized Capitalism*. Oxford: Polity Press.

Rodríguez-Garavito, César. 2005. "Global Governance, Cross-Border Organizing, and Labor Rights: Codes of Conduct and Anti-Sweatshop Struggles in Global Apparel Factories in Mexico and Guatemala." *Politics & Society* 33 (2).

Santos, Boaventura de Sousa. 1995. *Toward a New Common Sense: Law, Science and Politics in the Paradigmatic Transition*. New York: Routledge.

2001. (Ed.). *Globalização: Fatalidade ou Utopia?*. Porto: Afrontamento.

2002. *Toward a New Legal Common Sense*. London: Butterworths.

2004. "A Critique of Lazy Reason: Against the Waste of Experience." In *The Modern World System in the Longue Durée*, edited by Immanuel, Wallerstein. New York: Free Press.

Santos, Boaventura de Sousa. and Jane Jenson. (Eds.). 2000. *Globalizing Institutions: Case Studies in Regulation and Innovation*. Aldershot: Ashgate.

Sen, J., A. Anand, A. Escobar, and P. Waterman. 2004. *World Social Forum: Challenging Empires*. New Delhi: Viveka Foundation.

Simon, William. 2003. "Solving Problems v. Claiming Rights: The Pragmatist Challenge to Legal Liberalism." Public Law Research Paper, No. 03-58, Stanford Law School and Columbia Law School.

United Nations. 2000. *Global Compact Primer*. New York: United Nations (www.unglobalcompact.org).

Vargas, Virginia (s/d). *Los aportes y los retos feministas en el Foro Social Mundial*. (www.alainet.org).

Waterman, Peter. 2003a. *First Reflections on the World Social Forum, Porto Alegre, Brazil*. Library of Alternatives, WSF (www.forumsocialmundial.org.br).

2003b. *Second Thoughts on the WSF: Place, Space and the Reinvention of Social Emancipation on a Global Scale*. Library of Alternatives, WSF (www.forumsocialmundial.org.br).

CHAPTER 3

NIKE'S LAW: THE ANTI-SWEATSHOP MOVEMENT, TRANSNATIONAL CORPORATIONS, AND THE STRUGGLE OVER INTERNATIONAL LABOR RIGHTS IN THE AMERICAS

César A. Rodríguez-Garavito

3.1 INTRODUCTION

Just as sweatshops have become the symbol of the perverse effects of neoliberal globalization, the transnational anti-sweatshop movement lies at the heart of the struggle for social justice in the global economy. In the global North, the reemergence of sweatshops in such cities as New York and Los Angeles entails the return of the economic and legal realities of the nineteenth century (Bonacich and Appelbaum 2000; Ross 1997). In the South, the exploitative labor conditions and the unfulfilled promise of employment and growth have turned *maquilas* into an icon of the failure of late twentieth-century neoliberalism. In bridging the North–South divide through highly plural, dynamic, and decentralized transnational advocacy networks (TANs), the anti-sweatshop movement holds out the prospect of a revamped, twenty-first century labor internationalism (Evans, forthcoming; Moody 1997).

Beyond its political and symbolic importance, the anti-sweatshop movement offers a privileged vantage point to examine the role of law in counter-hegemonic globalization for two reasons. First, in terms of social movement theory (Snow *et al.* 1986), the "framing" of the anti-sweatshop cause has crucially relied on law and legal discourse. Given that abuses committed in global sweatshops – from physical violence to sexual harassment and misery wages – undermine fundamental conditions of human dignity, TANs have framed their struggle as a vindication of basic human rights. This has not only lent a potent moral force to the movement but has also placed the mobilization of human rights rules and discourses at the center of TANs' strategies. Secondly, as I will argue below, the anti-sweatshop movement can be best understood as a component of a broader movement to regulate the operation of transnational corporations (TNCs) in the global economy. A key stake in this global field of confrontation pitting TNCs against TANs – and the myriad governmental and non-governmental organizations siding with each camp, as well as the lawyers, consultants, and academics providing the legal and intellectual ammunition to each – is the definition of the rules establishing the rights of corporations and workers in the global economy (Cavanagh 1997:49). As Wallerstein has put it, "the creation of these legal structures as well as their real enforcement becomes therefore one of the prime political arenas of conflict in the world-system" (Wallerstein 2002:64). Thus, as I set out to show in this chapter, the counter-hegemonic potential of the normative vision and legal strategies of the anti-sweatshop movement can be assessed only if seen in relation to the hegemonic visions and uses of law through which TNCs and their supporters seek to consolidate their dominance in the global economy.

The legal tools available to actors in the confrontation over labor rights are highly heterogeneous and operate at different scales. In the absence of effective institutions of transnational governance, working conditions in global commodity chains are regulated through myriad public and private arrangements that constitute a legal kaleidoscope rather than a legal system.[1] Thus, in terms of sociolegal theory, the struggle for worker rights takes place in a context of legal pluralism in which national labor laws, ILO conventions, corporate codes of conduct, social clauses in bilateral and regional trade agreements, and unilateral sanctions overlap and clash (Arthurs 1996; Trubek, Mosher, and Rothstein 2000). This legal kaleidoscope involves both "soft law" created by private actors such as TNCs (e.g. codes of conduct) and NGOs (e.g. alternative treaties) as well as "hard law" backed by state apparatuses. Hegemonic and counter-hegemonic actors actively exploit and shape the unequal opportunities created by the tensions and contradictions within this pluralist legal arena.

The use of plural legal fields by social movements is a staple topic of sociolegal research. The existing literature, however, continues to be

---

[1] I take the concept of "legal kaleidoscope" from Santos and García's (2001) work on legal pluralism in Colombia.

largely focused on the local and national scales, thus missing the novel forms of legal pluralism and transnational political mobilization associated with globalization. Specifically in the Americas, the area on which this chapter focuses, two different trends have converged to produce this important blind spot in our understanding of contemporary law and social movements. In Latin America, the vibrant tradition of studies on the alternative use of law by popular actors has overwhelmingly focused on local processes of informal law creation within marginalized communities (Oliveira 2003; Santos 1991), or the mobilization of national courts by activists (García and Uprimny 2004). In the US, despite the recognition of legal pluralism, the literature on legal mobilization continues to be dominated by analyses of the use of litigation and domestic courts by social movement organizations (McCann 1994; Scheingold and Sarat 2004). In both scholarly traditions, therefore, the task of inquiring precisely how transnational social movements shape and are shaped by the plural array of rules regulating the world economy remains to be done.

The growing literature on transnational social movements offers some useful clues for this task (Keck and Sikkink 1998; Tarrow 2001). Particularly relevant is recent exploratory work on the role of NGOs in the "social construction of law" (Sikkink 2002). However, as Rajagopal (2003) has noted, social movement research has yet to systematically examine the use of legal institutions and discourses as frames and arenas of contentious political action across borders.

Based on ethnographic research on anti-sweatshop activism in the apparel industry in Mexico, Guatemala, and the US, in this chapter I set out to contribute to filling this void by examining the way in which the transnational anti-sweatshop movement has combined political and legal strategies to advance the cause of international labor rights. Since a central premise of my analysis is that such counter-hegemonic use of law should be understood in the context of the ongoing struggle to define the rules regulating capital and labor in the global economy, I also discuss the strategies of hegemonic actors (namely, TNCs targeted by anti-sweatshop TANs) to constrain the reach, the scope, and the enforceability of international labor regulations.

My argument is threefold. First, I claim that at the heart of the anti-sweatshop movement lies the effort to realign legal responsibility and corporate economic power. In seeking to establish de facto or de jure joint liability for labor conditions in the global apparel industry, activists seek to cut through the fiction of the Northern manufacturers and retailers and their Southern contractors as independent entities. Conversely, corporate responses to the movement are largely aimed at maintaining this fiction and the existing legal arrangements that support it. Secondly, contrary to approaches focusing on the functionality of legal pluralism and novel forms of "soft law" for the smooth operation of the global economy, I argue that global legal fields are sites of uneven political contention where hegemonic and counter-hegemonic actors struggle to set the hierarchy and the content of competing legal rules. As the study of the field of international labor rights shows, the privileged scale of regulation (whether global, national, or local) and the "hardness" or "softness" of the law are themselves objects of political contention rather than the result of a systemic trend toward global governance and soft law. Thirdly, I posit that transnational hegemonic and counter-hegemonic coalitions pragmatically exploit the tensions and contradictions of this kaleidoscopic legal landscape. TNCs' and TANs' strategies constantly shift among different scales and types of law, as well as between political and legal strategies. For instance, TANs simultaneously engage in efforts to bolster national states' regulatory capacity, create effective global corporate codes of conduct for labor and promote direct action campaigns to boycott the products of targeted TNCs at the regional level. Similarly, while strategically invoking their abidance with weak national labor laws to fend off attempts at cross-border regulation, TNCs strive to maintain the non-enforceable character of codes of conduct and use the political muscle stemming from their capacity to shift production away from inhospitable regulatory environments.

In order to substantiate these claims, in what follows I explore the three key issues of contention between anti-sweatshop TANs and their corporate targets. I begin by analyzing the struggle over *whether* to create a global regulatory system on labor. Then, I examine the battle over precisely *how* to regulate working conditions in the global economy. In the third section, I consider the conflict over the privileged *scale* of regulation. Finally, I offer some conclusions.

Before proceeding, a note on data is in order. The empirical evidence used in this chapter was collected as part of a broader research project on cross-border organizing campaigns and labor rights in the apparel industry of North and Central America (see Rodríguez-Garavito 2005). The project included detailed case studies – based on participant observation, factory visits, and interviews with key actors in Guatemala, Mexico, and the US – of exceptional campaigns that resulted in the unionization of *maquila* workers.[2] Prominent among them is the campaign at Kukdong, a Korean-owned Nike contractor located near the city of Puebla, Mexico. Since the Kukdong case vividly illustrates the core legal issues of the anti-sweatshop movement in the Americas and has become an icon of the accomplishments of the latter, I will use it to empirically ground the discussion throughout this chapter.[3]

The basic facts of the case are as follow.[4] On January 9, 2001, more than 600 out of the 850 Kukdong workers occupied the yard of the factory to vindicate their right to form an independent union and demand the improvement of the worm-infested cafeteria food. Management reacted by firing the strike's leaders and suing them for "destruction of private property." After two days of protests, the police forcefully evicted the strikers. The violent reaction of management and the state authorities escalated the conflict and prompted the activation of a budding US–Mexico anti-sweatshop TAN as well as of the code of conduct monitoring systems that had been recently set up under pressure from US student organizations as well as Mexican and US NGOs and unions. By organizing demonstrations at Nike stores in the US and summoning independent monitoring organizations from both countries, the TAN put heavy pressure on Nike (as well as on Reebok, a Kukdong customer at the time) to in turn pressure management to enforce the code of conduct and abide by local labor laws guaranteeing workers' right to organize. The campaign achieved rapid success and resulted in the reinstatement of all the workers and the founding of an independent union in March 2001. Mexican labor authorities, under strong international pressure, officially recognized the union in September 2001. The union signed a labor contract with management in October 2001 that included a 40 percent wage increase and considerable improvements in working conditions. Kukdong's union, which continues to thrive several years after its foundation, is the first (and still the only) independent union in the Mexican apparel industry.

---

[2] Fieldwork, which was carried out between 2001 and 2004, was made possible by grants from the Institute for Law and Society at New York University and the Tinker-Nave fund at the University of Wisconsin-Madison.

[3] After the episode of labor unrest described below, the factory changed its name to Mexmode. However, given that the case became internationally known by the former name of the plant, I will refer to it as Kukdong.

[4] For a detailed analysis of this case, see Rodríguez-Garavito (2005).

3.2 THE STRUGGLE OVER JOINT LIABILITY RULES ACROSS BORDERS

As economist John Commons wrote in 1901, "the term 'sweating,' or 'sweating system,' originally denoted a system of subcontract, wherein the work is let out to contractors to be done in small shops or homes" (1977:44). In contrast with the "factory system," in which workers toiled under the same roof under contract with the manufacturer, in sweatshops they were "isolated and unknown" (Commons 1977:45). Moreover, subcontracting made it possible for manufacturers to deny responsibility for violations of labor rights in sweatshops, which they could now conveniently blame on the infamous "jobbers" or "sweaters" owning the supplier workshops.

The first anti-sweatshop movement, organized by apparel workers in Northern countries in the early twentieth century, sought to fight exploitative working conditions and to restore through law the link between manufacturers and contractors that had been blurred by the subcontracting system. In the US, for instance, striking workers in garment factories (most famously at the Triangle Shirtwaist Company in New York City in 1911) not only inaugurated a national labor movement that was to last for most of the twentieth century but also signed union contracts with manufacturers that made the latter responsible for the wages and conditions of their contractors. Union manufacturers were required to use union contractors. Such joint liability arrangements, which spread through the industry and were incorporated in nascent labor law systems around the world, strike at the heart of the sweatshop system (Howard 1997:155).

The second, contemporary anti-sweatshop movement faces the same basic challenge as its predecessor. Compounding its task, however, is the fact that production has now been decentralized across borders, particularly in sectors such as apparel. With profits in the apparel sector concentrated in design, marketing, and retailing operations, dominant actors in the industry have abandoned their production activities (if they ever undertook them) and contracted them with suppliers in the global South. The concentration of revenue and power in this buyer-driven commodity chain is such that large retailers and branded merchandisers have the requisite muscle to set prices and conditions on myriad suppliers scattered around the globe (Gereffi, Korzeniewicz, and Korzeniewicz 1994). This allows retailers such as Wal-Mart to boom on low prices squeezed from their suppliers and enables brand merchandisers such as Nike to thrive on the careful cultivation of an image associated with a life style.

Just as early twentieth-century jobbers, global retailers and manufacturers seek to disentangle themselves from legal responsibility for labor conditions in supplier factories. At stake here, then, is the very possibility of subjecting TNCs to labor regulations. The infamous quote from a former CEO of General Electric – "Ideally, you'd have every plant you own on a barge" – embodies the extreme version of TNCs' efforts to exploit the opportunities of globalization and capital mobility to exempt themselves from labor regulations (quoted in Ross 2004:16). While not as extreme as the barge fantasy, instances of heavy deregulation of apparel production abound, as the exemption of Export Processing Zones factories from labor and tax laws in several Southeast Asian and Central American countries bears witness (Ross 2004:53).

The TNCs' balancing act consists in nurturing the legal fiction of complete separation vis-à-vis their contractors even as they remain deeply involved in the day-to-day operation of the factories and set the prices that constrain workers' wages. This largely successful endeavor relies on three strategies to which sourcing and "social responsibility" corporate divisions devote considerable resources. Challenging these strategies in order to subject TNCs to labor regulations through a global regulatory system of joint liability is the central goal of the anti-sweatshop movement.

First, transnational retailers and brand merchandisers zealously protect the secrecy of their contracting arrangements. Based on admittedly shaky arguments on the need to protect "trade secrets," TNCs staunchly resist activists' demands to disclose the identity and location of their suppliers, let alone the wages paid to workers. As joint liability crucially depends on information on the links between transnational retailers and manufacturers and their local suppliers, transparency has been one of the key issues of contention between TNCs and TANs. Requirements on the disclosure of the location and identity of contractors, for instance, are one of the key differences among systems of code of conduct monitoring in the US (Rodríguez-Garavito 2005). While some systems such as the student-organized Worker Rights Consortium (WRC) demand full disclosure from producers of collegiate apparel and are now seeking to extend transparency to information on wages, other systems such as the Fair Labor Association (FLA), Social Accountability International (SAI), and the Worldwide

Responsible Apparel Production Certification Program (WRAP) allow manufacturers to keep this information confidential. Secrecy is the rule also inside the walls of the factories. As interviews with sweatshop workers in Guatemala and Mexico showed, factory managers take pains to conceal labels and information that would reveal the identity of buyers.

Secrecy, however, is a limited strategy. For today's suppliers are usually not small local workshops but world-class factories built with transnational capital and employing hundreds or thousands of workers. Kukdong, for instance, is a high-tech factory with a capital investment of over US$30 million owned by a Korean TNC with headquarters in Seoul and Los Angeles. Sitting on the side of a major highway, its large facilities topped by Korean and Mexican flags flying in the wind are hard to miss. Moreover, local unions and NGOs as well as transnational activists compile and spread information on the location of the factories and the identity of their buyers.

In light of this, TNCs resort to a second strategy to thwart joint liability regulations: the denial of control over (and thus responsibility for) what goes on in their contractors' factories. The baseline corporate position on the matter is illustrated by the answer of Nike's general manager in Indonesia to a question on labor abuses in supplier factories in that country: "I don't know that we need to know" (quoted in Cavanagh 1997:39). One decade later, after intense anti-sweatshop campaigning, TNCs' public statements had been moderated but their basic position remained unchanged: in the words of Gap's senior vice president for global affairs, "we are not the all-powerful Oz that rules over what happens in every factory ... Do we have leverage? Yes. Is it as great as our critics believe? Not by a long shot" (Kaufman and Gonzalez 2001).

TANs and academic analysts contest the claim of lack of control (Bonacich and Appelbaum 2000). My own research suggests that manufacturers have much greater leverage than they are willing to admit. Some brands have adopted a business model that involves long-term relations with relatively few contractors over which they exert considerable control. This is clear in the following statement by the sourcing manager for Guatemala of one such brand, Liz Claiborne:

> We know day to day the factory situation ... for example, the factories that we have in Guatemala, basically I know most of the people, even workers ... so I go to the factories every single day ... You know, we

71

have control. I have people who control the fabrics, and we do all the details daily … what style, what's in production, how many production lines, so we can keep track of what we are doing, all of our production in Guatemala.[5]

While following a more decentralized business model, other brands also have substantial leverage over supplier factories of which they are major buyers. The fact that visits to Kukdong require the authorization of Nike is indicative of the considerable influence exerted by the latter over the details of the production process and labor relations. As is common in the industry, in its capacity as a major client Nike assigns delegates to closely control the quality of the garments during production and work with management to tackle production and labor issues.

Indeed, Nike's leverage over Kukdong created the opportunity for the nascent union and the TAN to put outside pressure on management to respect the workers' right to organize. Under the combined pressure from students picketing Nike stores in the US, pro-worker NGOs (notably the WRC, the International Labor Rights Fund, Global Exchange, and the Mexico-based Centro de Apoyo al Trabajador), international code of conduct monitoring organizations (notably Verité) and international unions (the AFL-CIO and the Korean House of Solidarity), Nike and Reebok used their considerable muscle to get Kukdong's management, the factory's corrupt pro-business union and the corporate-friendly government of the state of Puebla to back off. As the Program Director of the AFL-CIO's Solidarity Center for the Americas put it, although Nike and Reebok "were not necessarily natural or organic allies of the workers … for practical purposes they were allies" as they felt the pressure to enforce the clause in their codes of conduct guaranteeing the right to organize.[6]

Once the cross-border unionization campaign succeeded, Nike used its leverage to prompt Kukdong to make substantial improvements in labor conditions and wages. Among the changes was the installation of costly equipment to enhance health and safety conditions as well as a 40 percent wage increase as part of the first contract with the union in October 2001. This and other cases show that, *pace* corporate claims of lack of control over suppliers, the degree of TNCs' involvement in the

---

[5] Interview with Liz Claiborne's sourcing manager for Guatemala and Central America, Guatemala City, July 25, 2002. This quote is a verbatim transcription of an excerpt from the interview, which was conducted in English.
[6] Interview with the Program Director of the AFL-CIO's Solidarity Center for the Americas, Dallas, March 28, 2003.

protection of labor rights in global sweatshops is a function of the outcomes of the political struggles over de facto or de jure joint liability. Currently waged on a case-by-case basis, the struggle ultimately aims to establish a global legal regime of joint liability modeled after the one achieved by the first anti-sweatshop movement.

The efficaciousness of corporate discourses and legal schemes and discourses seeking to preserve secrecy and deny the existence of control over suppliers ultimately rests on the coercive power of a third strategy to which TNCs and their suppliers resort all too frequently: the explicit or veiled threat to cut and run to avoid stringent labor law enforcement and labor militancy. Shifting production elsewhere (or threatening to do so) is thus capital's form of "direct action" supplementing legal and ideological moves to thwart global labor regulation. In terms of Gramsci's (1971) concept of hegemony, this pervasive strategy embodies the coercive element of the hegemony of the economic/juridical system of global subcontracting and neoliberal regulation. By virtue of this system, for instance, Nike could credibly threaten to shift production to any of its 1,181 supplier factories around the world.[7] The exit option also gives suppliers the proverbial stick they usually wield to squash labor mobilization inside the factories. It also enables manufacturers and suppliers (with the support of free marketeers and pro-business governments) to frame anti-sweatshop TANs as Northern protectionist coalitions seeking to drive employment away from the global South.[8] In the Kukdong case, for example, the local corporate media couched the unionization drive as a conspiracy by US organiza-tions – led by United Students Against Sweatshops (USAS) – to eliminate much-needed jobs in the *maquila* sector. "The risk of Kukdong's closing is imminent, thanks to hundreds of US college students' threatening [Nike and Reebok] to stop consuming their products if they resume orders to the factory," wrote a local reporter at the height of the campaign (Ramos 2001:4). "We'll do even the impossible to avoid Kukdong's leaving the state of Puebla," declared the Economic Development Secretary of the state of Puebla a few weeks later (Sánchez 2001a:7). In the apparel sector at large, as inter-views with union leaders in Mexico and Guatemala revealed, the

[7] The figure on suppliers is taken from information provided by the FLA. See "First Public Report: Towards Improving Workers' Lives" (www.fairlabor.org, 2003), 56.

[8] For a much-debated criticism against the anti-sweatshop movement along these lines, see the 1999 "Third World Intellectuals and NGOs Statement Against Linkage (TWIN-SAL)" (www.columbia.edu/~jb38); see also Bhagwati (2000). For a reply, see Miller (2003).

numerous episodes of overnight plant closings and relocations aimed to stem unionization efforts have a strong dissuasive effect on discontented workers.[9]

This "hegemonic despotic" element of global production (Burawoy 1985) is reinforced by the considerable obstacles that the subcontracting system poses to workers' resistance. As Bonacich and Appelbaum have put it, "no better system has yet been devised to keep workers fragmented and powerless" (2000:3). Physical separation among workers producing for the same manufacturer across the world is magnified by language and cultural differences. Compounded by the secrecy shrouding the structure of global production, a similarly great divide exists between workers in the South and consumers in the North.

In the light of this, TANs' distinctly political strategies seek to reestablish the connections between workers and consumers as well as among workers. To this end, they engage in multifarious forms of direct action in different locales to exploit the vulnerabilities of global subcontracting – namely, the sensitivity of manufacturers, especially TNCs such as Nike, to negative publicity campaigns that can harm their most valuable asset: their carefully cultivated brand image (Klein 2000). To link up workers, pro-labor NGOs, and unions across borders, anti-sweatshop TANs pursue a wide array of schemes, from worker exchange and education programs to joint investigative and organizing teams, to solidarity campaigns in support of striking workers in sweatshops (see Ansley's chapter in this volume; Williams 1999). The plurality of actors and strategies typical of this "new labor internationalism" (Santos and Rodríguez-Garavito, forthcoming; Waterman 1998) was evident in the Kukdong case. In a model that I have called "triangle organizing," the nascent Kukdong union was supported by unions in the countries where the factory, the manufacturer, and the investor are based – respectively Mexico, the US, and Korea (Rodríguez-Garavito 2005). Independent Mexican unions and pro-labor NGOs provided essential logistical support during the strike and the subsequent legal battle to have the union recognized by the state. The AFL-CIO, through the Mexico office of its Solidarity Center for the Americas, contributed funds, elicited statements of support from progressive members of the US Congress and facilitated the visits of

---

[9] Interview with Blanca Velásquez and David Alvarado (Centro de Apoyo al Trabajador, CAT), Atlixco, Mexico, July 10, 2002; interview with Secretary General of FESTRAS (Guatemalan union federation), Guatemala City, July 29, 2002.

USAS delegations to Puebla. The Korean House of Solidarity launched a campaign in the Korean media and Congress to denounce the wrong-doings of Kukdong International in its Mexican plant and sent a delegation to Mexico that visited the factory and pressured management to negotiate. All along, the campaign was supported by coalitions of human rights NGOs, feminist and faith-based organizations, and ethical consumers, among them the Maquila Solidarity Network, the Coalition for Justice in the Maquiladoras, and the International Labor Rights Fund.

Other forms of political action explicitly seek to create links between workers and consumers. In an image-dependent industry thriving on the abysmal wage and purchasing power differentials between workers in the South and buyers in the North, consumer–worker alliances are a core component of the anti-sweatshop struggle (Frank 2003; Williams 1999). Forms of direct action embodying this type of alliance include consumer boycotts, speaking tours, and delegations providing opportunities for face-to-face interaction between *maquila* workers and apparel consumers, and the creation of "no sweat" factories and labels. In the Kukdong case, picket lines at Nike stores organized by USAS to protest the firing of striking workers as well as speaking tours by Kukdong union leaders on campuses across the US during the negotiations of the contract provided the requisite leverage to convince Nike to step in.

In addition to pursuing political strategies, anti-sweatshop TANs mobilize legal instruments both to push forward specific campaigns and to gradually create a global system of joint liability. Thus, like other networks and coalitions within counter-hegemonic globalization, they pragmatically combine direct and institutional action (Santos 2002; Santos and Rodríguez-Garavito's chapter in this volume). In the next sections I focus on the latter by examining the plurality of legal tools that TANs (and TNCs) create and use in the struggle over international labor rights, as well as the scales at which this competition takes place.

3.3 THE STRUGGLE OVER "HARD" V. "SOFT" LAW

Over the last decade, one of the most important developments and terrains of contention in the field of international labor regulation has been the formulation of corporate codes of conduct (whereby TNCs voluntarily commit to working with suppliers to ensure respect for workers' rights in the factories) and the creation of monitoring systems to oversee compliance with such codes. In the apparel sector, numerous TNCs have adopted codes of conduct and joined monitoring systems in response to mounting pressure from TANs and high-profile exposés of labor abuses in supplier factories. Nike is a case in point. In 1991, after the release of damaging reports on labor conditions in its Southeast Asian contractors' facilities, Nike drafted a code of conduct for labor and declared that it would ask all its suppliers to comply with it. Nike's failure to enforce the code, together with its position as the largest maker of athletic footwear and apparel in the world (with annual profits totaling US$945 million on sales of US$12.3 billion in 2004),[10] made it a privileged target of the nascent anti-sweatshop movement. Widespread denunciations of Nike's labor practices became a full-blown campaign after *Life* magazine published a picture showing a 12-year-old Pakistani boy slaving over a Nike football (Litvin 2003:242). By 1998, the pressure put on Nike by Global Exchange, the National Labor Committee, USAS, and other activist organizations was such that the firm's chairman and founder, Philip Knight, acknowledged that "Nike has become synonymous with slave wages, forced overtime and arbitrary abuse" and announced a package of measures aimed to strengthen the enforcement of Nike's code of conduct.[11]

Prominent among those measures was Nike's decision to join the FLA, a voluntary monitoring system involving a dozen TNCs and established at the initiative of the Clinton administration.[12] Several studies have documented the origins and details of the FLA and other code of conduct systems (including the WRC, WRAP, and SAI), as well as the differences and disputes among them (Bartley 2003; O'Rourke 2003; Rodríguez-Garavito 2005). For the purposes of this chapter, the significance of these systems lies in that they constitute a paradigmatic instance of a regulatory model – most commonly dubbed "soft law" or "governance" – that has been at the center of recent political and theoretical debates on international labor rights and global governance at large.

---

[10] See "Nike Profit Increases 23 Percent" (www.msnbc.msn.com, published June 25, 2004).

[11] Quoted in Financial Times (1998).

[12] The FLA originally involved several unions and pro-worker NGOs (including the AFL-CIO and the International Labor Rights Fund), most of which withdrew later on in protest over the FLA's slow progress in improving the transparency and independence of its monitoring scheme. Nike also signed the "Global Compact," a UN-sponsored voluntary declaration of principles on ethical investment and production involving major TNCs in the apparel and other sectors (Elson 2004).

I have elsewhere offered a critical review of the prolific, multi-faceted governance literature (Rodríguez-Garavito 2005). Important differences among them notwithstanding, the leitmotiv in studies and proposals on the governance model is the potential of non-state-centered forms of coordination to tackle the regulatory dilemmas of the global economy. In contrast to state-centered, top-down, "hard law," the governance model relies mainly on flexible, "soft law" formulated through collaboration among private actors (firms, secondary associations, and so on) and participatory problem solving (Dorf and Sabel 1998; Simon 2003). In the domain of labor relations, for instance, the "hard law" approach of labor laws formulated and implemented by the state's bureaucracy and courts contrasts with the "soft law" approach of voluntary codes of conduct and consensual monitoring involving firms, commercial and independent monitors, civil society organizations, and other private "stakeholders."

The terms of the contrast between hard law and soft law vary widely across different contributions to the debate on governance. While the most compelling analyses see an affirmative state and an empowered civil society as complementary and mutually reinforcing (Cohen and Rogers 1995; Fung and Wright 2003), studies focusing on the virtues of private self-regulation tend to view the latter as an alternative to top-down state regulation, thus envisioning "a paradigm shift from a regulatory to a governance model" (Lobel 2003:3). In a neo-Weberian twist, the latter version is based on the implicit or explicit claim that just as the regulatory model had an elective affinity with Fordist capitalism, the governance model (with its emphasis on flexibility and networks of private actors) is attuned to the realities of a global, post-Fordist world economy.

Empirical examination of the process of construction of global governance in the field of international labor rights calls into question sweeping claims of the shift from regulation to governance, from hard law to soft law. Rather than a spontaneous process of replacement of the new for the old based on structural affinity between economic and legal models, the process at work is one of struggle over the type of labor law applicable to TNCs. In other words, the "hardness" of international labor standards is in and of itself a key object of contention between TNCs and their critics.

Hegemonic and counter-hegemonic actors do not have fixed preferences for hard or soft law across the board. Instead, they pragmatically privilege one or the other depending on the object of regulation and the specific circumstances at hand. TNCs, for instance, strategically shift among calls for strengthening national and global hard law in matters essential to the profitability of their business (e.g. intellectual property rights), proposals for soft law and self-regulation in other areas (e.g. voluntary codes of conduct for labor), and deregulation in yet other domains (e.g. financial markets). Thus, neoliberal globalization relies neither on "disciplinary" regulation (Gill 2004) nor on corporate self-regulation or deregulation associated with the "retreat of the state" (Strange 1996). Rather, neoliberal global governance consists in a mixture of both: hard law to protect corporate rights and soft law to regulate social rights. This is most evident in the contrast between the strict, top-down, global regulatory framework on intellectual property rights – embodied by the WTO Agreement on Trade-Related Aspects of Intellectual Property Rights (TRIPS) and the detailed rules imposed by the US in its bilateral trade agreements – and the loose and largely voluntary international system of labor regulation (Elliot and Freeman 2003:24).

TANs are equally pragmatic in their use of hard and soft law. On the one hand, they exploit the obvious contradiction within TNCs' strategies of selectively defending and attacking state-backed regulation. They do so by simultaneously calling for the softening of corporate-friendly regulation (e.g. through limitations to intellectual property rights for reasons of public health, as illustrated by Klug's chapter in this volume) and for the hardening of social regulations. In the labor rights field, this strategy entails initiatives to improve the regulatory capacity of national states as well as the enforcement capabilities of international organizations, notably the ILO (Giraldo and Ossa 2004; ILRF 2001). On the other hand, TANs engage in ongoing struggles to establish and determine the conditions of soft law regimes, namely, code of conduct monitoring systems. Numerous national and global unions, NGOs, and solidarity organizations in the North and the South have strived to turn existing monitoring systems from corporate public relations ploys into transparent and effective mechanisms for enforcing labor rights. In the Americas, this has involved such organizations as the Centro de Apoyo al Trabajador and Factor X in Mexico; the Commission on the Verification of Codes of Conduct, and the Federation of Foodstuffs Workers (Festras) in Guatemala; ILRF, USAS, AFL-CIO, and US/LEAP in the US; the Maquila Solidarity Network in Canada; and the regional office of the International Textile, Garment and Leather Workers Federation (ITGLWF).

Albeit most of the apparel industry continues to be covered by weak corporate codes of conduct (e.g. WRAP, which includes such large retailers as Wal-Mart) or monitored by commercial auditing firms of questionable independence, the work of these and other activist organizations has led to changes in monitoring systems (e.g. the FLA and SAI) and the creation of stringent codes and models of monitoring (notably the WRC).

The Kukdong case offers a vivid illustration of the interplay between TNCs' and TANs' strategies on the ground. By joining the FLA, Nike had committed to enforcing this umbrella monitoring organization's code of conduct, which guaranteed workers' freedom of association and right to bargain collectively. Also, the fact that Kukdong produced Nike (and Reebok) sweatshirts for US universities that had joined the WRC (the student-organized alternative to the FLA) made the factory subject to the WRC's more demanding code and monitoring system. Tellingly, Nike had aggressively fought the WRC's "hard law," confrontational approach to monitoring. Viewing the WRC as an activist-controlled organization inimical to corporations (which, unlike in the FLA system, do not sit on its board), Nike's CEO, Phil Knight, withdrew a US$30 million donation to his alma mater, the University of Oregon, after the latter joined the WRC in 2000. A few months later, Nike rescinded contracts with the University of Michigan and Brown University for the same reason.

The opportunity created by the WRC and the FLA codes was not lost on the Kukdong workers who led the unionization drive and the organizations that launched the cross-border coalition in their support. As recounted by the workers and members of the key local support organization, the Centro de Apoyo al Trabajador, international pressure on Nike and Reebok by virtue of the code of conduct commitments was instrumental for the rise and continuation of the movement in the face of management's and state authorities' violent resistance.[13] The arrival in Puebla of independent monitors summoned by the WRC and the brands to verify the facts shortly after the strike, as well as the presence of delegates from USAS, international unions, and NGOs, not only raised the profile of the case in the local and international media but also put further pressure on Nike, Reebok, Kukdong, the

---

[13] Collective interview with Kukdong union leaders, Atlixco, July 12, 2002; interview with Blanca Velásquez and David Alvarado (CAT).

state authorities, and the factory's corrupt pro-business union to allow the formation of an independent union.[14]

Breaking the state authorities' and Kukdong's resistance would also require the mobilization of state and national courts. With the support of a local public interest law firm, Kukdong workers faced the countless hurdles put in their way by state courts intent on twisting the law to the point of openly making up new "legal" requirements to block the official recognition of the union.[15] After a nine-month legal battle that involved an appeal to the Mexican Supreme Court, the union was formally recognized by the state in early October, 2001. However, as the union's lawyer acknowledged, the success of this "hard law" strategy, and of the organizing campaign writ large, ultimately lay on the union's and the TAN's ability to effectively exploit the opportunities created by Nike's code of conduct commitments.[16] Given the long-standing tight alliance between the Mexican government, economic elites, and corrupt pro-business unions, it took Nike's external pressure (in turn prompted by TANs' pressure) to make state authorities and the factory management comply with the law. "In the last instance, the law that mattered was Nike's law," in the words of Huberto Juárez, an economist who participated in the negotiations leading to the rehiring of the striking workers.[17] "Sadly, things with the government here are too difficult, so we prefer to go straight to the codes," declared one of the Kukdong union leaders in our interview.[18]

3.4 LEGAL PLURALISM AND THE STRUGGLE OVER THE SCALES OF LABOR LAW

Enhancing the complexity of the legal field of hard and soft standards is the coexistence of labor regulations at different scales. Now overlapping, now conflicting, factory and local labor regulations operate alongside national laws and regional agreements as well as global standards embodied in ILO conventions and codes of conduct. Just as the determination of the "hardness" of the applicable law, the privileged scale of regulation in any given case is the object of a struggle involving TNCs, TANs, state authorities, and international organizations. Far from privileging a

---

[14] Interview with Arturo Alcalde (union-side labor lawyer), Mexico City, July 15, 2002.
[15] Interview with Samuel Porras (Kukdong union's lawyer), Puebla, Mexico, July 15, 2002.
[16] Ibid.
[17] Interview with Huberto Juárez, Puebla, Mexico, July 8, 2002. See also Juárez (2002).
[18] Collective interview with Kukdong union leaders.

particular scale, hegemonic and counter-hegemonic actors simultaneously pursue strategies at different scales and exploit the legal and political opportunities offered by the tensions and contradictions within and among local, national, regional, and global regulations.

This is evident, for instance, in the strategies of apparel TNCs and their suppliers with regard to the national labor regulations of producing countries. A strikingly recurrent statement in interviews with brand delegates, factory managers, and business associations' staff members is that – in the terms used by the Director for Labor Relations of VESTEX, the Guatemalan apparel business association – "all the development of the sector is based on compliance with national laws."[19] From the viewpoint of global brands, Liz Claiborne's representative in Guatemala put it in the following way: "[E]ach country we go to, we have to respect that country's law. I mean, [for instance] we have to let our people know, all our contractors, that they must pay the minimum salary that's recognized by the government of each country."[20]

Regardless of the accuracy of these statements,[21] what is worth noting for present purposes are capital's selective invocation of and double-sided strategy vis-à-vis national labor law. On the one hand, through explicit or implicit threats to move production to countries with lax labor regulations (e.g. China), global brands and contractors exert downward pressure on labor standards of countries desperate for jobs. The indirect pressure coming from individual mobile firms has a collective, institutional counterpart in retailers', brands', and contractors' associations' lobby on Southern countries to further "flexibilize" labor regulations. Through unconditional trade agreements and structural adjustment programs, neoliberal governments in the North and the South as well as international financial institutions support capital's case for labor market "deregulation." Viewed from this perspective, therefore, national labor laws appear as obstacles to be removed. At the same time, however, as evidenced by the quotes above, brands and producers invoke compliance with the thus heavily eroded national labor law as a proof of corporate citizenship. For instance, with legal

---

[19] Interview with VESTEX Director for Labor Relations, Guatemala City, July 26, 2002.
[20] Interview with Liz Claiborne's sourcing manager for Guatemala and Central America (verbatim transcription of an excerpt from the interview, which was conducted in English).
[21] Violations of national labor laws in Guatemalan and Mexican apparel *maquilas* are widespread and have been documented by monitoring organizations, human rights NGOs, and researchers. On Guatemala, see Human Rights Watch (2002) and COVERCO (2001b). On Mexico, see Juárez (2005).

minimum wages driven below subsistence levels (let alone living wage levels), compliance with the law, as VESTEX's representative put it, is indeed "good for business."[22] In this second face of hegemonic strategies vis-à-vis regulation at the national scale, labor law is no longer an obstacle, but rather an excuse.

At the regional and global scales, TNCs' strategies follow a different path. With the exception of the European Union, regional and global labor regulations remain embryonic at best. Thus, corporate efforts have focused on thwarting the further development of such regulations on two fronts. First, TNCs have opposed the inclusion of "hard law" clauses on labor into regional and global trade agreements. With the intellectual backing of free marketeers warning about the deleterious impact of the linkage between trade and labor rights on growth and employment in the South (see Bhagwati 2004), TNCs have lobbied to block or considerably water down labor provisions in trade agreements, from the WTO and NAFTA to the recent bilateral agreements signed by the US, among them those with Chile and Central American countries. Together with opposition to increasing funding and enforcement powers for the ILO, this strategy has frustrated the rise of an effective governance system of labor relations at the international level. Secondly, as explained in the previous section, TNCs have responded to criticisms of abuses stemming from this regulatory void by developing global codes of conduct as part of "corporate social responsibility" programs. Given their voluntary character, most codes offer a corporate-friendly alternative to regional and global labor laws (Rodríguez-Garavito 2005; Shamir's chapter in this volume).

Anti-sweatshop activists are equally pragmatic in promoting and mobilizing legal tools at different scales. At the local and national scales, they sue contractors before the producing countries' courts and bring legal challenges against brands in the jurisdictions where TNCs' headquarters are located. The latter strategy is part of a broader trend toward transnational litigation as a means to hold TNCs accountable for their actions around the globe. Prominent instances of this trend are the lawsuits against TNCs for human rights abuses brought before US courts by public interest law firms and NGOs on the basis of the Alien Tort Claims Act of 1789 (Shamir's chapter in this volume).

At the regional scale, TANs have launched campaigns to introduce effective labor clauses in trade agreements. Activists' pressure, for

---

[22] Interview with VESTEX Director for Labor Relations.

instance, led to the creation of a side agreement to NAFTA, the North American Agreement on Labor Cooperation (NAALC). Even when, as in NAALC, labor clauses have a largely symbolic, non-enforceable character, TANs have creatively used them to bring attention to widespread labor abuses even as they have pressured for their amendment (Graubart 2002; Human Rights Watch 2001). In addition, they have formulated alternative, region-wide model labor regulations based on fair trade (as opposed to free trade) principles and open-border immigration policies. A host of such "alternative treaties" have been produced through participatory and deliberative processes involving progressive NGOs, unions and grassroots organizations coming together on the occasion of "peoples' summits" that meet parallel to the closed-door summits of political and economic elites in which neoliberal institutions are forged. In the Americas, the most salient example is the effort to build a hemispheric social alliance around concrete and viable alternatives to the existing plans for a Free Trade Area of the Americas (FTAA). Launched at the Peoples' Summit of the Americas in Santiago (Chile) in April 1998, the initiative has produced, among other things, the *Alternatives for the Americas*, a detailed regulatory proposal on labor, the environment, foreign investment, intellectual property rights, and other key social and economic areas.[23] With its explicit goal of challenging the claim that "there is no alternative" to neoliberal institutions, its detailed institutional blueprint for a different type of globalization, and its participatory processes, this and other alternative treaties have become an integral part of the global movement for social justice and constitute a paradigmatic form of subaltern cosmopolitan legality (Santos 2002; Santos and Rodríguez-Garavito's chapter in this volume).

TANs have undertaken similar initiatives at the global scale, as the campaign to include a labor clause in the WTO and the alternative treaties emanating from the World Social Forum bear witness. However, given the considerable political and logistical difficulties involved in ratcheting up labor regulations to the global level, these efforts have yet to match the progress attained at the regional level. For instance, North–South divisions around the potentially protectionist use of labor clauses by Northern states have nipped in the bud proposals for a labor clause in the WTO. In light of this, TANs have pursued two

---

[23] See the proposal's text at www.web.net/comfront/alts4americas/. On grassroots alternatives to the FTAA, see ILSA (2004).

complementary strategies. On the one hand, they have supported initiatives to turn the international conventions on core labor rights into a global labor constitution whose enforcement would be entrusted to a revamped ILO (ILRF 2001). On the other hand, they continue to participate in the above-mentioned debates and campaigns to make global codes of conduct for labor transparent and enforceable.

The politics of scale can be seen at work in the Kukdong case. The transnational coalition in support of the nascent union simultaneously mobilized state and national laws, regional agreements, international ILO conventions, and global codes of conduct. In the early stages of the unionization campaign, it was Nike and Reebok's codes that provided the requisite legal leverage to force Kukdong to rehire the strikers and start negotiations with the independent union. Kukdong responded with a largely local legal strategy which entailed mobilizing the corporate-friendly state courts and government to criminally prosecute strikers as "trespassers" and fraudulently block the official recognition of the union. In an ironic twist illustrative of capital's strategic use of local and national laws, Kukdong's legal counsel described this move to the media as an effort to "reestablish the company's rule of law" (Sánchez 2001b:6).

The globalization of the Kukdong case was furthered by the presence of delegations from the ILO and international public interest law NGOs (notably the ILRF) with experience in transnational labor litigation. At the same time, a Mexico–US trade union coalition threatened to bring the case before the NAALC agencies, thus tapping the legal and political tools available at the regional scale.

It was only when the case had been thus internationalized that the TAN resorted to local and national legal strategies. In what Keck and Sikkink (1998) have called a "boomerang effect," the TAN put pressure on international corporate and state and inter-state actors (the brands, Kukdong's headquarters, the US government, the Korean government, and the ILO) to in turn pressure local actors (Kukdong's management, corrupt business union federations, and the governments and courts of Mexico and the state of Puebla) to abide by national labor laws and allow the formation of the union and the signing of a labor contract. As stated by the union's leaders and legal counsel in the interviews, local legal strategies succeeded only because of the effect of international pressure.[24]

---

[24] Collective interview with Kukdong union leaders; interview with Samuel Porras (Kukdong union's lawyer).

Interestingly, the practice of local lawyers representing the union is a far cry from the image of the cosmopolitan, well-connected attorneys that emerges from studies on other fields of transnational lawyering (see Dezalay and Garth 2002). This is brought home by the work of the pro-bono attorney who pushed forward the union's petition for official recognition through the maze-like system of regulations and ad-hoc requirements set by the state authorities to frustrate the consolidation of the union. Attesting to the local and conventional character of his practice, the Mexican Labor Code is the only book sitting on the desk of his austere office in downtown Puebla. When asked about the legal tools he used in defending the union's cause, he referred only to national labor laws even as he explained in detail the corporatist practices whereby business, corrupt unions, and the local and national states collude to frustrate the application of such laws. Tellingly, he was not aware of the content of the brands' codes of conduct, dismissing them as non-legal "unilateral declarations" even as he acknowledged the crucial political opportunity created by the codes in the case.[25]

Although it took eight months and numerous appeals (including one to the Mexican Supreme Court on constitutional grounds) to break the resistance of the courts, this legal strategy finally came to fruition when the combined pressure on the courts, the brands, the state of Puebla, and Kukdong forced the state's government and courts to officially recognize the union in early October 2001.

3.5 CONCLUSION

The successful Kukdong campaign vividly illustrates two central traits of counter-hegemonic legal strategies in the context of globalization. On the one hand, it involved a continuous combination of political and legal schemes whereby protest (from the strike and the occupation of the factory to the picketing of Nike stores) went hand in hand with the mobilization of juridical instruments (from Mexican labor law to codes of conduct). Without the former, the case would have joined the ranks of the countless attempts at forming independent unions that have been blocked by the Mexican state. Without the latter, the political pressure could not have translated itself into stable agreements with management and Nike that entailed a considerable improvement of working conditions at the factory. On the other hand, the success of the

---

[25] Interview with Samuel Porras (Kukdong union's lawyer).

cross-border organizing drive crucially depended on the combination of strategies at several scales. This allowed the TAN to simultaneously put pressure on corporate actors located in different nodes of the global apparel commodity chain, from US brands to the Korean multinational supplier.

As I have sought to show in this chapter, the Kukdong case is part of a broader struggle over the existence, the content, and the scale of enforceable international labor rights. In this dispute, TANs and TNCs strategically exploit the tensions and contradictions within the existing kaleidoscopic field of "hard" and "soft" labor laws at several scales, even as they formulate new legal frameworks and clash over the details of novel enforcement mechanisms.

Albeit the newness of this field of confrontation advises against concluding with general predictions, two trends can already be seen at work that are likely to influence its outcome. First, with regard to the issues in dispute, as so-called "protective rights" (which concern such issues as health and safety, minimum wage, overtime, and so on) have been incorporated in codes of conduct and other global regulatory frameworks, TANs have raised the stakes by moving to press for the protection of rights with broader political and economic connotations – namely, the right to a "living wage" and "enabling rights" (that is, freedom of association and the right to collective bargaining) (see Maquila Solidarity Network 2004). As the argument in this chapter would have predicted, TNCs and international financial institutions have risen to the challenge through strategies aimed to tame or postpone TANs' demands. This is evident, for instance, in recent efforts to develop a version of "worker empowerment" congruent with corporate visions of social responsibility (World Bank 2003) as well as in attempts to discount discussions of a living wage as premature. Together with continuing debates over international protective rights, therefore, the nascent discussion over a living wage and enabling rights will be at the center of the confrontation over international labor rights.

Secondly, with regard to the actors and the strategies involved, the campaigns and regulatory experiments that took place over the last decade have produced divergences within corporate and activist circles that will likely shape the process and the outcome of political and legal disputes over labor conditions in the Americas. Within corporate circles, some apparel TNCs (e.g. Gap and Liz Claiborne) have experimented (albeit timidly) with independent monitoring of their factories in Central America (COVERCO 2001a; 2001b), while others (e.g.

Nike) hold steadfastly to monitoring mechanisms such as those of the FLA that rely on commercial auditors. Within activist circles, some NGOs and unions (e.g. USAS and the National Labor Committee) pursue confrontational tactics while others (e.g. Human Rights First) have sought to maintain a space for collaboration and negotiation with TNCs. Yet others (e.g. ITGLWF, the global union of the apparel sector) combine both approaches. How the different tactics of such "confronters" and "engagers" (Winston 2002) interface with potentially diverging corporate approaches (as well as with national state policies) will affect the prospects of effective transnational labor regulation.

Whether this ongoing process leads to the construction of a cosmopolitan legal framework effectively protecting labor rights at the global level, or whether it results in the deepening of neoliberal regulation, will depend on the success of the hegemonic and counter-hegemonic strategies examined in this chapter. More broadly, the rise of a cosmopolitan labor law hinges on the fate of the larger struggle over the rules of the global economy. In this endeavor, the anti-sweatshop movement joins ranks with the fair trade movement, the mobilization against exclusionary regimes of intellectual property rights, campaigns for debt relief and the reform of international financial institutions, and other forms of counter-hegemonic globalization and subaltern cosmopolitan legality.

References

Arthurs, Harry. 1996. "Labor Law Without the State?" *University of Toronto Law Journal* 46: 1–45.

Bartley, Tim. 2003. "Certifying Forests and Factories: States, Social Movements, and the Rise of Private Regulation in the Apparel and Forest Product Fields." *Politics & Society* 31: 433–464.

Bhagwati, Jagdish. 2000. "Why Nike is on the Right Track." *Financial Times*, October 23 or www.columbia.edu/~jb38.
    2004. *In Defense of Globalization*. Oxford: Oxford University Press.

Bonacich, Edna, and Richard Appelbaum. 2000. *Behind the Label: Inequality in the Los Angeles Apparel Industry*. Berkeley: University of California Press.

Burawoy, Michael. 1985. *The Politics of Production: Factory Regimes Under Capitalism and Socialism*. London: Verso.

Cavanagh, John. 1997. "The Global Resistance to Sweatshops." Pp. 39–50 in *No Sweat: Fashion, Free Trade and the Rights of Garment Workers*, edited by Andrew Ross. London: Verso.

Cohen, Joshua, and Joel Rogers. 1995. *Associations and Democracy*. London: Verso.

Commons, John. 1977. "The Sweating System." Pp. 44–46 in *Out of the Sweatshop: The Struggle for Industrial Democracy*, edited by Leon Stein. New York: Quadrangle.

COVERCO. 2001a. *First Public Report: Gap Inc. Suppliers in Guatemala.* Guatemala: COVERCO.

——— 2001b. *Un Informe Especial de COVERCO: El Código de Conducta de Liz Claiborne Inc. y la Sindicalización de Dos Fábricas Proveedoras en Guatemala.* Guatemala: COVERCO.

Dezalay, Yves, and Bryant, Garth. 2002. *The Internationalization of Palace Wars: Lawyers, Economists, and the Contest to Transform Latin American States.* Chicago: University of Chicago Press.

Dorf, Michael, and Charles Sabel. 1998. "A Constitution of Democratic Experimentalism." *Columbia Law Review* 98:267–473.

Elliot, Kimberly, and Richard Freeman. 2003. *Can Labor Standards Improve Under Globalization?* Washington, DC: Institute for International Economics.

Elson, Diane. 2004. "Human Rights and Corporate Profits: The UN Global Compact – Part of the Solution or Part of the Problem?" Pp. 45–64 in *Global Tensions: Challenges and Opportunities in the World Economy*, edited by Lourdes Benería and Savitri Bisnath. New York: Routledge.

Evans, Peter. forthcoming. "Counter-Hegemonic Globalization." In *Handbook of Political Sociology*, edited by Thomas Janoski, Alexander Hicks, and Mildred Schwartz. Cambridge: Cambridge University Press.

Financial Times. 1998. "Corporate Citizenship." June 15.

Frank, Dana. 2003. "Where Are the Workers in Consumer–Worker Alliances? Class Dynamics and the History of Consumer–Labor Campaigns." *Politics & Society* 31:363–379.

Fung, Archon, and Erik Olin Wright. 2003. "Countervailing Power in Empowered Participatory Governance." In *Deepening Democracy*, edited by Archon Fung and Erik Olin Wright. London: Verso.

García, Mauricio, and Rodrigo Uprimny. 2004. "Corte Constitucional y Emancipación Social en Colombia." Pp. 163–204 in *Emancipación Social y Violencia en Colombia*, edited by Boaventura de Sousa Santos and Mauricio García. Bogotá: Norma.

Gereffi, Gary, Miguel Korzeniewicz, and Roberto Korzeniewicz. 1994. "Introduction: Global Commodity Chains." Pp. 1–16 in *Commodity Chains and Global Capitalism*, edited by Gary Gereffi and Miguel Korzeniewicz. Westport: Praeger.

Gill, Stephen. 2004. "Toward a Stark Utopia? New Constitutionalism and the Politics of Globalization." Pp. 13–26 in *Global Tensions: Challenges and Opportunities in the World Economy*, edited by Lourdes Benería and Savitri Bisnath. New York: Routledge.

Giraldo, Mauricio, and Martín Ossa. 2004. *El ALCA y el Derecho al Trabajo.* Bogotá: ILSA, Colección ALCA Temas.

Gramsci, Antonio. 1971. *Selections from the Prison Notebooks of Antonio Gramsci*. New York: International Publishers.

Graubart, Jonathan. 2002. "The Intersection of Transnational Activism and Soft Law: How Activists Exploit NAFTA's Labor and Environmental Accords." PhD Dissertation. University of Wisconsin-Madison.

Howard, Alan. 1997. "Labor, History, and Sweatshops in the New Global Economy." Pp. 151–172 in *No Sweat: Fashion, Free Trade and the Rights of Garment Workers*, edited by Andrew Ross. London: Verso.

Human Rights Watch. 2001. *Trading Away Rights: The Unfulfilled Promise of NAFTA's Labor Side Agreement*. New York: Human Rights Watch.

2002. *From the Household to the Factory: Sex Discrimination in the Guatemalan Labor Force*. New York: Human Rights Watch.

ILRF. 2001. "Developing Effective Mechanisms for Implementing Labor Rights in the Global Economy." In *Workers in the Global Economy*, edited by Cornell University ILR, ILRF, IPS, and EPI. Ithaca: ILR.

ILSA. 2004. *Colección ALCATEMAS*. Bogotá: ILSA.

Juárez, Huberto. 2002. *Rebelión en el Greenfield*. Puebla: Universidad Autónoma de Puebla.

2005. *Allá ... Donde Viven los Más Pobres: Cadenas Globales y Regiones Productoras en la Maquila del Vestido*. Puebla: BUAP.

Kaufman, Leslie, and David Gonzalez. 2001. "Labor Standards Clash with Global Reality." *New York Times*, April 24.

Keck, Margaret, and Kathryn Sikkink. 1998. *Activists Beyond Borders: Advocacy Networks in International Politics*. Ithaca: Cornell University Press.

Klein, Naomi. 2000. *No Logo*. New York: Picador.

Litvin, Daniel. 2003. *Empires of Profit: Commerce, Conquest and Corporate Responsibility*. New York and London: Texere.

Lobel, Orly. 2003. "The Fall of Regulation and the Rise of Governance in Contemporary Legal Thought." Paper presented at the Conference on "Regulation, Governance, and Law in the 21st Century: Towards a New Legal Process?" University of Wisconsin, Madison, October 1.

Maquila Solidarity Network. 2004. "2003 Year End Review: Emerging Trends in Codes and their Implementation." Toronto: MSN.

McCann, Michael. 1994. *Rights at Work: Pay Equity Reform and the Politics of Legal Mobilization*. Chicago: University of Chicago Press.

Miller, John. 2003. "Why Economists Are Wrong about Sweatshops and the Antisweatshop Movement." *Challenge* 46:93–122.

Moody, Kim. 1997. *Workers in a Lean World: Unions in the International Economy*. London: Verso.

Oliveira, Luciano. 2003. "Legal Pluralism and Alternative Law in Brazil: Notes for a Balance." *Beyond Law* 26:67–90.

O'Rourke, Dara. 2003. "Outsourcing Regulation: Analyzing Non-Governmental Systems of Labor Standards Monitoring." *Policy Studies Journal* 31:1–29.

Rajagopal, Balakrishnan. 2003. *International Law from Below: Development, Social Movements and Third World Resistance.* Cambridge: Cambridge University Press.

Ramos, Jesús. 2001. "Kukdong de Atlixco podría cerrar." *Síntesis*, July 17.

Rodríguez-Garavito, César A. 2005. "Global Governance, Cross-Border Organizing, and Labor Rights: Codes of Conduct and Anti-Sweatshop Struggles in Global Apparel Factories in Mexico and Guatemala." *Politics & Society* 33(2).

Ross, Andrew. 1997. *No Sweat: Fashion, Free Trade, and the Rights of Garment Workers.* London: Verso.

2004. *Low Pay, High Profile: The Global Push for Fair Labor.* New York: New Press.

Sánchez, Wendy. 2001a. "Haremos Todo lo Posible para que la Empresa Kukdong No Cierre: Sedeco." *La Jornada*, August 14.

2001b. "Sin Solución Conflicto Laboral en Kukdong Internacional." *El Sol de Puebla*, January 11.

Santos, Boaventura de Sousa. 1991. *Estado, Derecho y Luchas Sociales.* Bogotá: ILSA.

Santos, Boaventura de Sousa, and Mauricio García (Eds.). 2001. *El Caleidoscopio de las Justicias en Colombia.* Bogotá: Universidad de Los Andes.

Santos, Boaventura de Sousa, and César A. Rodríguez-Garavito. forthcoming. "Introduction: Expanding the Economic Canon and Searching for Alternatives to Neoliberal Globalization." In *Another Production is Possible: Beyond the Capitalist Canon*, edited by Boaventura de Sousa Santos. London: Verso.

Scheingold, Stuart, and Austin Sarat. 2004. *Something to Believe In: Politics, Professionalism, and Cause Lawyering.* Stanford: Stanford University Press.

Sikkink, Kathryn. 2002. "Transnational Advocacy Networks and the Social Construction of Legal Rules." Pp. 37–64 in *Global Prescriptions: The Production, Exportation, and Importation of a New Legal Orthodoxy*, edited by Yves Dezalay and Bryant Garth. Ann Arbor: University of Michigan Press.

Simon, William. 2003. "Solving Problems v. Claiming Rights: The Pragmatist Challenge to Legal Liberalism." Paper presented at the Conference on "Regulation, Governance, and Law in the 21st Century: Towards a New Legal Process?" University of Wisconsin, Madison, October 1.

Snow, David, E. Burke, Steven Worden, and Robert Benford. 1986. "Frame Alignment Processes, Micromobilization, and Movement Participation." *American Sociological Review* 51:464–481.

Strange, Susan. 1996. *The Retreat of the State: The Diffusion of Power in the World Economy.* Cambridge: Cambridge University Press.

Tarrow, Sidney. 2001. "Transnational Politics: Contention and Institutions in International Politics." *Annual Review of Political Science* 4:1–20.

Trubek, David, Jim Mosher, and Jeffrey Rothstein. 2000. "Transnationalism in the Regulation of Labor Relations: International Regimes and Transnational Advocacy Networks." *Law and Social Inquiry* 25:1187–1210.

Wallerstein, Immanuel. 2002. "Opening Remarks: Legal Constraints in the Capitalist World-Economy." Pp. 61–64 in *Transnational Legal Processes: Globalisations and Power Disparities*, edited by Michael Likosky. London: Butterworths.

Waterman, Peter. 1998. *Globalization, Social Movements and the New Internationalism*. London: Continuum.

Williams, Heather. 1999. "Mobile Capital and Transborder Labor Rights Mobilization." *Politics & Society* 27:139–166.

Winston, Morton. 2002. "NGO Strategies for Promoting Corporate Social Responsibility." *Ethics and International Affairs* 16:71–87.

World Bank. 2003. *Strengthening the Implementation of Corporate Social Responsibility in Global Supply Chains*. Washington, DC: World Bank.

CHAPTER 4

CORPORATE SOCIAL RESPONSIBILITY: A CASE OF HEGEMONY AND COUNTER-HEGEMONY

Ronen Shamir

4.1 INTRODUCTION

One general observation is shared among scholars of the global political economy regardless of their disciplinary, analytic, or ideological inclinations. Namely, that corporate global rule is already here. Positive evidence abounds. Multinational corporations (MNCs) dominate the global economy, accounting for two-thirds of global trade in goods and services. Of the one hundred largest world economies, fifty-one are corporations. The top two hundred corporations generate 27.5 percent of the world gross domestic product and their combined annual revenues are greater than those of the 182 states that contain 80 percent of the world population. The combined sales of four of the largest corporations in the world exceed the gross domestic product of the whole of Africa (Chomsky 2002; Davidsson 2002; Ellwood 2002). Economic figures tell only part of the story. As a result of their vast wealth, MNCs have accumulated significant political and cultural powers as well. Economic globalization and trade liberalization have given them powers that match and often surpass that of national governments. In rich and poor countries alike, albeit in different ways, MNCs often enjoy decisive powers to shape public policy, to encourage or bar legislative measures, to promote or discourage social reforms, and to influence governmental action in key areas including employment, the environment, and social and civil rights.

As corporations emerge as global private authorities, and as governments undergo structural adjustments, "we are back to the independent realm of economic action as a major locus of political power" (Beck, Giddens, and Lash 1994). Indeed, economic globalization in general and the enhanced powers of MNCs in particular have given rise to new types of political initiatives that focus on the role of market players and on their inadequate accountability to the vast populations affected by their business practices. MNCs are increasingly perceived as sharing disproportionately too small a burden in assuring the just distribution of social goods and of assuming too small a share in remedying the unequal social distribution of harms and risks. In impoverished countries, MNCs are increasingly regarded as bearing responsibility for a variety of plights such as mass displacements of populations as a result of development projects, direct and indirect exploitation of cheap labor, cooperation with oppressive regimes, impoverishment of natural resources and habitats, and the destruction of indigenous cultures. In the richer countries of the North, corporate practices – coupled with a corresponding privatization of the state – are perceived to be responsible for unemployment due to industrial "adjustments," for the McDonaldization of working conditions, and for the creation of chronic employment uncertainty. Beyond labor issues, corporations are perceived to colonize and monopolize the public sphere, to suffocate small businesses, and in general to transform the citizens into submissive consumers (Klein 1999). But, even more importantly, and as will be discussed in more detail below, some key struggles to contain the power of MNCs bring together "first world" and "third world" concerns.

Consequently, MNCs have begun to experience the heat of popular protests, consumer boycotts, legal suits, and a variety of public shaming campaigns addressing their misconduct or lack of adequate response to a variety of social wrongs. In tandem with the emergence of transnational market forces, emerge transnational networks of grassroot movements, loosely organized "corporate bashing" and "corporate watch" groups and a host of NGOs that shift their attention and gaze to MNCs (DeWinter 2001). The basic dialectic can be summarized as follows: the more the public domain is privatized, the more that the private is politicized and becomes a matter of public concern. Santos articulates this dialectic in arguing that neoliberal hegemonic globalization,

> while propagating throughout the globe the same system of domination and exclusion, has created the conditions for the counter-hegemonic forces, organizations and movements located in the most disparate regions of the globe to visualize common interests across and beyond the many

differences that separate them and to converge in counter-hegemonic struggles embodying separate but related emancipatory social projects.

(Santos 2002:446)

Santos, following up on this dialectic, uncovers, analyzes, and theorizes the conditions for counter-hegemonic practices (see also Santos and Rodríguez-Garavito's chapter in this volume). Yet explorations for the conditions of possibility of counter-hegemonic social projects must also take into account capitalist responses. Simply put, capitalists and capitalist entities do not sit still when faced with threats and chal- lenges. Corporations and corporate executives constantly mobilize a host of agents (e.g. NGOs, research institutions, business associations, state bureaucrats, etc.) to maintain their ideological and practical supremacy (Sklair 1997). Capitalism, write Boltanski and Chiapello, "has always relied on critiques of the status quo to alert it to any untrammeled development of its current forms and to discover the antidotes required to neutralize opposition to the system and increase the level of profitability within it" (1999). Therefore, it seems to me that any effort to explore and to theorize counter-hegemonic practices must also deal with capitalist responses to such threats. Concretely, any effort to explore counter-hegemonic efforts to curb corporate global rule should address corporate counter efforts to silence, evade, oppose, and coopt such unwarranted political pressures.

In this paper I demonstrate this point by looking at the emergent field of action commonly known as "corporate social responsibility" (CSR). In general, struggles to tame MNCs and to bring them under effective mechanisms of social control are one important tenet of the efforts to curb contemporary hegemonic neoliberal globalization. Specifically, law has a potentially transformational role in subjecting MNCs to enforce- able rules concerning their duties and responsibilities towards the public good. However, the field of corporate social responsibility is not a mere derivative of these new pressures. Rather, it is corporate response to such pressures that eventually allows for the emergence of a field.

Indeed, corporations no longer submit to the classical view that they are only answerable to shareholders and that their only commitment is to the maximization of profits (Dickerson 2002). To a greater or lesser degree, corporations begin to speak, albeit often in utilitarian terms, about their responsibilities to a multitude of "stakeholders." The CSR field thus evolves as a site where counter-hegemonic pressures and hegemonic counter-pressures begin to assume a more or less definitive structure, with "authorized" agents who occupy certain "recognized" positions from which they assert "what is at stake" and from which they try to control the definition and scope of the very notion of "responsibility." The field of CSR thus functions not simply as a buffer against corporate-bashing, but more generally as a constitutive force in shaping the relationship between business and society in contemporary global capitalism. As such, I believe it is worthwhile to take a closer look at corporate strategies designed to prevent the politicization of the market and to contain the counter-hegemonic projects such processes may unleash.

In the first part of the paper I consider the general contours of the CSR field. I look at various corporate strategies designed to preempt mounting pressures to introduce what Santos calls "counter-hegemonic forms of legal globalization," namely, the use of law as means for bringing about social emancipation from corporate tyranny. Specifically, I analyze a set of corporate practices relating to CSR and show how they shape the notion of responsibility in ways that diffuse its potentially radical application to MNCs and in ways that fit the hegemonic neoliberal framework.

In the second and third parts of the paper I look at some of the agents that mobilize the CSR field. In the second part, I discuss the establishment of corporate-sponsored and corporate-oriented NGOs and analyze the role they play in structuring the CSR field. In the third part, I consider the hybrid nature of counter-hegemonic movements. All in all, I offer some tentative reflections about the practical, conceptual, and institutional impediments to the ability to imagine and act upon alternatives to hegemonic practices. At what may be called a meta-theoretical level, I also briefly reflect on the ability to act outside the neoliberal blueprint of civil society and the institutional form that seems to have become dominant in it, namely, the non-governmental organization. While in the first part of the article I point at de-radicalization tendencies, in the second part I move to consider the corporatization of civil society as it is reflected in the activities of some NGOs in the field.

4.2 THE DE-RADICALIZATION OF CORPORATE SOCIAL RESPONSIBILITY

There is a growing recognition among scholars and activists alike of the widening gap between the transnational character of corporate activity and the availability of transnational regulatory structures that may be effectively used to monitor, assess, and restrain corporations irrespective of any specific territory in which they may happen to operate at a given moment. The problem is twofold. On the one hand, individual countries find it increasingly impossible or undesirable to tame the activities of MNCs. Poor or impoverished countries, often in desperate need to attract direct foreign investment, are reluctant to introduce legal measures that may deter MNCs from investing or that may cause MNCs to relocate their production sites in countries whose (underdeveloped) legal systems are more user-friendly from the corporate point of view (e.g. legal systems that do not endorse or enforce minimum wage requirements, child labor prohibitions, health and safety standards, environmental protections, collective bargaining rights, etc.). Moreover, MNCs are in a position to effectively escape local jurisdictions by playing one legal system against the other, by taking advantage of local legal systems ill-adapted for effective corporate regulation, and by moving production sites and steering financial investments to places where local laws are most hospitable to them.

On the other hand, there is an increasingly recognized 'remedial gap' in international law when it comes to regulating MNCs. For example, while MNCs are able to effectively push for transnational regulatory regimes that enhance the protection of their property rights (e.g. the TRIPS agreement of the World Trade Organization that protects intellectual property rights in all member states), international law fails to "articulate the human rights obligations of corporations and to provide mechanisms for regulating corporate conduct in the field of human rights" (HLR 2001). It is in this light that we should understand stark statements such as the one contained in a recent report of a sub-commission of the United Nation's Economic and Social Council, which states that "post colonial exploitation of developing countries by transnational corporations had become intolerable."

Counter-hegemonic efforts to curb corporate power through law operate at two distinct levels. First, there are growing attempts to envision and develop blueprints for regulating MNCs by subjecting them to a set of universal standards that will apply to corporations above and beyond the demands of any specific locality. Social theorists thus argue that "the task now is to create and entrench such institutions of effective political action as can match the size and the power of the already global economic forces and bring them under political scrutiny and ethical supervision" (Bauman 2002:73; also see Held 2002). Human rights and environmental organizations such as Amnesty

International, Global Witness, and the World Wildlife Fund (WWF) argue that the only effective means of ensuring effective governance of corporate social performance is through binding norms. James A. Paul, Executive Director of the Global Policy Forum, advocates a legal framework, including monitoring, that must be developed to govern corporate behavior, arguing that "multinational corporations are too important for their conduct to be left to voluntary and self generated standards" (www.commondreams.org). And Oxfam International, a non-governmental organization that increasingly focuses on corporate practices, suggests in a White Paper submitted to the British government that "what is needed is a set of verifiable and enforceable guidelines covering all aspects of corporate activity." Attempts at this level include pressures on international bodies like the United Nations, on regional entities like the European Union, and on international institutions like the World Bank to develop enforceable legal frameworks, in the form of treaties and multilateral agreements, subjecting MNCs to universal social standards of operation that can be systematically monitored, assessed, and, when necessary, enforced.

So far, attempts to move CSR into the enforceable domain of formal regulation seem to have made little headway. For example, the European Commission recently rejected proposals to adopt a regulatory approach that would have subjected corporations to mandatory social and environmental reporting. The EC emphasized the "voluntary nature of corporate social responsibility" and stated that it would not impose responsible behavior on companies by means of compulsory regulation. Further, it excluded from the outset debates on the advantages or disadvantages of enforcing social standards through legally binding codes. The position of the EC, in turn, has to be understood in the context of the fierce resistance to compulsory regulation put forward by the International Chamber of Commerce and other corporate-friendly organizations. These groups expressed their views that corporate practices are spread more effectively by example rather than by binding codes, and that the social responsibilities of corporations must remain unregulated in order to safeguard the flexibility needed "to address the diversity of European corporate culture" (Davidsson 2002). Likewise, attempts to subject MNCs to the recently established International Criminal Court (ICC) on grounds that MNCs are to be held liable for violations of international norms of human rights have also been aborted, establishing that the jurisdiction of the ICC would not cover "legal persons" (Clapham 2000).

Secondly, activists who try to curb corporate power through law enlist and mobilize the "developed" legal systems of rich countries in order to police and sanction corporate practices that take place in impoverished and exploited countries. A case in point concerns the relatively concerted attempts to invoke an old statute in US federal courts in order to sue MNCs for human rights violations outside the United States. For example, in a series of cases known as the ATCA cases (Alien Tort Claims Act of 1789), corporate giants have been accused of complicity in human rights violations in impoverished countries (Shamir 2004a).

One case applying ATCA to corporate practices was filed in 1996 against Unocal, a giant enterprise engaged in energy resource projects around the world.[1] The plaintiffs argued that Unocal relied on Burmese army units for building a gas pipeline and that the latter, with the tacit knowledge of Unocal, resorted to extreme methods of forced labor and forced relocation of villagers in the course of construction. The plaintiffs argued that Unocal should be held liable for the human rights abuses committed by the military under either joint venture or vicarious liability theories and sought monetary compensation accordingly. Another case was filed against Texaco.[2] In this case, the plaintiffs alleged that from 1964 to 1992 Texaco improperly disposed of waste while extracting oil from the Ecuadorean Amazon, resulting in environmental damages that amounted to a violation of human rights on three counts: cultural genocide, ethnic discrimination, and infringing on the indigenous population's right to a healthy environment.

In another case, the plaintiffs sued Royal Dutch Shell for conspiring with the Nigerian government against the Ogoni people.[3] The plaintiffs alleged that the Nigerian military – with the knowledge and cooperation of the defendant – arrested and convicted nine members of a Nigerian environmental movement in order to suppress that movement. These arrests, that were part of a widespread intimidation campaign, led to the false conviction and execution of Ken Sero-Wiwa, a Nobel Prize winner and a leader of the movement. Another noteworthy case was brought against Coca-Cola.[4] The plaintiffs argued that Coca-Cola should be held liable for the activities of paramilitary units who terrorized and murdered union organizers at a bottling plant in

[1] *Doe* v. *Unocal*, 110 F. Supp. 2d 1294 (CD Cal. 2000).
[2] *Aguinda* v. *Texaco*, 142 F. Supp. 2d 534 (SDNY 2001).
[3] *Wiwa* v. *Royal Dutch Petroleum Co.*, 226 F. 3d 88 (2nd Cir. 2000).
[4] *Sinaltrainal* v. *Coca-Cola Co.* (SD Fla.).

Colombia that exclusively catered to Coca-Cola. Among the human rights violations cited in this case were murder, extra-judicial killings, kidnapping, unlawful detention, and torture. The plaintiffs also argued that Coca-Cola and its affiliates were liable for the denial of the plaintiffs' right to associate and organize, in violation of internationally recognized human rights. The plaintiffs alleged that Coca-Cola was jointly and severally liable for all the acts of its subsidiaries and/or vicariously liable for the acts of its alleged agents, the paramilitary units. A few dozen claims against MNCs have since been brought before US courts, alleging various corporate violations of human rights and seeking compensation for resultant damages. However the attempts to use the aforementioned ATCA as a means of taming MNCs also face serious obstacles and draw strong opposition from the US administration (Shamir 2004a).

Alongside legal action, activists around the globe have launched numerous campaigns of corporate public shaming, using non-legal measures such as consumer boycotts, divestment programs, and popular protest in order to pressure MNCs to adopt responsible business practices. For example, in early 2003, Oxfam International launched a "Fair Trade Coffee" campaign against Kraft Foods and Procter & Gamble, mobilizing public opinion against the low prices they pay to coffee growers in Africa, Latin America, and Asia. Arguing that these MNCs are responsible for plummeted prices that seriously risk the livelihoods of millions, Oxfam had used measures such as protest at shareholders meetings in order to press for a minimum "floor price" for coffee. Indeed, on the basis of such activities we may agree with Sklair (1995) that "[t]he contemporary level of monitoring of corporate activities is historically unprecedented. There are thousands of organizations actively seeking out corporate malpractices all over the world" (1995:68). Yet again, it seems that the attempts to tame MNCs, whether at the principled level or through direct legal action, have so far yielded limited results (Sethi 2002; Winston 2002).

Of course, it is plausible to argue, as some do, that we are witnessing only the initial phase of a worldwide process geared toward the taming of MNCs. After all, it was only around the mid-1990s that concerted efforts to curb corporate power began in earnest (Corporate Watch was established in 1996; the first ATCA corporate case was filed in 1996; and the first Nike scandal, bringing to broad popular attention the links between consumer goods in rich countries and the sweatshop conditions of their production in impoverished countries, only surfaced in late 1997). However, it seems that at least part of the difficulty in taming MNCs above and beyond episodic outbreaks of consumer anger and above and beyond a more or less successful campaign against a single MNC or even a particular corporate sector has to do with the way MNCs have learnt to respond to the mounting pressures. It is this corporate strategic response that interests me here.

The fundamental strategy adopted by MNCs in the wake of various "production scandals" that threaten their corporate image has been to become active players in the area of CSR. To wit, the fundamental corporate strategy has not been to shirk responsibility or to deny the social obligations of corporations. On the contrary, corporations have assertively embarked on the CSR bandwagon, gradually shaping the very notion of CSR in ways amenable to corporate concerns. By and large, corporations and a host of other affiliated players in the field tend to associate the concept with voluntary notions of "good citizenship." This assigned meaning is naturalized as an extension of an age-old tradition of capitalist philanthropy. Yet while philanthropy was strictly separated from the core practice of the business, the two are united in the field through the idea that "charity is good for business." One important locus where this utilitarian principle is cloaked with scientific authority is the business school, where ideas of "corporate citizenship" are packaged for MBA students as tools for enhanced corporate success. The old academic interest in philanthropy moves from religious studies departments to the business school, and the old field of business ethics – heretofore marginal to business studies – enjoys a late blooming, as notions such as transparency and accountability are incorporated into the general conceptual package of "social responsibility" (Castro 1996).

New conceptions of corporate responsibility are integrated into the old models of how to successfully manage a business enterprise and how to ensure its reputation. Often presented as the product of scientific research, the new models teach prospective corporate executives how to act as a "good corporate citizen." For example, the good corporate citizen "sponsors community events, supports employee voluntarism, donates to charities, contributes products and services, supports community organizations," and its senior management is "active in the community." This model of citizenship is incorporated into other models that develop and measure "cause related marketing," "social branding," "brand loyalty," and "employee loyalty" as means for achieving financial success. Thus, unlike traditional bourgeois philanthropy that was strictly separated from the business, "corporate social respon-sibility" speaks the language of instrumental-rationality that ties "doing good" to profits (Bollier 1996). Accordingly, practically every major MNC now launches widely publicized philanthropic campaigns of various sorts, establishes charitable foundations and publicly endorses ideas about "giving back to the community." Often, charitable campaigns coincide with corporate image crises. Thus, for example, major pharmaceutical companies announced campaigns for the free distribution of HIV/AIDS medicines when faced with allegations that the prices they charged for these drugs augmented the AIDS crisis in South Africa (Shamir, forthcoming).

At any rate, the field of CSR goes way beyond charity. The single and most distinctive common denominator of all corporate-oriented and corporate-inspired notions of "social responsibility" is the volun-tary, non-enforceable, and self-regulatory meaning of the term. The principle of self-regulation has become the corporation's most crucial frontline in the struggle over meaning and an essential ideological locus for disseminating the neoliberal logic of altruistic social participation that is to be governed by goodwill alone. The grounding of this parti-cular meaning of responsibility – aided and legitimized by experts, academics, social science, and business management theories, and a host of institutional players – has become a major form of corporate activity.

Accordingly, hundreds of MNCs – with the active involvement of the International Chamber of Commerce – recently joined the United Nations' voluntary and unenforceable "Global Compact," intended to display corporate commitment to various social expectations across the globe. Another case in point has to do with ensuring that "social responsibility" plans channeled through the European Union will remain voluntary and non-binding. The European Commission issued a Green Paper to promote a framework for corporate social responsi-bility in July 2001. The Green Paper suggested measures to enhance the social accountability of corporations such as improved reporting by corporations on their social performance, the introduction of "social labels" on products informing consumers about the producer's social responsibility commitments, and the further development of corporate "codes of conduct." Yet the Commission excluded any debate on enforcing social standards through law, and expressed explicit reluc-tance to introduce legally binding codes on corporations. The Green Paper thus fully endorsed the self-regulation approach advocated by groups that promote the corporate point of view. For example, the position of the International Chamber of Commerce that advocates the idea that good corporate practices are spread more effectively by example rather than by binding codes and regulations and the position of CSR Europe – a non-profit organization representing corporate interests – that argues that the social responsibility of business needs to be unregulated in order to ensure the flexibility it needs to address the diversity of European corporate culture (Davidsson 2002).

Blueprints for voluntary "codes of conduct" abound (Westfield 2002). The United Nations Global Compact sets out nine principles with respect to human rights, labor standards, and the environment that corporations are advised to follow. The International Labour Organization adopted a Tripartite Declaration of Principles Concerning Multinational Enterprises and Social Policy, ready to be adopted by willing corporations, and the Organization for Economic Cooperation and Development (OECD) has set out Guidelines for Multinational Enterprises. Moreover, there are numerous corporate initiatives designed to promote and consolidate the voluntary principle while cooperating with non-governmental organizations that seek "constructive dialogue" with MNCs. Codes of conduct have been adopted throughout the European fashion industry and toy industry and similar initiatives have taken place in the United States in sectors as disparate as the garment and furniture industries. The Ethical Trading Initiative, a UK-based alliance of companies, non-governmental organizations, and trade union organizations committed to working together to identify and promote ethical trade, also issued a model code of conduct for MNCs. Consequently, corporate activities currently encompass a variety of "codes of conduct," "mission statements," and "social auditing schemes," all of which are designed to display corporate acceptance of the general idea that they do bear "social responsibilities." Concurrently, new corporate positions are created, from vice-presidents for human rights to new corporate citizenship and community relations departments, displaying the new corporate commitment to CSR in its unenforceable self-regulatory format.

Moreover, a whole commercial market develops around shaping, assessing, and consulting on the desired dimensions of social responsibility. A new breed of strategic consultants is also emerging in this new, potentially lucrative field. With a typical background in public relations, these experts sell strategic CSR models and advise corporations on how to develop CSR campaigns, to monitor them, and to end up with "impact assessment" reports. Thus, the field emerges as non-profit and for-profit entities begin to compete among themselves over the selling of various CSR models and SustainAbility programs (as one such for-profit British consultant firm chose to call itself). Law firms also begin to appreciate the business opportunities this field seems to be offering. The American Bar Association, for example, recently established a taskforce and published a report in which the concept of CSR is constructed in terms of corporate "accountability" and "transparency" as means of securing investors' confidence.[5] And, in the public relations and advertising industries, a new line of "social branding" is adopted by copywriters and graphic designers trained in the art of associating products and services with "morally good" notions like saving the planet, educating the poor, reaching out to communities, and preparing children for life in the global village.

Accounting firms also embark upon the CSR bandwagon, developing special expertise in "social auditing" and offering their commercial services to interested corporations. The issue of auditing, in general, seems to be the fastest growing area of high-revenue expertise related to CSR. Unlike financial auditing that already enjoys a rather broad base of agreed standards, the measurement of CSR performance is only in its early stages of development. The Green Paper, mentioned above, establishes that a "global consensus needs to evolve on the type of information to be disclosed, the reporting format to be used, and the reliability of the evaluation and audit procedure." The problems are manifold: What are the criteria of adequate CSR performance? Are they measurable? What should be the basis for comparison among corporations? How does one compare one industrial sector with another? How does one compare between service-oriented MNCs (e.g. airlines, hotels), industrial MNCs, and financial MNCs? Here again, a host of commercial entrepreneurs, corporate entities, and (nominally) non-profit organizations who hope to become the field's standard-setting authority compete over the development of rating systems for measuring corporate behavior. For example, the non-profit organization Social Accountability International (SAI) has developed the SA8000 standard for workplace conditions and a system for independently verifying factories' compliance with that standard. SAI operates as a non-profit organization with major funding from the Open Society Institute of George Soros, as well as from the McArthur,

[5] Preliminary Report of the ABA Task Force on Corporate Responsibility, July 16, 2002.

Ford, and Rockefeller foundations, and also engages in training accounting firms to act as social auditing experts. Another player striving to establish social measuring and reporting guidelines is the Global Reporting Initiative, a non-profit organization that is sponsored by corporations such as Ford, General Motors, Nike, and Royal Dutch Shell. The Triple Bottom Line Initiative is yet another non-profit venture engaged in the process of trying to set its own measurement and verification criteria as a corporate standard. Here again, the non-profit organization behind the project relies on the support of MNCs and business groups and also provides corporations such as IBM, Shell, Heineken, BASF, Philips, and Canon with training in CSR and SRI (socially responsive investment) programs.[6]

The competition over auditing techniques has implications far beyond the commercial and the technical. Through such initiatives, the notion of social responsibility undergoes a process of bureaucratization and standardization that transforms the heretofore politically loaded and morally debated notion of corporate responsibility into a measurable set of indicators that can then be exchanged and traded among shareholders and investors as any other commodity that adds "value" to the firm (or subtracts from it). Thus, as Parker notes, the emergence of this vibrant field of expertise and its various standards raises "questions about the extent to which they measure substance rather than procedure implementation" (2002:224). Largely dominated by players affiliated with corporations or dependent on them, social auditing may thus become monopolized in ways that will further tilt the meaning of "social responsibility" in the direction of business interests. In other words, while counter-hegemonic pressures often seek the backing of law and regulation, the CSR field evolves through corporate investment in self-regulatory schemes that have the capacity to preempt viable threats to corporate interests.[7]

---

[6] In discussing the contribution of non-profit organizations to the development of the CSR field in directions preferred by multinational corporations, I do not mean to suggest that all non-profit groups are thus coopted by, or work for, the advancement of corporate interests. For example, members of labor-support organizations, unions, and independent monitoring organizations across the global South risk their lives on a daily basis fighting the cooptation of CSR and other fields by MNCs. In this part of the paper, however, I refer to a growing corporate investment in nurturing friendly and nonconfrontational NGOs (see also Winston 2002).

[7] Of course, the dynamic of the field does not stop here. Counter-hegemonic forces do not stand idle in the face of hegemonic cooptation. Rather, "confrontational players" (Winston 2002) in the field, like independent unions, NGOs, labor support organizations, and other counter-hegemonic actors are experimenting with novel forms of independent monitoring of codes of

Oxfam's White Paper on globalization seems to capture this point. Under the title "Responsible Investment: A Corporate Imperative," the White Paper asserts:

> As public consciousness about the power and impact of TNCs has increased, corporations have responded by proclaiming their attachment to ethical standards, preferably as expressed through non-enforceable codes of conduct. High profile cases involving oil and biotechnology companies in which billions of dollars have been wiped off from share values because of public concern over corporate practices have added impetus to this process ... At their best, voluntary codes of conduct can act as a guide to corporate practice and set standards for others to follow ... At their worst, they are little more than a public relations exercise. But the deeper point is that corporate behaviour is too important for poverty reduction to be left in the field of voluntary codes and standards defined by the corporate sector itself ... What is needed is a set of verifiable and enforceable guidelines covering all aspects of corporate activity.[8]

The emergence of commercial activities in the field of CSR is an important mechanism in de-radicalization. De-radicalization is also significantly augmented by an increasing number of corporate-sponsored or otherwise corporate-oriented NGOs that aim to structure CSR as a field of private regulation. Dicle Kogacioglu, an insightful observer of this text, suggests the term MaNGO (market-oriented NGO) to describe old bodies like the International Chamber of Commerce and newer types of NGOs. Directly and indirectly sponsored by business, MaNGOs (market-oriented non-governmental organizations) are established in order to disseminate and actualize corporate-inspired versions of "social responsibility" while enjoying the aura of disinterestedness often bestowed on non-profit "civil society" entities. Their mission is to educate the corporate world about the merits of CSR practices, to initiate CSR projects, and to nurture ties with communities, civic groups, and other non-governmental organizations. There are dozens of such non-profit-yet-distinctly-market-players operating in Europe and the United States, facilitating yet another dimension of the evolving CSR field. Moreover, as will be discussed in the next part of this paper, the proliferation of MaNGOs is a strong indication of a sweeping process that can only be described as the persistent corporatization of civil society.

---

conduct that, while falling short of neutralizing hegemonic cooptation of the field, do "put up a fight" and lead to some successful experiences that make life less comfortable to global economic actors.

[8] See www.oxfam.org.uk/policy/papers/global/global2.htm.

4.3 THE CORPORATIZATION OF CIVIL SOCIETY

In this part of the paper, I would like to single out two main features of the MaNGOs that disseminate the idea of CSR. First, in substantive terms, MaNGOs tend to identify CSR with a variety of "civic virtue" activities aimed at "needy communities." The basic stance that follows not only gravitates toward charitable activities but also marks a tendency to disengage CSR from both the firm's core business practices and issues deemed to be "politically sensitive." A director of one MaNGO whom I interviewed thus told me that "the way to build corporate involvement in social issues is by looking for issues that are not politically sensitive, by looking for issues upon which everyone seems to agree that the contribution is for the greater social good." Likewise, corporate executives who attended training programs for CSR, organized by such MaNGOs, were discouraged from looking at CSR as a site of potential conflict between core business practices and social issues (Shamir 2004b). As a basic rule, explanatory narratives accounting for the rise of CSR and for thinking about the social role of MNCs were not cast in terms of a conflict paradigm but in terms of a rational linear evolution that led MNCs to "realize" their social missions. Accordingly, popular forms of resistance to the harms and risks posed by corporations were typically discussed as the changing "concerns" of consumers or the changing "needs" of communities.

Indeed, "community" is a key concept in the work of experts who disseminate the corporate-based version of CSR. The "community" replaces other sociological concepts such as gender, class, and race as a social category toward which CSR efforts should be directed. In fact these latter categories are devoured by the notion of the community in a way that allows for systematic de-politicization of the reasons for becoming "involved" in communities. In my study of several MaNGOs I have found a consistent bias in favor of community educational and training programs as the primary venue offered to corporations as means for actualizing their social responsibilities. The coupling of the vague notion of "community" with a repeated emphasis on the need for corporations to invest efforts in "educational programs" as a primary display of CSR ultimately invests both the term "responsibility" and the term "social change" with a distinctive a-political meaning.

In general, MaNGOs such as Business for Social Responsibility (corporate-oriented non-profit organizations operate under this name in Canada, Great Britain, and the US) spread a CSR model that seems to complement and further validate the neoliberal mode of operation characteristic of many service-oriented civil society organizations that rush to fill the void created by governmental retreats from the supply of public services. In a study of the transformation of social movements in Latin America into rationally structured NGOs, Taylor (1999) shows that many NGOs, adjusting to the tailored programs of donors, turn their attention to educational programs. Such programs, writes Taylor, "have subtly swapped a rhetoric of political empowerment for a rhetoric of socioeconomic empowerment by educating and equipping people with the skills and organizational tools for coping with the harsh realities of contemporary capitalism" (1999:273). At another level, but guided by the same approach, human rights often become a matter of launching educational programs for "democracy and tolerance." The version of CSR dispensed by MaNGOs is very similar. Through them, the idea that education is a primary means for social change becomes naturalized, and in fact also transforms the very meaning of the term "social change" from being one concerning political empowerment and participation to a question of skills.

This CSR model is also at a striking accord with the way Bourdieu describes the welfare state's "wholesale conversion to neoliberalism." The definition of public assistance, he writes, has been radically transformed

> [b]y the substitution of direct aid to individuals for older forms of support in the form of access to services ... In a perfect fit with the neoliberal vision, direct aid reduces solidarity to a simple financial allocation and aims solely at facilitating consumption ... without seeking to orient or to structure that consumption ... [T]he end result is a state charity, which is destined, just as it was in the good old days of religious philanthropy, for the "deserving poor."
>
> (Bourdieu 1999:184)

Consequently, this neoliberal mode of "intervention" turns potentially mobilized people into an aggregate of fragmented and isolated "disadvantaged" individuals (Bourdieu 1999: 184). In this way as well, the notion of corporate responsibility is abstracted from any political significance.

A second notable feature of MaNGOs that structure the CSR field is that "social responsibility is good for business." Hence, CSR has to be deployed as part of the corporation's marketing strategy and image-building machinery. In effect, MaNGOs are at the vanguard of preaching the idea that CSR must operate according to firm business models, should be based on equipping corporate executives with adequate "managerial tools" for realizing CSR projects, and must follow the general imperative of, in the words of one MaNGO executive, "applying business methods to worthy social causes." The construction of CSR as a business model seems to have two immediate implications. First, it allows for the unproblematic integration of CSR into the corporation's marketing and branding apparatuses, hence subjecting social considerations to commercial ones. This, almost necessarily, acts as a strong antidote against corporate involvement in controversial issues and against developing CSR in ways that can even remotely collide with core business practices.

Secondly, and not the least importantly, the "business model" formula often signifies the transformation of CSR into an element of the corporation's normative control apparatus over its own employees. In fact, a curious reversal of the notion of "community" happens at this juncture. One MaNGO executive says: "The community is first and foremost the community of employees. It is important to let them feel [through CSR projects] that they are partners." Another explains: "Over time, I understood that the important thing here is not our customers but our employees. The social involvement of business has a faster and stronger impact on employees than on customers. Employees that work for an organization that is involved are more satisfied and loyal." Indeed, such ideas have already become part of the "scientific managerial theory" that develops in the field, as consultants and other experts confirm that corporate employees develop stronger commitments to socially responsible companies than they do to indifferent ones.

In this sense, the de-radicalization of CSR also finds expression in its penetration right into the heart of official and quasi-official corporate culture. Corporate culture, writes Kunda, is the "shared rules governing cognitive and affective aspects of membership in an organization, and the means whereby they are shaped and expressed" (1992:8). The deployment of normative control through corporate culture consists of attempts to guide employees to act in the best interests of the firm by creating an internal commitment and strong identification with company goals (Kunda 1992:11). By focusing on employee participation in CSR projects, by enlisting them to contribute time, money, and knowledge, and by sharing with them the company's reputation as socially responsible, the normative control is deployed by transforming employees into a "community" and by turning labor relations into a question of employees' satisfaction and loyalty. Corporate executives specializing in CSR, therefore, simultaneously function as agents in the CSR field and as agents of the corporation's normative control apparatus.

In sum, MNCs, with the help of MaNGOs, business groups and associations, academic experts, and commercial consultants gradually embrace CSR as a business opportunity, treating CSR as a "project" that has to be managed with an eye to the strategies, goals, and methods of the business enterprise as a whole. Increasingly, the purpose of such enterprise is to create business opportunities for the firm, to consolidate a loyal cadre of employees, to build a market for the firm's products, and to develop a positive reputation for the firm. In this way, corporations transform the idea of social responsibility into a marketing device and into a commodity that conceals the power relations that underlie the relationship between global capitalism and social inequality, social harm, and social wrongs.

4.4 FINAL REMARKS: TENTATIVE REFLECTIONS ON COUNTER-HEGEMONIC POSSIBILITIES

The proliferation of MaNGOs is but one indication of an overall process in the course of which MNCs have learnt to deploy and mold the non-profit sector to fit a hegemonic neoliberal version of civil society. The general trend of deploying the non-profit sector for enhanced corporate social and political influence, and the specific trend of molding the CSR field to fit the self-regulatory ideology of MNCs, is thus an important factor that must be considered when analyzing the trajectory of counter-hegemonic transnational coalitions. In fact, "civil society" has become saturated with a multitude of nominally non-profit organizations that blur the lines between the old categories of state, market, and civil society. We must not forget that many NGOs, even if nominally free from direct corporate influence, are nonetheless heavily funded by foundations and trust funds that have been established in earlier rounds of corporate philanthropy. Of course, there are many NGOs who struggle to preserve their institutional and ideological independence, and there are many grassroots movements that struggle to protect their autonomy from both market and state intervention. Still, we cannot ignore the fact that an increasing number of NGOs are established or indirectly governed by both governments (GoNGOs) and market players (MaNGOs). Corporations infiltrate public local and transnational institutions through an invigorated emphasis on "partnerships," tying corporations to NGOs, governments, and international institutions. A case in point is the aforementioned Global Compact of the United Nations. Independent groups such as Corporate Watch, Human Rights Watch, and Amnesty International view the Global Compact with suspicion, warning against a "partnership" model which is too close for comfort, against the prospects of corporate "bluewash," and against the corporatization of the United Nations.

A second factor that we must weigh when assessing the conditions for counter-hegemonic action is the observation that the transnational networks that MNCs nurture and some of the transnational advocacy networks (Keck and Sikkink 1998) that struggle to tame corporate power share some fundamental social characteristics. A core issue here is that an increasing number of non-profit groups and civic associations are embedded within a culture of professional expertise that is not unlike the one around which corporations are organized. In what follows, therefore, I try to offer some critical reflections on some typical counter-hegemonic coalitions or otherwise joint confrontational campaigns.

Santos (2002) argues that conditions are ripe for new types of coalitions between "the subaltern of West and rest." For example, transnational coalitions for the elimination of sweatshops include labor unions, consumers' organizations, religious groups, human rights NGOs, independent monitoring agencies, students' organizations, and other umbrella agencies (see Rodríguez-Garavito's chapter in this volume). Similarly, consider the identity of the plaintiffs in the previously discussed ATCA cases. In many such cases, indigenous, poor, and oppressed people have been able to advance a claim because they were aided, funded, and represented by institutional players elsewhere. In the case against Unocal, Burmese farmers were represented by lawyers of EarthRights International, the New York-based Center for Constitutional Rights, and two commercial law firms specializing in civil rights cases and class action suits. In the case against Texaco, members of three indigenous tribes from Ecuador were aided by a wide coalition: an Ecuadorean lawyer working in the US initiated the case and was joined by an American commercial law firm specializing in class action lawsuits, a group of law professors from Boston, the Massachusetts Environmental Law Society, Earth Justice International, and Amazon Watch. In the case against Shell in Nigeria, family members of Ken Sero-Wiwa were represented by the New York-based Center for Constitutional Rights and aided by EarthRights International. In the case against Coca-Cola, the Colombian union Sinaltrainal was aided and represented by the American United Steel Workers Union and by the International Labor Rights Fund. The latter also assumed representation in a case against ExxonMobil in Indonesia.[9] ATCA cases thus blur the lines between civil law and public law, national law and international law, public interest lawyers and private lawyers, non-profit organizations and commercial law firms, labor unions and civil rights groups, and environmental concerns and class action interests. These hybrid coalitions are not limited to the legal domain alone. Other corporate-bashing campaigns also require cooperation and effective communication between "First World" and "Third World" activists. This is also the case with Oxfam International's recent "Fair Trade Coffee" campaign mentioned above. Here again, Oxfam relies on active cooperation with farmers and indigenous communities in Africa, Latin America, and Asia.

The dispute over the constitutionality of a South African law infringing upon the patent rights of the global pharmaceutical industry is another case in point.[10] In 1997, in an attempt to respond to a widespread AIDS crisis, the South African government introduced amendments to the South African Medicines and Related Substances Control Act of 1965. The theory behind the amendments was that the high cost of AIDS/HIV drugs – protected by patent rights held by major pharmaceutical companies – had put them beyond the reach of many infected people relying on public health services. In 1998, the Pharmaceutical Manufacturers' Association of South Africa (PMA), acting on behalf of the world's forty largest pharmaceutical companies (e.g. Bayer, Bristol-Myers, Glaxo-Wellcome, Merck, and Hoffman-La Roche), challenged the constitutionality of the amendment Act in the High Court of South Africa. Additionally, the PMA argued that the law also violated the WTO's TRIPS (Trade Related Aspects of Intellectual Property Rights) agreement which South Africa was obliged to respect. Prompted by the strong lobby of PharMA (the American Pharmaceutical Manufacturers Association), as well as by major pharmaceutical companies, the US government adopted the view that the South African law was in violation of TRIPS and subjected South Africa to trade pressures.

---

[9] *Doe* v. *ExxonMobil Corp.*, (DDC) No. 01CV01357.
[10] On this dispute, see also Klug's chapter in this volume.

However, the legal challenge of the PMA met strong opposition which had been directed in South Africa by a non-profit organization operating under the name of Treatment Action Campaign (TAC). Underlying the South African dispute was the attempt of the industry to preserve the crucial boundary separating *legally protected* business interests from *voluntary* practices of corporate social responsibility. Yet it was precisely that line that the TAC sought to undermine, arguing that the cost of drugs had a direct impact on access to medical care. The TAC has formulated what it labeled as a "multi-dimensional" process designed to force the pharmaceutical companies to reduce the prices of drugs and to withdraw their legal action.

On the one hand, TAC organized demonstrations and mass protests in front of corporate headquarters and relevant embassies across the globe, enlisting the active support of over 250 NGOs outside South Africa. Three international NGOs were particularly important in the globalization of the South African dispute: Médecins Sans Frontiers (operating in the United States under the name "Doctors Without Borders"), Oxfam International, and Ralph Nader's Consumer Project on Technology (CPT). These three organizations became highly instrumental in countering the lobbying efforts of PharMA in general and in urging the United States government and the EU to drop the sanctions against the South African government in particular.

On the other hand, within South Africa, TAC was substantially aided by the AIDS Law Project (ALP). The ALP is a research and resource center specializing in the social, legal, and human rights issues relevant to AIDS. The ALP is also a collaborating center of the United Nations Joint Program on AIDS (UNAIDS) and a partner of the Canadian HIV/AIDS Legal Network (CHALN). The ALP itself is part of the reputed Center for Applied Legal Studies (CALS) that operates at Witwatersrand University in Johannesburg. CALS provided the TAC with a resourceful team of lawyers that effectively struggled for the inclusion of TAC in the judicial process. Once successful in their bid to be heard, the pharmaceutical companies withdrew their case, fearing that the evidence provided by the TAC and its broad network of affiliates would severely damage their reputation as "responsible" market players. In this respect, the South African case is a prime example of the potential impact that well-organized coalitions may have. Working across borders and bringing together an amalgam of concerns (health, human rights, consumerist, and humanitarian) and a broad range of participants (AIDS activists and grassroots groups with first-rate experts in the areas of health and law) may serve as a blueprint for the effective deployment of counter-hegemonic law.

Still, it is noteworthy that, in all the examples cited above, the transnational coalitions are typically based on the ability of indigenous groups, local grassroot movements, and activists in impoverished countries to establish discursive and organizational ties with relatively resourceful experts and with often highly professionalized NGOs. Such hybrid coalitions are not free from the structural constraints imposed by an increasingly corporatized and de-radicalized civil society. Searching for a normative methodology for both analyzing and facilitating counter-hegemonic struggles, Santos argues that, instead of a theory that unifies this immense variety of struggles and movements, what we need is a theory of translation – that is, "a theory that rather than aiming at creating another (theoretical) reality over and above the movements, seeks to create mutual understanding, mutual intelligibility among them so that they may benefit from the experiences of others and network with them: instead of our rarified descriptions the procedure of translation rests on thick descriptions" (2002:465).

It seems to me that such a theory of translation must take heed of the emergent character of civil society organizations under corporate rule. Namely, such a theory of translation must come to grips with, and identify the pitfalls of, working from within the non-governmental-organization institutional paradigm, because the latter is heavily biased toward the corporate hegemonic model of organization and implementation. When we speak about "translation," then, we must also worry about the way the perceived grievances of oppressed, marginal, and exploited populations (Santos' subaltern "rest") are transformed into a meaningful political and legal voice by relatively affluent and secured career-situated experts who often speak the language of and deploy the instruments of hegemonic rational organizational and managerial systems characteristic of contemporary capitalism.

The point here is that, whether we talk about nation-states, or about multinational corporations, or about non-governmental organizations, there seems to have emerged a hegemonic cultural-institutional model concerning the "right way of doing things." This right way of doing things purports to be divorced from actual substance as it deals with models, blueprints, protocols, procedures, key words, and key concepts alone. When it comes to states, as Meyer (1997) shows, a world cultural model determines what a polity should do in order to look like a state, from establishing borders, through the collection of statistics along predefined criteria, to actually filling forms in a competent way. When it comes to NGOs, they are increasingly expected to demonstrate to donors that they are capable of implementing projects because of their organizational and skill capacities, technical competence, managing systems, and cost-effectiveness capabilities. In fact, regardless of substantive goals, many NGOs resemble their corporate counterparts in their reliance on experts and knowledge systems, in their drive to perform well in terms of economic sustainability. In a most grounded sense of everyday life, many NGOs resemble their corporate powers in their dedication to the PowerPoint way of framing problems, solutions, and all which is in between them.

In sociological theory, Gouldner's (1979) concept of the "new class" provides some useful tools for identifying the elective affinities between business concerns and social responsibility concerns, or between the concerns of the "excluded" (the poor and the suffering) and the concerns of the "included" (the post-material concerns of affluent citizens and consumers). Now one need not accept the whole theoretical package developed by Gouldner in order to consider the "new class" as a useful heuristic device. In conceptual terms, Gouldner spoke of a heterogeneous stratum composed of intellectuals and technical intelligentsia whose control over expert-based knowledge serves as its social capital, provides its foundation for claims of prestige and authority, and equips it with a *general* managerial-type orientation to social action. This general orientation consists of the belief that experts can solve "the fundamental requisites of the universal grammar of social rationality: to reunite both power and goodness" (Gouldner 1979:86). Yet this general outlook may find very different expressions. It may relate to the rational investment of capital and to theories of scientific management, to movements for governmental reform, to the drive to use brain trusts and experts in public policy, and to concerns with consumer rights, human rights, and environmental issues (Gouldner 1979:16–17). It may relate, in other words, to both corporate-inspired beliefs in self-regulatory CSR (advocated by experts located in MNCs and MaNGOs) and to counter-hegemonic pressures to subject MNCs to an enforceable legal framework (advocated by experts located in so-called confrontational NGOs). Hence, to some extent, the struggles in the CSR field, including at least some which are substantively confrontational and seek to impose an enforceable regime of duties on multinational corporations, are struggles that take place between different fragments and factions of the new class. Thus, above and beyond substantive disagreements and overt ethical and political conflicts, the inherent tensions between various factions of the new class or between conflicting institutional positions occupied by members of this class are often dealt with and framed in terms of a scientific, expert-based, professional-managerial language.

In this sense at least, some NGOs are able to become key players in world politics because they speak the same language as that of their corporate counterparts, because they employ similar methods of justification, and because they deploy similar models of action. In this regard, part of the effort to develop what Santos calls a theory of translation requires constant attention to the constraints imposed by hegemonic models of organizational action and hegemonic languages of expertise. Within this configuration, many NGOs assume the task of "normalizing" the quality of life at the societal level by the means available to the new class: framing a moral discourse as an imperative that has to be rationalized, legalized, codified, and regulated. At present, the most readily available means to that end is the language of social and human rights. However, this language is increasingly deployed both by that faction of the new class that nurtures models of self-regulation and blueprints of corporate governance and that faction of the new class that seeks to transform this language into a set of legally guaranteed and sanctioned goods such as access to health, education, housing, consumer and environmental protection, and purposefully redistributive, sustainable development. We can therefore observe that hegemonic economic globalization is the very force that produces its dialectic social counterpart, although of course the future implications of this process cannot be determined at this historical moment. At the same time, the study of counter-hegemonic movements in law should be embedded within the context of a social terrain monopolized by MNCs at both the substantive and the formal-organizational levels. This, after all, is the sense in which we talk about hegemony in the first place.

References

Bauman, Zygmunt. 2002. *Society under Siege*. Cambridge: Polity Press.

Beck, Ulrich, Anthony Giddens, and Scott Lash. 1994. *Reflexive Modernization: Politics, Tradition and Aesthetics in the Modern Social Order*. Stanford: Stanford University Press.

Bollier, David. 1996. *Aiming Higher*. New York: Amacom.

Boltanski, Luc, and Eve Chiapello. 2002. "The New Spirit of Capitalism." Paper presented to the Conference of Europeanists, March 14–16, 2002, Chicago.

Bourdieu, Pierre, et al. 1999. "The Abdication of the State." Pp. 181–188 in The Weight of the World: Social Suffering in Contemporary Society, edited by Pierre Bourdieu, Prisilla Parkhurst Fergusan, and Alain Accardo. Stanford: Stanford University Press.

Castro, Barry. 1996. Business and Society: A Reader in the History, Sociology and Ethics of Business. New York: Oxford University Press.

Chomsky, Judith B. 2002. "Fighting for Justice Abroad Through Litigation at Home: Multinationals in US Courts." Paper presented at the 2002 Meeting of the Law and Society Association, Vancouver, Canada.

Davidsson, Pall A. 2002. "Legal Enforcement of Corporate Social Responsibility within the EU." Columbia Journal of European Law 8:529.

DeWinter, Rebecca. 2001. "The Anti-Sweatshop Movement: Constructing Corporate Moral Agency in the Global Apparel Industry. Ethics and International Affairs 15:99–115.

Dickerson, Clair Moore. 2002. "Human Rights: The Emerging Norm of Corporate Social Responsibility." Tulane Law Review 76:1431.

Ellwood, Wayne. 2002. The No Nonsense Guide to Globalization. London: Verso.

Gouldner, Alvin W. 1979. The Future of the Intellectuals and the Rise of the New Class. Oxford: Oxford University Press.

Harvard Law Review. 2001. "Corporate Liability for Violations of International Human Rights Law." Harvard Law Review 114:2025.

Held, David. 2002. "Globalization, Corporate Practice and Cosmopolitan Social Standards." Contemporary Political Theory 1:59–78.

Keck, Margaret and Kathryn Sikkink. 1999. Activists Beyond Borders: Advocacy Networks in International Politics. Ithaca: Cornell University Press.

Klein, Naomi. 1999. No Logo: Taking Aim at the Brand Bullies. New York: Picador.

Kunda, Gideon. 1992. Engineering Culture: Control and Commitment in a High-Tech Corporation. Philadelphia: Temple University Press.

Meyer, John, et al. 1997. "World Society and the Nation State." American Journal of Sociology 103:144–181.

Parker, Christine. 2002. The Open Corporation: Effective Self-Regulation and Democracy. Cambridge: Cambridge University Press.

Santos, Boaventura de Sousa. 2002. Toward a New Legal Common Sense: Law, Globalization and Emancipation. London: Butterworths.

Sethi, S. Prakash. 2002. "Corporate Codes of Conduct and the Success of Globalization." Ethics and International Affairs 16(1):89–106.

Shamir, Ronen. 2004a. "Between Self-Regulation and the Alien Tort Claims Act: On the Contested Concept of Corporate Social Responsibility." Law and Society Review 38: 4.

2004b. "Mind the Gap – The Commodification of Corporate Social Responsibility." Unpublished manuscript.

forthcoming. "South Africa and the Pharmaceutical Industries: A Test for Corporate Social Responsibility." In *Global Perspectives on Cause Lawyering*, edited by Austin Sarat and Stuart Scheingold. Oxford: Oxford University Press.

Sklair, Leslie. 1995. *The Sociology of the Global System.* Baltimore: Johns Hopkins University Press.

1997. "Social Movements for Global Capitalism: The Transnational Capitalist Class in Action." *Review of International Political Economy* 4:514–538.

Taylor, Lucy. 1999. "Globalization and Civil Society – Continuities, Ambiguities and Realities in Latin America." *Indiana Journal of Global Legal Issues* 7:269–295.

Westfield, Elisa. 2002. "Globalization, Governance, and Multinational Enterprise Responsibility: Corporate Codes of Conduct in the 21st Century." *Virginia Journal of International Law* 42:1075.

Winston, Morton. 2002. "NGO Strategies for Promoting Corporate Social Responsibility." *Ethics and International Affairs* 16:71–87.

CHAPTER 5

CAMPAIGNING FOR LIFE: BUILDING A NEW TRANSNATIONAL SOLIDARITY IN THE FACE OF HIV/AIDS AND TRIPS

*Heinz Klug**

5.1 INTRODUCTION

In a dramatic display of political astuteness, six hundred volunteers under the banner of the Treatment Action Campaign, a non-government organization dedicated to ensuring access to treatment for the millions of South Africans infected with HIV/AIDS, commemorated human rights day in South Africa in 2003 by marching on the same police station at Sharpeville where anti-apartheid protestors had been gunned down on March 21, 1960. Symbolizing the number of South Africans dying each day from HIV/AIDS-related illnesses, the demonstrators demanded that the government immediately agree to establish an antiretroviral treatment program in the public health sector. At the same time, fellow TAC protestors in Durban and Cape Town highlighted the urgency of their demands by laying formal charges of culpable homicide against the Minister of Health as well as the Minister of Trade and Industry whom they accused of negligently failing to act and thus of causing the deaths of thousands of AIDS sufferers.

This campaign reflects a situation in marked contrast to the day nearly a decade before in May 1994, when Nelson Mandela, in his first official exercise of power as President of South Africa, announced that free health services must be provided to all children under the age of six and to pregnant women. Yet, unlike the over forty-year struggle against

* Research for this article was based in part on support gratefully received from the University of Wisconsin Graduate School.

apartheid, within a year the government had conceded that the public sector must provide treatment and was instead embroiled in a debate over the pace of implementation of the promised program. While it is indeed sad, as the Reverend Douglas Torr, the Anglican priest who led the TAC marchers in prayer at Sharpeville told the crowd, "that those who fought to liberate South Africa from apartheid needed to fight again," this paper argues that this new social movement, built in the context of the HIV/AIDS pandemic and in response to the extreme disparities in access to affordable medicines, has provided the impetus for a new transnational solidarity which has important implications far beyond South Africa and the immediate struggle for treatment.

In his opening address to the 13th International AIDS Conference in Durban, South Africa, in July 2000, Judge Edwin Cameron of the High Court of South Africa, claimed to embody in person "the injustice of AIDS in Africa." Cameron pointed out that he could live "only because, on a continent in which 290 million Africans survive on less than one US dollar a day, I can afford medication costs of about $400 per month." Accusing manufacturers of imposing prices which made drugs "unaffordably expensive," Cameron noted that the international patent and trade regime prevents the production and marketing of affordable drugs – despite earlier experience in India, Thailand, and Brazil, which he argued demonstrates the feasibility of producing key drugs at costs that would be within reach of the developing world. Yet the global brand-name pharmaceutical industry seemed to remain deaf to these arguments and continued to insist that the cost of patented drugs is directly proportional to their research and development expenditures which they argue guarantee the innovation necessary to produce future generations of miracle drugs. However, a growing movement of solidarity between HIV/AIDS activists, and health, consumer, and development-oriented NGOs, as well as cooperation among developing countries in international fora, brought increasing pressure to bear on both the companies and first world governments, leading over a four-year period to a dramatic reduction in the international prices of HIV/AIDS medications, including antiretroviral therapies.

The international framework for patent rights evolved rapidly in the late twentieth century. Historically, the protection of patent rights, while pursued internationally through the adoption of international agreements, was fundamentally a prerogative of national sovereignty. In fact, before the issue was put on the agenda at the Uruguay Round of trade talks in 1986, approximately forty states did not issue patents for pharmaceuticals, leading in some countries to a proliferation of copies of patented drugs. At the international level, the Paris and Berne Conventions impose only very general rules guaranteeing national treatment, but not the protection of all intellectual property rights. The international regime of intellectual property protection prior to 1994 provided no guarantee of protection for intellectual property-intensive industries; instead, its protection depended upon the rights each jurisdiction offered its own citizens. Switzerland, for example, benefited from participation in the Paris Convention yet refused to issue patents domestically until 1887. This ensured that Swiss corporations received the same protection for their intellectual property rights as local companies in other member states, yet Switzerland provided no protection of patent rights in its territory at all. So long as both Swiss and foreign corporations were denied protection equally, Switzerland remained true to its obligations under the treaty (Moy 1993). In other cases, such as India, patent law distinguished between different sectors and in the case of pharmaceuticals provided only process and not product patents, thus enabling generic manufacturers to reverse engineer patented drugs and legitimately produce the same product so long as they worked out a different production process. It was in this context that the intellectual property-intensive industries sought some minimum protection of their rights, and in the negotiations over TRIPS focused on creating a new international regime (see Ryan 1998; Sell 2003).

Despite adoption of the 1970 Patent Cooperation Treaty, increasing the World Intellectual Property Organization's (WIPO) institutional capacity to provide technical support services to national patent offices, the pharmaceutical industry continued to complain about commercial losses they attributed to the weakness of intellectual property rights protection, particularly in newly industrializing countries. For the pharmaceutical industry the goal was the establishment of minimum standards of patent protection allowing the increasingly multinational corporations that dominate the industry to operate in a single global market. The minimum standards now recognized under TRIPS represent important gains for the industry, including: an extended period of protection – to twenty years; the requirement that all technologies receive equal treatment – precluding lesser protection for pharmaceuticals; and limits on compulsory licensing.

For the brand-name industry, however, this is just the beginning as they continue to strive for what is often termed TRIPS-plus. These goals include: a complete ban on compulsory licensing and parallel imports; pipeline protection for inventions still under development; no early registration or stockpiling of generics prior to the termination of the patent period; and liberal rules allowing for patent extension. While the pharmaceutical companies assert that the protection of their intellectual property rights is an essential prerequisite to the continuing development of life saving drugs, the reality for the majority of people around the world is that they cannot afford to enter the private market and instead rely on their national public health services to address their health needs.

It is the tension between specific local needs, in this case the need to provide access to affordable medicines, and the international commitments developing countries must make in order to participate in the global economy that highlights the significance of the struggle to reconstitute international solidarity. Bringing together civil society, developing country governments as well as international non-governmental organizations, this new movement aims both to pressure states and to empower them to demand a rebalancing of the social needs of their citizens and the claims of "economic globalization." Using the case of South Africa's need to obtain affordable medicines and surveying the international debate over the interpretation of the TRIPS agreement, this paper will argue that the emergence of a global HIV/AIDS pandemic has fundamentally transformed the context within which this debate is being carried out.

Furthermore, I will argue that the struggle over access to affordable medicines is providing an hospitable arena within which to demand a reasonable balance between social needs and claims based on the assertion of property rights. While demands for access to medicines are empowered by the emergence of a new social movement in the face of the HIV/AIDS pandemic, producing major concessions from both the global pharmaceutical industry and developed countries such as the United States, these concessions have thus far been limited to voluntary price reductions and agreement on a highly complex exception to the limitations on compulsory licensing contained in TRIPS. Changes, both at the domestic level in response to social activism and at the international level, provide examples of how increased solidarity between social movements across the world and between developing countries, may achieve the desperately needed reconfiguration of, on the one hand, the social needs of citizens, which can only be adequately addressed by the provision of public goods, and, on the other hand, the demands of private rights claimants who rely on public guarantees of their property to exercise market power.

5.2 CHANGING THE FACE OF SOUTH AFRICA

South Africa's democratic transition was marked by the embrace of constitutionalism as a means of both facilitating and guaranteeing the creation and consolidation of a democratic state (Klug 2000). Given a history of racially structured deprivation the African National Congress (ANC) recognized that a commitment to constitutionally enshrined civil rights would merely entrench the economic distributions of apartheid unless supplemented by a commitment to at least the basic guarantees of socio-economic rights. In addition to these constitutional commitments, the new government began to implement its Reconstruction and Development Programme (RDP) on which it had campaigned for election. The essence of the RDP was a strategy to achieve economic growth and development through the redistribution of social resources. The RDP thus contained the dual goals of seeking to address the basic inequalities in social distribution legally enshrined by apartheid as well as promoting policies geared toward economic expansion which would be key to absorbing the vast numbers of unemployed and underemployed people who had been marginalized during the apartheid era.

In the health sector, the RDP immediately established a Presidential lead project to provide free health services to children under six and pregnant women, while the ANC's National Health plan envisaged a broader goal of making "basic health care available to all South Africans, giving priority to the most vulnerable groups." Emphasizing "[m]aternal and child care, the protection of the environment, services in the rural areas, women's health and the care of the disabled," the plan also promised that there would be "a focus on the prevention and control of major risk factors and diseases, especially AIDS, tuberculosis, measles, gastro-intestinal disease, trauma, heart disease and common cancers" (ANC 1994b). This policy process was capped with the adoption of the "final" 1996 Constitution which guarantees, among other socio-economic rights, the right to have access to "health care services" (section 27(1)(a)).

Introducing a constitutional right to health in a context of vast inequality and limited resources soon produced a tragic but classic confrontation between the health authorities and a patient who required access to renal dialysis in order to prolong his life. When the case *Soobramoney*, reached the Constitutional Court in 1997, the court drew a distinction between the right not to be refused emergency medical treatment in terms of section 27(3) and the progressive realization of the right to health care guaranteed in section 27(1). Rejecting Soobramoney's claim of a right to receive treatment, the Constitutional Court in effect recognized that certain medical decisions – in this case the decision to limit access to those patients whose medical condition made them eligible to receive kidney transplants – are best made by medical personnel and should not be second-guessed by the courts.

Subsequently, in a challenge to the government's limited provision of Nevirapine to prevent mother-to-child transmission of HIV (TAC, 2001), the Constitutional Court rejected the government's attempt to draw an analogy between the "medical decision" in *Soobramoney* and the question of whether Nevirapine should be made available beyond the eighteen test sites established by health authorities. While the medical status of individuals who need kidney transplants is clearly a medical question, the court held that the issue of whether public sector doctors may prescribe a registered drug where medically indicated is not. Even if the relationship between the availability of donated kidneys and the possibility of a successful transplant, as determined by the health of the donee, may be considered a medical question, the issue of whether it makes sense to provide a particular patient or group of patients with a particular treatment is not solely a medical judgment. Where the public sector is failing to provide a particular treatment regime, medically indicated and available in the private sector, then the issue is clearly one of health policy and resources and thus implicates the progressive realization of the right to health care services. The court's decision to require the government to extend the provision of Nervirapine throughout the public health system represented a major success for civil society and legal strategies to enforce socio-economic rights.

5.3 THE PHARMACEUTICAL SECTOR AND THE STRUGGLE FOR AFFORDABLE MEDICINES

The structure of South Africa's pharmaceutical industry as well as the pharmaceutical supply system is particularly marked by the legacy of apartheid. While the industry is dominated by subsidiaries of the multinational pharmaceutical corporations, the market this industry is geared to serve reflects the apartheid divide. Although the highest value for the industry lies in supplying the small, predominately white, middle class who are served by the private health system, the vast bulk of drugs produced are distributed through the public health system. Yet this latter segment represents only a fraction of the value of the industry's sales, since the government purchases in bulk and obtains substantial discounts from the manufacturers.

Thus, although pharmaceutical firms made only a small profit on the supply of drugs to the public system, they were able to charge relatively high prices to private consumers. While the high cost of drugs in the private market might have been mediated by the introduction of generics, the very structure of the South African market discouraged generic drug manufacturers from entering the market. Brand manufac- turers thus provided the bulk of the drugs consumed in the country, either to the public sector at close to generic prices, or directly to the private market. While this bifurcated structure of the pharmaceutical market reflected the old apartheid system, where the majority of those served by the public sector had little or no political power, the new government's goal of broadening access to health care by integrating the public and private health care systems changed this equation. This is particularly the case in relation to the supply of medicines: the goal of improving standards through the creation of a greater public–private partnership tied to ideas of equalization and cross-subsidization through some form of social or national health insurance program based on the goal of sharing costs – possibly including a more extensive system of co- payments – makes the cost of medicines in the marketplace a central concern to the new system.

In response to this situation, the new government published a National Drug Policy in January 1996. As a way of attacking the comparatively high cost of drugs in the South African market, the new policy promoted the use of generic drugs and suggested several ways to reduce unacceptably high retail prices, including allowing the state to facilitate the availability of affordable drugs in the private sector. It was this policy imperative that led to the passage of the Medicines and Related Substances Control Amendment Act in December 1997 (Act 90 of 1997), with the aim of bringing down the cost of medicines. Although the new Act was designed to fundamen- tally change the distribution practices of the pharmaceutical manufac- turers – prohibiting, for example, industry employees from serving on the Medicines Control Board, and blocking manufacturers and whole- salers from providing bonuses, rebates, or other incentives to doctors – the key feature of the Act was the "measures to ensure supply of more affordable medicines." These measures included empowering the Minister of Health "to prescribe conditions for the supply of more affordable medicines ... so as to protect the health of the public ... notwithstanding anything to the contrary in the Patents Act," and to "prescribe the conditions on which any medicine which is identical in composition, meets the same quality standard and is intended to have the same proprietary name as that of another medicine already registered in the Republic," may be provided. The effect of these provisions would have been to allow the parallel importation of medicines, generic substitution without the consent of the prescriber, and even compulsory licensing.

While the amendments to the Medicines Act were initially viewed as a simple adoption of World Health Organization (WHO) recommended measures to improve access to essential medicines, the changing health conditions as well as the growing international conflict over the implementation of TRIPS and the expanded protection of patent rights suddenly placed these reforms under the international spotlight. At the same time, the new government's changing economic policies, from a domestic focus on reconstruction to a focus on global reengagement, including a full embrace of the World Trade Organization (WTO) and TRIPS, heightened the sensitivity of the government to external pressure, particularly when these pressures seemed to directly threaten the policy of attracting foreign capital and increasing industrial capacity domestically as a means of supplying the regional or even the continental market. These changing circumstances were further intensified by the recognition in 1996 that antiretroviral therapies had the potential to dramatically transform the profile of the HIV/AIDS pandemic from a death sentence to a chronic but manageable illness. The simultaneous advent of these developments, including changes in economic policy and law as well as the exploding HIV/AIDS epidemic, set the stage for a protracted confrontation with ramifications in both the domestic and the international arenas.

5.4 GLOBAL COMMITMENTS AND DOMESTIC RESPONSES

During the final stages of South Africa's negotiated transition to democracy, the African National Congress agreed to join the government's delegation participating in the Marrakesh Conference which concluded the Uruguay Round of multilateral trade negotiations.

South Africa, long excluded from international multilateral meetings, signed the treaty (WTO 1994) creating the WTO, and accepted the TRIPS agreement, on April 15, 1994. Thus, while April 1994 marks the moment of South African national self-determination, it also marked its reentry as an active participant in the international economic arena through its participation as a founding member of the WTO. As an official in the Department of Trade and Industry later remarked, "South Africa was a founding member of the GATT and would of course embrace all the obligations included in the new international trading system" (author's interview, Pretoria, 1999). Endorsing this self-image as a bastion of free trade, despite the very recent history of international sanctions against apartheid, the South African government, merely days before the country's first democratic elections, eschewed the special transitional provisions for developing countries and accepted the immediate implementation of the agreement. The advocates of free trade believed that this early adoption would enhance South Africa's comparative advantage at the moment it was reentering the global economy and hoped for a wave of post-apartheid foreign investment. However, it was precisely this enthusiasm, reflecting the general confidence of a successful political transition, which led the country to immediately embrace all the commitments of the WTO agreement, including those contained in TRIPS, and which soon embroiled the new government in its first major international controversy.

South Africa's attempt to improve access to essential medicines by creating a more competitive market by considering parallel importation and even compulsory licensing soon attracted the attention of the international pharmaceutical industry and the US government in particular (see Bond 1999). In fact, the US government was active in the debate from very early on, with the United States Trade Representative (USTR) writing a letter to South Africa's United Nations representative in April 1997 querying South Africa's implementation of TRIPS and raising questions about compulsory licensing. By the time the amendment Bill was before parliament, US opposition was already evident; the US embassy in Pretoria presented the US government's views at a parliamentary hearing on the proposed amendments, while the US ambassador to South Africa made frequent public and private statements against the legalization of parallel imports.

Within two months of the amendment Act's adoption, the Pharmaceutical Research and Manufacturers of America (PhRMA) requested the USTR to designate South Africa a priority country under section 301 of the United States Trade Act of 1974 because "South Africa has become a 'test case' for those who oppose the US government's long-standing commitment to improve the terms of protection for all forms of American intellectual property, including pharmaceutical patents" (Consumer Project on Technology, 1999). Bristol-Myers Squibb (BMS) specifically complained about South Africa's decision to permit registration of a generic form of the cancer drug Paclitaxel (BMS brand name Taxol), an issue which the USTR took up during a WTO Trade Policy Review of South Africa a year later in Geneva. One month later, on May 1, 1998, the USTR put South Africa on the Special 301 Watch List. In June 1998, the Clinton administration announced that four items for which South Africa had requested preferential tariff treatment under the Generalized System of Preferences program would be put on hold until adequate progress was achieved in the protection of intellectual property rights in South Africa. At the end of October 1998, the United States Congress passed an omnibus appropriations Bill containing provisions cutting off US aid to the South African government pending a Department of State report outlining its efforts to "negotiate the repeal, suspension, or termination of section 15(c) of South Africa's Medicines and Related Substances Control Amendment Act No. 90 of 1997."

The local response to the Medicines Act was led by the Pharmaceutical Manufacturers' Association of South Africa, which filed suit on behalf of forty-two parties, including local companies, subsidiaries of transnational corporations, and the multinational corporations themselves, challenging the constitutionality of the 1997 amendment to the Medicines Act. They made a number of constitutional claims but argued most specifically that the Act's provisions, which empower the government to determine the extent to which rights granted under a patent in South Africa shall apply, and which allow the Minister of Health to prescribe conditions for the supply of more affordable generic medicines, together deprived owners of intellectual property in the affected pharmaceutical products and thus of their constitutionally protected property rights.

Significantly, the domestic litigation initiated in this case, facilitated by the financial resources of the multinational corporations, took on a form unique in the South African context. The plaintiffs engaged a major private law firm, and state attorneys soon found themselves completely snowed under with the volume of filings and alternative

127

lines of attack (author's interview, 1999). Not only did the plaintiffs initiate the litigation with a request for an interim interdict preventing the law from being implemented, they soon followed with a series of claims in alternative fora – to the Public Protector and the Competition Board – respectively challenging government statements about the high cost of drugs and calling for an inquiry into an alleged anti-competitive attempt by pharmaceutical distributors to create a joint company to engage in the parallel importation allowed under the Act.

In a notice of motion filed in the High Court of South Africa (Transvaal Provincial Division) in Pretoria on February 18, 1998, the plaintiffs articulated an extraordinary array of claims against the Act's validity. In addition to asserting that the Act violated their patent rights as well as South Africa's legally incorporated international obligations under TRIPS, the plaintiffs claimed that the powers granted the Minister of Health amounted to an unconstitutional delegation of legislative authority to the executive because it failed to set out policy considerations or guidelines that would limit the Minister's power. The plaintiffs also charged that various provisions of the amendment Act were unconstitutional as they violated the basic values and principles governing public administration included in section 195 of the Constitution. As if this was not enough, the plaintiffs then argued in the alternative that the Act conflicted with the legislature's constitutional obligations to take into consideration the recommendations made to the Portfolio Committee on Health and the Select Committee on Social Services in the National Council of Provinces – South Africa's second chamber – requesting in the process that the legislature transmit to the Constitutional Court a transcript of all the proceedings on the Bill which preceded the passage of the Act. In her founding affidavit, M. T. Deeb, Chief Executive Officer of the Pharmaceutical Manufacturers Association, argued that section 15C was in conflict with the TRIPS agreement and went so far as to claim that "Parliament ought not to have made a law which is in conflict with South Africa's international obligations" (Deeb 1998a:para. 10.2.5).

This linking of the domestic constitutional claim with international trade issues continued when in a supplementary affidavit to the plaintiff's amended particulars of claim filed on July 23, 1998, Deeb argued that the USTR's placing of South Africa on the Special 301 Watch List "demonstrates that the provisions in the Amended Act which affect intellectual property are seen to be at least potentially in conflict with

South Africa's international obligations and hence I submit that it cannot be regarded as being in the public interest as it may lead to the imposition of sanctions against this country and in fact may already have led to an undermining of investor confidence in South Africa" (Deeb 1998b:para. 20.6).

5.5 BALANCING INTERNATIONAL COMMITMENTS AND FORA

This threat of wider economic repercussions highlights the conflict between the domestic initiative to reduce drug prices and the global environment in which the policy was reflected. It is also important to recognize that even at the international level there are often tensions between the approaches taken by different government departments in their pursuit of different policies. While the 1997 amendment put South Africa into a direct bilateral trade conflict with the United States, these tensions were not confined to the trade arena but also surfaced at the World Health Assembly (WHA, the governing body of the WHO) where South Africa was active in trying to reshape the debate over patent protection for pharmaceuticals. At the same time, South Africa's leadership in the WHA was in stark contrast to the government's unilateral decision not to implement the law – pending further legal proceedings – and the growing policy conflict over the government's response to HIV/AIDS, which included questioning the very biomedical basis of the epidemic. Here the law may be seen to be simultaneously facilitating, delaying, and providing a space for different players to achieve a variety of goals in their struggles: to gain access to affordable medicines; to further particular economic policies; or to protect their property interests.

At the end of April 1999, the USTR scheduled an "out-of-cycle" review for South Africa under Special 301, arguing that South Africa's barriers to trade included: parallel imports; compulsory licensing; registration of generic forms of Taxol; and taking a leading role at the World Health Assembly. According to the USTR: "During the past year, South African representatives have led a faction of nations in the World Health Organization (WHO) in calling for a reduction in the level of protection provided for pharmaceuticals in TRIPS" (Consumer Project on Technology, 1999). Thus, from the perspective of the USTR, the problem was not only the protection of patent rights in South Africa but also the position South Africa was taking in the international debate over TRIPS. Although it is broadly understood that the TRIPS agreement introduced a new set of minimum standards for the protection of intellectual property rights, there remained wide disagreement as to the meaning of the embedded exceptions to those rights. More significantly, the broad language of the exceptions contained in TRIPS meant that the degree of legal uncertainty remained broad, allowing member states to assert very different interpretations.

In this context, the WHO began questioning the relationship between the new international trade regime and its own mandate to promote world health. In January 1998, just over a month after the adoption of the new South African law allowing parallel importation, the Executive Board of the WHA recommended the adoption of the "Revised Drug Strategy," calling upon member states to "ensure that public health interests are paramount in pharmaceutical and health policies," as well as "to explore and review their options under relevant international trade agreements, to safeguard access to essential drugs." In May 1998, when the WHA began discussing the recommendation at its meeting in Geneva, the proposal came under heated attack from the developed countries including the US, the EU, and Japan. Supporting the proposals and leading the negotiations for the African countries was Dr. Olive Shisana from the South African Ministry of Health.

Although action on the resolution was initially deferred, a bitter conflict erupted over the strategy. An Ad Hoc Working Group of fifty-nine countries met in October 1998 with South Africa and the United States representing the polar opposite positions. South Africa advocated for a strong public health statement while the United States represented the pharmaceutical industry's point of view (Consumer Project on Technology 1999). In January 1999, the WHA Executive Board met and approved the Revised Drug Strategy in the course of which South African health official, Dr. Desmond Johns, made comments which emphasized the strategy's openness to the parallel importation and compulsory licensing of pharmaceuticals. This interpretation was in conflict with the understanding of US officials and PhRMA who had a diametrically opposite interpretation of these developments (Consumer Project on Technology 1999).

Shaping the interpretation and understanding of the scope of internationally recognized intellectual property rights as well as the exceptions to them, takes place simultaneously in different settings. These include various international fora, in bilateral trade negotiations and conflicts, as well as in domestic legal arenas. This plethora of opportunities to pursue particular goals presents a clear advantage to those nations, industries, and organizations with the resources to participate at every level; however it also provides a differentiated arena in which coalitions of developing countries, NGOs, and other actors may productively intervene. The emergence and sustainability of these coalitions is, however, not preordained. In the struggle over access to affordable medicines it was the devastating impact of the HIV/AIDS pandemic in sub-Saharan Africa that provided the impetus for solidarity among a range of activist and policy-oriented organizations including: Act-Up and the Consumer Project on Technology in the United States; MSF, Oxfam and the South Centre in Europe; and the Treatment Action Campaign in South Africa. These interventions eventually led to a coordinated challenge from African member states in the TRIPS Council which later included other developing or newly industrializing countries at the WTO.

5.6 SOCIAL MOBILIZATION AND A CHANGING TRADE REGIME

The debate over intellectual property and trade underwent a dramatic shift from the beginning of 1999. In response to popular pressure from AIDS activists the Congressional Black Caucus began to link international HIV/AIDS policy and the question of trade disputes involving compulsory licensing, parallel imports, and other intellectual property issues. In February 1999, Representative Jesse Jackson Jr. introduced House Resolution 772, the "Hope for Africa Bill." Section 601 of the Bill proposed cutting off funding to any department or agency of the US government that sought "through negotiation or otherwise, the revocation or revisions of any sub-Saharan African intellectual property or competition law or policy that is designed to promote access to pharmaceuticals or other medical technologies," as long as those laws complied with TRIPS.

Two months later, in April 1999, several hundred protestors in downtown Washington DC demonstrated support for the Hope for Africa legislation and for compulsory licensing for HIV/AIDS and other essential medicines. Act-Up, a prominent US organization with a long history of activism on the issues of HIV/AIDS, called upon the US Department of Health and Human Services to give the WHO and foreign governments the right to use US government use rights in patents obtained as a result of federally funded research. Within two months, HIV/AIDS activists began a campaign to disrupt Vice President Gore's presidential election campaign to draw attention to US trade sanctions against South Africa and Thailand. These protests had an immediate effect. When Representative John Mica held hearings in Congress on US trade policy and the global AIDS crisis, Joseph Papovich from the USTR testified that the USTR no longer objected to parallel importing or compulsory licensing of pharmaceutical drugs in South Africa, if TRIPS compliant.

Finally, despite three years of needless delay by the government's lawyers, the South African case brought by the pharmaceutical companies against the government came to court in Pretoria and was withdrawn after the court accepted the intervention of the Treatment Action Campaign. The TAC had been demanding that the government provide access to medicines for both the treatment of HIV/AIDS-related opportunistic infections and to retrovirals for pregnant women and their newborn babies, but now sided with the government by arguing that the pharmaceutical industry was blocking attempts to reduce the prices of medicines needed to save the lives of those infected with HIV. Although the government remained resistant, even after the withdrawal of the case, to providing the drugs through the public health system (insisting that the case was not about HIV/AIDS drugs), it remains true that it was the public relations impact of the claim that the pharmaceutical companies were attempting to deny access to these drugs to the millions of HIV-positive South Africans that forced the hand of the companies. Not only did the companies concede that the law did not violate either the South African Constitution or TRIPS, they also agreed to pay the government's legal costs. The government, on the other hand, responded by arguing that they understood the new law as allowing for the parallel importation of patented drugs, but not necessarily the compulsory licensing of patented drugs, thus relieving the industry of one of its major concerns.

On September 17, 1999, the USTR announced that South Africa had agreed to implement the Medicines Act in a manner consistent with its obligations under the rules of the WTO "enabling us to set aside this issue from our bilateral trade agenda." Just over a week before, PhRMA had announced the suspension of the lawsuit brought against implementation of the Medicines Act in South Africa. Furthermore, officials at the office of the USTR said that they were now considering removing South Africa from the Special 301 Watch List. From the South African side there was a commitment to revisit the Act, although it was predicted that it would be some time before the government implemented the law.

The impact of these developments were not limited to South Africa. After Congress failed to enact section 601 in the Hope for Africa Bill, President Clinton issued an executive order on May 10, 2000, stating that in "administering sections 301–310 of the Trade Act of 1974, the United States shall not seek, through negotiation or otherwise, the revocation or revision of any intellectual property law or policy of a beneficiary sub-Saharan African country, as determined by the President, that regulates HIV/AIDS pharmaceuticals or medical technologies if the law or policy of the country: (1) promotes access to HIV/AIDS pharmaceuticals or medical technologies for affected populations in that country; and (2) provides adequate and effective intellectual property protection consistent with the … TRIPS Agreement." While it would seem that a partial resolution to the direct conflict between the South African and the US governments had been found, the international legal regime established under TRIPS remained uncertain.

5.6.1 The Doha Declaration on TRIPS and public health

In dire need of success the WTO was able to declare the launching of a new round of trade negotiations at the end of its ministerial conference on November 14, 2001. An essential ingredient was the issuing of a separate declaration on TRIPS and public health. Despite concerted opposition from multinational pharmaceutical corporations and a group of developed countries led by the United States, Switzerland, and Japan, the 140 trade ministers gathered in Doha, Qatar, agreed that the TRIPS agreement "does not and should not prevent members from taking measures to protect public health … [and] that the agreement can and should be interpreted and implemented in a manner supportive of WTO members' rights to protect public health and, in particular, to promote access to medicines for all." At first glance, the developing world gained a major success. Not only is this interpretation extended to all aspects of public health, not just pharmaceuticals, but it also emphasizes the need to interpret the WTO agreements in more holistic ways. In essence, it accepts that an interpretation reducing barriers to free trade is not automatically the sole or correct understanding of the agreements.

Despite their opposition to a broad public health exception, their own threats to override Bayer's Cipro patent – in response to the mailed anthrax attacks after September 11, 2001 – completely undercut the claims of the United States and Canada that stronger patent protection was the most effective means of securing access to required medicines. With their prior arguments severely compromised and with no other effective means of addressing the ongoing HIV/AIDS pandemic, accepting the demands of developing countries became the easiest way to save the talks. Addressing what had been an intense debate within the TRIPS Council, the declaration specifically clarified the right of members: to grant compulsory licenses; to determine what constitutes a national emergency or other circumstances of extreme urgency; and that each member is free to establish its own regime for the exhaustion of intellectual property rights. It also encourages developed countries to promote technology transfer to the least developed countries and extends the initial transition period for pharmaceutical products in these countries until January 1, 2016. This understanding of the TRIPS agreement and its future implementation amounts to a major shift in the rhetoric about the protection of intellectual property rights, embracing as it does most of the positions of the developing world – with much of the language for the declaration coming directly from the proposal put forward by Zimbabwe on behalf of the Africa Group and other developing countries.

5.6.2 Paragraph 6 of the Doha Declaration and the problem of capacity

The Doha Declaration, with its broad interpretation of the TRIPS agreement and its future implementation, amounted to a major shift in the global intellectual property regime, yet, given the realities of pharmaceutical production and distribution, it did not go very far toward ensuring access to urgently needed HIV/AIDS-related medications. Despite acknowledging that many countries have "insufficient or no manufacturing capacities in the pharmaceutical sector" and therefore cannot make effective use of compulsory licensing, the declaration failed to accept the developing countries' interpretation that they have the right to grant a compulsory license to a producer in another country having manufacturing capacity in order to gain access to medicines. Instead, the Declaration instructed the TRIPS Council to find a solution to this issue and to report to the WTO General Council by the end of 2002. Without the capacity to produce under compulsory license or import generic equivalents of the necessary medications, the problem of access for the millions infected or suffering from life-threatening diseases in developing countries remained unresolved. It took the TRIPS Council a further twenty-one months, to late August 2003, to reach agreement on the problem of access to medicines for countries that do not have manufacturing capacity.

Heralded at first as the solution to the problem of lack of capacity, the pre-Cancún agreement has since been criticized for placing so many preconditions on its implementation as to make it unworkable. These limitations include the requirement of proof by a country that it does not have: (1) production capacity; (2) access to affordable medicines; and (3) an existing health emergency. Although the Canadian government is discussing changing Canadian law to make the export of medicines made under compulsory license possible, the international brand-name pharmaceutical industry has begun to raise questions about whether Canada is precluded from supplying these medicines under the NAFTA agreement. Furthermore, even the Canadian government seems to be limiting its proposals to drugs designed to address only HIV/AIDS, malaria, and tuberculosis, a restriction rejected by the developing countries and the pre-Cancún agreement.

Once again it seems that the question of access to essential medicines is being displaced by an assertion of prior legal commitments – the idea of *pacta sunt servanda*, in which concerns over the rights of patent holders and an interpretation of the TRIPS agreement as a contractual arrangement place notions of unrestricted trade before the health needs of millions of people around the world. While all participants in the debate deny any intention to restrict access, or even such an effect (IIPI 2000), it seems hard to deny that the failure to resolve this issue, since it was first raised by the international pharmaceutical industry in its 1997 case against the South African law which was implementing an essential drugs program, has in fact frustrated attempts to broaden access. Even if it is accepted that the TRIPS agreement initially failed to accommodate the complexities of a global health emergency such as HIV/AIDS, it is hardly unreasonable to suggest that the principle of changed circumstances, or *rebus sic stantibus*, brought about by both new understandings of the magnitude of the pandemic as well as the emergence of effective medicines to address it, should have been applied to interpretations of TRIPS in order to facilitate all attempts to address this exploding crisis. At the least, such an approach would justify the assertion of an Article 30 exception under the TRIPS agreement. Instead, there has been a constant emphasis upon the rather unique protection of private rights contained in TRIPS and a denial of the legal effect of the so-called soft law exceptions and principles of interpretation which are also part of international trade law, including TRIPS.

5.6.3 The Treatment Action Campaign and the struggle for antiretroviral treatments

The domestic struggle over access to affordable medicines in South Africa did not end with the government's victory in the case brought by the Pharmaceutical Manufacturers Association or the Doha Declaration. The next phase of legal activity, initiated by the Treatment Action Campaign (TAC) and given its impetus by the consolidation of a new broad-based social movement including TAC branches and the People Living with AIDS organization as well as support from the trade union movement and the communist party, included two legal challenges. The first challenged the government to provide mothers and their new-born babies access to Nevirapine, an antiretroviral which, when administered to both mother and child during birth and shortly thereafter, more than halved the rate of mother-to-child transmission of HIV. Secondly, the TAC brought a complaint before the Competition Board alleging that a number of the major pharmaceutical corporations had colluded in maintaining the high price of particular medicines. The impact of these two initiatives was to dramatically alter the debate over access to antiretroviral treatment and to set the stage for a major reduction in the price of medicines.

In the mother-to-child transmission (MTCT) case, the Constitutional Court essentially upheld a High Court decision requiring the government to provide mothers and new-born babies in public health facilities access to Nevirapine. Relying on the constitutional guarantee of a right to the progressive realization of access to health care services, the Constitutional Court argued that, under the circumstances, in which the cost of the drug and the provision of appropriate testing and counseling to mothers was less burdensome than the failure to provide Nevirapine, the government had a constitutional duty to expand its program beyond the eighteen test sites the health authorities had already planned.

In the second case, the TAC, pursuing its aim to lower drug prices and thus expand access to antiretroviral treatment, launched a complaint with the newly created Competition Commission against two of the major pharmaceutical corporations active in South Africa – GlaxoSmithKline (GSK) and Boehringer Ingelheim – accusing them of engaging in excessive pricing of medicines. After the Commission found that the companies had colluded to fix prices, the companies reached an out-of-court settlement with the government which included granting at least three generic pharmaceutical companies voluntary licenses on three major antiretrovirals, thus allowing more competition into the market and lowering the price of the drugs in the South African market. Despite these dramatic interventions and legal victories, the problem of access remains unsolved. For the majority of HIV-infected South Africans, even the reduced price of the drugs on the private market is unaffordable and until the government manages to roll out the public sector program they will continue to be denied access.

5.7 CONCLUSION

After twenty years, the HIV/AIDS pandemic has finally been recognized as a global health crisis, yet the debates over access to public goods which are essential to defeating this scourge continue to be shaped less by principles of public health than by concerns over unrestricted trade and intellectual property rights. Within the legal field, the claims of the international patent-based pharmaceutical corporations are framed as rights to property, while the claims of NGOs and developing country governments seeking access to affordable medicines are characterized as legal exceptions to free trade or as the soft law contained in general preambular statements. These formal legal distinctions, based upon the interpretation of international agreements created in a context of asymmetrical power, are now relied upon to delay and avoid recognizing the urgent needs of those whose very lives and futures are at stake. But the emergence of a new social movement, both domestically and transnationally, based on a new solidarity which places public needs over corporate claims of property rights has begun to shift the balance of power (Santos 2002).

Driven by this new solidarity – which brings together a unique yet loose alliance of health, human rights, and development activists together with some governments and parts of the pharmaceutical industry, particularly generic producers – the international intellectual property and trade regime has begun to change. First, there is a new acceptance of a human rights perspective, in which the health impact of any particular legal option or interpretation is an equally legitimate consideration in evaluating the validity of any particular intellectual property or trade rule. Secondly, there is recognition that both health and human rights considerations are an essential corrective to the present distinction between so-called hard law obligations and soft law principles or commitments. Thirdly, the acceptance of these approaches to the interpretation of the TRIPS agreement may facilitate access to medicines by emboldening private investors to accept compulsory licenses or other exemptions as sufficient to secure their needed investments in generic production. Finally, such an approach should also provide developing countries with a means to justify decisions to privilege policies securing access to medicines over concerns about their international trade commitments or threats from patent holders. Instead of relying on thin strands of legal flexibility, NGOs, international organizations, and governments attempting to address the global HIV/AIDS pandemic might look to the building of this new, multifaceted, and complex solidarity to assert a human rights-based interpretation of the international trade and intellectual property regime – one which places public health ahead of property claims.

References

African National Congress. 1994a. "A National Health Plan for South Africa." Prepared by the ANC with the technical support of WHO and UNICEF, May.

1994b. "RDP White Paper Discussion Document." September.

Bond, Patrick. 1999. "Globalization, Pharmaceutical Pricing and South African Health Policy: Managing Confrontation with US Firms and Politicians." *International Journal of Health Services* 29(4):765.

Consumer Project on Technology. 1999. Cptech, Appendix B: Time-Line of Disputes over Compulsory Licensing and Parallel Importation in South Africa, http://www.cptech.org/ip/health/sa/sa-timeline.txt, August 5, 1999.

Deeb, M. T. 1998a. Founding Affidavit, February, 18 High Court of South Africa.

1998b. Supplementary Affidavit by M. T. Deeb, July 23, High Court of South Africa.

Department of Health, "National Drug Policy for South Africa." January.

International Intellectual Property Institute. 2000. *Patent Protection and Access to HIV/AIDS Pharmaceuticals in Sub-Saharan Africa.* Washington, DC: International Intellectual Property Institute.

Klug, Heinz. 2000. *Constituting Democracy: Law, Globalism and South Africa's Political Reconstruction.* Cambridge: Cambridge University Press.

Minister of Health v. *Treatment Action Campaign* 2002 (5) SA 721 (CC).

Moy, Carl R. 1993. "The History of the Patent Harmonization Treaty: Economic Self-Interest as an Influence." *John Marshall Law Review* 26:457

Ryan, Michael. 1998. "Knowledge Diplomacy: Global Competition and the Politics of Intellectual Property." Washington, DC: Brookings Institution.

Santos, Boaventura de Sousa. 2002. *Toward a New Legal Common Sense: Law, Globalization and Emancipation.* London: .Butterworths.

Sell, Susan K. 2003. *Private Power, Public Law: The Globalization of Intellectual Property Rights.* Cambridge: Cambridge University Press.

Soobramoney v. *Minister of Health, KwaZulu-Natal* 1997 (12) BCLR 1696 (CC).

WTO. 1994. Final Act Embodying the Results of the Uruguay Round of Multilateral Trade Negotiations.

CHAPTER 6

NEGOTIATING INFORMALITY WITHIN FORMALITY: LAND AND HOUSING IN THE TEXAS COLONIAS

Jane E. Larson

6.1 INTRODUCTION

Among the manifest expressions of the amorphous phenomenon called "globalization" is the intensification and spread of informality in many social and economic practices. Long recognized and studied in the developing world, informality is increasingly visible inside the United States. Most studies of informality inside the United States have focused on labor, production, and distribution, examining sweatshops, home piecework manufacture, or street vendors. Informal housing is hardly recognized as existing in this country, and certainly is not included in state policy as a legitimate means of housing production. Whether the subject is informal labor or informal housing, nowhere in the United States has the formal legal system crafted a coherent, much less productive, policy toward the departures from regulation that define informal economic activity.

Yet, within the Texas stretch of the United States–Mexico border-lands, more than half a million people now live in settlements of informal housing known regionally as "colonias." Although there are colonia-type settlements in other border states of the United States, the vast majority of such settlements inside the country are found in Texas (LBJ School 1997:1).[1]

---

[1] More than half of the long international boundary that links the United States with Mexico crosses the State of Texas, and this is the most populated and economically vital stretch, with large cross-border urban areas at Brownsville/Matamoros, McAllen/Reynosa, Laredo/Nuevo Laredo, and El Paso/Ciudad Juárez .

In this region, the word "colonia" refers to a semi-rural subdivision of substandard housing that lacks some or all basic physical infrastructure and public services, in particular, clean water, sanitary sewage, or adequate roads. (This is a regional usage of the word "colonia." In Spanish, the word means simply "neighborhood.") This chapter focuses on informal housing settlements in Texas. There are also thousands of such settlements along the Mexican side of the border (Dwyer 1994). Nearly all people on both sides of the border are congregated in "twin cities," urban areas that are physically contiguous to one another on opposite sides of the boundary line, and colonias ring these booming border cities on both sides of the line. An integrated demographic or sociological perspective would examine housing settlements in both Mexico and the United States, but because this chapter focuses on legality and its relationship to informality, the boundaries here are those of the nation and state, which bounds law's reach.

This chapter describes colonias as "informal housing." Informal economic activity takes place outside the domain of governmental regulation, in particular labor, health and safety, land use, and environmental laws. Worldwide, a common form of informal housing begins with squatting or land seizure, an illegal form of housing production. But colonias in the United States are better described as *extra-legal*. When residents and developers created existing colonias, subdivision and sale of rural land for residential construction without provision of basic infrastructure or access to public services was lawful, and no building codes set housing standards. Yet, where the state fails to regulate activities that in other settings are regulated according to accepted patterns, a kind of informality develops that is built on legal and material nonconformity rather than illegality (Castells and Portes 1989:12).

Colonias surfaced alongside the emergence of a globalized economy in the United States border region. It is here, beginning in the 1980s, that the country saw one model of what might be ahead in the new economic paradigm. Policies of trade liberalization and the border's strategic location created an economy of low-wage work that attracted new migrants and shifted long-time residents away from the traditional pursuit of agricultural labor to work in manufacture and assembly, transport, warehousing, and construction. In these same years, government cuts in social welfare spending (as much a part of the globalization agenda as free trade) took hold and ended or restricted programs for income support and affordable housing at all levels of government. The poor working families that made up the labor force for the border's economic development were left to negotiate a world of privatized social provision with the limited economic resources provided by low wages and uncertain job security.

The explosive growth of colonias in Texas during these same years is evidence these workers turned to informal housing as an economic survival strategy (Larson 2002:142). This dynamic also explains the broader sphere of informal economic activity growing inside the United States, as Sassen, among others, contends the informal economy and the global economy are intrinsically linked (1998:79). Households cannot make it on below-poverty wages and must find ways to supplement income, often by working off-the-books. Families cannot afford goods and services produced and sold in the formal economy, and so support a parallel economy of street vendors and flea markets. Housing, typically the greatest expense families face, triggers the same resort to informality. Within the United States, the poor are already mostly shut out of formal markets in housing finance or construction, and thus from home ownership. And, for low-wage workers, even rental markets have become unaffordable. Where cheap land is on the market, where unpaid family labor is available, and where laws are loose enough, self-help housing is one solution.

In this sense, informal housing is what Santos calls a process of "localized globalism," or "the specific impact of transnational practices and imperatives on local conditions that are thereby destructured and restructured in order to respond to transnational imperatives" (1997:4–5). In the crucible of a globalizing regional/transborder economy, the housing practices of self-built housing and extra-legal settlement long-established in Mexico crossed the line. Such a marked local change in the modes and expectations of housing production is a response to globalized economic and political imperatives.

This chapter situates the growth of informal housing in the United States within this broader context, and asks how the formal regulatory system will and should respond to the informality in our midst. In the arena of housing, this chapter argues that existing models of land development and housing quality regulation establish unattainable standards that hinder the poor in their effort to provide for basic shelter. The other side of the regulatory coin (deregulation) might tolerate but does not legitimate the informal sector, and abandons any aspiration to improve conditions for this sector over time. In light of the widening disparities of wealth and shrinking social welfare commitment that drive informality, as well as the appearance of these new social practices not contemplated when the existing regulatory alternatives were adopted, formal law appears to have no viable tools with which to respond. Without rethinking conventional regulatory strategies and expanding the legal tools available, there is little doubt the United States will make unproductive, indeed unjust, policy even as informality grows in our midst.

As an alternative, I argue in this chapter that regulatory policies should support and neither punish nor prohibit those who shelter themselves informally. This policy is called "regularization." Regularization is not across-the-board deregulation, nor is it negotiated or discretionary enforcement of rules. Regularization is an alternative regulatory strategy created in the developing world and designed for conditions of extreme economic constraint. Regularization loosens some regulatory standards, thus "legalizing" some previously illegal housing conditions, and gradually imposes other retooled standards, accompanied by assistance in reaching those standards, all in a program aimed at encouraging self-help housing.

Consider the example of Mexico. Mexico has built its current housing and social policy around informal housing production, abandoning an earlier policy that treated these settlements as illegal social problems to be erased. Mexico now not only tolerates informal housing, but seeks to encourage its production. Governments at all levels recognize informal settlements as a response to housing shortages and a useful form of economic investment. Through a variety of policies and programs, Mexico helps such settlements regularize, and thereby seeks to integrate them into the society, economy, and polity (Staudt 1998; Ward 1991). Many other countries of the developing world have adopted similar policies (Farvacque and McAuslan 1992; Payne 1997).

Although these countries have moved from prohibition to integration of informality, there is no level of government in the United States that follows such a policy. To move in that direction would require more than just innovative reforms in law; it demands a rethinking of some basic presumptions about law and legality prevalent in the United States. Conventional regulation establishes universal standards and obliges full and immediate compliance. Universality and enforcement are the twin pillars of what "the rule of law" has traditionally meant in this legal system. Regularization, by contrast, sets standards relative to the resources available to the regulated, and allows gradual and flexible standards of compliance, with the goal of progressive improvement rather than immediate and unqualified compliance. Could such "pro-gressive" or "flexible" modes of regulation be translated into the United States?

Looking for a legal technology appropriate for regulating the infor-mal economy under conditions of extreme economic constraint, I borrow a model of "progressive realization" from international human rights law.[2] As applied to housing, progressive realization would com-mit both government and families (the regulated) to standards of adequate shelter, but would demand in compliance no more than that the regulated commit the maximum available resources to attain-ment of those standards. Under this model, each must comply, but only to the extent of his or her resources. Compliance is thus always possible under the "maximum available resources" rule, and continuing progress toward the standard is always demanded by the requirement of "pro-gressive realization."

The chapter proposes to build a domestic program for regulating housing quality and land development around the progressive realiza-tion of standards. Such a program would better balance the regulatory burden on diverse populations, the public interest in adequate housing, and would importantly retain an aspirational commitment to elevating living standards in pursuit of social equality. Linked to a comprehensive program of regularization, progressive realization places law behind, rather than against, the activities of informals.

Progressive realization is a new idea within the United States legal tradition. Indeed, the United States has not adopted the international agreement that created the concept (the International Covenant on Economic, Social and Cultural Rights), arguing that an obligation that creates anything short of absolute and immediate compliance is not really "law" (Alston and Quinn 1987:158). Yet, in informality, we find ourselves facing a new reality that, given its structural link to globalization, can only be expected to become more the norm for certain sectors of the population. Retooling a standard from inter-national law for domestic application fits with the globalized character of this new reality. To the extent that informality is linked more broadly to globalization, any effort to find regulatory tools appropriate to its character should sensibly draw on international experiences, practices, and ideas.

[2] I thank my colleagues Heinz Klug and Berta Hernandez-Truyol for helping me bring the idea of "progressive realization" home to domestic regulation.

6.2 INFORMAL HOUSING IN THE UNITED STATES

Although observed since the 1950s, colonias began to grow exponentially in the 1980s. This explosive growth is linked to the border's emergence as a place of economic development, liberalization and intensification of trade, and strategic geographical location in the global economy. The border region as a whole grew dramatically; the Texas border cities have been among the fastest growing areas in the United States for a decade. Yet, despite this growth and economic development, the southern border remains among the poorest regions of the country. Colonias are a response to this growth without prosperity.

Living conditions vary greatly in the Texas colonias, depending on differences in age, size, location, service provision, security of land tenure and title, housing consolidation, settlement density, and community solidarity. But there are common features, in particular the ways in which these settlements depart from the norms established by formally regulated land and housing development, and by formal markets for housing finance and production. Notably, the ways in which the colonias are nonconforming inside the United States are also the ways in which these settlements share the characteristics of informal housing settlements throughout the world. Thus, colonias are not an ad hoc peculiarity of our borderlands, but rather a patterned alternative to what the United States knows as the "normal" practices of housing development.

Typically, colonias, like other informal housing settlements, grow up on cheap land located at the distant periphery of a fast-growing urban center. Residents may bypass law altogether and squat on the land, or may purchase lots from developers in illegal or nonconforming subdivisions. In either case, settlers and developers follow a conscious strategy of avoiding regulation. Nonconformity with law is a means of gaining access to land not otherwise available for development, and access to housing not otherwise affordable for the settler population.

Once they have land, settlers move quickly to construct temporary shelter. Without secure legal title, the investment of time, labor, money, and materials is risky. Yet, they must risk enough to "signal" to authorities and to other people seeking land a determination to hold onto the land and develop it as housing.

Informal settlements usually lack access to water and sewer hookups at the beginning, leading to improvised and inadequate solutions for storing drinking water and disposing of human waste. Some communities gradually receive public services; others never do; and temporary solutions can become permanent ones. Residents without water or sewer hookups improvise by drilling shallow wells, purchasing water and storing it, or taking water from nearby irrigation ditches. Human waste may be disposed of in a pit, outhouse, or septic system. Lack of adequate water or sewerage undermines housing quality and spreads disease (Larson 1995:189–192).

The incremental process of owner-construction often begins with a provisional shelter in the form of a used trailer or mobile home, or a shack. Such shelter is often unsafe, overcrowded, or otherwise unsuitable for the family. The family slowly constructs the permanent structure nearby or even around the shell of the trailer or shack. Construction is usually piecemeal, with the household providing both labor and capital. The household often builds with nonstandard materials and techniques around a shell of the existing structure (such as a trailer or a shack), allowing the family to live and build at the same time. Self-builders purchase materials as money becomes available; when money is tight, work stops. Construction can take years to complete, and families may live in provisional housing for a decade or more. Once completed, the resulting permanent structure rarely meets conventional building codes, and irregular wiring, plumbing, insulation, etc. cause safety and health problems for inhabitants. The speed of housing consolidation depends, obviously, upon household income. Where land costs are high or increasing, a newly settling household may never "graduate" from a temporary to a permanent shelter, and the community's housing quality deteriorates.

Depending on governmental policy, informal settlements may or may not gradually "regularize," casting off their illegal or nonconforming status and gaining services and infrastructure. Regularization policies typically take two forms: legal regularization clears or grants formal legal title to the land; physical regularization provides infrastructure and access to public services. Physical regularization is usually gradual, with provision and upgrading over time of a basic level of public services such as potable water, sewers, and roads. Some governments also assist housing consolidation, subsidizing credit or offering technical support and materials for builders (Gilbert and Ward 1985).

This approach to housing production upends what residents of the developed world know as the "normal" sequence of land and housing development, which begins with planning, followed by servicing, and ends with housing construction. In informal housing, the homebuilding comes first, and everything else follows.

The Texas colonias developed by this pattern. Until 1995, rural land was mostly unregulated, allowing substandard subdivision and self-building. Developers lawfully bought and carved up agricultural land outside the border cities, offering unimproved half- and quarter-acre lots for sale to those willing to build their own shelter and do without piped water, flush toilets, and paved roads. Developing a colonia in this legal setting meant little more than buying a field, drawing a grid, grading a few dirt roads, and opening a sales office (Larson 1995).

In some transactions, developers fraudulently promised buyers future access to water, sewerage, and other infrastructure. Most buyers, however, were aware of the tradeoff they were making. They did so, my research suggests, with the expectation that the government could be pressed to provide infrastructure at some later date. This expectation was based in part on familiarity with the housing policies and practices of Mexico, in which regularization is both policy and practice,[3] and in part on the opportunities created by Texas' historic hostility to land regulation (Larson 1995). As one activist put it, "The people found a loophole in the law that allowed them to build their own homes, and they walked right through it."[4]

During these years of open development, quarter-to-half-acre colonia lots cost an average of US$100 down and US$50–150 per month for an ultimate purchase price of US$10,000–12,000. Sellers conveyed lots by means of contract for deed, an installment arrangement for the purchase of land similar to a "rent-to-own" arrangement, offering seller financing backed by the threat of forfeiture. Interest rates were high at 12–14 percent. The contract for deed mechanism worked by creating a source of financing for buyers otherwise priced out of formal credit markets. Median household income in the Texas counties with concentrated colonia development is about half of the per-capita income for the rest of the nation (Larson 2002:148–149, 209).

Informality is thus a strategy by which people exploit themselves as a means of creating economic opportunity not otherwise available. Despite the inadequacy of much colonia housing, the increase in accessibility of the housing market due to colonia development is

---

[3] Latina/os make up 82 percent of colonia residents (LBJ School 1997:38). Although 85 percent of colonia residents are citizens and three-quarters were born in the United States, many are first- or second-generation immigrants who retain strong ties to Mexico (Larson 1995:193–195).

[4] Interview with David Arizmendi, Proyecto Azteca, San Juan, Texas, August 4, 2002.

striking. Eighty-five percent of colonia households own their own homes (LBJ School 1997:38), compared to a national home ownership rate of 66.8 percent for households of all income levels, and 45.5 percent for Hispanics (HUD 2000:3). When comparing similarly poor neighborhoods, the effect is even more salient: nationally, only 27 percent of very low income families with children own their own homes (HUD 1995).

Informality creates opportunity, but also limits it. Houses not built to code are not insurable, which means a catastrophic loss is just that for the family involved. The contract for deed arrangement makes ownership legally insecure, as do the irregular business practices of colonia developers. Finance institutions will not make home equity loans in colonias due to the uncertainty over ownership, which prevents self-builders from taking out home improvement loans to hasten construction or upgrading. Without secure tenure, many families put their life savings into houses that cannot easily be sold.

Colonias thus create housing opportunity, but they do so by avoiding regulation and all its protections. Economically marginal buyers can get affordable single-family housing, as well as a means of financing that purchase, but only at high interest rates and without basic consumer protections. Although land use regulation and building codes would enhance living conditions, the families who bought into the existing colonias in Texas could not have afforded that better-quality housing and environment. Thus housing quality remains both unregulated and substandard, opening doors for self-builders but with significant health, welfare, and environmental costs for families, the settlements, and the surrounding communities.

6.3 "YOU HAVE TO TAKE WHAT THE COMMUNITY IS DOING AND MAGNIFY IT, EXTEND IT"

Political struggles over colonia policies have been ongoing in Texas since the late 1980s. Beginning in the mid-1980s, groups of colonia residents, often organized as self-help groups within particular communities, and sometimes working in broader political empowerment groups modeled after the Industrial Areas Foundation model, used many avenues of action and communication to demand redress from developers and assistance from the state in remedying the profound physical deficits of colonia settlements. Women proved especially committed activists in keeping communities organized and pressing issues forward. These groups captured media attention, staged demonstrations demanding water for their children, confronted local political officials at meetings, allied with progressive NGOs in the state, and eventually captured national attention as the media became interested in Texas when then-Governor George W. Bush became a candidate for President.

In 1995, the state finally acted, adopting a broad package of legislation it hoped would "solve" the colonia problem once and for all. From the perspective of the colonias, the results of these laws have been mixed. The state tightened subdivision requirements so as to prevent new colonias and to drastically limit growth in existing settlements. The new standards require fully serviced land before lots in any subdivision can be sold for housing construction. The state also began a remedial program to bring water and sewerage services to many existing settlements.[5] The overall message of the state's policy was that the colonias were a temporary problem caused by greedy developers exploiting vulnerable and ignorant buyers, and not a permanent housing stock for a permanent and growing low-wage labor force essential to the region's free-trade economy. Developers have created few new subdivisions since 1995 under the tougher development rules because the required infrastructure so significantly increases land costs that those who would buy into colonias are priced out of the market.

With land prices higher, those who do buy into the new, fully serviced subdivisions have little left over to invest in housing. Those who cannot afford lots in the new subdivisions either buy existing homes, rent, or live on internally subdivided lots in older colonias. Without the incentive of ownership, the renters do not build permanent dwellings. Those who buy the tiny lots carved out of larger lots are crowded and often lack sufficient space to replace a trailer with a house, or to construct a safe septic system. Local observers believe housing quality has declined in the few colonias developed under the new standards and in the internally subdivided lots in pre-1995 colonias. An unknown number of families are again resorting to living on raw land in unplanned (hence illegal) subdivisions without access to electricity or water.[6]

---

[5] Although slow, the program has built water and sewerage systems in the larger and better-organized settlements, and those closest to the cities.
[6] Interview with David Arizmendi.

The 1995 legislation "grandfathered-in" existing houses in pre-1995 colonias, an attempt to soften the impact of the new regulations by not making homes "illegal" overnight. This humane stance does nothing, however, to address the structural reasons for the existence of colonias in the first place. Enforcing only against "newcomers" will not bridge the gap between wages and housing for the local population. Only by permitting colonias to grow, i.e. giving newcomers the same opportunities existing residents have taken, can colonias ease the housing crisis for the working poor of the region.

Similar tensions between conventional regulation and the reality of the colonias have played out in more recent political struggles over building and housing codes. To date, housing quality remains unregulated in areas of Texas located outside of cities. Rural and semi-rural areas fall within the jurisdiction of counties. As part of the 1995 legislation, there were proposals to give the border counties the power to adopt building codes supported by lawmakers and state officials sincerely determined to publicize and eradicate substandard conditions in the colonias. They saw informal housing as a symptom of inequality and sought to end it as a step towards equal standards of dignity and habitability for all persons.

Outside of the state capital and on the ground, however, grassroots groups opposed adoption of building codes in the counties.[7] Self-help groups all along the border region organized as Iniciativa Frontera, and allied with NGOs in the Border Coalition for Low-Income Housing, to educate legislators and state policymakers on their position. Colonia residents rode buses from the border to the state capitol to confront legislators, expanding their political mobilization from the border to the state's political center. No building code provision made it into the final legislation.

In 1999, legislation was introduced to allow households to hook up to available utilities even if they lived in an illegal or substandard colonia. Blanca Juárez, a leader from the Starr County self-help group, Colonias Unidas, testified in the legislature in favor of the Bill. She recalls the distance between her lived reality and the mindset of the lawmakers, despite their apparent good intentions: "They were saying 'those people need to get out of those colonias, they are not livable.'" Juárez then asks,

---

[7] This position was supported by a few non-governmental organizations active in communities at the border, including the Texas Low-Income Housing Information Service and its Border Coalition for Low-Income Housing (Henneberger 2001; interview with David Arizmendi).

"Why would people leave their houses just because they don't have electricity and water? Where would they live, under a bridge? On balance, no water or electricity is better than no house."[8]

The issue of conventional standards will not die, and that is because it so plainly raises the tensions between the existing regulatory toolbox and the confounding realities of informal housing. In 2001, the Texas legislature again considered giving counties the power to regulate building standards. The Bill, introduced by a border legislator who has often been an ally on colonias issues, described its purpose as "to prevent the proliferation of colonias and substandard housing developments."[9] The Bill was defeated at the last moment, but by conservatives opposed to land use regulation in principle and not by the alternative understandings of law created by grassroots groups from the colonias.[10]

The building codes in widespread use throughout the United States are descendants of those first enacted in the early twentieth century when the Progressive movement pushed for basic sanitation standards in overcrowded urban tenements. Codes thus began as politically progressive reform measures, but modern codes require construction standards far above the minimum required for health and safety. The political process of drafting model codes explains why: model codes shape existing codes; most local jurisdictions adopt one or more of the handful of model codes, in whole or in part, often simply by reference. Model codes in turn are written by trade groups such as the construction and building materials industries, and labor unions, and close out self-builders by requiring costly materials and high-skill labor, and restricting use of prefabricated or manufactured components (Kelly 1996:350). The model code process is thus a confluence of economic interests for whom affordability is not a core policy goal.

What is the alternative perspective on housing quality coming from the colonias? How have they come to understand the tension between conventional regulation and informal housing, and thus to oppose the adoption of conventional building codes in the colonias? David Arizmendi, a long-time community organizer, says simply, "you cannot impose housing quality standards on people without giving them the

---

[8] Interview with Blanca Juárez, a founder of Colonias Unidas and now Defensora/Colonia Ombuds for Starr County, Rio Grande City, Texas, August 15, 2000.

[9] SB 517, 77th Leg., Reg. Sess. (Texas 2001) (adding Chapter 236 to amend the Local Government Code).

[10] Interview with John Henneberger, Austin, Texas, March 16, 2001.

resources to meet them."[11] He predicts that few existing colonia structures could meet existing building codes; many would be seriously
deficient, and a portion would have to be razed and rebuilt. Even if
existing structures were grandfathered, code standards would rule out
the typical construction practices of self-builders for any new housing,
including new or incomplete construction on already-purchased lots.
Such codes would thus have the practical effect of making new colonia
housing illegal and impossible.

Blanca Juárez, colonia resident and long-time activist, tries to educate policymakers in the debate over building codes by moving from the
abstract to the concrete: "It's a house or no house," she says. "Do you
honestly believe these people will leave their houses just because they
aren't safe or healthy?"[12]

Juárez makes clear that colonia residents are not ignorant or unaware
of the tradeoffs their condition forces on them. "It isn't that they don't
want to have a healthy life, and it isn't that they are used to living
without anything. Like they keep saying, 'Oh, they're from Mexico, and
they're used to living without water or electricity.' Well not all people
in Mexico live with nothing, and not everyone in a colonia is from
Mexico."[13]

Those who live in existing colonias, and the many who *would* buy
into such settlements if development opened up again, have few housing options, and all of them mean hardship and deprivation in one way
or another. Where there is no good choice (only better and worse
choices), arguments of principle or "either/or" solutions will work
perverse outcomes. Juárez captures the dilemma with characteristic
immediacy: "People here want good houses. I would like to live next
to Bill Clinton, but the truth is that I can't, I just can't. So I am going to
build whatever I can. I am not living under a bridge, and I am not asking
the government to give me a house. I am just doing the best that I can
to make a house for my children and to live as good a life as I can."[14]

For Juárez and Arizmendi, solutions to colonia problems lie in helping residents rather than penalizing them for their living conditions. In
the absence of political will to resolve the disconnect between wages
and housing prices, these local theorists believe that building up from
the community's solutions is the best policy. "The answer will have to

---

[11] Interview with David Arizmendi.   [12] Interview with Blanca Juárez.   [13] *Ibid.*
[14] *Ibid.*

come from the community," Arizmendi says. "You have to take what the community is doing and magnify it, extend it."[15]

The community has responded to the lack of affordable housing by building colonias. Thus, what might seem anti-progressive from the perspective of principle – to support informal housing knowing it leads to substandard conditions – is pragmatic, coherent, and strategic in the politics that the colonias have made of their conditions.

6.4 REGULATING UNDER CONDITIONS OF EXTREME ECONOMIC CONSTRAINT

If conventional regulation won't work, the first alternative that leaps to mind is deregulation. Yet eliminating government regulation removes a powerful tool for collective action in the struggle for economic justice, even as enforcement of unattainable standards burdens those already on the margins and increases reliance on informal solutions. Regulation at least tries to extend law's reach so as to integrate informal economic activity (albeit by prohibition), and thereby expresses an aspiration for the common good in its demand for better housing quality. Deregulation leaves informality at the margins and envisions no aspirational program of change over time. If we leave behind these recognized legal tools, is law capable of facilitating more adequate housing for populations under conditions of economic constraint without mandating unattainable standards?

In earlier work, I argued in general terms for the "gradual and progressive" imposition of minimal building standards in the colonias, paired with access to credit for home improvement and technical assistance for construction (Larson 1995:249–250). Saskia Sassen, too, has urged the creation of gradual and flexible forms of regulation that can bring informal economic activities within the regulatory framework at a minimal cost to the regulated. "Upgrading is likely to demand greater flexibility in the implementation of existing codes and acknowledgment ... that compliance may require several phases. Lower thresholds of regulatory compliance would be applied to new, small-scale businesses in low-income communities than to well-established businesses that have had an opportunity to recover start-up costs" (1998:166). But neither Sassen nor I specify the legal form for this flexibility. In this chapter and in other recent work (Larson

[15] Interview with David Arizmendi.

2002:177–181), I propose adopting the "progressive realization" model first articulated in international human rights law as the basis for a new regulatory template attuned to the realities of informality.

Human rights law is not a source typically consulted on what are in the United States the quintessentially local questions of land use and housing quality. Yet public international law is pioneering new understandings of "rights" that include positive as well as negative rights, which in turn is creating new understandings of what "law" is, and can be. Brought home to the domestic world of land and housing, these expanded understandings create new legal and social space, and extend the regulatory toolbox.

The International Covenant on Economic, Social and Cultural Rights (Economic Covenant) recognizes the human right of all people to "an adequate standard of living ... including adequate food, clothing and housing, and to the continuous improvement of living conditions" (Article 11(1)). Parties ratifying the Economic Covenant undertake an obligation to assure their people this basic level of sustenance. Many nations have signed the Economic Covenant, including many in which most of the people lack adequate housing. So do the positive rights guaranteed by the Economic Covenant have the force of law, or are they merely symbolic expressions of aspiration?

Indeed, the Economic Covenant does not guarantee immediate provision of adequate housing to all persons. As a practical matter, economic rights cannot be implemented in all the same ways as civil and political rights, and the Economic Covenant recognizes this.[16] The Economic Covenant requires these rights to be "progressively ... realiz[ed] ... to the maximum of ... available [governmental] resources." Thus, the Economic Covenant takes resource constraints into account; the rich nation must provide more than the poor one. Where there is extreme economic constraint, citizens will only gradually realize the right relative to the nation's resources. Nor does the Economic Covenant impose universal standards for measuring compliance. Parties to the Economic Covenant may have differing standards for judging the adequacy of shelter, for example, and the right may be

---

[16] States have direct power to establish structures that protect their citizens' civil and political liberties, such as police, courts, and constitutions, but they cannot create the natural or social resources to feed and house those citizens by the same measures. Yet states do have the power to influence the creation of wealth, and even more directly, to distribute and redistribute wealth, by structures such as property law, social welfare, and taxation. So economic rights are enforceable, but by different and more indirect mechanisms.

guaranteed in a wide variety of political settings with no particular approaches mandated.

By this model, there are no immediately enforceable rights to full compliance from all regulated parties. Speaking from within the United States legal tradition, some commentators have argued that enforceability is the mark of a legal right, and therefore class "progressive realization" of the Economic Covenant's rights as something less than law (Alston and Quinn 1997:155). The United States as a nation, for instance, maintains that economic, social, and cultural rights "belong in a qualitatively different category from other rights, that they should not be seen as rights but as goals of economic and social policy" (UN General Assembly, 1985).

In general, negative rights provide the norm of legal rules in the United States rather than positive rights. Negative rights prohibit the state from doing something, such as denying equal protection of the law or restricting freedom of speech. Positive rights impose an affirmative obligation on the state. The approaches governments take to assure these two kinds of rights generally differ, with programs of distribution and redistribution used for positive rights and programs of enforcement employed for negative rights.

Yet, if the law focuses on enforceability generally, as opposed to universal, immediate, and absolute compliance, the principle of progressive realization and the requirement of commitment of maximum available resources *do* bind parties equally and in legally enforceable ways. The principle of progressivity requires nations to create programs and policies to address housing needs, and to make steady progress over time to increase access to adequate housing. The requirement of progress consistent with available resources imposes an "immediate and readily identifiable obligation upon states parties," permits measurement, and hence allows for meaningful enforcement[17] (Alston and Quinn 1997:165–166).

"Progressive realization" provides a regulatory conception for imposing aspirational standards while calibrating compliance obligations to available economic resources. By adapting this legal technology to a domestic regulatory regime, governments may evenhandedly include both the poorest colonia and the wealthiest enclave under a universal

---

[17] The United Nations has weak enforcement powers under the Economic Covenant, and this weakness, as much as the positive rights critique, has led some to conclude that the Economic Covenant is not really "law." Nonetheless, the adaptation of the progressive realization model for domestic regulatory purposes could include adoption of effective enforcement mechanisms.

housing standard, obliging compliance from residents in each setting according to their realistic capacity to meet the standard. The model marries aspiration and attainability by committing both government and people to a common norm of decent housing for all persons, and requiring continuing progress toward the standard by the "progressive realization" principle.

A domestic program for regulating housing quality and development built around the progressive realization of standards would better balance the regulatory burden on diverse populations, the public interest in adequate housing, and a commitment to social inclusion expressed as a commitment to elevating living standards. To encourage compliance with modified regulations and enforcement practices, local regulators can offer self-builders technical and financial assistance as part of the long-term upgrading process. At any point when the household seeks governmental assistance, the regulatory structure may assess whether it has met the dual compliance obligations of continuous progress toward the standard and the commitment of maximum available household resources. By this approach, enforcement becomes a cooperative effort at progress rather than a punishment of the poor for where they live or the limits of their resources. Linked to such a comprehensive program of regularization, progressive realization places law behind, rather than against, the activities of informals.

6.5 CONCLUSION

Out of the effort to find some form by which law can engage informality on its own terms emerges the "progressive realization" model. It is an alternative model of law that respects the strategic choices of those struggling hardest to stay alive in the new world of cheap labor and privatized social provision. Lawyers must learn from social investigation of the historical and social particularities of the informal sector as it exists in our midst, and from social theorists who connect that knowledge to larger structures of politics and economy. But it is the task of lawyers to find material ways to embody these ideas in policy frameworks and regulatory tools. That is the aim of this chapter.

References

Alston, Philip, and Gerard Quinn. 1987. "The Nature and Scope of States Parties' Obligations under the International Covenant on Economic, Social and Cultural Rights." *Human Rights Quarterly* 9:156.

Castells, Manuel, and Alejandro Portes. 1989. "World Underneath: The Origins, Dynamics, and the Effects of the Informal Economy." In *The Informal Economy: Studies in Advanced and Less Developed Countries*, edited by Alejandro Portes, Manuel Castells, and Lauren A. Benton. Baltimore: Johns Hopkins University Press.

Dwyer, Augusta. 1994. *On the Line: Life on the United States–Mexican Border* London: Latin American Bureau.

Farvacque, Catharine, and Patrick McAuslan. 1992. *Reforming Urban Land Policies and Institutions in Developing Countries*. Washington, DC: World Bank.

Fernandes, Edesio, and Ann Varley. 1998. "Law, the City and Citizenship in Developing Countries: An Introduction." In *Illegal Cities: Law and Urban Change in Developing Countries*, edited by Edesio Fernandes and Ann Varley. London: Zed Books.

Gilbert, Alan, and Peter Ward. 1985. *Housing, the State and the Poor: Policy and Practice in Three Latin American Cities*. Cambridge: Cambridge University Press.

Kelly, Eric. 1996. "Fair Housing, Good Housing or Expensive Housing? Are Building Codes Part of the Problem or Part of the Solution?" *John Marshall Law Review* 29:349.

Larson, Jane E. 1995 "Free Markets Deep in the Heart of Texas." *Georgetown Law Journal* 84:179.

 2002. "Informality, Illegality, and Inequality." *Yale Law and Policy Review* 20:137.

Lyndon B. Johnson School of Public Affairs. 1997. *Colonia Housing and Infrastructure: Current Characteristics and Future Needs*, Policy Research Project Report No. 124, vol. 1. Austin: Lyndon B. Johnson School of Public Affairs.

Payne, Geoffrey. 1997. *Urban Land Tenure and Property Rights in Developing Countries: A Review*. London: Intermediate Technology Development Group.

Pinkerton, James. 1994. "Water Project Up and Running, But Most Still Lack Running Water." *Houston Chronicle*, 6 November.

Santos, Boaventura de Sousa. 1997. "Toward a Multicultural Conception of Human Rights." *Zeitschrift fur Rechtssoziologie* 18:1.

 2002. *Toward a New Legal Common Sense*. London: Butterworths.

Sassen, Saskia. 1998. *Globalization and Its Discontents*. New York: New Press.

Staudt, Kathleen. 1998. *Free Trade? Informal Economies at the United States–Mexico Border*. Philadelphia: Temple University Press.

Ward, Peter. 1991. "Political Pressure for Urban Services: The Response of Two Mexico City Administrations." *Development and Change* 12:379.

CHAPTER 7

LOCAL CONTACT POINTS AT GLOBAL DIVIDES: LABOR RIGHTS AND IMMIGRANT RIGHTS AS SITES FOR COSMOPOLITAN LEGALITY

Fran Ansley

This chapter will present two case studies from the global North – in fact, from the pinnacle of Northern power, the United States. It will take a vantage point grounded in what some have dubbed "the South in the North," meaning persons and communities in wealthy countries who are marginalized or otherwise disadvantaged by things as they are, groups like factory workers and low-income people of color, who have relatively little social power and who enjoy increasingly little economic security.

The two cases presented arguably constitute examples of what Santos calls "subaltern cosmopolitan legality" (2002:479), law-making and law-challenging projects that link the local and the global in ways that unsettle global inequality and exclusion (see also Santos and Rodríguez-Garavito's chapter in this volume). My hope is that the experiences recounted in these case studies will illuminate some of the challenges confronted by those who want to help realize the compelling and questionable dream that Santos and others have held up for our contemplation – that of egalitarian and emancipatory global transformation from below.[1]

Both efforts described here were triggered and enabled by what I am going to call "strategic global contact points." By that term I mean instances when (1) some kind of new, material, and social connection is made between a group of people in one part of the world, and a group

---

[1] There are many people critically pursuing this dream. For varied cases, see Prokosch and Raymond (2003); Nissen (2002); Brecher, Costello, and Smith (2002); Edwards and Gaventa (2001); Gaventa (1999); and Klein (2000).

of people in another; (2) the connection bears some close relation to the dynamics of contemporary globalization; and (3) the groups brought into contact through the connection are in some sense non-elite, that is, both groups are more on the receiving end than on the deciding end of the global forces that are currently in play. The contact points that interest me, the ones I believe are most strategic, are those that garner acute attention from one or both of the groups connected by the contact, and the ones that are sufficiently new (or at least newly visible) that they have not yet come to be seen as natural or inevitable. Both cases described below meet these rough criteria, and both are drawn from developments over the last few years in Tennessee, a state in the Southeastern United States where I live and work.

The first part of this essay will describe two sets of law-related activities that were triggered by the appearance of new global contact points in Tennessee. The second will discuss whether either of these efforts qualifies as an instance of the "cosmopolitan legality" Santos has urged scholars to seek out and study. I conclude that both efforts do qualify. However, I also point to some significant problems they encountered that are likely to confront similar South–North efforts in the future, due in large part to the gross asymmetries across which such global collaborations are required to operate.

7.1 TWO STORIES

7.1.1 First contact point: capital flight and job loss

For many years Tennessee was a receiving destination for light industry leaving the Northeast and Midwest in search of the low wages, the docile and unorganized workers, and the "business-friendly" regulatory environment for which the Southeastern Unites States has long been known. But in the late 1970s and 1980s, disinvestment and the attend-ant loss of blue-collar jobs became a major feature of the economic landscape. Many Tennessee manufacturing operations shifted to Mexico and other low-wage locations in the global South. Workers learned that they could be ordered unceremoniously to pack their machines and their unfinished work into cardboard boxes headed South, take up their pink slips, and go home. Most had precious little information with which to imagine the Mexican worker who would be unpacking that box at the other end of its journey.

In 1989, a coalition of labor, community, and religious groups from around the state came together for the purpose of fighting these plant shutdowns. Organizers with a fledgling group called the Tennessee Industrial Renewal Network (TIRN)[2] originally hoped they could put a brake on factory closures. Like the national plant closing movement of which it was a part, TIRN undertook an array of initiatives aimed at making footloose capital more accountable to workers and communities (Ansley 1993; Lynd 1982, 1987).

However, as TIRN organizers encountered closure after closure, talked with distraught workers, and sought repeatedly to find some ground upon which to stand and fight, and as they began to learn something about the destinations where these plants were going, the global dimensions of the phenomenon became increasingly apparent (Weinbaum 2004).

It also became evident that the laid-off workers TIRN encountered in its organizing were hungry for more information about these new global trends. They wanted to understand what was happening to them and to their communities, and why. Many were confused and angry as they witnessed the implicit post-World War II US social compact – thin as it surely was – coming unraveled before their eyes. TIRN organizers heard many bitter complaints about corporate greed and government collusion. They also heard comments about "those Mexicans" who were "stealing our jobs."

Accordingly, in addition to the work tied directly to plant closures, TIRN decided to mount an effort aimed at cross-border understanding between blue-collar workers in Tennessee and their counterparts in the booming export processing industry along Mexico's northern frontier. In 1991, the group sponsored its first two-way exchange, an experiential educational travel program that involved factory workers and activists from Mexico's *maquiladora* (or simply *maquila*) zone, in travel exchanges with factory workers and activists from Tennessee.

This long-term program, still ongoing today, has been chronicled in some detail elsewhere (Ansley and Williams 1999; Ansley 1998, 1995, 1992; Disney 2003; Williams 2002). For present purposes, suffice it to say that these trips have been intense. They expose US participants to the superheated world of the *maquilas*, with their glittering industrial parks and blistering squatter settlements, chaotic growth, glaring disparities, and breathtaking deprivations – all jumbled into a shocking

---

[2] The organization recently changed its name from the Tennessee Industrial Renewal Network to the Tennessee Economic Renewal Network – all for good reasons that are no doubt obvious. For simplicity's sake, in this primarily historical essay, I retain the original name throughout.

bundle that travelers regularly report to have been utterly unimaginable prior to their journeys. And yet the strangeness Tennesseans encountered on these trips was also laced with an eerie familiarity. As a result of the corporate connections that created this global contact point of capital flight in the first place, blue-collar members of TIRN delegations sometimes met up in northern Mexico with former supervisors and sparred with them about old times. Some travelers recognized the individual machines they had tended back home, now bolted in place on vast new Mexican shop floors staffed by armies of teenage operators.

One outcome of the exchange program was the development of a multi-faceted educational program. Returning delegations have given slide shows, written letters to the editor, spoken to meetings, led Sunday school classes, testified at hearings, organized workshops, and composed songs and poems about the downside of globalization and free trade. A widely circulated video is still well received (Ranney 2003:225; TIRN 1993).

Returning delegations also took action. They sent (modest) contributions of material aid to sister organizations, supported corporate campaigns that focused on the practices of particular multinationals, and started buying fair trade coffee. The first main way that TIRN found to engage members in action after these trips to the border was a campaign that focused on law.

As the organization began to learn about the *maquiladora* program, and as it met others who were also concerned about capital flight to low-wage havens, TIRN was introduced to a whole world of international trade and finance entirely new to most of the group's members. These homegrown plant-closure activists found themselves confronted with an array of international acronyms, programs, and entities. Few in the organization knew much if anything about "structural adjustment programs," or could recall hearing about the "debt crisis," or had any idea how to respond to an elected official when he started spouting theories of "comparative advantage." Much less could they interpret or understand the alphabet soup of GATT, WTO, IMF, TRIPS, and NTBs.

However, when the US, Mexico, and Canada announced they were going to negotiate a free trade agreement that would have to be voted on by the US Congress, it appeared that there might be a political handle that groups like TIRN could grab. (After all, many such groups *did* know how to lobby Congress, even if they were neophytes on the global economy.) The ensuing anti-NAFTA campaign brought together an array of different constituencies that had been working on issues of economic justice and environmental sustainability. It also gave them their first clue that their own government was busy pushing a set of new supranational rules about international investment that would positively restrict governments at all levels from enacting many of the very measures these groups had been lobbying their elected officials to adopt.

Groups that had often been pitted against each other – such as labor unions, critics of US foreign policy and war-making, small farmers, civil rights organizations, and environmentalists – now joined new coalitions to oppose NAFTA and the anti-democratic "fast-track" authority under which it was negotiated and approved. A legislative campaign directed at the US Congress allowed these networks to use familiar tools to make their views known and to attempt to affect federal policy.

Although on one level the fight against NAFTA looked like any other legislative battle that US groups might have mounted in the past, important things about it were newly cosmopolitan. If the tri-national structure of NAFTA created a framework that brought elite professionals together at the top (for instance, high-level trade negotiators, lawyers, and corporate executives from all three signatory countries), that very framework was also put to use as a common meeting ground for grassroots and trade union opponents at the bottom. Admittedly, these scrappy opponents lacked the lavish support enjoyed by state and corporate negotiators, but that did not prevent them from creating events and relationships. For instance, one strand of tri-national networking involved the creation of a loose international working group that began to hammer out an "alternative" to the official agreement. This network aimed for a set of concrete proposals and an animating vision that could serve as a practical and ideological counter to NAFTA and the neoliberal gospel that undergirded it.

In the earliest days of the negotiations, when the future of the agreement was still quite hazy, critics in Mexico, the US, and Canada searched energetically to identify and contact cross-national counterparts (Hathaway 2000). Beginning with a historic tri-national meeting in Zacatecas, Mexico, in 1991 (Ranney 2003:201–204), these aspiring partners organized meetings of their own at the same time and place that NAFTA trade negotiators convened. They became adept at capitalizing on such moments to go public in various ways, but also used their time together for consultation within and across national delegations. Later these networks would provide the basis for more advanced work along similar lines in the context of the greatly expanded reach of the Free Trade Area of the Americas (Cavanagh, Anderson, and Hansen-Kuhn 2001).

These early cross-border dialogues about alternatives to "free trade" were mainly peopled by academics and intellectuals from the three countries. However, some grassroots participants like TIRN were also included, and the working groups tried hard to feed their work back into the more popular networks that had begun mobilizing around the country. The importance of such outreach was highlighted as it became increasingly clear that significant strands of the domestic opposition to NAFTA in the US were isolationist, even xenophobic (Buchanan 1991; Perot 1993). As the politics of the anti-NAFTA campaign developed, a kind of de facto alliance emerged between internationalists and isolationists (including some groups that were strenuously anti-immigrant). This alliance held out the prospect of garnering more votes against NAFTA on the floor of the US Congress, but posed some real dangers as well, at least in the minds of some in the coalition. Questions about handling these tensions (for instance, whether to downplay or to highlight differences between the still ill-defined and overlapping camps, and whether to promote or reject a right–left coalition leading up to the NAFTA vote) were a continuing bone of contention among the anti-NAFTA forces.

The dialogue among the tri-national working groups on alternatives certainly did not resolve those tense questions. Nevertheless, they put a strong priority on building cross-border ties and articulating a cross-border perspective, and they churned out copious facts and arguments supporting a wholeheartedly internationalist case for the defeat of NAFTA (Hansen-Kuhn 2001). Meanwhile, more grassroots and rank-and-file sorts of cross-border contact, like the exchange trips organized by TIRN and by others, provided stories and perspectives that helped the alternatives working groups to understand what people closer to the ground in all three countries cared about, and what moved them (CBN 2002; Ojeda 1999).

In one sense, the mobilization to block or radically alter NAFTA ended in short-term defeat when the agreement was approved overwhelmingly by Congress. On the other hand, the movement forced some serious concessions, including a substantial appropriation for "trade adjustment assistance" to factory workers laid off as a result of NAFTA-related trade, and a novel set of labor and environmental "side agreements" not fully integrated into the main trade pact, but offering at least some mechanisms for bringing complaints, and providing another platform for tri-national cooperation among labor rights groups in the three countries.

Further, the unfavorable vote in Congress did nothing to dismantle the ideas and relationships that were begun during the campaign. To the contrary, those relationships continued to flourish. In this hemisphere, the original tri-national nucleus of anti-NAFTA activists has now expanded into a Hemispheric Social Alliance in step with the widening scope of the proposed Free Trade Area of the Americas (FTAA) and cognizant of worldwide arenas and players like the WTO. The new vistas and understandings opened by these encounters with the global economy and its new corporate-dominated constitutionalized legal order have raised profound questions for academic and grassroots participants alike about what is happening in the world and why (Alvarez 1997; Rupert 1995).

TIRN readily followed the path opened by the foregoing developments. Tennesseans attended assemblies of the Hemispheric Social Alliance in South America, and they accompanied delegations of grassroots groups from the US to meetings of the World Social Forum in Brazil and India. TIRN and its constituent organizations have taken repeatedly to the streets as well, turning out for demonstrations against the WTO and the FTAA in Seattle, Quebec City, Washington, DC, and Miami, and staging local actions back home to coordinate with those distant convergences.

7.1.2 Second contact point: immigration

The second strategic global contact point came close on the heels of the first. In the 1990s, mass labor migration of low-wage workers from Mexico and Central America surged into Tennessee communities previously made up almost exclusively of native-born whites and blacks (Mendoza 2002; Mendoza, Ciscel, and Smith 2001). In this second new-world moment, rather than watching as the familiar drained away, native-born Tennesseans watched as foreign others penetrated the familiar. From our previously "interior" location, insulated well toward the center of the nation's territorial mass, we witnessed international boundaries cropping up in grocery store lines, restaurant kitchens, construction sites, and Wal-Mart superstores all around us.[3]

---

[3] Of course Tennessee is not alone in experiencing this dramatic demographic shift (Aponte and Siles 1994; Fink 2003; Lowell and Suro 2002). Demographics are intensely watched in the US, in part because of their bearing on racial politics. The US Census reported that the US Hispanic

This shift was not only demographic: it brought legal change as well. Many new immigrants in Tennessee are "undocumented," meaning that they are in the US without authorization. That means they are legally prohibited from working and are subject to deportation if detected by immigration authorities. For most undocumented persons, present US immigration law offers no path to regularization of status. In Tennessee, although the overall number of Latinas and Latinos is still a relatively low percentage of the population, they are nonetheless a striking new presence. In some counties, the growth has been especially dramatic, with attendant impacts on schools and other institutions that are ill-prepared to cope either equitably or competently with the new-comers they are now challenged to serve (Mendoza 2002; Smith 2001).

Like the phenomenon of job loss attendant upon capital flight, mass labor migration satisfies criteria that suggest it might provide a favor-able platform for cosmopolitan legality. First, it is a signature phenom-enon of today's global economy, propelled by the dynamics of the neoliberal development model that now dominates the world. Secondly, it brings people who start from very different geographic and social locations into new sorts of contact with each other. Finally, the phenomenon is still new enough to appear quite strange and questionable to those of us who are watching it unfold. For most Tennesseans, for instance, even hearing another language spoken on the street was a novelty not so long ago. The idea of a whole new separately treated segment of the workforce, one that is both differen-tially disciplined by law, and visibly marked by color, still seems morally questionable and pragmatically ill-conceived to many ordinary citizens.

In the early 1990s, some of the same people who had been involved with TIRN's worker-to-worker exchanges began to take note of this growing immigrant presence and to wonder whether there could or should be any relationship between that and the organ-ization's work on the global economy. For instance, one factory worker soon after her return from Mexico wrote a letter to the editor criticizing anti-immigrant views that were aired in the local paper. A union that had helped sponsor TIRN's first trips to Mexico convened a workshop on immigration at one of its annual membership meetings.

These moments of connection showed that some of those involved in the campaigns around job loss and capital flight were also paying

---

population grew by 57.9 percent between 1990 and 2000, as compared with a figure of 13.2 percent for the US population as a whole. Of Hispanics counted, over half were of Mexican origin (Guzman 2001).

attention to this second global contact point. Nevertheless, such moments were relatively isolated, and none of them involved initiatives taken by immigrants themselves. For the most part, TIRN's globalization work continued to focus on issues of capital flight and on building opposition to the long train of proposed trade deals that continued to issue forth from the Clinton and Bush administrations.

In February 2000, the AFL-CIO announced a reversal of its former position on immigration. It called for an amnesty program for a large segment of undocumented workers already in the country and declared that labor would begin aggressively recruiting immigrants into its ranks. It is hard to overstate the potential significance of this development for the future of organized labor and immigration politics (Ely 2000).

At the same time, policy announcements from the top do not necessarily translate into real "buy-in," change or energy at the base. Certainly, little in Tennessee seemed to follow initially from the policy change. Few of the industries where Latinos were working had ever been organized to begin with, and, in any event, new workplace organizing drives of any kind are rare here as elsewhere.

Many grassroots community groups and social justice organizations that were part of TIRN or its circle of allies had by then become convinced they needed to hook up somehow with the immigrant community. But most of these groups, like the unions, were greatly hampered by a lack of Spanish-language capacity in their organizations and by their still quite rudimentary knowledge of the needs, culture, and concerns of the immigrant community. Meanwhile, not a single immigrants' rights organization was yet in existence in the state.

In the spring of 2001, an unlikely issue provided the seed around which these emerging trends and networks could crystallize: access to the driver's license for undocumented people. Beginning in 1998, Tennessee required applicants for a driver's license to provide a social security number, something generally only available to persons authorized to work in the US – mostly citizens and those who have been granted Legal Permanent Residency status with its accompanying "green card."

The effect of this requirement was to bar undocumented immigrants from obtaining a license to drive. The impact of this bar may be difficult for non-US readers to appreciate. In Tennessee, as in many other US locations, there is basically *no* local public transportation outside the tight central core of the larger cities. For the vast majority of people, including poor people, an automobile is therefore a virtual necessity for even the simplest acts of daily existence, including the task of getting to and from one's place of work. For undocumented immigrants, the inability to obtain a license functioned to criminalize another aspect of daily life in the US. The opportunities and temptations for police to engage in the most blatant racial profiling directed at those "driving while brown" were thereby multiplied a thousand-fold.

All who interacted regularly with Latinos knew this issue was universally seen as critical by the immigrant community. When the Roman Catholic Church announced that access to the driver's license would be one of its main agenda items for the 2001 legislative session of the Tennessee legislature, a state-wide network of other supporters soon emerged. A website and an e-mail list were created, and volunteers began finding their way to campaign. Dozens of people, including many immigrants, made a dramatic visit to the general assembly on Catholic Lobby Day, where some undocumented immigrants chose to tell their stories to startled legislators, who attentively heard them out. Astonishingly, the proposed bills made it into law. In short order, licenses were once again issued to undocumented persons in Tennessee.

Within days, masses of immigrants descended on driver's license stations around the state (Semien 2001; Whitaker 2001a). Long lines angered some natives who were unnerved to stumble onto these scenes and unhappy to be inconvenienced by the delay. Anti-immigrant organizations were quick to capitalize on these reactions and used them to fuel an immediate effort at repeal. Eventually, the lines diminished, and the bottleneck was over, but not the controversy (Whitaker 2001b).

The driver's license campaign represented the first time that Tennessee Latinas, Latinos, and their allies had come out into the open in a coordinated way to seek some kind of reform, and it was a dramatic experience for those involved. To tell the truth, many people who were involved were more or less dumbfounded at their success. Several had been dubious that the campaign would prevail in a first round effort, especially given the conservative tenor of the Tennessee legislature and the reservoirs of anti-immigrant feeling that they had reason to believe existed in the state. Pro-immigrant groups took real heart from the victory. Meanwhile, fights over access to the driver's license began to surface in other states as well. These were hotly contested, to be sure, but many observers nevertheless saw them as part of a generally brightening picture, in which talk of a broad amnesty was much in the air.[4]

---

[4] At the height of the complaints about long lines at driver's license stations, for instance, a member of the presidential cabinet in Mexico wrote a letter to *The Tennessean*, Nashville's daily

Such was the precarious but greatly encouraged mood in the summer of 2001. And then came the events of September 11.

The ensuing fallout for immigrants was intense at every level. Two particularly potent strands of American anger and anxiety intersected precisely on the terrain of our modest Tennessee driver's license victory. First was the fear of immigrants, such that many Americans began to express a widespread concern over the simple fact of immigrants' increasingly visible, uncontrolled, and transgressive presence in our midst. Second was the fear of immigrants' apparent ability to construct false identities using what were perceived as the ordinary, innocent workings of our own state and private bureaucracies of information. In the days and weeks after the attack, it seemed the media repeated endlessly that several of the 9/11 terrorists had been in possession of official state-issued driver's licenses. That all the terrorists had entered the country *legally* did nothing to reduce the cries of alarm about undocumented people in our midst, or the relentlessly repeated references to identity documents and the danger they posed to law-abiding citizens. Each time activists from the driver's license campaign read or heard those reports again, our hearts sank. In immigrant communities, the sense of dread and anxiety was palpable at every turn.

Immigrant advocates did not fall into paralysis. Since the initial trauma, they have worked unstintingly to control damage, to defend prior gains, and to identify small openings for reform, working at national, state, or local policy levels as the weather suggested (Smith and Sugimori 2003), and fights over immigrant access to the driver's license – some offensive and some defensive – have been prominent (FAIR 2002; NILC 2004, 2002). Meanwhile, they have faced a barrage of anti-immigrant measures, likewise put forward at multiple levels, all raising opportunities for education and debate, but also threatening serious setbacks. Signs of anti-immigrant feeling among the general population are still much in evidence.

In Tennessee, opponents of immigrant access to the driver's license have mounted strong efforts at repeal, and they have succeeded in chipping away at access. (Today, for instance, Tennessee licenses issued to drivers who lack a social security number are prominently marked to

newspaper, urging us to have patience and not go back on the decision to allow access to the driver's license for immigrants. In closing he remarked, "A year from now, when the kinks have been ironed out and other states have joined the handful already granting immigrants licenses, Tennessee will be proud to say it was among the first to recognize this important opportunity" (Hernandez 2001).

indicate that damaging fact.) Nevertheless, despite the furor after 9/11 and continuing heightened concern about security, immigrant groups have thus far succeeded in holding part of the ground they gained in the 2001 campaign.

More importantly, the human networks that were created during the driver's license campaign have continued to function and grow. Tennessee is now home to a formal organization, the Tennessee Immigrant and Refugee Rights Coalition, whose genesis was greatly boosted by the driver's license campaign, but whose agenda is now much broader. These days, more meetings are conducted in Spanish, and more leadership roles are filled by immigrants and refugees themselves.

7.2 BUT WAS IT COSMOPOLITAN?

Santos discerns at work in the world a form of globalization that links "social groups, networks, initiatives, organizations and movements" that oppose neoliberal globalization (2002:459). He calls this kind of globalization from below "cosmopolitanism of the oppressed" and argues that in present circumstances it represents a "necessary condition of social emancipation" (Santos 2002:466). Within this loose and far-flung assortment of local and international projects, Santos identifies law-focused activity, "cosmopolitan legality," as an important component that calls out for further study.[5]

Since this essay is in some sense a response to such a call (see Santos and Rodríguez-Garavito's chapter in this volume), it seems important to ask whether the two cases discussed here can rightly be seen as instances of cosmopolitan legality. I conclude that both of these exercises in legality displayed important "cosmopolitan" features, in the honorific sense that Santos mostly uses that term, but I also note that both efforts were affected by the constant gravitational pull of *anti*-cosmopolitanism (including the particularly virulent form which anti-cosmopolitanism often takes in the US). Based on these observations, I will offer a few tentative suggestions about ways that people who are situated in the global North and want to be part of creating "a new legal

---

[5] Santos uses "law" in a very broad sense, which includes non-official law and even illegal practices (2002:495). For more on the possibility of an emancipatory matrix between law and politics, see Stammers (1999).

common sense" might work to align their efforts more securely with a cosmopolitanism of the oppressed.

Three salient features seem especially worth pointing out. First, both cases involved *global boundary crossing*. Whether the boundaries were territorial, racial, legal, or otherwise, these cases brought about collaborations and alliances that linked people from different, usually quite separate, social/global locations. They brought denizens of two or more global sites into some new and striking contact that allowed the two groups to engage in peer exchange and sharing of perspectives.

Secondly, both efforts (admittedly the anti-NAFTA effort more than the driver's license campaign) involved an element of *horizontal understanding* – that is, they stressed solidarity between peers, rather than charity from generous superordinates toward needy subordinates. In this sense, the anti-NAFTA work called up an oppressed and cross-national "we" that stood out against an oppressive corporate "they." As a consequence, it provided a counter – first, to the more nationalist, anti-cosmopolitan frame that has traditionally been so strong in the US, and, secondly, to the quite different, elite-oriented cosmopolitanism suggested by the neoliberal world view of global markets and free trade.

Thirdly, in both cases, *legal strategies played a non-dominant part in a broader, deeper, longer political effort*. As many scholars have recognized, legal "rights" in the abstract, international or domestic, are highly contingent – equally capable of promoting egalitarian redistribution, or defending embedded privilege. Accordingly, movements bent on gaining or defending legal rights as a way of advancing the fortunes of oppressed people had best remain vigilant about their vulnerability to absorption and derailment. I agree with Santos that an important hedge against the capture of legal rights into the service of the status quo (whether as discourse or as social practice), is the integration of rights claims into political activity that regularly moves and sees beyond immediate legal claims. In both of the cases discussed above, law reform goals were prominent. But in both cases the law-centered work was accompanied by non-legal (sometimes even by massive illegal) activity, and was part of a long-term effort to build cross-boundary relationships for future dialogue and action.

In three important ways, then, the cases presented here display features of cosmopolitan legality. However, both cases manifest contradictory signs as well. The emergent cosmopolitanism of both efforts was subjected to constant pressure from the breathtaking social and economic distance between the Northern and Southern poles of their respective collaborations. Present global disparities, together with the privileges they entail, can make it difficult for citizens of the global North to move toward genuine peer-to-peer alliances with Southern counterparts.

The difficulties stem in part from the pull of self-interest and self-protection: Northerners of all kinds witnessing Southern realities can see risks of loss in addition to the promise of gain. But the difficulty stems from epistemological disadvantage as well. Privilege in the global economy often consists precisely in being distanced and sheltered from direct evidence of the disturbing conditions of life faced by others in less privileged locations and from direct experience with many of the instrumentalities that play such important roles in global maldistribution.

This kind of anti-cosmopolitan pressure is certain to recur in other efforts at South–North cosmopolitan legality. The strength of this pressure is directly related to the degree of asymmetry prevailing between the Northern participants in such cross-border efforts, and the Southern counterparts with whom they are brought together by the occurrence of new global contact points. A few brief examples should illustrate.

7.2.1 Global boundary crossing
Both efforts described above involved proposals for legal reform that were generated at sites where there was significant boundary crossing going on. Still, all boundary crossings are not equal. In the case of TIRN's cross-border labor rights exchanges, for instance, barriers of time, language, and other resources meant that trips by US participants to Mexico were brief, highly managed, exhausting, and filtered through human and all-too-uneven interpreters. Only rarely were the trips prepared for and followed up as thoroughly as the organizers and participants would have liked. Most travelers returned to disperse widely across our large state, reentering families and workplaces where few knew much about Mexico or the machinery of the global economy. Although most did find multiple ways to bring back news of their trip, the scope and duration of these efforts was limited. Maintaining significant direct contact between individual travelers to the border and the Mexican workers and activists they met there has proven to be extremely difficult. Conditions at the border are chaotic; resources for organizations there are thin; and no stable independent union locals exist at the border that could support and facilitate ongoing, in-depth communication.

In the case of the driver's license fight, of course the whole context was created by a massive wave of literal boundary crossings – the surge of undocumented immigrants across the US–Mexico border. However, the campaign itself did little in its public manifestations to encourage two-way crossing – that is, to help native-born Tennesseans explore the realities and life experiences of their new immigrant neighbors. The coalition made a decision to address the issue only in terms of the perceived self-interest and existing experience of US citizens. This internal focus may have contributed to the short-term success of the campaign, but it allowed only a severely curtailed set of issues to make it into the foreground. Perhaps as a tactical matter the choice was a correct one that will support stronger work in the future, but in the short-term certainly, this struggle lacked a cosmopolitan face.

7.2.2 Horizontal understanding

The two cases recounted here also differ on the second marker of cosmopolitan legality. TIRN's work was overtly and insistently horizontal in its rhetoric. The trips were billed as "worker-to-worker exchanges" that were intended to build global solidarity and understanding among workers who were being mutually and similarly exploited in the global economy, often by the self-same corporations. Orientation meetings stressed the difference between charity and solidarity, and many people talked about the common interests shared by workers in Tennessee and in Mexico.

Nevertheless, all of us participants were attempting to adopt this frame of reference against powerful pulls in the other direction. Deeply ingrained ideas about US superiority and Mexican subordination, about US resources and Mexican need, were hard to dislodge. Once present in Mexico, for instance, some well-meaning US travelers were overcome with the desire to help poor children, perhaps to pass out small change or candy they had stashed in their purses. Others rejected the notion of solving big social problems through tiny donations of material aid, but still found it hard to kick other versions of *noblesse oblige*. An observation I heard more than once was a remark to the effect that "we need to send some people down here to help them learn how to organize."[6] Horizontal understandings across sharp disparities are tough.

---

[6] I recall no apparent recognition of the irony embedded in this remark, given the precipitous decline in US union membership.

7.2.3 Legal claims integrated with politics

Although both of the efforts presented here were integrated into ongoing political mobilizations and coalition-building activity, both cases revealed problems likely to face groups that mobilize politically in the North around global issues.

Santos suggests that there is no single polis for cosmopolitan legality, that efforts will be "transcalar" and "voracious" in seeking local and global sites for doing law (2002:468). I agree. Nevertheless, it is important to recognize that Northern groups in general, and US groups in particular, have access to polities that are importantly constituted by global exclusion. They will and should mount activities in these exclusionary and privileged fora. But, when they do, they will face the pull of anti-cosmopolitan forces, and in a context where their global allies have no official right even to be heard, much less to demand accountability.

In the anti-NAFTA fight, for instance, one wing of the generally progressive coalition in the US was drawn into an intense focus on winning the vote in Congress, a focus that led them into alliances with anti-internationalist and anti-immigrant groups. A somewhat parallel dynamic was at work in the driver's license campaign. The point here is not to denounce all short-term coalitions. Nor is it to suggest that power differences and coalitional dilemmas would disappear if we could only transpose struggles around legality to some global level that transcended the exclusionary boundaries of spatial polities. But figuring out how to do internationalist politics within local or national polities clearly poses a serious challenge for cosmopolitan law-makers and law-breakers.

If Northern groups and individuals want to help make the politics that must be inseparable from cosmopolitan legality, we will need to adapt countervailing strategies that take into account the sharp disparities and power differences that privilege our positions and make it hard for us to read the world. Whether and to what extent a variegated and unequal "we" in the US, or in the global North generally, can succeed at such an effort is certainly an open question.

7.3 CONVERGENCE?

This chapter has reported on two embryonic efforts at cosmopolitan law-making that emerged from situations where the processes of world economic integration brought previously separated people into new kinds of contact. One effort was triggered by mass labor migration, the other by capital flight, two different phenomena associated with globalization, both of which impose powerful impacts on sending and receiving locations alike. Through the line of the narrative I have shared thus far, the two spheres of activity followed largely separate paths. In the fall of 2003, however, a high-profile national mobilization provided the occasion for a moment of local convergence between the two.

The high-profile national event was the Immigrant Workers Freedom Ride, launched by the AFL-CIO to dramatize its new position on immigrants' rights and immigration policy, and to help restart the momentum on immigrant legalization that had been lost in the turbulent wake of September 11. Together with a broad coalition of civil rights and immigrants' rights organizations, the labor federation announced that eighteen buses filled with immigrants and their supporters would set forth from locations all over the United States to converge on Washington, DC, and then caravan to a site overlooking the Statue of Liberty in New York harbor (Greenhouse 2003a, 2003b, 2003c). The ride was not designed to promote any one piece of legislation, but aimed instead to create a vivid symbolic event and to frame the question of immigration reform in a progressive way. The publicity stressed four key requirements for a just immigration policy: (1) a "road to citizenship" for immigrant workers (an implicit critique of any Bush-style guestworker programs offering no possibility of eventual legalization); (2) a right to family reunification; (3) protection of workplace rights and standards for all workers: and (4) civil rights and civil liberties for all people.

When plans for the ride were made public in spring 2003, conditions were ripe in Tennessee for local groups to get involved. The networks of people advocating for immigrants had become sufficiently strong and interconnected, and the unions had become sufficiently convinced about the importance of a new immigration policy for labor, that both were ready to sign on. Groups and individuals associated with TIRN's fair trade work joined forces with churches and with immigrants' rights organizations that had been active in the driver's license campaign to build local committees. Four buses ended up coming through the state, tracing two different routes to Washington, and stopping in many different Tennessee communities along the way.

In Knoxville, my home, the stop-over event was amazing. Over 200 people crowded around the steps at Sacred Heart Cathedral to await the freedom riders. When two long charter buses pulled up at the church, a mass of rumpled immigrants and their co-riders came piling off. They nodded and smiled toward our greetings, but were obviously intent on a task of their own, and they asked the crowd to go back inside the church and wait for them there. They wanted to make a proper entrance. We did as requested and had just gotten ourselves settled in the pews, when we heard a stir behind us. In a moment the whole assembly was on its feet, excited to see a spirited procession entering the building and starting down the aisle of the cathedral.

At the head of the column was a brown-faced Latino immigrant. Held high in his hand was a flaming torch, its base the familiar cone-shape of the one lifted by the Statue of Liberty. In the low light of the church sanctuary, it cast a brilliant glow on the torchbearer's face. He was smiling broadly, as were the people who walked in a multiracial line immediately behind him, a US flag stretched between them at chest height. A long procession of cheering freedom riders flowed out behind these leaders and swept past us, down the aisle and toward the altar at the front of the sanctuary, as the long double file and the whole cathedral full of people chanted with and to each other "¡Sí se puede! ¡Sí se puede! ¡Sí se puede!"[7] over and over, and not willing to stop –not for many minutes after the group of riders were all aligned before us, down front and beaming, in tired but glorious array.

In the jubilant pews that evening were a number of people who had been on TIRN trips to Mexico in past years, along with others who had worked on the driver's license campaign, and yet others I had never seen before. To someone like me who had been a participant-observer in both of the separate strands of aspiring cosmopolitan legality described here, it was a real high point to see and feel the two coming together. Over the clapping hands and cheering voices, I could see in the eyes of many others that they felt the same.[8]

Perhaps the feelings of hope and inspiration that washed over many of us that night suggest a closer look at the freedom ride. For all its brevity and superficiality, for all the difficulties it could not paper over, for all the ways it was nowhere near enough, for all the contradictions whose depths it did not plumb – I believe the Immigrant Worker Freedom Ride was a real and hopeful sign of nascent cosmopolitan

---

[7] "¡Sí se puede!" is the signature chant of the exuberant union of California farm workers led by César Chávez in the 1960s. It has since become a widely shared expression used by immigrants' rights and other social justice groups, Latino and otherwise. It translates to something like "Yes, it can be done," "Yes, it is possible," "Yes, we can do it."

[8] Photographs and a brief description of the Knoxville stop ended up on the website of the national Immigrant Workers Freedom Ride Coalition. See www.iwfr.org/knoxville.asp.

legality. In its iridescent, unstable, simultaneous evocation of the
national and the global, it may be pointing toward possible solutions
to some of the problems I have tried to outline above. A couple of weeks
after that night at the cathedral, I received the following e-mail, sent
out over a listserv that links lawyers and others interested in the rights
of low-wage immigrant workers:

> I am back [in Washington state] after the Immigrant Workers Freedom
> Ride, exhausted and exhilarated at the same time, and want to share
> with you a bit of the experience.
>
> The Seattle bus consisted of 50 incredible people from 22 different
> countries. We sang in Indonesian and learned to say, "¡Sí se puede!" in
> nine languages. We rallied with meatpacking workers in Washington,
> Iowa and Nebraska, farmworkers in Idaho, janitors in Ohio and DC.,
> and members of many immigrant communities, including a memorable
> dinner in Columbus with members of the large Somali community
> there. We cried at the amazing stories of the struggles and bravery of
> the people on our bus, shared some tense moments when an elusive INS
> check point outside of Denver was rumored to be in our future, and
> cheered each other on as our bus members spoke of their own lives and
> related them to the struggles of immigrants from every country who live
> in this country. For the first time in my adult life, I felt comfortable
> carrying a [US] flag to rallies, because our bus was a true reflection of the
> face of this country, and of our most sacred principles.[9]

All people in all nations who aspire to be part of something like a
cosmopolitanism of the oppressed will meet challenges concerning
which people can best reflect the face of their country, and what
principles should be deemed its most sacred, and how those faces and
principles relate to the larger world. I hope the two case studies presented
here have provided some food for thought on the possibilities and
challenges facing those of us in the US and in the global North, who
surely confront these problems in a particularly sharp and urgent way.

References

Alvarez, José. 1997. "Critical Theory and the North American Free Trade
Agreement's Chapter Eleven." *University of Miami Inter-American Law
Review* 28:303–312.

Ansley, Fran. 1992. "North American Free Trade Agreement: The Public Debate."
Georgia Journal of International and Comparative Law 22:329–468.

[9] E-mail to author, dated October 6, 2003, from Rebecca Smith, sent out over the Immigrant
Employment Rights listserv of the National Employment Law Project.

1993. "Standing Rusty and Rolling Empty: Law, Poverty and America's Eroding Industrial Base." *Georgetown Law Journal* 81:1757–1896.

1995. "The Gulf of Mexico, the Academy, and Me." *Soundings* 78:68–104.

1998. "Rethinking Law in Globalizing Labor Markets." *University of Pennsylvania Journal of Labor and Employment Law* 1:369–427.

2001. "Inclusive Boundaries and Other (Im)possible Paths Toward Community Development in a Global World." *University of Pennsylvania Law Review* 150:353–417.

Ansley, Fran, and Susan Williams. 1999. "Southern Women and Southern Borders on the Move: Tennessee Workers Explore the New International Division of Labor." In *Neither Separate Nor Equal: Women, Race and Class in the US South*, edited by Barbara Ellen Smith. Philadelphia: Temple University Press.

Aponte, Robert, and Marcelo Siles. 1994. "Latinos in the Heartland: The Browning of the Midwest." Research Report No. 5, Julian Samora Research Institute, Michigan State University, East Lansing, MI (www.jsri.msu.edu/RandS/research/irr/rr05abs.html).

Brecher, Jeremy, Tim Costello, and Brendan Smith. 2002. *Globalization from Below: The Power of Solidarity*. Cambridge, MA: South End Press.

Buchanan, Patrick. 1991. *America Asleep: The Free Trade Syndrome and the Global Economic Challenge: A New Conservative Foreign Economic Policy for America*. Washington, DC: US Industrial Council Educational Foundation.

2002. *The Death of the West: How Dying Populations and Immigrant Invasions Imperil Our Country and Civilization*. New York: St. Martin's Press.

Cavanagh, John, Sarah Anderson, and Karen Hansen-Kuhn. 2001. "Crossborder Organizing Around Alternatives to Free Trade: Lessons from the NAFTA/FTAA Experience." In *Global Citizen Action*, edited by Michael Edwards and John Gaventa. Boulder: Lynne Rienner Publishers.

Crossborder Network for Justice and Solidarity (CBN). 2002. "About" and "History" (www.crossbordernetwork.org/about.html).

Disney, Kristi. 2003. "Building a Movement on Both Sides of the Border." In *The Global Activists' Manual: Local Ways to Change the World*, edited by Michael Prokosch and Laura Raymond. Boston: South End Press.

Edwards, Michael, and John Gaventa (Eds.). 2001. *Global Citizen Action*. Boulder: Lynne Rienner Publishers.

Ely, Jacob. 2000. "LION Immigration Policy: Local Labor/Community Alliance Participates in the Change in AFL-CIO Immigration Policy" (www.laborcenter.berkeley.edu/immigrantworkers/lionsactions.shtml).

Federation for American Immigration Reform (FAIR). 2002. "FAIR's Work Against Licenses for Illegal Aliens" (www.fairus.org/Research/Research.cfm).

Fink, Leon. 2003. *The Maya of Morganton: Work and Community in the Nuevo New South.* Chapel Hill, NC: University of North Carolina Press.

Gaventa, John. 1999. "Crossing the Great Divide: Building Links Between NGOs and Community Based Organizations in North and South." In *International Perspectives on Voluntary Action: Reshaping the Third Sector,* edited by David Lewis. London: Earthscan Publications.

Gordon, Jennifer. 1995. "We Make the Road by Walking: Immigrant Workers, the Workplace Project, and the Struggle for Social Change." *Harvard Civil-Rights Civil-Liberties Law Review* 30:407–450.

Greenhouse, Steven. 2003a. "Riding Across America for Immigrant Workers." *New York Times,* September 17.

2003b. "Immigrant Workers Share a Bus and Hopes." *New York Times,* September 28.

2003c. "Immigrants Rally in City Seeking Rights." *New York Times,* October 5.

Guzman, Betsy. 2001. "The Hispanic Population: Census 2000 Brief." Washington, DC: US Census Bureau (www.census.gov/prod/2001pubs/).

Hansen-Kuhn, Karen. 2001. "Opposition to Free Trade is Internationalist, Not Isolationist." Washington, DC: Development GAP (www.art-us.org/docs/isolationists/).

Hathaway, Dale. 2000. *Allies Across the Border: Mexico's "Authentic Labor Front" and Global Solidarity.* Cambridge, MA: South End Press.

Hernandez, Juan. 2001. "Immigrants Want to Obey the Law." Letter to the editor, The Tennessean, June 19.

Klein, Naomi. 2000. *No Logo.* New York: Picador.

Lowell, B. Lindsay, and Roberto Suro. 2002. *How Many Undocumented: The Numbers Behind the US–Mexico Migration Talks.* Washington, DC: Pew Hispanic Center.

Lynd, Staughton. 1982. *The Fight Against Shutdowns: Youngstown's Steel Mill Closings.* San Pedro: Singlejack Books.

1987. "The Genesis of the Idea of a Community Right to Industrial Property in Youngstown and Pittsburgh, 1977–1987." *Journal of American History* 74:926–958.

Mendoza, Marcela. 2002. *Latino Immigrant Women in Memphis.* Memphis: University of Memphis Center for Research on Women.

Mendoza, Marcela, David H. Ciscel, and Barbara Ellen Smith. 2001. *Latino Immigrants in Memphis, Tennessee: Their Local Economic Impact.* Memphis: University of Memphis Center for Research on Women.

National Immigration Law Center (NILC). 2002. "Immigrant Driver's License Proposals and Campaigns: Surprising Progress Since 9/11." *Immigrants' Rights Update,* web edition, May 14 (www.nilc.org/immspbs/).

2004. "2004 State Driver's License Proposals" (www.nilc.org/immspbs/DLs/state_DL_proposals/).

Nissen, Bruce. (Ed.). 2002. *Unions in a Globalized Environment: Changing Borders, Organizational Boundaries, and Social Roles*. Armonk, NY: M. E. Sharpe.

Ojeda, Martha. 1999. "Coalition for Justice in the Maquiladoras: An Interview with Martha Ojeda." Albany, CA: Information Services Latin America (www.isla.igc.org/Features/Border/mex2.html).

Perot, H. Ross (with Pat Choate). 1993. *Save Your Job, Save Our Country: Why NAFTA Must Be Stopped – Now!* Westport, CT: Hyperion Press.

Prokosch, Michael, and Laura Raymond. (Eds.). 2003. *The Global Activists' Manual: Local Ways to Change the World*. Boston: South End Press.

Ranney, David. 2003. *Global Decisions, Local Collisions: Urban Life in the New World Order*. Philadelphia: Temple University Press.

Rupert, Mark. 1995. "(Re)Politicizing the Global Economy: Liberal Common Sense and Ideological Struggle in the US NAFTA Debate." *Review of International Political Economy* 2:658–692.

Santos, Boaventura de Sousa. 2002. *Toward a New Legal Common Sense: Law, Globalization, and Emancipation*. London: Butterworths.

Semien, John. 2001. "Driver's License Stampede: Stress Runs High at Testing Stations." *Commercial Appeal*, June 18.

Smith, Barbara Ellen. 2001. *The New Latino South: An Introduction*. Memphis: Center for Research on Women.

Smith, Rebecca, and Amy Sugjmori. 2003. "Low Pay, High Risk: State Models for Advancing Immigrant Workers' Rights." New York: National Employment Law (www.nelp.org/iwp/reform/state/low_pay_high_risk.cfm).

Stammers, Neil. 1999. "Social Movements and the Social Construction of Human Rights." *Human Rights Quarterly* 21:980–1008.

TIRN. 1993. "From the Mountains to the Maquiladoras" (video). Knoxville: TIRN.

Weinbaum, Eve. 2004. *To Move a Mountain: Fighting the Global Economy in Appalachia*. New York: The New Press.

Whitaker, Monica. 2001a. "Immigrants Jam License Lines: Delays Spur Complaints to Workers, Lawmakers." *The Tennessean*, May 17.

2001b. "Lines Thinning at Stations for Driver's License Testing: Effort Continues to Repeal Law Easing Process of Immigrants." *The Tennesseean*, July 11.

Williams, Susan. 2002. "The Power of Voices: The Tennessee Industrial Renewal Network." In *Teaching for Change: Popular Education and the Labor Movement*, edited by Linda Delp, Miranda Outman-Kramer, Susan J. Schurman, and Kent Wong. Los Angeles: UCLA Center for Labor Research and Education.

PART TWO

TRANSNATIONAL SOCIAL MOVEMENTS AND THE RECONSTRUCTION OF HUMAN RIGHTS

CHAPTER 8

LIMITS OF LAW IN COUNTER-HEGEMONIC GLOBALIZATION: THE INDIAN SUPREME COURT AND THE NARMADA VALLEY STRUGGLE

*Balakrishnan Rajagopal**

8.1 INTRODUCTION

Popular struggles have an ambivalent relationship with the law. At one level, they tend to see law as a force for status quo and domination, which must either be contested as part of a larger political struggle or largely ignored as irrelevant. Yet, they can hardly avoid the law as it also provides them space for resistance. Indeed, there is an increasing sensibility that law is a terrain of contestation between different actors including social movements and states, and that a theory of law or adjudication that ignores this fact is inadequate. There are several reasons why this is so under conditions of globalization. First, law operates at multiple scales under globalization, that is, simultaneously at the international, national, and local levels. As such, it provides much greater opportunity to use law as a tool of contestation by social movements who can deploy legal tools at one level against another (Klug 2000; Santos 2002). Secondly, the forces that social movements are up against in their counter-hegemonic struggles are often a combination of local and global elites, and that in turn defines the space for a

* I thank Prashant Bhushan for providing generous access to the legal papers, including submissions of counsel, relating to the Narmada dispute. Much work on this paper was done during my sabbatical stay as a Visiting Fellow at the Centre for Law and Governance, Jawaharlal Nehru University, Delhi, and the Madras Institute for Development Studies, Chennai, during spring 2004. I am grateful to both institutions for their support. I thank the editors of this volume, Boaventura de Sousa Santos and César A. Rodríguez-Garavito, and Sally Engle Merry and Upendra Baxi for their helpful comments on a previous draft. Responsibility for all errors is mine.

politics of resistance that is neither purely local nor global (Klug 2000:50–51; see also Esteva and Prakash 1998). This is particularly so in the case of contestations over development (Khagram, Riker, and Sikkink 2002) and especially over large dams (World Commission on Dams 2000). Thirdly, there is a great deal of hybridization of law, not simply in the mode of *lex mercatoria* (Dezalay and Garth 1997), but through such means as judicial globalization (Slaughter 2000), world constitutionalism (Ackerman 1997), and global rule of law programs (Carothers 1998). Fourthly, there is an increasingly vertical and horizontal growth of international legal norms in areas such as human rights, indigenous peoples' rights, environment and sustainable development, and a proliferation of international judicial and political arenas where domestic decisions could be contested. This in turn creates political opportunities for making claims that derive their force from comparative and international legal developments.

Despite this encouraging pluralization of normative opportunities for contestation, the outcomes of social movements' engagements with the law are highly uncertain in terms of their impact either on law or on the movements themselves. Put differently, the pluralization of the normative space and the ability to contest seem to offer neither a guarantee of success for social movements that choose to engage law as part of their political mobilization nor propel law in the direction that is most helpful to movement goals. The outcomes of the dialectic between law and social movements seem to depend on a number of scripts that are both internal and external to law, and seem to depend on particular *local and national* contexts. These scripts need to be unearthed and examined to properly appreciate the role of law in counter-hegemonic globalization.

Furthermore, it is unclear how to judge the success of the outcomes of social movements' deployment of law and courts in their struggle. Both in law and social sciences, much debate surrounds this issue. Legal scholarship tends to celebrate the heroic role played by judges and lawyers, especially in "constitutional moments" when fundamental conflicts exist in society over the terms of political and social life. This tendency, no doubt more pronounced in common law jurisdictions, tends to reduce historical evolution of law to episodic interventions by charismatic judges, divorced from the social context in which such judges act (Strauss 1996). In the social sciences, it is hard to know how to evaluate the role played by law and courts in popular movements. Does one judge by the change in outcomes and, if so, should one focus on changes in public policy or private conduct? Should the focus be on the change in processes of decision-making and, if so, at what level? Or should the focus be on something more fundamental, on the changes in social and ethical values that are being contested? At the bottom of this debate is the question of to what extent law is separate from the social and the cultural.

In this chapter, I offer an analysis of the role of law in the Narmada Valley struggle, especially that which was waged by one of India's most prominent social movements in recent years, Narmada Bachao Andolan or NBA (Save the Narmada), with a specific focus on India's Supreme Court. The NBA rose in reaction to the Indian government's plan to construct a large number of dams along the Narmada River, contesting the relief and rehabilitation provided for displaced families at first, and subsequently challenging the dams themselves as being destructive. While the NBA is not the only social movement of the displaced people in the Narmada Valley, it is easily the most prominent and perhaps the largest, but I do focus on the struggle as a whole where it is appropriate. The focus in this chapter on the role played by law at multiple scales and by the Indian Supreme Court in the struggle waged by the NBA is particularly useful for understanding the role of law and courts in counter-hegemonic globalization for several reasons.

First, the resistance in the Narmada Valley is well known for its transnational character, both in the composition of the actors and in the terms with which the resistance in the valley was conducted. The resistance movement consisted not only of the displaced people in the valley, consisting of farmers, women, tribals, and local NGOs but also Western NGOs, transnational social movements, and other overseas actors, including individuals from the Indian Diaspora who were concerned about the social and environmental aspects of the dam projects. The protagonists of the dams included Western dam building multinational corporations, the World Bank, local Indian corporations, several Western governments, Indian state and federal governments, a plethora of local and foreign analysts and consultants, and sections of the Indian Diaspora. The actors were thus a mix of local, national, and global actors. The resistance was framed not simply in terms of local laws and the Indian constitution, but also in terms of international law and global public policy.

Secondly, the normative and institutional framework for the Narmada dam projects operated at many scales, from the global scale (international

institutions, global norms, and foreign investment), national scale (constitutional norms, statutes, and administrative mechanisms), to the local
scale (local criminal law, tribal rules, customary norms, and informal
property rules). At any given moment, the NBA was simultaneously
engaged with norms and institutions at multiple levels.

Thirdly, the Indian Supreme Court played a major role in the political
struggle of the NBA, by allowing it to contest the raising of the height of
a dam on the river, at first as part of a series of victories that the NBA was
notching up globally in the early 1990s, and then dealing it a major blow
in 2000 by allowing the height of the dam to be increased and the
construction to proceed with some conditions. As such, understanding
the role played by the Indian Supreme Court in the struggle waged by the
NBA may offer valuable lessons in understanding the relationship
between law, resistance, and courts in the context of globalization.

Fourthly, the Narmada Valley struggle may also offer some sobering
lessons in just how difficult it is to judge the role played by law and
courts in counter-hegemonic globalization. This is partly due to the
vast time frame within which the resistance evolved, at least over a
period of more than two decades and the episodic interaction between
the law and the actions of the NBA. It is also due to the difficulty of
deciding at just what point one must judge whether law has been
operating in either the hegemonic or the counter-hegemonic mode.
I would suggest that this compels us to adopt a much longer, historical
perspective on the law and globalization linkage.

In the light of these issues, I probe answers to several questions in this
chapter. They include: what levels of law (international, national, local)
did the NBA engage, and where and when was it able to have an impact
on the legal terrain? Conversely, how did law shape the NBA's strategies
and goals? Did its resort to law produce a hegemonic or a counter-
hegemonic outcome (Santos 2002; Santos and Rodríguez-Garavito's
chapter in this volume)? The remainder of the chapter is divided into
five parts. In the first part, I analyze the relationship between law,
globalization, and counter-hegemonic globalization, and try to identify
some key theoretical issues which are relevant to the NBA struggle. In
the second part, I discuss the evolution of the NBA's struggle and provide
background to the litigation before the Indian Supreme Court. In the
third, I discuss the judgment of the Indian Supreme Court and critique
what I call the dominant scripts that reveal the limits of law in counter-
hegemonic globalization and more broadly in the use of law in social
movement struggles. In the fourth section, I discuss three possible modes

of assessing the relationship between the NBA struggle and the law, and find that, while the relationship between the NBA struggle and the law was more positive at the international level, at the national and local levels it was much more oppositional. In the fifth part, I draw the overall conclusions on the role of law in counter-hegemonic globalization in the light of the NBA's experience.

8.2 LAW, SOCIAL MOVEMENTS AND COUNTER-HEGEMONIC GLOBALIZATION: SOME THEORETICAL ISSUES

There are several theoretical issues in thinking about the relationship between law and social movements in the context of counter-hegemonic globalization that are of relevance to the NBA's struggle. First, the distinction between international and domestic spheres that is so central to the self-constitution of law, with its disciplinary boundaries around the doctrine of sovereignty, makes little sense when we consider what social movements do. Social movements are increasingly organized to engage in political struggles at multiple levels from the local to the global (Khagram et al. 2002) whereas law structures social relations at multiple levels as well. As such, social movements use norms and institutions at multiple levels in framing their demands and engaging in action (Rajagopal 2003b). On the other hand, state sovereignty and the power it provides for groups who are in charge of the state continue to be dominant in determining the outcomes of social struggles. In particular, the outcomes of social movements' engagements with the law depend on the extent to which they can frame their demands and engage in struggles that avoid a direct confrontation with state sovereignty and its ideological foundation of developmental nationalism (Nandy 1992; Rajagopal 2003a). This confrontation cannot be avoided by social movements by taking recourse to law because law and courts share this ideology of developmental nationalism. The tension between the increasing ability of social movements to operate at multiple levels beyond state borders and the continuing importance of state sovereignty needs to lead to a critique of the ideological foundations of state sovereignty.

Secondly, the distinction between law and policy or between the domains of adjudication and administration continues to influence whether, how, and to what extent social movements will use law in their struggles and to what extent law will prove to be emancipatory. The self-image of law and adjudication as apolitical provides an ideological cover for the pursuit of private, partisan ends which are often dressed up as public interest (see Kennedy 1998). This operates in two ways. First, it operates to remove certain facts from the domain of public policy – and therefore of social movement pressure – on the ground that the "law" governs it. An example would be the way Article 262 of the constitution of India makes the adjudication of inter-state water disputes subject to the exclusive jurisdiction of specialized water disputes tribunals and, in that process, seeks to exclude both public participation in the settlement of water disputes and even judicial review by higher courts. Making water disputes an exclusive domain of bargaining and adjudication between states takes popular politics out of it. It also provides little incentives for social movements to try to influence the law that applies to water disputes as they are not given the right to do so. A second way in which the law–politics distinction works in determining whether law will be emancipatory is in drawing a sharp line between adjudication and administration. When faced with specific issues that raise questions of distribution of resources – such as most questions involved in development projects – the courts often take the view that their institutional role prevents them from acting on those issues. This may be due to a combination of factors including the institutional boundary between the courts and the executive, the lack of necessary expertise by judges to adjudicate complex policy questions, a concern over whether judicial orders will be enforced by the executive, the need for democratic accountability in decision-making processes that involve the distribution of resources and the very self-image of what judging is all about (Rosenberg 1991). Nevertheless, the consequence of this boundary drawing is that social movements are often prevented from successfully using law and the courts in challenging administrative or policy processes that do not operate in the public interest.

Thirdly, there are significant tensions between the internal logic of the law – its language, method, and sources of legitimacy – and the logic of social movement struggles (Rajagopal 2003a). The language of the law is specialized, measured, and, in postcolonial countries, often in a Western language. The language of social movements is explicitly oriented toward communicative action, and is therefore popular and local. These languages can often collide, producing moments of incompatibility that cannot be easily resolved. Social movements use methods of contestation that include the media, for instance. Once social movements judicialize their struggle by going to the court, they run into problems when they attempt to "speak" publicly on issues that are considered by the court to be *sub judice*. The courts may find it offensive and even contemptuous that social movements do not accept the finality of recourse to the judiciary and abandon their agitational strategies, but instead treat legal recourse as part of their agitations. This tension between the logic of the law and the logic of social movements is relevant to the NBA's engagement with the law, as I discuss below.

The source of law's legitimacy is also different from that of social movements. Law depends traditionally on sovereignty – and, by extension, on the latter's normative and institutional expressions in the constitution and formal democratic institutions. In the post-World War II era, the state – and therefore law – has also depended, for its legitimacy, on the idea of development, a substantive moral vision for the transformation of traditional societies into more modern ones in order to achieve better living standards (Nandy 1992). Social movements are often in tension with these sources of legitimacy. They may contest the constitution itself as morally and politically inadequate, as when they attempt to change approved constitutional doctrines and structures as enunciated by the judiciary and the legal elite (Siegel 2002). These interpretive acts by ordinary people, while unauthorized and even illegal, are in fact ubiquitous and a central part of the legal systems of most countries, taken in their totality. This argument is not novel but has been a staple of law and society scholarship (Fernandes and Varley 1998; Santos 2002) as well as constitutional law scholarship (Baxi 1987, 2003; Shivji 1995; Siegel 2002). They may find that formal democratic institutions fail them and therefore contest the meaning of democracy itself (Mamdani, Mkandawire and Wamba-dia-Wamba 1993). Social movements also often contest the ideology of development that is sought to be promoted by the state, when they find that such an ideology violates their rights. Indeed, as we will see, this was the case with the NBA. As such, the logic of law and the logic of social movements have certain basic tensions which influence the outcome of social movements' engagement with the law.

Fourthly, the role of the domestic judiciary in a social movement campaign with transnational dimensions, such as that of the NBA, needs to be understood better. Currently, the dominant theoretical framework for understanding transnational social movement networks and their domestic impact on norm-creation and implementation, is to be found in the field of international relations (IR) theory (Keck and Sikkink 1998; Risse, Ropp, and Sikkink 1999). That framework usefully explains how domestic and transnational movements combine to bring pressure from "above" and "below" to compel governments to abide by human rights standards. Domestic NGOs, social movements and national opposition groups ally with members of transnational networks consisting of NGOs, churches, etc. and convince powerful external actors such as international organizations, foreign donor institutions, and other states to put pressure on the domestic government to alter its norm-violating behavior (Risse 2000:189). Models about how this dynamic between transnational and domestic social movements has an impact on enforcement of international human rights law are useful (Risse *et al.* 1999). But this model pays insufficient attention to the impact of domestic law on the dynamic, especially that of the domestic judiciary, and remains overwhelmingly focused on international law. Domestic judiciaries are embedded in their legal cultures and have distinctive traditions for incorporating international norms into domestic law which may impede the movement dynamics that IR theorists model. For example, a country such as South Africa, whose constitution explicitly asks its judiciary to interpret domestic laws in the light of applicable international law, is likely to be easier for the sort of transnational–local social movement linkages posited by IR theory. On the other hand, in countries such as the US, whose courts are notoriously unwilling to pay attention to international law while interpreting domestic law, or in India, where courts are unpredictable in reading international law into domestic law, domestic social movements often find it more difficult to link with transnational networks to enforce human rights.

Domestic judiciaries may intervene in movement dynamics in ways that reframe the issues, shift crucial resources available to social movements (such as moral capital) and generally depoliticize domestic social movements that in turn weakens its link with transnational social movement networks. Domestic judiciaries may do so, even when they adopt ostensibly progressive rulings using counter-hegemonic discourses such as human rights. IR theory does not pay sufficient attention to these issues. As will become clear during the discussion of the Indian Supreme Court's role in the NBA struggle, linkages between transnational and local social movements alone cannot explain why movements fail or succeed. After all, in the case of the Narmada Valley struggle, a vigorous dynamic continued to exist between transnational and local social movements, putting pressure on the governments from above and below, and yet it did not succeed in enforcing human rights and environmental norms partly because of the role played by India's Supreme Court and its legal framework. Domestic laws and institutions matter, and the constitutional texts – the literal and the social – matter too, in determining when counter-hegemonic globalization would be successful locally.

8.3 THE EVOLUTION OF THE NARMADA VALLEY STRUGGLE

In this section, I shall describe the evolution of the struggle in the Narmada Valley from 1979 until now, and the ways in which the Narmada struggle engaged with the law at multiple levels from the local to the international. It is not my intention here to provide an exhaustive factual background to the struggle but only to focus on the general outline and those specific facts which are relevant to the role of law in the struggle.[1]

8.3.1 Background

The Narmada River is India's fifth-longest river and one of the last major rivers to be dammed. The desire to build dams across the Narmada River, a westward-flowing river in the middle of India that crosses three state boundaries (Madhya Pradesh, Maharashtra, and Gujarat), in order to harness its water for drinking, irrigation, and power, had existed at least since the 1940s. But disputes soon arose between the states of Gujarat, Maharashtra, and Madhya Pradesh over the sharing of the costs and benefits of the project. To resolve the differences between these riparian states, the federal government of India constituted the Narmada Water Disputes Tribunal (hereinafter "the Tribunal") in 1969 under India's Interstate Water Disputes Act of 1956. The deliberations of the Tribunal were halted when Rajasthan and Madhya Pradesh moved the Supreme Court in 1972, thus involving the Court in a long and difficult relationship with the river valley projects that lasts even to today (Jayal 2001:155). After a political deal was made between the states on the availability and allocation of the water between the states, the height of the dam and the level of the canal from the dam, Madhya Pradesh and Rajasthan withdrew their petitions from the Supreme Court. Thereafter, in 1974, the Tribunal recommenced its work and gave its final award in 1978, which came into effect in December 1979.

---

[1] Several book-length studies and exhaustively researched chapters exist on the Narmada Valley struggle. See e.g. Fisher (1995); Baviskar (1995); Sangvai (2000); Jayal (2001); and Khagram (2002). See also Rajagopal (2003a:122–127).

8.3.2 The struggle in and around the law: 1979–1994

There were three stages in the evolution of the struggle in the Narmada Valley between 1979 and 1994 which have a major bearing on their relationship to law. The first stage was between 1979 and 1988 when the key issue was the content of the resettlement and rehabilitation package for the people who would be displaced. The second stage, from 1988 to 1991, saw a stalemate and hardening of the positions between the protagonists and antagonists, an increasing focus on environmental issues and mass action, and more state repression and confrontation. During these two stages, the forces in favor of the dam projects as well as the resistance against the projects were operating at multiple levels, from the local to the global, but the domestic courts played a minor role in the struggle. During the third stage, between 1991 and 1994, the Narmada Valley struggle became both less internationalized as the World Bank funding stopped in 1993, as well as more judicialized due to the involvement of the Indian Supreme Court. Local and international legal norms, as well as local and international institutions including the courts, were significantly influential in determining the direction and pace of the struggle in the valley, but the degrees of influence varied across the three stages.

The dam projects were already embedded in a maze of local laws that determined the outer limits of what claims the struggle against the dams could make. Applicable land law was governed by a range of instruments including the Indian Forest Act 1927, the Forest Conservation Act 1980, the Land Acquisition Act 1894, the Transfer of Property Act 1882 and the Indian constitutional provisions concerning right to property and special provisions concerning the right of tribal people over their land. They also potentially included land rights under private law doctrines and religious law. But none of these laws provided land rights to the tribal inhabitants of forests who lacked formal titles of ownership. Even land owners were afforded only cash compensation in case of acquisition, under the Land Acquisition Act. Indeed, it is perhaps for these reasons that India never had (and still does not have) a national policy on resettlement and rehabilitation. It is in that light that one must view the award of the Tribunal in 1979, which was a watershed in offering land for land as compensation, but fundamentally flawed because it left tribal and other affected peoples out of its ambit.

In addition to the land laws and the Tribunal's award, the struggle against the dams was also embedded in other local laws, such as local criminal laws that enabled state repression including section 144 of India's Criminal Procedure Code (which imposes a curfew and prevents the assembly of more than four persons) and the Official Secrets Act. Within the limits of these laws, the people affected by the dams were severely restricted not only in *making* certain claims but also in *using* certain methods to claim their rights. Their land rights were not recognized; they could not get information about the projects; and they could not assemble to protest or stage peaceful demonstrations without inviting state violence. As such, the political opportunity structures for the struggle against the dams were severely constrained.

The projects were transnationalized from their conception. The World Bank sent its first mission in late 1979 to Gujarat and helped to get US$10 million from the United Nations Development Program (UNDP) for the basic planning of the projects (Khagram 2002:210). The involvement of the Bank transnationalized the projects at three levels.[2] First, it functioned as a seal of approval that brought several other foreign actors into the projects. Secondly, the Bank's involvement opened the door for a transnationalization of the political arena and the entry of transnational NGOs who used international legal norms relating to human rights and the environment to hold the Bank and the borrower country accountable. Thirdly, the Bank's own internal policies, known as Operational Manual statements, provided a set of soft international law standards for judging the performance of the projects on the ground in areas such as involuntary resettlement.[3]

The popular resistance to the Narmada projects began barely a week after the Tribunal had given its award in 1979 (Khagram 2002:209), though in some parts of Madhya Pradesh, agitation had begun as early as 1978 (Jayal 2001:162). In what is perhaps the first encounter between the popular resistance and the courts, a group of tribals moved the Gujarat High Court in early 1984 with the assistance of Arch-Vahini, a local NGO, to enforce promises made by the government regarding resettlement and rehabilitation (Patel 1995:183). The government was forced to compromise. Disagreements over the rights of tribal people who did not have formal property rights to their land emerged as the main one in the negotiations between the government of Gujarat and the World Bank over the loan agreement, which was

---

[2] I borrow this framing from Fisher (1995:19).
[3] See e.g. Operational Manual statement 2.33, February 1980, on involuntary resettlement (since superseded by OMS 4.30, June 1990); OMS 2.34, 1982, on tribals in Bank projects; and OMS 2.36, 1984, on environmental guidelines.

signed in 1985. After a futile wait for a new policy from the government of Gujarat on this issue, and for the release of the World Bank loan document which had been signed, Arch-Vahini and other NGOs moved the Supreme Court for the first time in 1985. Although the government of Gujarat stated in the proceedings that encroachers had no rights (Khagram 2002:214), the court issued an interim injunction against displacement (Patel 1995:187). Independently of this, another group, the Narmada Dharangrasta Samiti, had filed legal challenges to land acquisition at the local courts in Maharashtra, but without success (Sangvai 2000:154). Despite this brief involvement of the courts in the struggle against displacement, they remained marginal. The injunctions had not been against construction of the dam per se, and the courts never grappled with the question of what rights the so-called encroachers actually had under Indian law (Patel 1995:188). As a result, the construction of the dams continued even as Arch-Vahini and other groups managed to extract a progressive policy on resettlement and rehabilitation from the government of Gujarat in 1987, ensuring a minimum of five acres of land for land owners and extending its package to encroachers as well. However, this policy was constantly breached. Thus, until 1988, the focus of domestic mobilization remained largely on obtaining better terms of resettlement and rehabilitation for the displaced people in the valley, and the access to courts was a notable but not a particularly significant part of this mobilization.

The groups working on resettlement and rehabilitation had better success at the international level. An alliance between Arch-Vahini and Oxfam UK led to the formation of a transnational campaign focused on the role of the World Bank in the project (Khagram 2002). The World Bank also came under pressure from NGOs like Survival International, which charged that India was violating the rights of tribal people under International Labour Organization (ILO) Convention No. 107, to which it was a party, due to the dam construction. In 1986, NGOs petitioned the ILO's Committee of Experts to investigate possible violations of Convention No. 107 relating to the rights of indigenous peoples. That led to a warning from the Committee of Experts to the World Bank and the Indian government which acknowledged their duty to comply with the Convention. Although the World Bank pressured the Gujarat government to improve its package for the displaced people, in the end it signed the loan agreement in 1985 with the government. Put differently, the Narmada Valley struggle had some limited impact on the international legal rules and institutions concerning resettlement and on the World Bank. Domestic policy on resettlement in Gujarat was formally changed due to the struggle but implementation on the ground remained very poor.

On the environmental front, there were major encounters between the Narmada Valley struggle and the law. In the late 1980s, a new transnational environmental coalition emerged and used the political opportunities provided by the World Bank's own 1984 guidelines as well as emerging norms of international environmental law, for the struggle in the valley. At the core of this coalition was a domestic social movement, the NBA. The NBA was formed in 1989, as a social movement of affected communities, domestic NGOs, and individuals drawn from all over India but consisting mainly of the Narmada Dharangrast Samiti from Maharashtra, the Narmada Ghati Navnirman Samiti from Madhya Pradesh, and the Narmada Asargrastha Sangharsh Samiti from Gujarat (Jayal 2001:163).

A successful international campaign led by the NBA, with the participation of NGOs drawn from several countries from Europe, North America, and Japan, forced the World Bank to commission an unprecedented independent review of the dam projects in 1991 which found that the World Bank had failed to comply with its own guidelines (Morse and Berger 1992). Meanwhile, domestic agitations in the valley intensified and confrontations with the state increased as the state pursued more and more aggressive tactics to counter the successes of the Narmada Valley movement. The construction of the Sardar Sarover dam had continued as there had been no injunction against it. The Gujarat state in particular, began treating the dam construction as part of an ideology of cultural nationalism, and branding all opponents as "enemies of Gujarat" (Jayal 2001:164). In 1989, Gujarat politicians from across various party lines criticized the dam critics as anti-national agents of foreign interests and adopted a resolution in the state assembly supporting the project. A sophisticated media campaign was launched by the proponents of the dam, led by Sardar Sarover Nigam Limited.[4] Meanwhile, the NBA had intensified mass resistance through direct action in the valley, and the goal of the struggle had changed at this stage to demand a comprehensive reevaluation of the whole project, not just better terms of resettlement and rehabilitation. Thus, the goal of the struggle in the valley had shifted from a focus on

---

[4] Sardar Sarover Nigam Limited was established in April 1988 in Gujarat as an autonomous corporation responsible for the implementation of the Sardar Sarover dam project.

resettlement to a comprehensive questioning of the whole project through confrontation and mass action from 1988 to 1991.

Between 1991 and 1994, the Narmada Valley struggle became even more internationalized as well as more judicialized. The independent review team, appointed by the World Bank, concluded in its report in June 1992 that the project was "flawed" and that the World Bank should "step back" from the project. Citing hostility in the valley and local opposition to the project, the report also stated that "progress will be impossible except as a result of unacceptable practices" (Morse and Berger 1992:356). As a result, the World Bank worked out a face-saving formula with the Indian government whereby the Indian government would announce that it was asking the World Bank to cancel the remaining US$170 million of the US$450 million loan and that it would complete the project on its own.[5] This was announced in March 1993.

Despite this success at the international level, the situation in the valley was grim and the NBA and its allies were taking recourse to courts in desperation. A flurry of legal action followed. As early as 1990, the villages that were scheduled to be submerged were beginning to be cleared in Maharashtra. The submergence and the displacement were challenged in the Bombay High Court in 1990, which restrained the government from forcible evictions which it had, in an earlier case,[6] eloquently declared as unconstitutional. Despite this, the construction of the Sardar Sarover dam proceeded apace, even as forced evictions and agitations continued. In 1991, Dr. B. D. Sharma, the Commissioner of Scheduled Castes and Tribes, a statutory authority in India, filed an interlocutory appeal in a case concerning tribal rights in the Supreme Court. In its order,[7] the court laid down some provisions concerning resettlement, including the provision that resettlement should be completed at least six months before submergence (Sangvai 2000:154) and directed the three state governments to ensure that rehabilitation would be consistent with Article 21 (right to life) of the constitution. However, the court also declared that it would like the work on the dam to be expedited, even though it had not been asked to pronounce on the viability of the dam itself (Jayal 2001:185). For the movement in the valley, it would be a foretaste of things to come, as the court had already

---

[5] Some think that the Indian government merely ended up diverting World Bank funds from other sectoral loans to India toward the Narmada dam project (Udall 1995:220).

[6] See *Olga Tellis v. Bombay Municipal Corporation*, AIR 1986 SC 180.

[7] *B. D. Sharma v. Union of India*, 1992 Supp (3) SCC 93.

taken sides in the more fundamental debate over the viability of the project, that the movement had put on the agenda since 1988. Several legal challenges were also leveled in local courts and the Bombay High Court in Maharashtra in 1992 and 1993, against forced evictions, deforestation, and police atrocities, but these cases got nowhere as the courts either avoided cases emerging from the valley or were awed into silence by the specter of confrontation with the forces behind India's largest development project (Sangvai 2000:155).

Meanwhile, direct non-violent confrontation was escalating in the valley. A new *satyagraha* (a non-violent struggle) at Manibeli, launched by the NBA during the monsoon in 1993, forced the federal government to announce that there would be a review of the project. A five-member expert review panel was appointed by the government to review the project, though without the power to revisit the viability of the project itself. Despite this somewhat favorable outcome for the NBA, repression by state police forces continued in the villages in Maharashtra and Gujarat. A petition filed by the Lok Adhikar Sangh, an oustees' rights group in Gujarat, in 1991, resulted in a judgment by the Gujarat High court in April 1993 (Sangvai 2000:155). That court ruled that the submergence of the first six villages without resettlement was illegal, and in February 1994 ruled that no further work on the dam which would cause further submergence could proceed. Despite this, the Gujarat government and the Sardar Sarover Nigam Limited (SSNL) continued their work on the dam and, in February 1994 closed the sluice gates of the dam, causing the waters to rise and leading to permanent submergence (Sangvai 2000:155). The struggle in the valley was in a desperate situation as a result, and the NBA decided to approach the Supreme Court for relief.

8.3.3 The struggle through the law?: 1994–2000

The NBA filed a petition before the Supreme Court in May 1994, challenging the Sardar Sarover project on many grounds, calling for a comprehensive review of the project, and prayed for a court order stopping all construction and displacement until such a review was done. This petition was admitted by the court as a form of public interest litigation[8] by a bench which had a pro-human rights, liberal

---

[8] See Baxi (1987); and Desai and Muralidhar (2000).

character.[9] The decision to approach the court had been taken after much internal deliberation and disagreement within the NBA as there were many who felt that the courts were elitist and not favorably disposed toward the struggle in the valley (Patkar 1995; Sangvai 2000:152). As counsel for the NBA said, at first the NBA was reluctant to approach the court as it was felt that the courts were "protectors of the powerful."[10] Nevertheless, the NBA had to approach the Supreme Court because of the desperate situation in the valley and its inability to obtain relief through either the lower judiciary or governmental mechanisms.[11] Water was rising in the valley as a result of the decision of the SSNL to close the sluice gates of the dam in February 1994, and the lower judiciary was being openly defied by the Gujarat government. It was a classic example of the lack of any legal remedy for gross violations of law and human rights.

The first significant act of the court was to order the report of the five-member expert panel, which had been released in July 1994, to be made public. That report was accordingly made public in late 1994, and it confirmed the findings of the World Bank's independent review. It concluded that the hydrology of the river was not known, and it criticized the poor record of resettlement and rehabilitation. The Supreme Court also ordered the federal and state governments to make submissions on all aspects of the dam and to discuss all the issues arising out of the five-member panel report in a Narmada Control Authority (NCA) meeting (Sangvai 2000:70).

Meanwhile, in early 1994, the new Chief Minister of Madhya Pradesh, Mr. Digvijay Singh, had openly begun campaigning for reducing the height of the dam from 455 feet to 436 feet.[12] This move was intended to save 30,000 people and 6,500 hectares of land in Madhya Pradesh from submergence (Jayal 2001:188). Taken together, the release of the five-member panel report and the decision of the Chief Minister of Madhya Pradesh, effectively operated to reopen the Narmada water dispute which had purportedly been finally settled by the Tribunal's award in 1979. Indeed, in the Chief Minister's own

---

[9] The bench that accepted the petition consisted of Chief Justice M. N. Venkatachalliah, Justice J. S. Verma, and Justice S. P. Barucha. At least the first two justices had a pro-human rights, liberal reputation by that time. The importance of having friendly justices on the bench would become more and more obvious in the coming years.
[10] Interview with Prashant Bhushan, counsel to NBA, New Delhi, February 17, 2004.
[11] Ibid.
[12] He had sent a letter to that effect to the Prime Minister in March 1994 (Sangvai 2000:67).

words before the state assembly on December 16, 1994, "the Supreme Court has virtually reopened the whole issue and now we are no longer bound by the Narmada tribunal award … no further construction on the SSP would be allowed if the oustees were not rehabilitated at least six months before the submergence."[13] Combined with two negative Madhya Pradesh state assembly reports on the dam project in 1994 (Jayal 2001:190), the inter-state dimension of the dispute reared its head once again. Protests in the valley continued in late 1994, with the affected people engaging in various forms of direct political action such as *dharnas* and indefinite fasts. In the light of these developments, and in view of the Supreme Court proceedings, the NCA decided to suspend the river bed construction of the dam in December 1994. In May 1995, the Supreme Court confirmed this decision through a stay order on further construction of the dam. The NBA's struggle in the valley seemed to have achieved victory, but it would prove to be fleeting.

Even as the river bed construction of the dam was suspended formally by the NCA and the Supreme Court, the construction continued on the ground in violation of these orders. To contest this, the NBA organized a massive march on Delhi in late 1995 which resulted in suspension of the construction work (Sangvai 2000:70). The construction of the dam remained suspended for four more years until 1999. But, indisputably, the struggle in the valley had become much more dependent on and intertwined with the law and the court. The momentum behind the struggle slowly waned over these years as the NBA recognized that it had deprived itself of its traditional repertoires of more direct political action (Jayal 2001:194).

In July 1996, the court ordered the states to resolve their differences before appearing before it, as the matter had once again become an inter-state dispute, especially between Madhya Pradesh and Gujarat. Following this, a meeting of the Chief Ministers of Gujarat, Madhya Pradesh, Maharashtra, and Rajasthan was convened by the Prime Minister in the summer of 1996, and an agreement was purportedly reached to raise the dam to a height of 436 feet and, following a hydrological review, to increase it to its planned height of 455 feet (Jayal 2001:191; Sangvai 2000:71). This agreement came undone when it was revealed that Madhya Pradesh and Rajasthan had not accepted the agreement and that it was basically a political decision of the Prime

---

[13] Quoted in Sangvai (2000:68).

Minister (Jayal 2001:191–192). The NBA organized a protest march against this decision in Delhi in early August 1996.

Meanwhile, the Supreme Court refused to lift the stay order against the construction of the dam in a hearing in August 1996, and expressed its concern over human rights violations, especially relating to resettlement and rehabilitation.[14] This ruling was confirmed by the court in March 1997, and again in a final ruling in April 1997, when it decided to constitute a five-member constitution bench to decide the issues relating to its jurisdiction. The latter decision resulted from the fact that the federal government and the Gujarat government had consistently opposed the court's jurisdiction to reopen the Narmada dispute which they argued had been finally settled under section 11 of the Inter-state Water Disputes Act read with Article 262 of the constitution. The court's July 1996 order to the states to resolve their differences before appearing in front of it, so that it could confine its focus to the issues arising from the constitutionality of resettlement and rehabilitation, had not been implemented. The reality of political differences between states over the allocation of costs and benefits between them, as well as the complex intertwining of the costs and benefits with resettlement and rehabilitation, made this impossible.

During 1996, the struggle in the valley also began to transform itself. As the construction of the dam had stopped, the NBA began to focus on positive reconstruction rather than confrontation, and it began to branch off into national and global political action. In 1996, the NBA took the lead in establishing the National Alliance of Peoples' Movements (NAPM), an umbrella of like-minded peoples' movements and trade unions from all over India, and also contributed to the formation of the World Commission on Dams in 1998. But even as the NBA was notching up victories abroad, it was facing trouble back home. For reasons that can only be guessed at,[15] from 1998, the Supreme Court began to dispense with the need to decide the jurisdictional question which it had assigned to a constitution bench in 1997 (Sangvai 2000:72). It also limited itself to the resettlement and

---

[14] During the course of the hearing, Justice Verma said, "we have to rise above the law for the protection of human rights" (quoted in Sangvai 2000:153).

[15] The most plausible reason is that Chief Justice Venkatachalliah and Justice Verma, who had been friendlier to the NBA's cause, retired, and the new bench consisted of Chief Justice Anand, and Justices Barucha and Kirpal. Prashant Bhushan, counsel for the NBA, feels that the jurisdictional issues were "implicitly decided" in the 2000 judgment (interview with the author).

rehabilitation question, though it had previously asked counsel for the states and the federal government to be prepared to argue all aspects relating to the project. Thus, the NBA's hope that the court would order a comprehensive review of the whole project, and that the constitution bench would set important legal precedent for settling disputes over large projects and peoples' rights, had been dashed. Also, the struggle in the valley had been witnessing lower levels of participation and energy after the Supreme Court stayed the construction of the dam in May 1995 (Jayal 2001:193). It was in this context that the Gujarat government wanted the stay order to be lifted so that construction could proceed beyond the height of 80.3 meters where it had remained since May 1995. The Gujarat government was also interested in sending a signal to international investors that India was open for business, especially in crucial sectors like power which were beginning to be disinvested. As its counsel argued before the court in a hearing in February 1999, "a strong signal should go from this Court to the outside world, that the work on the dam is on . . . only then would the foreign aid come . . . only then would the people move out from their villages" (quoted in Sangvai 2000:72). The Bharatiya Janata Party (BJP), a Hindu nationalist party, had also come to power in Gujarat and at the federal level, whose leaders had been strong supporters of the dam project. It was in this climate that the Supreme Court gave an interim order on February 18, 1999, allowing the construction of the dam to go ahead by another five meters (Sangvai 2000:72). In a further order on May 7, 1999, it allowed further construction of the dam by another three meters of humps over 85 meters, and approved an in-house Grievance Redress Authority appointed by the Gujarat government which was to submit reports to the Supreme Court on the rehabilitation of oustees in Gujarat (Sangvai 2000:72–73). The political winds were beginning to transform the legal landscape against the struggle in the valley. A clear indication of where the Supreme Court itself was heading came in June 1999, when it contemplated[16] – but did not impose – sanctions against the NBA for contempt of court because of its media advocacy tactics and direct political action, such as *satyagraha* (Sangvai 2000:74).

After the hearings were concluded, the final order of the Supreme Court came on October 18, 2000, landing like a bombshell on the

---

[16] Statement by K. K. Venugopal, Supreme Court of India, 1999. He had been appointed by the court as *amicus curiae*.

NBA.[17] In its order,[18] the court (a) allowed the construction of the dam to proceed up to ninety meters (which the Relief and Rehabilitation Sub-Group of the NCA had already allowed) and announced that the priority was to complete the construction of the dam as soon as possible; (b) ordered that further raising of the height of the dam will be *pari passu* with the implementation of rehabilitation and environmental measures and after clearance by the Relief and Rehabilitation Sub-Group and the Environmental Sub-Group of the NCA at every additional five meters; and (c) ordered the states concerned to comply with the decisions of the NCA, particularly relating to land acquisition and rehabilitation, and asked the NCA to prepare an action plan in this regard. The decision of the court left no doubt that the final decision-making authority belonged to the political arena, and declared that in case the Review Committee of the NCA could not decide any issue, it shall be referred to the Prime Minister, whose decision shall be final. It was clear that completing the construction of the dam was more important to the court than the social and environmental costs it imposed. The court also extolled the virtues of large dams.

Thus the decision by the NBA to approach the Supreme Court had backfired, as many within the NBA itself had feared. Critics of the judgment were many, in the Indian media[19] and elsewhere,[20] but it was clear that the struggle in the valley had reached a dead-end and necessarily had to explore newer forms of political action to continue. The Supreme Court's Delphic pronouncements carry almost mythical power in India, and its seal of approval for the project, as well as its criticisms of the NBA, dealt major blows to the NBA's legitimacy and moral capital. The struggle from 1994 to 2000 had been waged in and through the Supreme Court and it had proved to be very costly.

8.4 THE POLITICS OF THE SUPREME COURT AND BEYOND

8.4.1 The Narmada judgment and its scripts

Why did the Supreme Court decide as it did in 2000? Answering this question is important in order to appreciate what role, if any, courts and law play in counter-hegemonic globalization, a classic instance of which is the struggle in the Narmada Valley. It would also help us

---

[17] *Narmada Bachao Andolan v. Union of India*, 10 SCC 664.   [18] *Ibid.*, pp. 768–770.
[19] Too numerous to list here. See e.g. Rajagopal (2000).   [20] See Jain (2001).

understand the important role played by domestic legal institutions, especially courts, in globalized struggles such as the Narmada one. The court's decision could be attributed, at first glance, to the change in the composition of the bench that decided the case. This explanation is believed by NBA's counsel to lie behind the judgment.[21] There may be much to commend this explanation. Indeed, it is well recognized by observers of the Indian judiciary that, especially in the area of public interest litigation, outcomes of cases often depend on the ideology of individual judges,[22] despite cautionary notes from within the judiciary itself about the importance of treating the court as a single institution with one voice rather than an assemblage of individual judges.[23]

An entirely different set of explanations emerge, however, when the judgment itself is examined closely. These explanations suggest, I shall argue, that there are several dominant scripts in the legal reasoning itself, which are responsible for the conclusions that the court reached. Strictly speaking, these scripts come from outside the law itself, but are so ingrained in legal reasoning and judicial craft as to be able to influence the very process of framing and perceiving the "facts" of the dispute. In other words, the court examined the facts of the dispute through lenses which were themselves biased in ways that approved only one version of the facts. That the court was not only deciding the "law" on the basis of settled "facts," should be settled in advance. Indeed, the estimate of costs and benefits of the project was itself contested by the governments and the NBA before the Supreme Court in 2000. As such, the court's role was not simply to decide the law on the basis of settled facts, but rather to decide which version of the facts trumped the others. The law was simply one more terrain on which the NBA struggled over the social recognition and political legitimation of human suffering, and was not independent of or prior to the establishment of social facts. By recognizing one version of the facts presented by the governments as valid, the Supreme Court delegitimized the human suffering that the NBA was trying to draw attention to.

The techniques through which the court performed this task will be evident when the dominant scripts of the judgment are examined closely. A first script could be termed *evolutionary*, in that the court

---

[21] Interview with Prashant Bhushan.   [22] See Desai and Muralidhar (2000:180).

[23] See the remarks of R. S. Pathak, J. (as he then was) in *Bandhua Mukti Morcha* v. *Union of India* (1984) 3 SCC 161.

subscribes to a view of human progress in which the modern is always epistemologically superior to the traditional. As the court says, "the displacement of the tribals and other persons would not per se result in the violations of their fundamental or other rights ... The gradual assimilation in the mainstream of the society will lead to betterment and progress" (pp. 702–703). This evolutionary ideology enables the court to rationalize the displacement, even though its position is factually tenuous. Almost 140 out of a total of 193 villages in Madhya Pradesh that are slated for submergence consist of a mixed population in the plains of Nimar, with a well-developed economy. For the people of this region – where the resistance to the dam has been fierce – displacement is unlikely to lead to "betterment and progress." Even in the case of the rest of the people to be displaced, who are tribals, the idea that their displacement would lead to betterment depends on an ideological position that a forest-based, river-based economy is backward when compared to a modern one. Further, it also depends on a belief that rehabilitation packages would in fact be implemented and land would be made available. This was, to say the least, highly dubious, as recognized by the court itself in its order (p. 769).

A second script of the judgment could be called *nationalist*, in the way in which it extols the importance of the dam for securing India's border with Pakistan as well as for ensuring national development, including through better infrastructure, food security, and electricity supply. While discussing the benefits of the Sardar Sarover dam, the court says, "apart from bringing drinking water within easy reach, the supply of water to Rajasthan will also help in checking the advancement of the Thar desert. Human habitation will increase there which, in turn, will help in protecting the so far porous border with Pakistan" (p. 764). The discourse about the dam had, over the years, pointed out that the border between Gujarat and Pakistan was porous, partly due to poor human habitation, and expressed the hope that bringing drinking water to the dry regions of Kutch, Saurashtra, and North Gujarat would improve India's own security. Indeed, discourses of Gujarati nationalism and Indian nationalism tended to overlap a lot in calling attention to the security dimensions of the dam project. It is because of this that any criticism of the dam project was attacked by pro-dam elements as anti-national, and mob violence against the dam critics has been orchestrated by all political parties in Gujarat over the years (Jayal 2001:196; Sangvai 2000:140–143). The workers at the dam site have also been charged with sedition for demanding better wages (Jayal 2001:195).

A nationalist framing also suppresses any rational evaluation of the costs and benefits by the jingoistic fervor that immediately accompanies the discourse of nationalism. In addition, the court also praises the value of river valley projects in increasing India's self-sufficiency in food (pp. 764 and 766) and water, the provision of which is seen as a primary duty of the government (p. 761). Once the project was seen in this manner, it placed an impossibly heavy burden on the NBA, which it could not discharge.

A third script of the judgment could be termed *developmentalist* in that it emphasizes the value of dams per se as tools of development, and casts the overall utilitarian argument in terms of public welfare that justifies the sacrifice of some for many. The court also understands development in a particular way that makes the building of dams almost compulsory. To begin with, the court extols the value of dams per se, though it had not been asked to decide the viability of dams as tools of development, including their costs and benefits. Indeed, the court's characterization of the NBA as an "anti-dam organization" (p. 695) – rather than as a "human rights organization" or an "environmental NGO" – gives some sense of the court's disapproval of anyone critical of dams per se. In addition to the "vital role" dams play in "providing irrigation for food security, domestic and industrial water supply, hydro-electric power and keeping flood waters back" (p. 701), dams are seen by the court to contribute positively to the living standards of the displaced persons as well as to the environment. Thus, the court declares that "a properly drafted [resettlement and rehabilitation] plan would improve the living standards of displaced persons after displacement ... It is not fair that tribals and people in undeveloped villages should continue in the same condition without ever enjoying the fruits of science and technology for better health and have a higher quality of lifestyle" (p. 765). It says that dams are "instruments for improving the environment" (p. 765) and that "hydroelectric power's contribution to the greenhouse effect is negligible and it can be termed ecology-friendly" (p. 768). These bald assertions, unsupported by facts (Jain 2001), serve an ideological role in leading the court to justify the project as a whole.

The court sees the sacrifice of some in the interest of the many as being inherent in the public welfare argument that lies behind the construction of the dam. As it says, "displacement of these people would undoubtedly disconnect them from their past, culture, custom and traditions, but then it becomes necessary to harvest a river for the larger good" (p. 765). This argument, recalling American jurisprudence on property rights in the nineteenth century when developmental and utilitarian arguments dominated (Horowitz 1977), enables the court to provide the ideological justification for displacement and, therefore, for the project. Also, the court understands development in a particular manner which makes the building of dams compulsory for its realization. Taking per capita consumption of electricity as one of the indicators of living standards (p. 767), for example, makes dams important for ensuring energy consumption even though the court ignores the internal tension that this approach creates with its own commitment to the environment.

A fourth script of the judgment is *statist*, and puts the emphasis on the efficiency and equity of the system that is responsible for designing and executing the project as well as in taking ameliorative measures. Put differently, faced with substantive critiques in the areas of rehabilitation or environment, the court puts its faith in the setting up of state agencies and the fulfillment of procedures, rather than coming up with answers to the critiques. For example, faced with the question of whether environmental clearance by the Ministry of Environment and Forests in 1987 was given without proper data and planning and was therefore contrary to law, the majority puts much emphasis on the process through which the decision was arrived at, including the fact that it was finally cleared by the Prime Minister himself. As the court says, "care for the environment is an ongoing process and the system in place would ensure that ameliorative steps are taken to counter the adverse effect, if any, on the environment with the construction of the dam" (p. 729). This could be contrasted to the view of Justice Barucha, the dissenting judge, who says that the environmental clearance was based on "next to no data ... and was, therefore, contrary to the terms of the then policy of the Union of India in regard to environmental clearances and, therefore, no clearance at all" (pp. 775, 776, and 781). Similarly, with regard to displacement, the majority of the court says that "with the establishment of the [Resettlement and Rehabilitation] Sub-Group and the constitution of the grievance redress authorities by the states of Gujarat, Maharashtra and Madhya Pradesh, there is a system in force which will ensure satisfactory resettlement and rehabilitation of the oustees" (p. 745). This reasoning of the court overlooks the fact that the state agencies had no intention, judging by their record, of ensuring either resettlement and rehabilitation or environmental protection as per the award of the Tribunal. The multiplication of state agencies is, in this view of the court, a substantive response to the failure to ensure resettlement and rehabilitation or to protect the environment. But the NBA's plea for an independent agency to evaluate and monitor the project is rejected.

A fifth script of the judgment could be termed *legalist/dominant* in that it sees the dispute as something that has been settled by law which the Supreme Court has little power to change. In this view, the role of the court is to dispense justice in accordance with the law and, if the law clearly favors the work on the dam to go ahead, there is little that the court can do. As the court says, "the Court has not forsaken its duty and role as a court of law dispensing justice in accordance with the law .... No directions are issued which are in conflict with any legal provisions" (p. 762). This could be contrasted with views expressed previously by the court, including in previous proceedings in the same case, that, when the law is in conflict with fundamental rights, the law must give way. The law that the court refers to here, against which it is purportedly helpless, is of two kinds. First, the law governing the settlement of inter-state water disputes, contained in Article 262 of the constitution and the Inter-State Water Disputes Act, prevents the jurisdiction of the Supreme Court over water disputes and provides no right of appeal. Although the court had reopened the water dispute by admitting the petition in 1994 and by suspending the work on the dam for four years, it now takes the position that its only job is to ensure that the award of the Tribunal is enforced (pp. 768 and 769). This position seems to have been prompted by the court's desire to assert the dominance of the constitution and the power of the federal government over the procedure for deciding inter-state water disputes. This was because of its concern that the federal constitutional scheme for settling water disputes between states was coming unstuck because Madhya Pradesh was trying to reopen the whole dispute, taking some political cover under the NBA's agitation for the rights of the displaced people. At several places, the court notes that the award of the Tribunal is binding on states (pp. 696, 697, and 766). While this is a legitimate concern, the court's duty, especially in a public interest litigation alleging violation of constitutional rights, is to first safeguard rights if there is evidence of violation. The court failed to do this.

A second legalist reason for the Court's decision has to do with the doctrine of laches, which, according to the majority, prevents the NBA from prevailing in the case. According to the Court's reasoning, since the NBA did not approach the Court until 1994, that is, after construction of the dam began in 1987 and after environmental clearance was obtained, it is guilty of laches. Apart from the fact that the Supreme Court is rarely concerned with traditional procedural issues in public interest litigation,[24] this decision of the Court is also factually inaccurate and in bad faith. The Court was, as noted above, first approached in 1991, and the NBA had approached a number of lower courts quite successfully over the years even though it could not get the judicial orders enforced. It was only after trying virtually every governmental and judicial authority and failing that the NBA approached the Supreme Court. Therefore, the Court's decision on this point seems hard to comprehend.

A sixth script that runs through the judgment may be termed *adjudicatory*, and seeks to rest its reasoning on the institutional role of the Court (as opposed to the Executive), which is to decide only law and not policy. As the Court says, "the conception and the decision to undertake a project are to be regarded as a policy decision ... The courts, in the exercise of their jurisdiction, will not transgress into the field of policy decision. Whether to have an infrastructural project or not and what is the type of project to be undertaken and how it has to be executed, are part of policy-making process and the courts are ill-equipped to adjudicate on a policy decision so undertaken" (pp. 761 and 762). Imposing this interpretive framework on itself gives the Court enough wiggle room to avoid difficult legal questions, such as the conflict between individual rights and state rights or the role of the Court in inter-state water disputes when important constitutional questions other than riparian rights of states are at stake. The adjudicatory script also helps to mask the ideological hand-me-down of the Court behind the façade of democratic accountability. This is doubly ironic because of the well-established record of the Court in actively making policy decisions through public interest litigation. Indeed, perhaps no other country's highest court has intervened in so many areas of public policy in fields ranging from criminal justice, environment, human rights, women's rights, and public accountability. Yet, when it comes to development projects such as dams, the Court suddenly discovers the virtues of judicial self-restraint.

The seventh script that is evident in the judgment may be called *selective cosmopolitanism*; through it the Court justifies its reasoning by

---

[24] The Indian Supreme Court is famous for innovating new procedural rules in the domain of public interest litigation. For a review, see Desai and Muralidhar (2000).

appeal either to a universal human interest or to global sources of law, but does it in a manner that is highly selective. The Court was asked by counsel to the NBA whether "the forcible displacement of tribals and other marginal farmers from their land and other sources of livelihood for a project which was not in the national or public interest was a violation of their fundamental rights under Article 21 of the constitution of Indian read with ILO Convention 107 to which India is a signatory" (p. 697). Counsel for the NBA contended that ILO Convention No. 107, read into Article 21 of the constitution, makes the displacement illegal as there was no free consent and the project itself is not in the national or public interest due to its unacceptable social, economic, and environmental costs (pp. 697 and 698). The Court rejects this argument by taking a strict constructionist view of Convention No. 107 and concludes that the exception clause in the Convention allows displacement because land-for-land compensation was assured by the states (p. 701). This overlooks two factors. First, land-for-land compensation had not been guaranteed in practice, as the Court itself acknowledged. Secondly, the ILO itself had written letters of concern to the Indian government about the violation of Convention No. 107. More importantly, the Court's positivistic refusal to engage in a liberal reading of Convention No. 107 is notably in tension with the Court's overall record in reading international law into domestic law.[25] Later, the Court's refusal to recognize the relevance of the "precautionary principle" for assessing environmental compliance also shows a selective approach, as it neither comports with the Court's recent activism in environmental law,[26] nor with the current state of international environmental law.[27] But, while the Court freely departs from current international legal norms relating to the precautionary principle in environmental protection, it is ready to praise the importance of water as a human right even though the status of that norm under international law is, at best, that of a soft law norm. The Court says that "water is the basic

---

[25] See e.g. *Vishaka* v. *State of Rajasthan* (1997) 6 SCC 247 (reading provisions on sexual harassment from the Convention on the Elimination of Discrimination Against Women into Indian law); and *Vellore Citizens' Welfare Forum* v. *Union of India* (1996) 5 SCC 647 (reading a precautionary principle into Indian law, relying upon a report of the International Law Commission).

[26] See *Center for Environmental Law WWF-I* v. *Union of India* (1999) 1 SCC 263; and *Vellore Citizens' Welfare Forum* v. *Union of India* (1996) 5 SCC 647.

[27] See *Gabcíkovo-Nagymaros Project (Hungary/Slovakia)* (Merits), ICJ Reports, Judgment of 27 September 1997 (especially the concurring opinion of Judge C. G. Weeramantry).

need for the survival of human beings and is part of the right to life and human rights as enshrined in Article 21 of the constitution of India" (p. 767), and cites a UN resolution as the legal basis for this conclusion while justifying the dam project as one that will fulfill this need. In a remarkable example of the hegemonic use of counter-hegemonic discourse, the state of Gujarat had argued[28] that it had a responsibility to guarantee the human right to water to its population and that the dam was needed for this purpose among others. The Court's readiness to accept this and its remarkable activism in con-juring law out of politics is sorely missing when it focuses on the issues that seem to favor the NBA.

8.4.2 Post-judgment woes: towards electoral politics?
Since the judgment of the Court in 2000, which led to much criticism and an attempt by the Court to muzzle its critics (Venkatesan 2002), the NBA has been on the defensive and searching for new political vistas. There has been no proper resettlement and rehabilitation, despite the directions of the Court in 2000. Therefore, the judgment has not ended the role of the Court itself.[29] The NBA filed a fresh review petition before the Court in May 2002, which was dismissed. The state of Madhya Pradesh has also filed a petition in the Court in 2004, challenging aspects of the 2000 judgment. Thus, the role of law in the Narmada Valley struggle has not formally ended. But, the dam's height has been gradually increased and approval has now been given for a height of almost 110 meters, despite opposition from the NBA and the Madhya Pradesh government (Sharma 2004a). For the Gujarat government, the Sardar Sarovar dam's height has become one of the key barometers of its own political success. The NBA, having run out of other options, has decided to enter electoral politics (Sharma 2004b). The struggle in the valley has had a long relationship with electoral politics (Jayal 2001; Sangvai 2000), but the NBA itself has not actively entered politics so far. Whatever the reason behind the new winds of change may be, it is a factor that must be taken into account when assessing the limits of law and institutions concerned with formal political participation, in processes of counter-hegemonic globalization.

---

[28] Interview with Prashant Bhushan.   [29] Ibid.

8.5 ASSESSING THE ROLE OF LAW IN THE NARMADA VALLEY STRUGGLE

What can one make of the role of law in the Narmada Valley struggle? What was the impact of the struggle on law itself? The difficulties in answering these questions must be evident. Not only has the struggle in the valley been both local and transnational at the same time, it has also extended over a long time. As such, it is hard to come to any snap judgments about the relationship between law and the Narmada Valley struggle. However, one could start by debunking many common suppositions about the relationship between law and social movements. First, it is clear that law is very relevant to social movement struggles both in shaping the political opportunity structures that movements have at specific moments and also in sanctifying and legitimating the identities and strategies that movements deploy. This conclusion should be seen against the common social science predilection either to take law for granted or to dismiss it as irrelevant to social struggles (Fernandes and Varley 1998).

In the Narmada Valley struggle law was always very relevant. From private law relating to land acquisition, to constitutional rights, to international human rights law, the struggle in the valley was profoundly affected. The political opportunities for the struggle were severely constrained by private law, for instance in the kinds of claim that the movement could legitimately advance within the system. While private law and regulatory law relating to the environment were more relevant during the initial years of the struggle, international law became more relevant later and constitutional law was crucial in more recent years. Secondly, the meaning of "law" has changed irrevocably from a normative order within territorial states to a global normative order. As such, this requires a broad framework that is capable of appreciating the local and global engagements between law and social movements. This could be contrasted with traditional assessments of the role of law in social movement struggles which remain centered on national law. In the case of the Narmada Valley struggle, law operated at virtually all conceivable levels and the role of international law was crucial. Thirdly, the "law" that social movements engage with includes not only state law, but inter-state, sub-state, and non-state law as well. Therefore, the question of whether law can be emancipatory (Santos 2002; Santos and Rodríguez-Garavito's chapter in this volume) cannot be answered easily but depends on the dynamics between various levels of law. In the case of the struggle in the Narmada Valley, operative tensions between law at different levels were resolved differently at different times, largely due to the impact of the struggle on the law. For example, the relationship between international law and national law was resolved in favor of the former while the World Bank was still involved with the project (until 1993), but the dynamics sharply changed after the struggle in the valley succeeded in compelling the World Bank to pull out. Fourthly, the role of domestic institutions, especially that of the judiciary, cannot be taken for granted. This must be seen against the background of intense debates about whether domestic courts help or hinder social movements (Epp 1998; Rosenberg 1991; Siegel 2002) in which opinions tend to be cast in an "either/or" fashion. This seems problematic, but it is more likely that domestic courts could both help and hinder a movement. While national legal cultures within which the judiciaries function are impor- tant, the assessment of the role of the judiciary in social movement struggles becomes more difficult due to the longevity of social move- ment struggles. Another crucial issue is the tension between the logic of judicial decision-making and movement politics. In both their finality and their temporal aspects, judicial decisions work against the logic of movements which do not easily accept finality, while the courts find the duration and continuity of social movements hard to fit into their adversarial mode of resolving disputes. In the Narmada Valley struggle, all these propositions proved to be true.

Looking at the relationship between law and the Narmada Valley struggle through these issues, one could begin to come to some conclu- sions. In order to make sense, however, these conclusions will have to rest on a framework that is broader than simply the question of whether the movement achieved a change in *outcome* by its engagement with the law. One also has to take two other dimensions of evaluation, namely, whether the movement led to any change in the *process* of decision-making, and whether the movement was able to change the *values* that underlie the dispute.[30] Using this triangular framework of outcome change, process change, and value change, one could come to the following conclusions.

The struggle did lead to *outcome change* but this was more evident at the international level. The NBA's involvement led to the pull-out of the World Bank from the project, and the establishment of the World

---

[30] I borrow this framework from Rochon and Mazmanian (1993).

Commission on Dams which has significantly contributed to the global public policy discourse on development. At the domestic level, the major successes of the struggle included winning a better resettlement and rehabilitation policy from Gujarat in 1988 and the stay order of the Supreme Court in May 1995, but, judging by the overall outcome, the struggle failed. The juggernaut of construction of the dam and the displacement could not be stopped. The struggle had a moderate impact on decision-making *process*, both at the international and domestic levels. The struggle led to the establishment of the complaints panel at the World Bank in 1993, a new information policy at the World Bank to improve transparency, and the support of the World Bank for the World Commission on Dams. At the domestic level, the struggle led to the establishment of the environmental and rehabilitation sub-groups of the NCA as well as the Grievance Redress Authorities in the three states concerned. The decision-making process relating to large projects has been somewhat democratized at the international and domestic levels, but not as much as the NBA hoped. In terms of *value change*, the struggle in the valley has perhaps had better success in general, and more so at the international level. The norms relating to sustainable development have been significantly affected by the struggle in the valley (Khagram 2002) because the cultural dimensions of counter-hegemonic globalization in this area have been shaped by the struggle. Human rights norms relating to internal displacement are beginning to be changed to include development-induced displacement (Robinson 2002), while foreign investors shy away from large projects which have significant social and environmental costs. At the domestic level, the struggle has led to much polarization between groups who have diametrically different moral compasses on issues relating to development and its costs, but has not been able to ensure its values prevail. However, it cannot be denied that the struggle has had a counter-hegemonic effect at the domestic level in India.

8.6 CONCLUSION

This chapter has analyzed the role of law and courts in counter-hegemonic globalization by examining the relationship between law and the struggle against displacement in the Narmada Valley in India, especially that of the role played by the NBA. The struggle began in the early 1980s against a massive river valley development scheme along India's Narmada river consisting of hundreds of dams, which planned to flood the lands of both tribals and prosperous farmers across three states, Gujarat, Maharashtra, and Madhya Pradesh. A transnational coalition was formed to fight the displacement and environmental destruction and led to major successes including the pull-out of the World Bank from the project. The success of the movement continued when, in 1995, it obtained a stay order from the Supreme Court against further construction of the dam. However, a major blow was struck when the Supreme Court cancelled the stay order in 1999, and ruled against the movement in 2000. The struggle in the valley is now focusing on formal electoral politics as a major avenue of action.

The role of law in the struggle was complex. It was conducted at multiple levels, using different alliances and tactics, over two decades. While the movement succeeded in having a significant impact on the values that underlie the development discourse, especially at the international level, the movement was unable to have much success domestically. The role played by the domestic judiciary in this outcome was crucial. My conclusions challenge conventional debates about the role of law in social movement struggles, as well as the impact of social movements on the making and enforcement of law itself.

References
Ackerman, Bruce. 1997. "The Rise of World Constitutionalism." *Virginia Law Review* 83:771.

Austin, Granville. 1999. *Working a Democratic Constitution*. Delhi: Oxford University Press.

Baviskar, Amita. 1995. *In the Belly of the River: Tribal Conflicts over Development in the Narmada Valley*. Delhi: Oxford University Press.

Baxi, Upendra. 1987. "Taking Human Suffering Seriously: Social Action Litigation Before the Supreme Court of India." In *The Role of the Judiciary in Plural Societies*, edited by Neelan Tiruchelvan and Radhika Coomaraswamy. New York: St. Martin's Press.

2003. "A Known But an Indifferent Judge: Situating Ronald Dworkin in Contemporary Indian Jurisprudence." *International Journal of Constitutional Law* 1:557–589.

Carothers, Thomas. 1998. "The Rule of Law Revival." *Foreign Affairs* 77(2):95–106.

Desai, Ashok H., and S. Muralidhar. 2000. "Public Interest Litigation: Potential and Problems." In *Supreme But Not Infallible: Essays in Honour of the Supreme Court of India*, edited by B. N. Kirpal, Ashok H. Desai,

Gopal Subramanium, Rajeev Dhavan, and Raju Ramchandran. New Delhi: Oxford University Press.

Dezalay, Yves, and Bryant Garth. 1997. *Dealing in Virtue: International Commercial Arbitration and the Construction of a Transnational Legal Order*. Chicago: University of Chicago Press.

Epp, Charles R. 1998. *The Rights Revolution: Lawyers, Activists, and Supreme Courts in Comparative Perspective*. Chicago: University of Chicago Press.

Esteva, Gustavo, and Madhu Suri Prakash. 1998. *Grassroots Postmodernism: Remaking the Soil of Cultures*. London: Zed Books.

Fernandes, Edesio, and Ann Varley (Eds.). 1998. *Illegal Cities: Law and Urban Change in Developing Countries*. London: Zed Books.

Fisher, William (Ed.). 1995. *Toward Sustainable Development? Struggling over India's Narmada River*. Armonk, NY: M. E. Sharpe.

Horowitz, Morton. 1992. *The Transformation of American Law, 1870–1960*. Cambridge, MA: Harvard University Press.

Jain, L. C. 2001. *Dam vs. Drinking Water: Exploring the Narmada Judgment*. Parisar: Pune.

Jayal, Niraja Gopal. 2001. *Democracy and the State: Welfare, Secularism and Development in Contemporary India*. New Delhi: Oxford University Press.

Keck, Margaret, and Kathryn Sikkink. 1998. *Activists Beyond Borders: Advocacy Networks in International Politics*. Ithaca: Cornell University Press.

Kennedy, Duncan. 1998. *A Critique of Adjudication*. Cambridge, MA: Harvard University Press.

Khagram, Sanjeev. 2002. "Restructuring the Global Politics of Development: The Case of India's Narmada Valley Dams." In *Restructuring World Politics: Transnational Social Movements, Networks and Norms*, edited by Sanjeev Khagram, James Riker, and Kathryn Sikkink. Minneapolis: University of Minnesota Press.

Khagram, Sanjeev, James Riker, and Kathryn Sikkink (Eds.). 2002. *Restructuring World Politics: Transnational Social Movements, Networks and Norms*. Minneapolis: University of Minnesota Press.

Kirpal, B. N., Ashok H. Desai, Gopal Subramanium, Rajeev Dhavan, and Raju Ramchandran (Eds.). 2000. *Supreme But Not Infallible: Essays in Honour of the Supreme Court of India*. New Delhi: Oxford University Press.

Klug, Heinz. 2000. *Constituting Democracy: Law, Globalism and South Africa's Political Reconstruction*. Cambridge: Cambridge University Press.

Kothari, Smitu. 1995. "Damming the Narmada and the Politics of Development." In *Toward Sustainable Development? Struggling over India's Narmada River*, edited by William Fisher. Armonk, NY: M. E. Sharpe.

Mamdani, Mahmood, Thandika Mkandawire, and E. Wamba-dia-Wamba. 1993. "Social Movements and Democracy in Africa." In *New Social Movements in the South*, edited by Poona Wignaraja. London: Zed Books.

215

Morse, Bradford, and Thomas Berger. 1992. *Sardar Sarover: Report of the Independent Review*. Ottawa: Resources Futures International.

Nandy, Ashis. 1992. "State." In *Development Dictionary: A Guide to Knowledge as Power*, edited by Wolfgang Sachs. London: Zed Books.

Patel, Anil. 1995. "What Do the Narmada Valley Tribals Want?" In *Toward Sustainable Development? Struggling over India's Narmada River*, edited by William Fisher. Armonk, NY: M. E. Sharpe.

Patkar, Medha. 1995. "The Struggle for Participation and Justice: A Historical Narrative" In *Toward Sustainable Development? Struggling over India's Narmada River*, edited by William Fisher. Armonk, NY: M. E. Sharpe.

Rajagopal, Balakrishnan. 2000. "The Supreme Court and Human Rights." *The Hindu*, December 6.

  2003a. *International Law from Below: Development, Social Movements and Third World Resistance*. Cambridge: Cambridge University Press.

  2003b. "International Law and Social Movements: Challenges of Theorizing Resistance." *Columbia Journal of Transnational Law* 41:397–433.

Risse, Thomas. 2000. "The Power of Norms Versus the Norms of Power: Transnational Civil Society and Human Rights." In *The Third Force: The Rise of Transnational Civil Society*. Washington, DC: Japan Center for International Exchange, Tokyo, and Carnegie Endowment for International Peace.

Risse, Thomas, Stephen Ropp, and Kathryn Sikkink (Eds.). 1999. *The Power of Human Rights: International Norms and Domestic Change*. Cambridge: Cambridge University Press.

Robinson, Courtland W. 2002. *Risks and Rights: The Causes, Consequences and Challenges of Development-Induced Displacement*. Washington, DC: Brookings Institution.

Rochon, Thomas R., and Daniel A. Mazmanian. 1993. "Social Movements and the Policy Process." *Annals of the American Academy of Political and Social Science* 528:75–87.

Rosenberg, Gerald. 1991. *The Hollow Hope: Can Courts Bring About Social Change?* Chicago: University of Chicago Press.

Salve, Harish. 2000. "Justice Between Generations: Environment and Social Justice." In *Supreme But Not Infallible: Essays in Honour of the Supreme Court of India*, edited by B. N. Kirpal, Ashok H. Desai, Gopal Subramanium, Rajeev Dhavan, and Raju Ramchandran. New Delhi: Oxford University Press.

Sangvai, Sanjay. 2000. *The River and Life: People's Struggle in the Narmada Valley*. Mumbai: Earthcare Books.

Santos, Boaventura de Sousa. 2002. *Toward a New Legal Common Sense*. London: Butterworths.

Sharma, Kalpana. 2004a. "Gujarat Given Permission to Raise Narmada Dam Height." *The Hindu*, March 17.

2004b. "Medha Patkar Forms Political Front." *The Hindu*, March 18.

Shivji, Issa. 1995. "Constructing a New Rights Regime: Promises, Problems and Prospects." *Social and Legal Studies* 8:253.

Siegel, Reva B. 2001. "Gender and the Constitution from a Social Movement Perspective." *University of Pennsylvania Law Review* 150:297–351.

Slaughter, Anne-Marie. 2000. "Judicial Globalization." *Virginia Journal of International Law* 40:1103.

Strauss, David A. 1996. "Common Law Constitutional Interpretation." *University of Chicago Law Review* 63:877.

Udall, Lori. 1995. "The International Narmada Campaign: A Case Study of Sustained Advocacy." In *Toward Sustainable Development? Struggling over India's Narmada River*, edited by William Fisher. Armonk, NY: M. E. Sharpe.

Venkatesan, J. 2002. "Arundhati Roy Jailed for Contempt of Court." *The Hindu*, March 7.

World Commission on Dams. 2000. *Dams and Development: A New Framework for Decision-Making*. London: Earthscan.

CHAPTER 9

THE MOVEMENT OF THE LANDLESS (MST), JURIDICAL FIELD, AND LEGAL CHANGE IN BRAZIL

*Peter P. Houtzager**

9.1 INTRODUCTION

What forms of legal change can social movements set in motion to diminish systemic and durable forms of social exclusion? And when are movements successful at doing so? This chapter explores these two questions in the context of the struggle for land waged by the Movement of the Landless' (MST) in Brazil, a country which has one of the most unequal land distributions in the world. It focuses in particular on the movement's emergent juridical strategy and that strategy's contribution to legal change. The MST rarely initiates legal action itself, and in fact does not have standing to bring cases to expropriate land for agrarian reform, which is the preserve of federal government. In recent years, however, its reactive juridical strategy – in civil and criminal cases *brought against it* – has grown increasingly sophisticated. The movement has helped produce watershed legal precedents, contributed to a broader process of constitutionalizing law, and made access to land more equitable in parts of Brazil by redefining property rights in practice.

* An early draft of this chapter was presented at the workshop on "Fundamental Rights in the Balance: New Ideas on the Rights to Land, Housing and Property," October 16–18, 2003, Institute of Development Studies (IDS), Brighton, UK. The paper owes much to discussions with Eugênio Facchini Neto, Jacques Távora Alfonsin, Ipojucan Vecchi, Avelino Strozake, Claudio Pavão, Luís Cristiano, and Adrián Gurza Lavalle. The editors, Boaventura de Sousa Santos and César A. Rodríguez-Garavito, made gentle suggestions that improved the chapter. Daniel Guimarães Zveibil provided valuable research assistance.

These outcomes have been achieved at a world historic moment when powerful international institutions are committed to globalizing a new "classic" interpretation of liberal property rights. The creation of rural and urban land markets, modeled on a mythologized account of Western property regimes, has become a pillar of many international programs of structural reform and to combat poverty.[1] The MST's emergent juridical mobilization offers some insights into countervailing possibilities – that is, establishing more equitable access to, and forms of, property – and the role movement engagement with juridical actors and institutions can play in realizing these possibilities (see Santos and Rodríguez's chapter in this volume).

This chapter explores legal change that occurs through what Bourdieu (1987) calls the juridical field. Changes in law that reduce deep-rooted social exclusion can result from many sources, including from legislative or executive action, shifts in public opinion, and civil society monitoring of public or private action. Legal change is produced by an array of juridical protagonists, such as judges, private lawyers, public prosecutors, law school professors, law reform NGOs, and so forth. The most visible changes in law these juridical protagonists – the socially authorized interpreters of legal code – produce are watershed court rulings in the juridical field, but more legal change occurs in less visible forms, and often involves a multitude of diverse actors, many situated far outside the courthouse.

The chapter sets out a two-step argument. It argues first that the MST's ability to convert movement energy into juridical energy has played a central role in setting legal change in motion through the juridical field. The movement's capacity to concentrate the talents of diverse juridical actors on defending its claims has made it an important catalyst for legal change through the juridical field. It has been able to concentrate juridical talent by pursuing a strategy that Santos (1995, 2002) argues is most likely to succeed in the counter-hegemonic use of law and rights: it integrates juridical action into broader political mobilization, politicizing struggles before they become juridified, and mobilizing sophisticated legal skills from diverse actors.[2] This strategy

---

[1] USAID, the World Bank, and other international actors have used structural adjustment programs, a variety of types of loan, poverty reduction programs, and broader legal reform programs to spread a "classic' interpretation of property rights in the wake of the collapse of Eastern European political economies and the failure of structural adjustment programs in Africa.

[2] The prior politicization, Santos (1995:386) suggests, makes possible the construction of the conflict in ways that neutralize its individualization by law.

enabled the MST to engage in the type of sustained and broad litigation – both geographically and across issues – that Epp (1998) suggests is central to redefining legal terrain.[3]

Secondly, the chapter argues that the MST has contributed to *substantial legal change* when dynamics in the movement field and the political arena converged to alter that of the juridical field. In the absence of such convergence, the MST's mobilization across multiple fields helped to produce important but *small-scale and incremental change*. Such change has been far more common. In the 1990s, the transition to democracy, the rising prominence of the Workers' Party, and shifts within the Catholic Church produced a series of shifts in the movement and juridical fields that created new opportunities to set in motion juridical modalities of change.

The movement and juridical fields in contemporary Brazil have a variety of particularities, and the chapter does not attempt broad generalization. Its value is in identifying emerging juridical forms of cosmopolitan legal change – that is, change processes in which juridical actors play a prominent role and that alter authoritative legal norms or their application. The chapter examines three particular modalities of change that altered legal practices. The MST has worked with or through juridical actors and institutions to (1) compel public authorities to implement or enforce existing legislation and constitutional mandates in ways that alter legality in practice; (2) create novel interpretations of substantive rights and obligations, and institutionalize these through jurisprudence (i.e. judge-made law); and (3) innovate in the contest over juridical time, by using novel procedural instruments that increase the pace of judicial proceedings to more closely match that of social movements.

9.2 THE LOGIC OF FIELDS

Encounters between movements and judiciaries are complicated and unsettling affairs, for the parties involved and for society at large. It is not that movements are forces of progressive change and judiciaries are guarantors of conservative status quo. There are innumerable reactionary movements and many instances of progressive judicial action.

---

[3] Epp (1998:3) notes that the judicial process is "costly and slow and produces changes in the law only in small increments." In the case of Brazil, which has a federal system that grants state judiciaries a high degree of autonomy and which lacks *stare decisis* (binding legal precedent of court rulings), legal change through litigation is particularly costly and slow.

Rather, social movements and judiciaries have profoundly contrasting logics. It takes little contact with social movements and judiciaries to intuit that they not only look and feel very different, but also function in different ways. Movements have a quick and sometimes reckless pace, and acquire much of their social and political significance from mass public displays and from collective trespassing of legality. In contrast, judiciaries plod cautiously along the path of due process. They obtain their significance through individual, almost private, performances that reinforce existing legalities. Movement and juridical discursive styles, and construction of the issues at the heart of social conflict, tend to be worlds' apart. Movements' need of media attention is matched only by the judiciaries' ambivalence toward such public scrutiny (witness the ongoing debate over the presence of cameras in the courtroom).

The contrasting logic of the social movement and juridical fields establishes broad boundaries within which movements can set juridical modalities of change in motion. The logic of each field substantially constrains actors' agency and points to the need to take "field effects" into account when explaining legal change.

Bourdieu's sociology of practice makes visible and open to interpretation the sources and nature of these logics. Bourdieu (1987:831) suggests that the juridical field converts "conflict between directly concerned parties into juridically regulated debate between professionals acting by proxy." When parties enter the field it "implies tacit acceptance of the field's fundamental law ... [that] conflicts can only be resolved *juridically* – that is, according to the rules and conventions of the field itself" (1987:831). For him, the logic of the juridical field has two principal sources: the specific power relations between protagonists in the field, which give the field its structure and order competitive struggles; and the "internal logic of juridical functioning [according to existing norms and doctrine] which constantly constrains the range of possible actions and, thereby, limits the realm of specifically juridical solutions" (1987:816). The competitive struggles are, in large measure, over the control of the field's primary source of power vis-à-vis the rest of society – "the technical competence to *interpret* a corpus of texts" (1987:817).

The need to reproduce society's perception of the juridical field's autonomy, neutrality, and universality – that is, its sources of legitimacy – is central to this internal logic. The power of judiciaries and other actors in the field in the larger society resides primarily in the symbolic effectiveness of their action – they are *signalers* par excellence (Bourdieu 1987:839; Galanter 1981). The outcome of court proceedings therefore is the product of interpretative struggles between actors (possessing unequal talents and juridical power), not just inside the court room, but within a larger field of juridical practices.

The logic of the movement field could hardly be more different. It is shaped by the competition over legitimate representation of social groups or values, and by the establishment of the deserving nature of these groups' interests or values. Movements engage in disruptive or expressive collective action to communicate the importance and righteousness of their cause, and the number, worthiness, and commitment of their members (McAdam, Tarrow, and Tilly 2001).

Accumulating this kind of capital requires a complicated balancing act. Movement action must disrupt the ordinary and routine to build and display its power. Movements' reliance on the mass media to communicate with the public and to build its political influence reinforces the need for short and expressive bursts of collective energy, as well as for a degree of risk-taking. Yet movements also have to maintain the support of broad segments of the general public, or of more powerful actors who may tolerate inconvenient disruptions but not a sustained paralysis of valued institutions. Movements of the poor, because they are short on material resources or specialized knowledge (such as legal knowledge) in particular require access to allies' resources, knowledge, political support, and influence. And, movements must keep the costs of collective action to participants as low as possible. To balance disruption, broad support, and acceptable cost, they generally seek to engage in forms of legitimate disruption, on the edges of legality, while developing discourses and a set of symbols that are far more radical than their actions and demands are in practice (Houtzager 2001a, 2001b; McAdam *et al.* 2001).

Bourdieu's sociology has sought to establish the autonomy of fields, their distinctive forms of power and logics, and how these are reproduced over time, but the task in this chapter is somewhat different. The chapter seeks to identify how movements such as the MST can produce changes in the logic of the juridical field. The juridical mobilization of the MST points to an important refinement in the sociology of practice if it is to be used to explore the possibilities for purposeful change. It suggests that action in one field – such as that of social movements – can alter the dynamics of another. The autonomy of the juridical, like that of the movement, is relative and varies over time.

How can movements alter juridical practices, when the juridical field has its own particular forms of capital, rules, and institutions, which are relatively resistant to conventional movement tactics such as mass mobilization or other disruptive practices? The MST has not produced change in the juridical field by directly "occupying" the latter. It has done so by bringing the movement and juridical fields into contact and redirecting the energy of important juridical actors toward its claims. Private and public lawyers, legal scholars, judges, and other authorized interpreters of law have deployed their particular juridical capital *within their field* to alter the dominant interpretations of property rights, legitimate forms of civil disobedience, and so on. Networks of progressive lawyers or judges, as well as political actors, have played a critical *bridging* role between the two fields, helping convert movement energy into juridical energy. In the case of Brazil, the role of the movement field in the creation of a transformative pole within the juridical field is difficult to overstate.

Summarizing, changes in the relations between fields can alter their respective internal logics. The movement and juridical fields therefore should not be decontextualized – that is, they need to be understood in relation to each other.

9.3 THE MST AND MODALITIES OF JURIDICAL CHANGE

The MST's principle agrarian reform strategy has been to pressure *executive* parts of federal and state governments – in particular, by large-scale occupations of agricultural land – to expropriate and redistribute privately-held land. Juridical mobilization has not been a core component of this strategy. A profound distrust of the judiciary runs through much of the MST and it has yet to acquire a legal identity that would allow it to be either a plaintiff or a defendant. For most leaders and activists, the judiciary is the enforcer of bourgeois property rights. Experience has taught them that, when social conflict becomes judicialized, the outcome is often the absence of legal change, and the criminalization of movement activity, or of the movement itself. Furthermore, the MST resists giving up control of the terms and direction of its struggles to juridical actors such as private lawyers. Its leaders and activists know that the struggle over the translation of social conflict into legal categories, and over tactical procedural matters, inevitably renders parties to a case dependent on their legal proxies.

Nonetheless, MST leaders are acutely aware that its struggle for land takes place in the shadow of the law and have learnt that land occupations become judicialized almost immediately.[4] And, while in the first decade of its existence (1980–1990),[5] the movement paid little attention to judicial institutions and legal instruments, since the early 1990s it has invested more in what is an increasingly sophisticated reactive juridical strategy. Exactly why this shift occurred is explored in the second half of the chapter.

The movement is not monolithic, but its leaders tend to see juridical mobilization primarily in political terms. Courtroom procedures are political moments in which the misdeeds of landowners, including the illegal possession of public land, can be made public and the importance and legitimacy of the movement can be reaffirmed. Victories in the courts are measured by their effect on public opinion, on forcing executive branch action, and of course in keeping movement leaders and activists out of prison. The MST has not, for example, engaged in public interest litigation to pressure the government to implement a coherent agrarian reform process. The possibilities for such litigation are few and relatively recent creations, but the 1988 Constitution does provide for public class action suits.

Nonetheless, the MST's ability to concentrate legal talent and resources in the juridical field is considerable. This reflects the fact that, during the 1990s, the MST became the politically most significant social movement in the country, with a substantial and highly organized

---

[4] An "average" occupation produces an array of cases. Those initiated by the landowners targeting the MST include civil cases, in particular possession orders (*reintegração da posse*), maintenance of possession orders (*manutenção da posse*), and damages (*danos*). A variety of "cases within cases" result, as each actor seeks to maneuver within the limits of the law, while not infrequently engaging in extra-legal activity on the side. Landowners also frequently file police complaints that can provoke preventative detention (*prisão preventiva*) and that usually initiate criminal prosecutions for adverse possession (*esbulho possessório*); the constitution of a criminal organization (*formação de quadrilha*); theft (*roubo*); private imprisonment (*carceraria privada*); and even homicide (*homicidio*). The MST is far less active as a plaintiff. If any of its leaders is imprisoned by local police or the court orders detention, lawyers who work with movements will file *habeas corpus* petitions. In rare cases, they might file a police complaint against landowner violence, which can result in a criminal case. In a few instances, it has filed abuse of authority cases (*mandado de segurança*) against public officials. The federal or state government (its executive branch, that is) will, for its part, bring a case against the landowner or the person/group in possession of the land if it decides to claim the occupied land for the purposes of agrarian reform. In these cases, the MST, notwithstanding its direct interest in the case, is not a party to the proceedings. The government's action can provoke the landowner into filing an abuse of authority case (*mandado de segurança*) and almost certainly a series of appeals.

[5] The MST as a national movement was formally established in 1985 but it emerged and began to identify itself as the "Movement of Landless Rural Workers" as early as 1980.

structure and a far-flung network of relations (Mançano 1996, 2000; Navarro 1997). The tens of thousands of families that have obtained land by participating in MST-led occupations are spread across the country in over 1,000 agrarian reform settlements. The movement's allies include prominently situated actors in diverse arenas: religious (through the progressive wing of the Catholic Church and pastoral organizations), political (through the Workers' Party, in particular), labor (through the labor organization Central Única dos Trabalhadores), academic, and within international advocacy groups and NGOs. It has dense relations with state actors and receives public funds to run primary and secondary schools on agrarian reform settlements. Its cooperatives have access to public agricultural credit and public agricultural extension.

The case of the Pontal do Paranapanema, in the state of São Paulo, shows how the movement's land occupation strategy and juridical mobilization can combine to set in motion different types of modalities of legal change. Three modalities are evident: state enforcement of a de jure legality that was ignored in practice; a significant procedural innovation that accelerated the judicial clock; and (once again) a shift in the source of law and a reinterpretation of substantive legal norms. What is recounted here is part of the juridical story. How the outcome in each story was obtained will become apparent later on in the chapter.

The MST in the state of São Paulo played a central role in altering legality on the ground by pushing the state government to reestablish public possession of property that had been illegally occupied by large landowner-squatters, and then redistributing these. Its government proxies in the juridical field also fought the *juridical time* battle and contributed to producing an important procedural innovation that made it possible to accelerate the pace of judicial process more in line with the pace of the movement. And, finally, the movement's *habeas corpus* appeal to free imprisoned leaders in the case produced a federal high court ruling that took a significant step in decriminalizing the movement and in legalizing its repertoire of collective action. The *habeas corpus* ruling expanded the breadth of direct action accepted as civil disobedience. In terms of creating new legalities in practice, the Pontal do Paranapanema, a triangular piece of land in the state's relatively poor southwestern corner, is the only region in Brazil that analysts agree is experiencing true agrarian reform. Juridically driven legal change has played an important role in the

225

widespread expropriation of illegally held land in parts of the region, and fundamentally remade rural land tenure and social and political relations.

These modalities of legal change were all activated by the judicialization of social conflict that MST land occupations initiated. In most of the country the MST occupies land that it argues fails to fulfill its constitutionally required social function, and therefore should by law be expropriated for agrarian reform. In Pontal do Paranapanema, however, the strategy was different. Its principal strategy since the early 1990s has been to occupy public land that is held illegally (in adverse possession) by large landowners. The local MST learnt that the São Paulo state government had surveyed the Pontal do Paranapanema back in the 1940s, and established that 444,130 hectares of the region was in fact public land held illegally by landowner-squatters, and that the legal status of another 519,315 hectares remained to be ascertained (Mançano 1996:160). The government at the time, however, did not take any further action to reestablish public possession of that land. Fifty years later, the MST calculated that the state government could be convinced to repossess and redistribute the lands that had already been declared public. Legally, this would not constitute agrarian reform, which is a function reserved for the federal government, but in practice it would be just that.

The movement launched a series of land occupations in 1991 to force the state executive branch to intervene in the region. The state government, fearing a violent confrontation, entered the fray and brought several types of case to reclaim the public lands. The MST did not have legal standing and was not a party to these cases, even though its occupations were their immediate cause. Although the occupied areas had already been declared public land, the government had to win possession cases in the courts before it could take the land and redistribute it. In legal terms, the only uncertainty in such cases was the amount the state would pay for improvements that had been made on the land – that is, for buildings, fences, etc. For government lawyers, the cases were primarily a bargaining tool used to pressure the large squatters to settle on the transfer of possession of the property on the government's terms.

Between 1990 and 1995, however, few settlements were reached. In a small number of cases the combined pressure of movement occupation and government litigation, which depressed land values and led to escalating legal costs forced landowner-squatters to give up possession.

The relatively attractive offer made by the state's land institute contributed as well.

One of the principal hurdles the government faced, however, was the gross discrepancy in the *time* operative in the movement and juridical fields. In particular, landowner-squatters were able to keep legal procedures running for many years on end – either in the belief that a newly elected state government would give up and go away (as in the 1940s), or in order to hold out for a better deal. One example suffices to illustrate the depth of the problem. Ironically, it involves a procedural request by the government that would have sped up the pace of legal proceedings. In one of the first possession cases, in 1992, the public attorney asked a local judge to sequester the land in question in public hands until legal proceedings concluded. This would allow MST families who had occupied the land to stay on the land and greatly increase the pressure on the landowner to negotiate a settlement. If the courts accepted this procedural move, it would set a crucial precedent in the region – one or two quick victories for the government would virtually ensure that the remaining squatters would settle cases before they went to trial. Four years later – an eternity in movement time and an entire electoral cycle for the state governor – the Federal Superior Court ruled in favor of sequestering the land. In the intervening period, however, a new state government was elected and sought to alter juridical time through an entirely different procedural instrument.

What changed between the first and second efforts to speed up the juridical field? First, the election of a center-left state governor, and, secondly, the MST's ability to escalate its land occupations, appear as the most important changes. Up until 1994, the public attorney's office in the region, closely tied to local political elites, also had limited interest in resolving the case juridically. Much like the state government at the time, it was not politically committed to agrarian reform and had a profound distrust of the MST. The governor elected in 1994, however, was generally sympathetic toward the movement's goals, if not to the movement itself, and was concerned that collective violence could break out in the confrontation between the landless and landowner-squatters, with substantial human cost and electoral implications. The governor made a political and social justice decision to mobilize part of the formidable legal-bureaucratic apparatus at his command to resolve the region's land conflicts. An integrated plan – the *Plano de Ação para o Pontal* – that included administrative, political, and juridical components was drawn up for the region (ITESP 2000:72–80).

To accelerate court proceedings, the state Secretary of Justice tried out a new procedural instrument that had just come into effect, called *tutela anticipada* (anticipated tutelage). The instrument allows the judge to accelerate the judicial clock by making a provisional ruling at the beginning of a case. Due process, the alibi of slow judicial proceedings, is tricky in cases where the time consumed by normal procedures substantially reduces the benefits the final ruling may have for the plaintiff.[6] Because *tutela anticipada* appeared to invert the long-standing logic of such provisional rulings – that they be made only in cases of *absolute necessity* – there was considerable uncertainty in the juridical field about how judges would interpret its use, and especially whether they would relax the restrictive conditions that applied to other provisional measures. In the absence of jurisprudence, lawyers and judges would have to construct interpretations of how and when the instrument could be deployed.

The local judge ruled in favor of *tutela anticipada* in late 1995. On appeal, the São Paulo Tribunal of Justice reversed the lower court's decision. The case then went on to the Federal Superior Tribunal. The state Attorney-General and the Secretary for Justice made regular pilgrimages to the Federal Superior Tribunal, their staff set up camp in the national capital, Brasilia, and the governor himself appeared before the court. After fifteen days of deliberation, the Tribunal upheld the request for *tutela anticipada*.

In this manner, the government was able to obtain 73,540 hectares through the judicial system in the four years spanning 1995–1998, enough to create 60 agrarian reform settlements and to settle around 3,000 families. By contrast, the government had only acquired enough land in the first 4 years of the decade to settle 151 families.

The process that led to this outcome had two important dimensions. One is the centrality of the media campaign pursued by each of the parties to the conflict. Government officials, MST leaders, and land-owner-squatters converged in their media strategies and all played up the volatility of the region. Each believed that building the perception that the Pontal do Paranapanema was on the verge of a local class war

---

[6] Time can be a decisive factor in the utility of the outcome of a case. A patient with a life-threatening condition, for example, will gain little from a ruling that guarantees access to needed medication if that ruling comes after the condition has run its full course. In such cases, a provisional ruling (*medida cautelar*) can be requested to accelerate the juridical clock. This shifts the balance between due process and the efficacy of the ruling toward the latter. However, up until 1995, provisional rulings could only be obtained under highly restrictive conditions.

would bring judicial intervention that would be favorable to their interests. The real threat of violence at the time is impossible to ascertain. Headlines in the papers, however, were emphatic. In late 1995, the local newspaper O *Imparcial* (October 18, 1995) screamed "Police Chief Fears Social Convulsion"; São Paulo's leading newspaper, *Folha de São Paulo* (October 28, 1995), headlined "Landowners Have Already Hired Armed Security Forces in the Pontal"; the national *Jornal do Brasil* (December 24, 1995) declared "Landless Will Ensure Invasions with Bullets"; and the national news magazine, *IstoÉ* (October 11, 1995) noted that "the Pontal is a barrel of gun powder ready to explode." Lawyers representing landowner-squatters used such news reports to have MST leaders arrested and to show how the MST threatened the entire property system of the region. The MST for its part was acutely aware that historically government intervention for agrarian reform occurred primarily in regions of heightened social conflict, and rarely in regions where there was no pressure from below. The state government had its own reasons. It needed to build political support for its intervention in the Pontal, and to secure federal agrarian reform money to cover the cost of such an intervention. In the juridical field, it had to convince judges of the need to dramatically speed up legal proceedings that would place the occupied lands into its hands.

The second dimension that should be explicated is the unprecedented and *tout court* campaign by the state government to obtain judicial support for *its* interpretation of *tutela anticipada*. The state Secretary of Justice and state prosecutors visited the local judge who would hear the case, the local public prosecutor who would argue the state's case, and the chief justice of the São Paulo Tribunal of Justice, and, when the case was appealed to the Federal Superior Court, appeared before the President of that body. The governor of São Paulo, the economic powerhouse of Brazil and indeed of Latin America, would himself appear before the Federal Superior Tribunal. In each instance, the state government argued from a procedural and a consequentialist position. It suggested that all the requirements for the provisional measure were present in the case and made clear the governor's great concern that the region might descend into violence and disorder. One participant called the latter socio-political form of argumentation, *ad terrorem*. That is, the Pontal do Paranapanema was on the verge of large-scale collective violence and, if the courts denied the state government the legal tools necessary to maintain the landless on the land, a social convulsion was likely to ensue. It added that, if the court set a favorable precedent in this first case, it would undo the legal logjam, and the other landowner-squatters whose land was occupied would settle quickly.

The MST set in motion a third modality of legal change in the Pontal do Paranapanema region when a different judge in the Pontal issued an arrest warrant for thirteen of its leaders. The movement's counter-mobilization in the courts and in the public arena led the Federal Superior Tribunal to issue a ruling that decriminalized the movement and expanded the notion of what constitutes civil disobedience. The ruling is widely cited, not the least because the decision's author, Luiz Vicente Quicchiarro, is a leading Brazilian jurist in penal matters.

The principal charge against the movement leaders was the formation of a criminal gang with the intent of illegally taking possession of land. The São Paulo Tribunal of Justice denied the *habeas corpus* petition to free the MST leaders and echoed the view of the movement and its activities that was prevalent in many of the country's courts: "To allow third parties to violate the property of others, under the pretext of the social question, will be the undoing of the country's entire legal order. Today rural properties are invaded … Tomorrow industries, factories and commercial establishments may be invaded, with guaranteed impunity, under the pretext of 'social problems.' This is the obituary of the state and of society organized by law. The judiciary cannot accept or tolerate this."

The Federal Superior Tribunal reversed the São Paulo Tribunal. As in the previous cases discussed above, the justices moved the definition of the legal issue to a constitutional ground, from the penal code this time, and took a consequentialist position. Its ruling juxtaposed the right to property and the right to claim rights, a political liberty, finding that the movement's land occupations could not be considered a criminal act because there was no criminal intent. Instead, the MST land occupations should be seen as exercising the rights of citizenship, particularly the civil right to pressure government to guarantee constitutional rights, in this case that of agrarian reform. For the same reasons, the MST should also be considered a popular movement claiming citizenship (see Strozake 2000).

This ruling has been extremely significant, in both political and juridical terms. It has not, however, stopped local judges from granting arrest warrants against MST leaders. Judges in Brazil are not bound by high court precedent and place a particularly high value on their autonomy. As recently as 2003, another judge in the Pontal region issued an arrest warrant for local MST leaders. Although the subsequent *habeas corpus* petitions are likely to succeed in the high court, such legal harassment has substantial costs for the movement and reveals that the MST's contribution to legal change is uneven and accumulates only slowly.

9.4 MOVEMENT AND JUDICIAL FIELDS IN LEGAL CHANGE

It is quite rare that encounters between movements and judiciaries set the entire chains of events depicted in motion. This section explores the changes that occurred in the movement and juridical fields that allowed their particular logics to synchronize to and produce cosmopolitan legal change. It focuses on the key components of the unique logics of the movement and juridical fields: the distinctive forms of power that operate in the two fields; institutionally situated actors who enjoy variable capacity for action; and, finally, the struggle over symbolic order.

9.4.1 The MST in the movement field

The contemporary social movement field in Brazil emerged in the late 1970s as part of the country's democratic transition, but in recent years it has undergone profound changes. At its foundational moment, the field's protagonists shared an oppositional stance toward the state, an emphasis on transgressive collective action, and a symbolic order structured by a prophetic utopian project. Since the early 1990s, there has been a shift toward increased contact with the state, a focus on citizen participation, and a discourse built around the construction of citizenship and influencing public policy. Changes in the field have contributed to the MST becoming one of its most prominent actors, a status that has greatly enhanced its ability to concentrate the energy of different types of actors in the juridical field.

An array of actors during the democratic transition (the late 1970s and 1980s) identified themselves as part of "the popular movement." In her noteworthy analysis of the movement field, Diomo (1995:68) suggests the popular movement was a multi-centric field defined by relations among actors who, notwithstanding diverse identities, shared a political commitment and discourse, and an involvement in cross-cutting networks. Its symbolic order revolved around a utopian and prophetic discourse that emphasized popular (mass) participation in direct action in the struggle for emancipation from capitalist exploitation and authoritarian social and political institutions (Diomo 1995:144). Along with independence from political parties and the struggle against the state, these provided elements for a new democratic and transformative project for society (Diomo 1995:29). The field's actors included not only rural social movements such as the MST and the Movement of the Displaced by Dams, but also urban movements such as the Housing Movement and the Union of Neighborhood Associations of Porto Alegre (UAMPA), which contributed to the creation of the participatory budget in Porto Alegre, and a large variety of popular education institutes and NGOs. For the MST, which grew directly out of the organizing work of liberation theology Catholic radicals, the oppositional stance vis-à-vis the state, and formal political institutions generally, and emphasis on popular engagement in direct action to obtain one's rights (by forcing state action) were particularly strong. Among movements it was, and remains, unique in its commitment to a prophetic mission and attention to reproducing the mystique of *a luta*, the struggle.

Diomo's analysis suggests that the movement field was shaped in profound ways by the struggle against authoritarian rule and by the role the Catholic Church played in these struggles. The church as an institution with remarkable organizational infrastructure and access to international resources, and Catholicism as a symbolic order with deep resonance among "the people," provided much of the structural and ideational underpinnings of the field. The latter also had strong influence from the Gramscian left, which may help account for the strong (and somewhat paradoxical) emphasis on rights.

In this foundational period, accumulating such capital involved strong ties to the Catholic Church and, in rural areas where the MST functioned, the skilled use of a radical political-religious discourse. As Mançano (2000:84) observes, the struggle for land was a "permanent struggle for dignity and for life," and what bound the movement together were popular religiosity and the "mass struggles in which the [landless] families participated" directly.

In the 1990s, a variety of processes came together to alter many core components of the movement field. These processes included the consolidation of democratic institutions, and particularly the Constitution of 1988; the conservative shift within the Catholic Church on the one hand, and the growing electoral power of the

Workers' Party and of its growing presence in the municipal government of several important cities on the other; changes in international funding as Western European agencies shifted agendas and geographic interests; and the state's greater decentralization and openness to the participation of civil society organizations in policy-making and implementation. The latter had, among other things, important resource implications for the field's actors.

The Catholic Church had lost much of its role in providing the field's structural and symbolic bases by the late 1980s, while that of the Workers' Party had grown considerably. New types of actors, with direct access to international funds, as well as government funds, became prominent in particular civil society coordinating bodies such as the Association of Popular Movements and ABONG (the Brazilian Association of NGOs) and well-funded and professionalized advocacy NGOs like Polis and IBASE. Older actors such as the MST became more institutionalized. The symbolic universe changed as well. The field lost its original utopian and prophetic content as the emphasis shifted to constructing citizenship and "citizenship in action," which included participation in constitutionally mandated policy councils, and influencing public policy and public debate (Diomo 1995:213). Ties between actors in the field and state agencies grew substantially.

Paradoxically, the MST's position in the field grew substantially during the 1990s and along with it the ability to concentrate social energy. More than any other actor in the field it resisted many of these changes, setting itself apart in striking ways. It maintained close ties to progressive segments of the Catholic Church and kept large transgressive collective action – in the form of land occupations, protest marches, and the occupation of government agencies and highways – as its principal strategy. Land occupations in fact spread throughout the country and grew substantially in number. Although the difficulty in compiling data on occupations is considerable, the DATALUTA project at the UNESP Presidente Prudente suggests that both the number of occupations and the number of participants in occupations rose more than threefold, from 421 in the 1990–1994 period to 1,855 in the 1995–1999 period (Mançano 2000:270–272).

The growth of the movement's visibility and support within the movement field, and more broadly within progressive quarters, gave it access to far greater legal, political, and material resources. In the 1990s, the MST became *the* nationally recognized movement for land reform, although rural workers' unions and other movements also engaged in land occupations and sought redistribution (Navarro 1997). Its combative rhetoric and transgressive action notwithstanding, the movement did follow the new logic of the field by developing pragmatic and extensive relations with sectors of the state and diversifying its resource base. Although the MST has remained distrustful of the judiciary, the 1990s did see a shift in the MST's definition of "the land question" toward a more secular and juridical one. In the earlier period, the struggle for land had been constructed in a political-religious form as an issue of social justice and human dignity, and as a basis for liberation from a capitalist system that enslaved the weak to the benefit of the national and international capital (Mançano 2000:81–83). It had set itself apart from other significant rural movements by rejecting the Land Statute of 1964 and demanding new legislation be created with the participation of rural workers, "with a basis in the practices and experiences of these [rural workers]" (Mançano 2000:81). In the 1990s, the discursive construction included, alongside a broad notion of social justice, the constitutional principle of the social function of land and the constitutionality of agrarian reform.

Within the movement itself, two important developments helped push it closer to the juridical field. One is the gradual learning process of its leaders as small victories accumulate in the courts and encounters with less conservative judges and lawyers become more common place. The other, and probably more importantly, is that out of necessity it has had to develop a concern with human rights. Many of its most important leaders are no longer "first-time offenders" in criminal cases, and hence face greater chances of long prison sentences. The growing legal burden and threat forced the movement to create a human rights department and engage in an ongoing way with allies in the juridical field.

Finally, the Workers' Party's growing power also helped to synchronize the movement and juridical fields. The MST and the Workers' Party emerged out of the same process of political mobilization that helped produce the transition to democracy, and they have since maintained close ties. The Workers' Party's political figures have been invaluable allies to the movement, including, in particular, in the case of the arrest of MST leaders in the Pontal do Paranapanema, when they helped the case move quickly from a local action in the juridical field to a national concern of the political field. Some of Brazil's most distinguished human rights lawyers, including a Workers' Party congressman, argued the *habeas corpus* petition in the

Superior Court. The growing number of Workers' Party administrations at the municipal and state levels also helped to shift the MST away from its long-standing state-as-enemy position.

9.4.2 The Brazilian judiciary and the juridical field

The juridical field underwent its own set of changes during the 1990s, albeit at a slower pace than those in the movement field. This helped make possible the juridical modalities of change the MST was able to set in motion. In public debate these changes and the tensions that accompanied them have been framed as "the crisis of the justice system." At the center of these changes is the gradual and highly contested constitutionalization of law, as members of the field have sought to rebuild the democratic legitimacy of judicial institutions and to adjust to the realities of a new democratic regime. The importance of this process cannot be overstated, not only because the civil code that was operative until 2003 was starkly liberal in its conception of property rights, and the individual nature of rights in general, but also because of the array of social and diffuse rights available in the 1988 Constitution. The constitutionalization of law has made possible the legal definition of social conflicts in ways that were closer to those in the movement field. Perhaps most importantly, the process has opened the door to a substantial expansion of the role of the judiciary and of judicial interpretation. Overall, efforts since the early 1990s to constitutionalize law and to reconcile legal norms that vary substantially in normative and substantive disposition have played a critical role in facilitating juridical modalities of change.

As in the case of the movement field, the types of actor in the juridical field also changed. In addition to the deservedly heralded federal and state public prosecutors offices (*Ministério Publico*), the formal and informal networks of judges and lawyers concerned with questions of social justice and with defining a new democratic role for judicial institutions and the legal profession were particularly important. These networks played a fundamental role in bridging the gap between the juridical and the movement fields and in helping to produce a new legal common sense in the former on matters related to the MST and land conflict.

The Pontal do Paranapanema case illustrates how the lower courts' application of legal norms serves to translate social conflicts that enter the juridical field into universal and socially abstracted categories. What the local judge had constructed as a narrow conflict over individual property rights, adopting what critics call the traditional proceduralist or positivist legal reasoning, the higher courts constructed as a conflict of fundamental rights and property rights, with important social consequences. The former would argue that constitutional principles are not law, and therefore implementing legislation (and hence the mediation of the legislator) is necessary to make them law and justiciable; the latter argue that fundamental rights and other constitutional principles impose immediate legal obligations and do not require further legislation to have binding force.

The two constructions of the case reflect the competing efforts to interpret the 1988 Constitution and have led to a profound split within the juridical field but have also brought it closer to that of the movement field. Constitutions in Latin America, including in Brazil, have been seen primarily as political documents rather than as law. With the 1988 Constitution, however, the trend toward constitutionalization that accompanied the creation of the welfare state in Europe appears to have reached Brazil. Accepting the Constitution as law greatly expands the competence of judges and, because of the nature of the Constitution's articles and its concern with substantive (and social) outcomes, requires that they engage in far greater interpretation and construction of law. This also flows directly from the expansion of collective social rights and legal instruments, such as public class action suits, that make it easier to transform individual legal battles into collective ones.

The state of São Paulo has a conservative judicial tradition, but judges committed to a constitutionalist view of law, human rights, and the democratization of the judiciary formed the Association of Judges for Democracy in 1991 and, specifically for criminal matters, the Brazilian Institute of Criminal Sciences (IBCCRIM) in 1992. The decision of the São Paulo judges to create independent and formal organizations paradoxically reflects their tenuous position within the state's magistracy. Since the early 1990s, these judges have seen the constitutionalization of law as vital for democratizing the law and for bringing a modern social context into the rigidly individualistic and de-contextualized application of the civil and criminal codes. They have also seen, correctly, that the process of constitutionalization entailed an acknowledgment of the expansion of judges' interpretative activities.

Networks of progressive lawyers are not new in Brazil, but during the 1990s the first national network of popular lawyers who work with rural and urban movements emerged. The National Network of Popular Lawyers (RENAP), formally constituted in 1996, played an important role in synchronizing the juridical and movement fields. Reflecting a general trend in progressive lawyering networks, RENAP is national in scope and more specialized – today it has approximately 420 law professionals distributed across twenty-two of the country's twenty-six states and focuses primarily on agrarian questions, and is closely tied to the MST.

RENAP has been an important bridge between the movement and juridical fields, and links inexperienced lawyers at the local level with nationally recognized jurists. Its lawyers have also played an important role in overcoming the movement's resistance to entering the juridical field and in building relations of trust between the movement and other juridical protagonists, including the informal networks of judges committed to social justice. Although the MST from its early days in the 1980s drew progressive lawyers into its orbit, it is only from the mid-1990s that it has sought to establish closer and ongoing relations to these. Prior to this, the movement sought out lawyers in piecemeal fashion to free imprisoned leaders and to battle the various forms of legal harassment and criminalization.

The network has also been deeply committed to the constitution-alization process within the juridical field and helped propagate new doctrinal bases from which to argue cases involving the MST. Perhaps the strongest evidence of the former is the remarkable campaign to create a new legal common sense on issues that affect the MST (Varella 1997). Through its magazine and periodical publications it circulates new jurisprudence that is favorable to the struggles for land. Two recent edited volumes contain essays by over thirty notable legal jurists on civil and criminal cases that involve the MST (see Strozake 2000, 2002). Contributors include members of the São Paulo network of Judges of Democracy and, of course, RENAP itself.

The publications reveal RENAP's impressive reach in the juridical field, and through it that of the MST. The volumes have been made available not only to RENAP members but also to hundreds of judges. This initiative is remarkable because both lawyers sympathetic to the MST, and local judges who may or may not be, have very tenuous access to sources containing jurisprudence. As several judges in São Paulo observed during interviews, there are magistrates who still apply parts of the 1916 civil code which have long been superseded. Once out of law school, even professionally committed judges find it difficult to

keep abreast with emerging jurisprudence, and even with new legislation (which is particularly voluminous in Brazil).

9.5 CONCLUSION

The MST's sustained engagement with the juridical field has set a
number of modalities of legal change in motion that, in the cases
discussed in this chapter, redefined important legal terrain on property
rights, as well as on civil disobedience. It also produced substantial
social results. The movement's ability to convert movement energy
into juridical energy, and to mobilize across multiple fields, has played a
central role in setting these modalities of legal change in motion.

The movement's capacity for this kind of strategic action, and the
impact of such action, however, has been contingent on broader
dynamics within the movement, party political, and religious fields
over which it has had limited control. Substantial shifts in each of
the fields during the 1990s greatly enhanced the movement's ability to
redirect and concentrate the energies of highly qualified legal experts
toward the civil and criminal issues it confronted. It is also during this
period, as a result of shifts in the respective fields, as well as its own
strategic action within these shifts, that the MST became the most
prominent social movement in contemporary Brazil. This particular
status within the movement field has enabled the movement to construct a breadth of alliances, in the juridical and other fields, that can be
matched by few other social movements in Brazil.

The MST's juridical mobilization nonetheless sheds light on some of
the ways in which social movements can use the law to create countervailing possibilities to the particular "liberal" property regime that is
being globalized from above. It has played a substantial role in altering a
highly exclusionary legality by compelling public authorities to implement existing agrarian reform legislation, by helping to create and
institutionalize novel interpretations of the social function of property
and an expanded notion of civil disobedience, and by pushing public
prosecutors to use procedural instruments in innovative ways that
dramatically increase the pace of judicial proceedings.

References

Barroso, Luís Roberto. 2002a. *O Direito Constitucional e a Efetividade de Suas
Normas: Limites e Possibilidades da Constituição Brasileira*. Rio de Janeiro:
Renovar.

2002b. "Fundamentos Teóricos e Filosóficos do Novo Direito Constitucional Brasileiro." *Jus Navigandi* 59:157.

Bourdieu, Pierre. 1987. "The Force of Law: Toward a Sociology of the Juridical Field." *Hastings Law Journal* 38:814–853.

Bourdieu, Pierre, and Loïc Wacquant. 1992. *An Invitation to Reflexive Sociology*. Chicago: University of Chicago Press.

Dezalay, Yves, and Bryant Garth. 1998. *Dealing in Virtue: International Commercial Arbitration and the Construction of a Transnational Legal Order*. Chicago: University of Chicago Press.

Diomo, Ana Maria. 1995. *A Vez e Voz do Popular: Movimentos Sociais e Participação Política no Brasil Pós-70*. Rio de Janeiro: ANPOCS/Relume Dumará.

Epp, Charles. 1998. *The Rights Revolution: Lawyers, Activists, and Supreme Courts in Comparative Perspective*. Chicago: University of Chicago Press.

Facchini Netto, Eugênio. 2003. "Fundamental Rights in the Balance: One View of the Cathedral, through a Judge's Eye." Paper presented at the International Workshop on "Fundamental Rights in the Balance: New Ideas on the Rights to Property, Land, and Shelter," 16–18 October 2003, Institute of Development Studies, Brighton, UK.

Galanter, Marc. 1981. "Justice in Many Rooms: Courts, Private Ordering, and Indigenous Law." *Journal of Legal Pluralism* 19:1–47.

Houtzager, Peter. 2001a. "We Make the Law and the Law Makes Us: Some Ideas on a Law in Development Research Agenda." *IDS Bulletin* 32(1):8–18.

2001b. "Collective Action and Patterns of Political Authority: Rural Workers, Church, and State in Brazil." *Theory and Society* 30(1):1–45.

Hunt, Alan. 1993. *Explorations in Law and Society: Toward a Constitutive Theory of Law*. New York: Routledge.

ITESP. 2000. *Mediação no Campo: Estratégias de Ação em Situações de Conflito Fundiário*. 2nd edition. Cadernos ITESP No. 6. São Paulo: ITESP, Paginas e Letras.

Mançano, Bernardo. 1996. *MST: Formação e Territorialização em São Paulo*. São Paulo: Editora Hucitec.

2000. *A Formação do MST no Brasil*. Rio de Janeiro: Vozes.

McAdam, Doug, Sidney Tarrow, and Charles Tilly. 2001. *Dynamics of Contention*. Cambridge: Cambridge University Press.

Merryman, John. 1985. *The Civil Law Tradition: An Introduction to the Legal Systems of Western Europe and Latin America*. Stanford: Stanford University Press.

Navarro, Zander. 1997. "Sete Teses Equivocadas sobre as Lutas Sociais no Campo, o MST e a Reform Agrária." In *A Reforma Agrária e a Luta do MST*, edited by João Pedro Stedile. Rio de Janeiro: Vozes.

2001. "'Mobilização sem emancipação' – as lutas sociais dos sem-terra no Brasil." In *Reinventando a emancipação social*, edited by Boaventura de Sousa Santos. São Paulo: Record.

Santos, Boaventura de Sousa. 1995. *Toward a New Common Sense: Law, Science and Politics in the Paradigmatic Transition*. New York: Routledge.

2002. *Toward a New Legal Common Sense: Law, Globalization, and Emancipation*. London: Butterworths.

Streck, Lenio. 2002. *Jurisdição Constitucional e Hermenêutica: Uma Nova Crítica do Direito*. Porto Alegre: Livraria do Advogado.

Strozake, Juvelino (Ed.). 2000. *A Questão Agrária e a Justiça*. São Paulo: Editora Revista dos Tribunais.

(Ed.). 2002. *Questões Agrárias: Julgados comentados e Pareceres*. São Paulo: Editora Método.

Varella, Marcelo. 1997. "O MST e o Direito." In *A Reforma Agrária e a Luta do MST*, edited by João Pedro Stédile. Petrópolis: Vozes.

CHAPTER 10

INDIGENOUS RIGHTS, TRANSNATIONAL ACTIVISM, AND LEGAL MOBILIZATION: THE STRUGGLE OF THE U'WA PEOPLE IN COLOMBIA

César A. Rodríguez-Garavito and *Luis Carlos Arenas*

10.1 INTRODUCTION

In an ironic twist, one of the most powerful challenges to globalization has come from the indigenous peoples whose localized, "pre-modern" existence was supposed to have crumbled under the pressure of modern capitalist projects – from that of the colonial project to that of the "development project" (McMichael 2000). Encapsulating the clashing forces of this historical short-circuit, the plight and transnational resistance of indigenous peoples expose with unique clarity the cultural, political, and legal issues at stake in the confrontation between hegemonic and counter-hegemonic globalization.

Several reasons explain the visibility and importance of the indigenous peoples in such a confrontation. First, the indigenous movement involves populations historically subjected to the cruelest forms of exclusion. In Latin America, depending on the area, between 50 and 90 percent of the indigenous population died during the first century of the Spanish conquest, and few tribal groups survived the assimilationist policies of the postcolonial states (Kearney and Varese 1995). Today, albeit comprising the majority or a large portion of the population in several countries (71 percent in Bolivia, 66 percent in Guatemala, 47 percent in Peru, and 38 percent in Ecuador), indigenous peoples continue to be "the poorest of the poor" (Psacharopoulos and Patrinos 1994). In Guatemala, while 53.9 percent of the population is poor, 86.6 percent of indigenous people fall under the poverty line. The gap is similar in Mexico, where 80.6 percent of the indigenous population is poor, as well as in Peru

241

(79 percent) and in Bolivia (64.3 percent) (Psacharopoulos and Patrinos 1994). Thus, if counter-hegemonic globalization focuses on the populations most harmed by hegemonic globalization (Santos and Rodríguez-Garavito's chapter in this volume), then the struggle of indigenous peoples is one of its core components.

Moreover, as we explain below, the rise of the transnational indigenous movement is explicitly rooted in a reaction against the expansion of the frontiers of predatory forms of global capitalism into new territories (e.g. the Amazon) and economic activities (e.g. the commercial exploitation of traditional knowledge and biodiversity). This expansion, in turn, is linked to the pressures to step up the exploitation of natural resources associated with increasing consumption in the North and economic dependence in the South. The examination of the indigenous movement thus allows us to see the new frontiers of neoliberal globalization and of the resistance to it.

The indigenous cause illustrates two particularly promising features of the global justice movement. On the one hand, it illustrates the combination of struggles and scales of mobilization that characterizes counter-hegemonic globalization. Indigenous peoples raise claims for self-determination and land that vindicate local customs, laws, and ancestral territories. However, in pursuing these local claims they have not only mobilized globally in alliance with indigenous peoples and transnational indigenous rights organizations but have also joined forces with the global environmentalist movement, the struggle of national ethnic minorities and other counter-hegemonic movements. By bridging movement frames and issues, indigenous peoples have challenged hegemonic actors at every scale, from local colonists and discriminatory national states to transnational corporations (TNCs) seeking to exploit natural resources in their homelands. On the other hand, the fact that the indigenous movement is identity-based brings into relief the distinctively cultural dimension of counter-hegemonic globalization – that is, the fact that global social movements are as much about difference as they are about equality.[1] Indeed, the iconic character of the Zapatista struggle (and the indigenous movement writ large) within the global justice movement lies in its capacity to bring together the aspiration to economic justice (as evident in its launching on the occasion of the entering into force of NAFTA in 1994) and the aspiration to ethnic, racial, and gender justice (Ceceña 1999).

[1] On this issue, see chapter 2 by Santos.

242

The very location of the indigenous cause at the crossroads of different movements, scales, and historical trajectories that accounts for its visibility and importance also explains its difficulties. Therefore, the study of the indigenous movement in action illustrates some of the main tensions and contradictions within counter-hegemonic globalization. Among them are the differences between the time frames and the agendas of Northern NGOs and indigenous peoples, and the ambiguous effects of the judicialization of indigenous rights struggles.

Finally, and particularly important for the purposes of this chapter, the transnational mobilization of indigenous peoples has unleashed a process of legal innovation with profound implications for national constitutional systems and the international human rights regime. Centered on the recognition of collective rights and embodied by myriad constitutional reforms and new international legal instruments, this "renaissance of indigenous peoples for the law" (Marés 2000) has shaken the individualist and Western-centric tenets of liberal legal thought and institutions and holds out the prospect for a cosmopolitan reconstruction of human rights (Anaya 1996; Kymlicka 1999; Santos 2002a, 2002b).

In this chapter, we examine the connection between politics and law in the transnational indigenous movement. To that end, we offer a case study of the struggle of the U'wa, an indigenous people of 5,000 members living in northeastern Colombia, against oil drilling in their territory. Waged in collaboration with national and transnational environmentalist NGOs and indigenous rights and human rights organizations, the decade-long, ongoing campaign of the U'wa people against Occidental Petroleum (Oxy) and the Colombian government vividly illustrates the potential and the limitations of transnational political mobilization in support of indigenous rights. Given that the struggle has revolved around the interpretation of the U'wa's collective right over territory, it has crucially involved judicial and quasi-judicial institutions (from the Colombian Constitutional Court and Council of State to the Inter-American Commission on Human Rights and the International Labour Organization) advancing contrasting discourses and agendas on law and human rights.

Our analytical focus is twofold. First, we examine the connection between local, national, regional, and global contentious mobilization in support of the U'wa. Thus, we give especial attention to the transformation of the membership, strategies, and impact of the pro-U'wa coalition as it shifted from the local and national scales to the regional and global scales – and then, in a "boomerang effect" (Keck and Sikkink 1998), returned to Colombian political and legal venues. Secondly, we engage the nascent literature on the role of law in counter-hegemonic globalization (see Santos and Rodríguez-Garavito's chapter in this volume) by focusing on the distinctively legal strategies of the U'wa coalition and assessing the potential and limitations of such strategies for the advancement of the U'wa cause and the movement for global justice writ large.

The chapter is organized as follows. In the first section, we locate the U'wa struggle in the broader economic, political, and legal context of the turn to neoliberalism and the rising indigenous movement in Latin America. In the second, we zero in on the U'wa campaign as it has unfolded in national and international settings. In the third section we step back to assess the achievements and limitations of the campaign along our two analytical axes. Finally, we offer some conclusions.

10.2 RESISTING THE "SECOND CONQUEST": NEOLIBERALISM, HUMAN RIGHTS, AND THE INDIGENOUS MOVEMENT

The simultaneity of the turn to neoliberalism and the rise of the indigenous movement in Latin America is not accidental. Beginning in the mid-1970s and gaining momentum in the 1980s, these two processes have developed in explicit confrontation with each other, as shown by the massive indigenous protests against neoliberalism since the early 1990s, from those that have driven neoliberal presidents in Bolivia and Ecuador out of office to those of the Zapatistas in Mexico.

The connection between "structural adjustment" programs and the plight and resistance of indigenous peoples is manifold. It includes, for instance, the effects of neoliberal policies that have rolled back land reform throughout the region and liberalized rural property rights that protected collective indigenous holdings such as the *ejido* system in Mexico (Bartra 2005). Together with the turn to export crops and the erosion of agricultural commodity prices in global markets, the unconditional opening of domestic economies has further depressed the marginalization of indigenous peoples (Stavenhagen 2002).

For our purposes, the most relevant link between globalization and the indigenous cause concerns the escalation of resource extraction. The combination of pressure for debt service and the dwindling income from agricultural products competing with heavily subsidized exports from the US have encouraged Latin American states to increase resource extraction, from timber to mining and oil. In Colombia, oil revenues amount to 25 percent of all export earnings. Ecuador depends on oil for approximately half of its export earnings, while devoting about half of the latter to service the debt (Brysk 1998:151).

The broader negative effects of a country's dependence on resource extraction (the so-called "resource curse") for economic growth, equity, and democracy have been well documented (Karl 1999). Specifically with regard to indigenous peoples, what is striking about this process is the overlap between the location of the most sought-after natural resources and indigenous territories (Jimeno 2002). Therefore, as Maybury-Lewis (1984:129) has put it, the ongoing, "second conquest" of indigenous peoples, "unlike the first one, is not particularly interested in Indian labor. It is interested in Indian land. The threat to the Indians is not this time one of slavery, but of expropriation of their lands and [the] total destruction of their way of life, if not their persons as well."

It is not surprising, therefore, that some of the most internationally visible and locally effective native uprisings have involved indigenous peoples resisting resource extraction in their territories. Also, since foreign investment and technology are invariably needed for the exploitation of the most profitable natural resources, TNCs have joined national governments as targets of indigenous mobilization. For instance, the Mayagnas in Nicaragua have waged a national and transnational struggle against Korean TNCs seeking to exploit timber in their territories, while the Huaorani, the Secoya, and the Cofán in Ecuador have been involved in a decade-long international campaign to hold Texaco accountable for massive oil spills in their territories.

Thus, faced with the deepening penetration of "the global triad of modernity" (states, markets, and Western culture) embodied by neoliberal globalization, these and other struggles have shaped the indigenous movement's "trio of core demands: self-determination, land rights, and cultural survival" (Brysk 2000:59). Self-determination entails political self-government in accordance with indigenous traditions and laws. In the large majority of cases, this claim points to some form of autonomy within a larger national state, rather than secession (Kymlicka 1999:281). The vindication of cultural difference concerns the right of indigenous peoples to negotiate on fair terms their engagement with the larger world, in opposition to assimilationist projects and other forms of imposition of Western culture (Anaya 1996).

Particularly prominent in struggles against predatory development such as the one waged by the U'wa is the demand on land. This claim is closely related to the affirmation of cultural difference, for the broader indigenous notion of "territory" radically departs from the conception of land as a factor of production and private property. From the indigenous perspective, "territory" includes both the space and the natural resources that are necessary to reproduce the economy and culture of a community. Thus, as Brysk has put it, "indigenous concepts of land also encompass location as a source of cultural reproduction: territory as identity" (2000:61). This notion includes environmental considerations, for land ("Mother Earth") is viewed as a living organism whose existence and integrity must be respected. "Among our principles – explained Gilberto Cobaría, the U'wa's spokesperson – is the awareness that we, the U'wa, are here to protect, take care and maintain the balance of the earth and of the existence in this planet."[2] Identity, land, and environmental preservation thus come together in the radical indigenous defense of collective land rights (Bartra 2005).

Indigenous claims have raised a formidable political and legal challenge to Latin American states and TNCs with interests in the region. In pursuing their demands, indigenous peoples have combined national and international mobilization. At the national scale, indigenous uprisings have been the most effective form of contestation of structural adjustment programs and placed the issue of indigenous rights at the center of political debate. The power of the national movements and indigenous organizations, especially in countries with a large native population, has risen since the 1990 March for Territory and Dignity in Bolivia and the nationwide *levantamiento* (uprising) in Ecuador in the same year. Today, the power of the Bolivian Katarista movement and the Ecuadorian Pachakutic party to destabilize national governments and press for structural constitutional reforms bears witness to the growing political clout of indigenous peoples (Dávalos 2005; Tapia 2005; Van Cott 2003). Local and national protests, marches, and acts of civil disobedience have been articulated with solidarity campaigns put together by coalitions of transnational indigenous rights organizations (e.g. the International Group on Indigenous Affairs, and Survival International), human rights NGOs (e.g. Human Rights Watch and the Washington Office on Latin America), anti-poverty organizations (e.g. Oxfam), faith-based coalitions (the World Council of Churches),

---

[2] Interview with Gilberto Cobaría, Bogotá, June 15, 2000.

and environmentalist organizations and networks (e.g. Rainforest Action Network and Oilwatch).

As for the distinctively legal dimension of the movement, transnational indigenous mobilization has given rise to one of the most potent challenges to national and international legal systems. Against the individualistic and monocultural slant of modern legal orders, indigenous peoples have vindicated a relational and collective understanding of rights (thus adding collective rights to the liberal repertoire of individual guarantees) and proposed multicultural legal frameworks guaranteeing the right to difference (Kymlicka 1999; Santos 2002a).

Demands for the protection of indigenous peoples' collective entitlements have led to profound transformations of national and international law. Since the late 1980s, constitutions across Latin America have recognized for the first time the multicultural character of the population and incorporated indigenous rights (Van Cott 2000). After the pioneer introduction of indigenous entitlements in the Nicaraguan constitution in 1987 in the wake of the conflict between the Miskito and the Sandinista government, a wave of new constitutions introduced specific provisions on indigenous rights: Brazil (1988), Colombia (1991), Mexico (1991), Peru (1993), Bolivia (1994), and Venezuela (2000). As shown below in the description of the way in which the U'wa resorted to the Colombian Constitutional Court to defend their right to territory, indigenous movements have integrated the newly established constitutional frameworks into their political struggle.

A parallel transformation has been taking place within the international system of human rights. Given the failure of the existing human rights system to deal with the claims of indigenous peoples, one of the central goals of the transnational advocacy network for indigenous rights has been the reform of the system (Anaya 1996; Kymlicka 1999). Two key instruments have resulted from this effort. First, the International Labour Organization (ILO) approved Convention No. 169 in 1989, which recognizes native peoples' right to political and cultural self-determination and territory within national states. Since entering into force in 1991, the convention has marked the turn of international law away from assimilationist views and provided a blueprint for legal reform and adjudication in favor of indigenous rights in Latin America and elsewhere. Secondly, the most comprehensive attempt at incorporating indigenous claims into the international system of human rights is the UN Draft Declaration on the Rights of Indigenous Peoples. The outcome of ten years of deliberation of the UN Working Group on Indigenous

Populations and vigorous NGO lobbying, the Draft Declaration is still working its way up to the UN General Assembly.

The final piece of the new legal repertoire used by cross-border solidarity coalitions is transnational litigation. In some cases, suits have been brought before the courts of the country of origin of the TNC accused of violating indigenous rights. This is illustrated by the failed *Aguinda* v. *Texaco* case, in which the participants in the above-mentioned campaign to hold Texaco responsible for environmental degradation in Ecuador filed suit against Texaco in the US courts. In other instances, the strategy consists in bringing cases involving violations of indigenous rights before regional judicial bodies. In Latin America, indigenous rights advocates have resorted on several occasions (including in the U'wa case) to the Inter-American Commission/Court of Human Rights. Despite the limitations of the legal instruments that provide the basis for these suits (namely, the fact that they protect only civil liberties as opposed to collective rights), litigation-oriented organizations participating in international indigenous coalitions (e.g. the US-based Indian Law Resource Center and the transnational Center for Social and Economic Rights) have creatively extended the interpretation of such instruments to include indigenous rights. This strategy led to the landmark decision of the Inter-American Court of Human Rights against Nicaragua in 2001 that supported the case of the Awas Tingni against logging in their ancestral territory, which expanded the notion of private property to encompass the collective entitlement of indigenous people to territory (Anaya and Grossman 2002).

In sum, indigenous peoples have allied with transnational coalitions to resist the second conquest through political and legal strategies at the local, national, regional, and global scales. In so doing, they have gained unprecedented political clout and prompted a radical revision of national constitutions and international law. All of these processes are vividly illustrated by the intricate path of the struggle of the U'wa people, to which we now turn.

10.3 THE U'WA CASE

10.3.1 Acting locally: the grassroots mobilization for territory

The U'wa (a name that means "people who think, people who know how to speak") currently occupy a swath of land of approximately 60,000 hectares in northeastern Colombia. However, their ancestral territory is considerably larger, encompassing areas of several Colombian provinces and extending to the western part of Venezuela (Osborn 1985).

The first signs of the second conquest of the U'wa territory and the origins of their political mobilization predated Oxy's arrival by several decades. In the 1940s, impoverished colonists fleeing from poverty and violence in the Colombian hinterland began slowly to eat away at the U'wa territory. Albeit coexisting peacefully with the newcomers, the U'wa began to organize in the early 1970s to resist the threats to their culture and the environment posed by the colonization process. In a process parallel to the one taking place across Latin America, the U'wa founded their first political association in 1976, which later became part of the rising nationwide indigenous movement and the National Indigenous Organization of Colombia (ONIC). The process of political organizations went hand in hand with a process of cultural affirmation, as shown by the community's decision in 1990 to repudiate the name the Spanish had given them (Tunebo) and revert to the original indigenous name of their people (U'wa) (Mesa 1996).

The vindication of the right to territory has been at the heart of the U'wa movement since its inception. Throughout the 1970s and 1980s, the U'wa pressed the Colombian government to recognize their collective entitlement on their land. This led to the creation of a 45,440-hectare reservation in 1974, which was expanded, after continuous mobilization by the U'wa and ONIC, to 61,115 hectares in 1987. This solution, however, was far short of what the U'wa had been demanding, for the new reservation did not include the territories occupied by the different U'wa communities, which, therefore, remained separated. Thus, in the early 1990s, encouraged by the recognition of indigenous rights in the 1991 Constitution, the U'wa and the national indigenous movement (through ONIC) resumed the campaign for their right to live together in a unified reservation in a portion of their ancestral territory (IDEADE 1996).

It was at the height of this two-decade-long struggle in 1992 that Oxy entered the scene, eventually prompting the internationalization and judicialization of the case. Upon signing a joint venture agreement with Colombia's oil company (Ecopetrol) and Shell to exploit a drill site (called Samoré Bloc) that partially overlapped with the U'wa homeland, Oxy applied for a license from Colombia's environmental authorities in May 1992. At around the same time, Oxy began geological testing on the site through a contractor (Project Underground 1998).

These developments prompted the first U'wa declaration against Oxy, released in March 1993. In it, the U'wa announced their opposition to any kind of oil exploration or exploitation in their territories. As Berito Kubaru'wa, a community leader, put it in our interview (and as the official U'wa communiqués have repeatedly stated), the radical nature of this stance stems from the U'wa view that the land "is a living organism like any of us ... So, just as we have veins through which our blood circulates and keeps our body warm, oil is for us the blood of Mother Earth."[3]

Between 1993 and early 1995, the conflict and the U'wa campaign would remain within Colombian borders. Over that period, the U'wa political authorities (organized in the community's council or *cabildo*) engaged the Colombian government to halt Oxy's preparations for oil drilling. Invoking their newly acquired constitutional right to be consulted before the license for oil exploration could be granted,[4] the U'wa (with the support of ONIC and Colombian human rights organizations) persuaded the national office for indigenous affairs to organize a meeting with Oxy and representatives of Ecopetrol, the Ministry of the Environment, and the Ministry of Mining and Energy. The meeting, held in January 1995, concluded with a joint communiqué whereby Oxy and the Colombian government ostensibly acknowledged the U'wa's right to participate in a process aimed at modifying the oil exploration project. The declaration also announced a second meeting of the parties in February of the same year.

In a surprising twist of events, the Ministry of the Environment granted the license for oil exploration on February 3, 1995. According to the Ministry, the January meeting had fulfilled the constitutional requirement of consultation with the U'wa. The blockage of institutional avenues that this decision entailed would radicalize the political mobilization of the U'wa, prompt the judicialization of the case, and bring the U'wa cause to the attention of international audiences. The turning point came two weeks later, when the second meeting of the U'wa with Oxy and the government took place as scheduled. Cornered by the executive's and Oxy's collusion in violating the Constitution and sensing the imminence of oil drilling, the U'wa announced that they would collectively commit suicide unless plans for exploration were halted, just as some of their communities had done several centuries earlier to avoid being enslaved by Spanish conquistadores:

---

[3] Interview with Berito Kubaru'wa, Madison, Wisconsin, July 20, 2000.
[4] This right is also established in ILO Convention No.169, which, as we will see, would also play a role in the case.

In view of a secure death as a result of the loss of our lands, the extermination of our natural resources, the invasion of our sacred places, the disintegration of our families and communities, the forced silence of our songs and the lack of recognition of our history, we prefer a death with dignity: *The collective suicide of our communities.*[5]

The wide diffusion of this declaration in the national and international media escalated the conflict to the point that it eventually became an icon of the worldwide resistance of indigenous peoples against predatory development and corporate globalization. However, the immediate outcome of international publicity was not the mobilization of transnational advocacy networks (a development that would have to wait two more years), but rather the judicialization of the struggle at the national scale. From then on, legal mobilization would be a core component of the movement in support of the U'wa.

10.3.2 Suing locally: the judicialization of the U'wa case

The entering of the highest courts of the land into the dispute was prompted by the Colombian Ombudsman's Office, which in August 1995 brought two legal challenges against the government, arguing that the license granted to Oxy violated the U'wa's constitutional right to effectively participate in the process. The Ombudsman's Office's legal strategies on behalf of the U'wa and the judicial processes they unleashed illustrate the tensions and contradictions within state apparatuses with regard to the handling of the conflicting demands of resource extraction and indigenous and environmental rights. On the one hand, the Ombudsman's Office asked the Constitutional Court to issue a writ to order the immediate suspension of seismic prospecting operations in the U'wa's homeland until a proper consultation process was implemented. Created by the 1991 Constitution, the Court had quickly established itself as the vanguard of an activist judiciary and a progressive "new constitutionalism" embracing an expansive understanding of human rights (Rodríguez-Garavito, García and Uprimny 2003). On the other hand, since the license had been granted by an administrative agency (the Ministry of the Environment), Colombian law required that the suit against the executive be brought before the highest administrative court, the Council of State. Fashioned after the French legal model, the Council of State had for decades represented the tradition of judicial restraint and the conservative conception of

---

[5] U'wa communiqué 1995; emphasis in the original.

rights embraced by the Colombian judiciary until the 1990s. With the case running on opposite judicial tracks, a distinctly legal layer of global contestation – the conflict pitting national governments and traditional courts against the "new constitutionalism" of activist courts around the world (Hirschl 2004) – was added to the U'wa struggle.

The timing and the effects of the foretold collision of the rulings of the Court and the Council reveal the high political stakes (for social movements, states, and corporations alike) of the local contests for judicial supremacy and the interpretation of rights taking place in Latin America and elsewhere. After more than one and a half years of legal proceedings that slowed down both the U'wa's political mobilization and Oxy's preparations for oil exploration, in February 1997 the Constitutional Court ruled in favor of the U'wa. Invoking the Constitution and ILO Convention No.169, the Court concluded that indigenous collective rights stand on a par with individual human rights. Thus, the state's and a corporation's interests in oil drilling is to be balanced with indigenous peoples' rights to cultural survival and territory through an effective process of consultation with the active participation of the affected communities (Corte Constitucional 1997). Since the January 1995 meeting had fallen far short of a meaningful consultation process, the Court ordered that a new meeting be held within thirty days to jump-start such a process.

Carefully timed to erode the effectiveness of the Court's decision, the ruling of the Council of State was handed down only one month later. Focusing on national laws rather than on constitutional or international law texts on indigenous rights, the Council found that the Colombian state was not legally obligated to consult and reach an agreement with native communities before granting licenses for oil drilling. Informing the affected communities about plans for resource extraction and eliciting the community's feedback, as the state authorities had done, satisfy the standard set by national laws (Consejo de Estado 1997). Making clear that its decision was to be regarded as the definitive one (thus disputing the jurisdiction of the Constitutional Court over the case), the Council authorized oil exploration to resume.

The head-on clash between two of Colombia's highest courts left the U'wa in a limbo. In fact, their struggle had metamorphosed into a contest for judicial supremacy. Magnifying the confusion and disappointment with the ambiguous outcome was the geographic and cultural distance between the Bogotá courts and the U'wa communities. Evaristo Tegría, a U'wa lawyer who worked as legal counsel in the case, described the episode as follows: "when the U'wa won the case before the Constitutional Court, they went up to the mountains, full of joy, to explain the decision to the communities. On their way down, they ran into fellow U'wa who were making the hike to bring the news of the decision of the Council of State [overturning the Court's ruling]."[6] Beyond the contradiction between the rulings, the U'wa were baffled that both courts had focused on their right to participate in the consultation process rather than on the substance of their claim, that is, their opposition to oil drilling on principled (as opposed to procedural) grounds, which they saw as nonnegotiable. As the U'wa put it in their communiqué on the Constitutional Court's ruling, "we do not understand why they will call us to participate in an audience if they already know what we have to say, which is what we have been saying since the beginning."[7]

In assessing the potential and the limits of law-centered tactics in the U'wa campaign in the next section, we will return to the political and cultural contradictions exposed by the judicialization of the struggle. For the purposes of the description of the case in this section, what is worth noting is that the outcome of the judicial phase effectively closed off the remaining institutional avenues within Colombia. This created the type of domestic blockage that, as Keck and Sikkink (1998) have noted, underlies the transnationalization of resistance. The U'wa cause was no exception to this pattern, as shown by the subsequent scaling up of political and legal tactics to the global level.

10.3.3 Acting and suing globally: the transnational coalition in support of the U'wa

In contrast to the sequence of political and legal tactics at the national scale, the transnationalization of the U'wa struggle took place simultaneously through political and juridical routes. Reacting quickly to the outcome of the judicial impasse in Colombia, the transnational advocacy network (TAN) that had been assembling pursued two strategies. On the one hand, in May 1997, the Amazon Coalition, a US-based environmentalist NGO, invited U'wa and ONIC leaders on a speaking tour of several US cities. The presentation of the case by U'wa leader Berito Kubaru'wa helped establish direct relations with transnational activists and NGOs that would prove instrumental in future phases of the campaign. On the

---

[6] Interview with Evaristo Tegría, Bogotá, June 15, 2000.
[7] U'wa communiqué, February 10, 1997.

other hand, while in Washington, DC on the same trip, Berito Kubaru'wa and the head of ONIC submitted a formal complaint against the Colombian government before the Inter-American Commission of Human Rights. Drafted by experts from transnational litigation-oriented NGOs (the Earth Legal Defense Fund, the Center for Justice and International Law, and the Colombian Commission of Jurists), the complaint added a regional layer to the protracted legal battle of the U'wa.

After the first visit of the U'wa to the US, the membership and activities of the TAN grew exponentially. Turned into icons of indigenous resistance against environmental degradation and ethnocide, Berito Kubaru'wa and other U'wa spokespeople have since split their time between work in their community and participation in multiple international fora. The number of U'wa international tours at the height of the campaign between 1997 and 2000 (seven in the US, seven in Europe, and many more in Latin America) illustrates the dynamism of the transnational campaign.

The TAN's membership and strategies are highly heterogeneous. In the US, the key organizations have been Rain Forest Action Network (RAN) and Amazon Watch, as well as the coalition of NGOs that established the U'wa Defense Project to serve as a coordinating node for the campaign. To put pressure on Oxy to withdraw from U'wa territory, US activists have pursued numerous strategies and forms of direct action. They have included negative publicity campaigns in visible media outlets such as the *New York Times*, the award of the US$100,000 Goldman Environmental Prize in 1998 to the U'wa, well-attended rallies against presidential candidate Al Gore (who has long-standing ties with Oxy) during the 2000 campaign, protests at Oxy's shareholders' meetings, and the targeting of Oxy's main institutional investor, mutual fund conglomerate Fidelity Investments, and demonstrations and direct actions at over seventy-five locations in the US, Japan, and the UK (Reinsborough 2004).

Acción Ecológica, a transnational environmentalist NGO based in Ecuador, coordinated the Latin American and European branches of the TAN. Through Oilwatch (a transnational coalition focusing on creating direct grassroots links among communities harmed by oil exploration), Acción Ecológica sponsored a trip by Colombian indigenous Senator Lorenzo Muelas to Nigeria in 1999, as well as a subsequent trip by Muelas and Berito Kubaru'wa to the land of the Ecuadorian Secoya, an indigenous community affected by Oxy's drilling in their territory. In Europe, activism by TAN members including the Italian

Green Party and London's Reclaim the Streets led to the decision of the Spanish government to award the U'wa the Bartolomé de las Casas Prize for their role in the defense of indigenous rights.

Thus integrated into the global justice movement, the U'wa case has been featured prominently at several events, from the rallies against the World Bank in Washington in 2000 to the 2004 Social Forum of the Americas in Quito and the annual World Social Forum. In a "boomerang effect" (Keck and Sikkink 1998), the new strength that such an outbreak of transnational solidarity infused into the movement shifted the correlation of forces at the local scale in the next round of confrontation between the U'wa, Oxy, and the Colombian government. From this point on, the local, national, and international threads of the conflict would become woven together in an intricate pattern that exposes the complexity, potential, and limits of political contention and legal mobilization across borders.

10.3.4 The boomerang effect

With a complaint against the Colombian state pending before the Inter-American Commission on Human Rights, a dynamic transnational coalition mobilizing against Oxy, and international awards enhancing the movement's symbolic and economic capital, the government and Oxy felt the pressure to reopen the local process of negotiation that the clash between the Colombian courts had left all but dead. Therefore, in May 1997, the government requested the intervention of the Organization of American States (OAS) to carry out a study of the conflict and to make recommendations to put an end to it.

The OAS put together a joint project with experts from Harvard University's Program on Nonviolent Sanctions and Cultural Survival (Macdonald 1998). Based on research *in situ*, the OAS/Harvard group issued a report in September 1997 recommending, among other measures: (1) an immediate suspension of oil exploration in the territory under dispute; (2) the granting of the long-standing petition of the U'wa to live in a unified reservation; (3) the establishment of a two-phase consultation process, whereby negotiations would be conducted first to identify the limits of U'wa territory (outside of which the suspension of oil operations could be lifted), and then to develop measures to prevent harm to the U'wa that might result from renewed oil exploration; and (4) technical assistance to the U'wa to ensure that they are "adequately prepared to evaluate and to decide on the issues under consideration" (Macdonald, Anaya, and Soto 1998).

The Colombian government and Oxy accepted the recommendations and informed the OAS of their interest in the continuation of the proposed process. The U'wa's and ONIC's reaction was cautious, as they were wary that the report could open the way to oil exploration inside U'wa territory. Arguing that "a dialogue in which one group convinces the other is not a dialogue, but an imposition," they expressed doubts about the deliberative character and openness of the proposed consultation.[8] The U'wa never sent the OAS the formal statement of interest that, according to the report, would be necessary for the implementation of the recommendations of the OAS/Harvard group. Hence, the OAS' mediation project was aborted and the case stalled once again.

The government sought to wrest itself out of the dilemma posed by the U'wa's radical resistance by pursuing a carrot-and-stick approach that entailed selectively implementing the recommendations of the OAS/Harvard report. On the one hand, it revived the process of land titling that the U'wa had been pressing for since the early 1970s. In meetings between the U'wa and representatives of the Ministry of the Environment and the national agrarian reform agency in early 1999, long dormant plans for a unified U'wa reservation were reconsidered on the basis of a recent "socioeconomic study" on the limits of the U'wa territory carried out by Colombian academics (IDEADE 1996). Albeit explicitly excluding from the territory thus demarcated the site of an oil well (called "Gibraltar I") that Ecopetrol and Oxy were planning to explore, in August 1999 the government finally granted the U'wa the title over the unified reservation. The U'wa celebrated the government's decision, but made clear that it "in no way compromises our position of disagreement vis-à-vis oil exploration either on or off our land."[9]

On the other hand, one month later, the government went ahead with plans for oil drilling by granting Oxy a new environmental license to explore the Gibaltrar I site. The fact that the drill site is located only 1,000 feet off the new reservation (and within the community's home-land as mapped in the above-mentioned socioeconomic study) incensed the U'wa and their local, national and transnational suppor-ters, thus sparking a new round of legal mobilization and litigation. Once again, the U'wa became entangled in a maze of bureaucratic procedures and in the technicalities of the struggle between conservative and progressive branches of the judiciary to authoritatively determine

[8] ONIC communiqué, October 1997.   [9] U'wa communiqué, August 23, 1999.

the content of indigenous rights. Now, the rules were less favorable to the cause of the U'wa, for the Colombian government had issued new regulations that heavily curtailed the right of indigenous peoples (as established by ILO Convention No.169) to participate in the process leading to the granting of licenses for resource extraction in their territories. Therefore, after one and a half years more of negotiations with the government and appeals to the courts, the U'wa petition for the revocation of the license was rejected in May 2000, thus opening the way for exploration of oil in indigenous territory.

This time around, however, litigation did not preclude or slow down political mobilization within and without Colombia. In response to the granting of the new license to Oxy, the U'wa launched a "civil disobedience campaign" involving nonviolent direct actions by members of the community as well as rallies and road blocks by peasants from the Arauca province, a neighboring region with a long record of violence and environmental degradation associated with oil drilling. After occupying the Gibaltrar I drill site in late 1999 and being evicted from it by the military, the U'wa called three general peasant strikes during the first semester of 2000 that brought the local economy to a halt and interrupted communications and transportation within the region. At the national level, in 2000 ONIC and other Colombian indigenous federations launched a "national mobilization for indigenous rights," in which the U'wa struggle was featured prominently along with new cases of threats to indigenous cultures and territories (notably those of the Embera Katío people) stemming from dam building and other development projects (ONIC 2003).

The stakes of the local and national conflict and the risk of violent confrontation had been raised by the entering into operation of Plan Colombia in 1998, a US-funded military initiative to crack down on drug trafficking and guerrilla groups. Particularly important for US oil companies, which were among the main supporters of Plan Colombia,[10] was an increased military presence in oil-rich provinces where guerrilla groups had continuously sabotaged their operations by blowing up oil pipelines. The U'wa feared that oil exploration would bring with it the panoply of actors of the Colombian civil war – from the Colombian military and US military advisors to guerrilla groups, paramilitary squads, and drug traffickers. Their suspicions were

---

[10] Oxy Vice-President testified before the US Congress in favour of President Clinton's US$1.3 billion military aid package to Colombia (Gedick 2003:97).

confirmed by two episodes that marked a tragic turn in the case. The first sign of the link between oil and violence (and of the risks of grassroots transnational activism) was the murder of three US members of the pro-U'wa coalition by the FARC, the largest guerrilla group in Colombia, during a visit to the community's territory. The second episode came in February 1999 when, during the eviction of the U'wa and the peasant strikers from the drill site in February 2000, three indigenous children were killed by the Colombian military.

Caught in the middle of the fire and under pressure from the government and Oxy to negotiate, U'wa resistance became at the same time more entrenched and more vulnerable. With institutional avenues all but exhausted, the campaign endured owing to a combination of grassroots support, continuous mobilization by the Colombian indigenous movement, and the support of a national coalition of environmentalist and human rights NGOs (notably Censat-Aguaviva and MINGA) working in collaboration with the organizations responsible for coordinating the above-mentioned international campaign, including Friends of the Earth and Oilwatch.[11] By the end of 2000, the stalemate between the U'wa coalition and the government and Oxy brought the case to a standstill even as the economic and political stakes of oil exploration in the area continued to increase.

10.3.5 Breaking the stalemate: the withdrawal of Oxy and the "victory" of the U'wa coalition

It would take an unexpected turn of events to change the course of the case. During its annual shareholders' meeting on May 3, 2001, Oxy announced that it was returning oil concessions on U'wa land to the Colombian government and abandoning its plans to drill in the region. Although Oxy declared that it was withdrawing because it had found no oil in the area, the decision probably had more to do with the persistence of the four-year transnational campaign in support of the U'wa and the risk it represented for Oxy's corporate image.

Oxy's announcement meant that the immediate goal of the campaign (the halting of Oxy's exploration activities) had been accomplished. However, it is worth noting the contrasting reactions of the U'wa and the international members of the TAN, for they expose an importance divergence between local and global struggles. Transnational NGOs, in need of short-term victories capable of

---

[11] Interview with Hildebrando Vélez and Tatiana Roa, Bogotá, June 1, 2000.

sustaining long-distance solidarity, celebrated the episode as the cul-mination of the campaign (Reinsborough 2004). Given the myriad other urgent cases competing for transnational NGOs' attention and resources, international members of the U'wa coalition focused on other campaigns. With Oxy's withdrawal, therefore, the cycle of trans-national contentious mobilization that started in 1997 came to an end.

The U'wa reacted differently. Accustomed to protracted struggles and wary of the intentions of the Colombian government and Oxy, they declared that, although "a battle has been won, the war to defend the earth and our territories is on."[12] They suspended their civil dis-obedience campaign, but expressed their concern that the government would not abandon for long the plans for oil drilling.

The U'wa's fear that Oxy's announcement did not mean the end of the struggle materialized when, in early 2002, Ecopetrol, the state oil company, resumed seismic prospecting in the drill site that Oxy had turned over to it. Since then, the U'wa have issued repeated "urgent calls" to "resume international solidarity."[13] The fact that international response has not been nearly as enthusiastic as during the first phase of the campaign bears witness to the premature demobilizing effect of Oxy's withdrawal.

The slowing down of the campaign is visible also in the latest international legal developments in the case. In late 2001, the ILO decided a complaint submitted by the Colombian national federation of trade unions (CUT) in support of the U'wa. The ILO found that the new Colombian legislation violates ILO Convention No.169 in as much as it fails to establish a clear obligation for the state to consult with indigenous groups before granting licenses to explore natural resources in indigenous territories. With the campaign in a lull, national and international organizations failed to use this decision to advance the U'wa's case. Also, the U'wa complaint against the Colombian government before the Inter-American Commission of Human Rights has stalled in the protracted procedures of the Inter-American system, despite the U'wa's declarations in 2003 and 2004 that they were interested in pushing the case forward.

At the close of 2004, there were signs of reactivation of the transna-tional campaign in response to escalating violence associated with the

---

[12] U'wa communiqué, July 31, 2001.
[13] U'wa communiqués, October 2002; February 12, 2003; March 4, 2003; March 6, 2003; November 12, 2003; January 16, 2004; January 21, 2004; and August 25, 2004.

expansion to U'wa territory of the four-decade-old civil war and the struggle over oil-rich areas pitting US-trained military units (supported through fresh Plan Colombia funds earmarked for the protection of oil pipelines) and guerrilla groups. The latest casualty of these develop-ments for the U'wa was the killing of one of their female leaders in January 2004 by the ELN, the second-largest guerrilla group in the country.

As shown by the description of the twists and turns of the case in this section, the itinerary of the U'wa struggle offers compelling evidence of the complexity, the potential, and the limits of transnational mobiliza-tion in defense of indigenous rights. In the next section, we briefly step back to take stock of the case in the light of my analytical focus on the combination of local, national, and transnational political mobilization and on the role of the law in it.

10.4 LAW AND POLITICS IN THE U'WA STRUGGLE

What does the U'wa case tell us about the potential and difficulties of counter-hegemonic globalization? What role did the law play in the struggle, and what is the balance of the combination of legal and political strategies pursued by the pro-U'wa coalition? As social move-ment analysts have observed, assessing the results of cross-border mobi-lization is not simple, as there is no single indicator of success or failure, and perceptions of the result may vary among local and international actors (Khagram, Riker, and Sikkink 2002). Also, as sociolegal analysts have noted, the net effects of legal mobilization for social movements cannot be evaluated simply by examining the immediate outcome of mobilization. Indirect and mediate effects (e.g. consolidation of activist coalitions through collaborative work on legal cases) must also be taken into consideration (McCann 1994).

These caveats notwithstanding, some observations on the achieve-ments and shortcomings of the U'wa campaign can be made that are of general relevance for analyses of the global justice movement and of subaltern cosmopolitan legality (see Santos and Rodríguez-Garavito's chapter in this volume). In terms of Keck and Sikkink's fivefold criteria for evaluating the outcome of transnational coalitions, the U'wa cam-paign has been largely successful insofar as it has managed to (1) create the issue of indigenous rights vis-à-vis resource extraction in Colombia, and raise international awareness about similar conflicts elsewhere, (2) influence the discourses of target actors (Oxy and the Colombian

government), (3) have an impact on institutional procedures (in particular, the process of consultation), (4) bring about (temporary) policy
changes in target actors, and (5) influence target actors' behavior (as
shown by Oxy's withdrawal).

The relative success of the campaign has stemmed from the two
factors highlighted throughout this chapter: (1) the combination of
grassroots mobilization at the local level with national and international support and solidarity actions, and (2) the simultaneous pursuit
of political and legal strategies. However, tensions and contradictions
within each of these dimensions of the movement are apparent. They
help explain the waning of solidarity after Oxy's withdrawal in 2001,
and the ongoing threat to the lives and territory of the U'wa.

Dislocations between local and transnational mobilization stem from
differences among coalition participants concerning time frames and
targets. While the U'wa view their current struggle as the latest phase
of a resistance movement spanning several decades (if not several centuries), transnational supporters tend to view it as a short-term campaign
to be evaluated in the light of immediate results. The reasons for this
divergence are as much cultural as they are organizational. Given that
transnational NGOs are under pressure to compete for scarce funding,
media attention, and activists' time, and are called to intervene in equally
important cases around the world, it is not surprising that they choose to
focus on short-term gains and shift their priorities as the sense of urgency
wanes. For affected communities such as the U'wa, however, this may
mean that victories are short-lived and that the causes of the struggle and
the threats they pose to cultural survival and the environment remain as
acute and in need of international solidarity after the "victory" as ever.[14]

A related disjuncture is observable with regard to the target of the
local and transnational struggles. While for the transnational coalition
the campaign clearly focused on Oxy, for the U'wa the campaign was
not just against Oxy but against the Colombian government and any
company (public or private, national or international) exploring for oil
in their territory, as well as against any legal or illegal armed group
threatening to disrupt peace in their territories. Again, this choice of
target is explained by the comparative logistical advantage of transnational NGOs to target TNCs. This fact also accounts for the relative
decline of the coalition after Oxy's withdrawal. However, as shown by

---

[14] Phone interview with Hildebrando Vélez and Tatiana Roa, Censat-Agua Viva, Bogotá,
September 6, 2004.

the recurrent calls of the U'wa for international solidarity and their increased exposure to the Colombian civil war, the fact that the Colombian oil company (rather than Oxy) is now ostensibly in charge of oil exploration has not reduced the risks for the survival and territory of the U'wa and for the social and environmental equilibrium of the region. Targeting the state-owned oil company in a country in dire need of foreign revenue has proven more difficult than targeting a wealthy TNC.

With regard to the role of law in counter-hegemonic globalization, the U'wa case also offers a window into the potential and limits of legal strategies. The U'wa's resistance has raised a potent challenge to and helped transform national and international legal frameworks and conventional conceptions of human rights. Within Colombia, the case unleashed one of the most visible rounds in the confrontation between the "old constitutionalism" of limited rights and conservative courts and the "new constitutionalism" of expanded social and collective rights enforced by progressive courts (Rodríguez-Garavito et al. 2003). Together with several other cases, it has marked a turn toward "multicultural constitutionalism" in the country (Van Cott 2000).

Despite contradictory court rulings and long-winded procedures, legal mobilization before national courts has considerably heightened the symbolic capital and the visibility of the movement, and has delayed oil exploration. At the regional level, the U'wa case has contributed to the above-mentioned trend toward the protection of indigenous rights by Latin American constitutions and the Inter-American system. It remains to be seen whether the U'wa petition to the Inter-American Commission on Human Rights will lead to a ruling of the Inter-American Court of Human Rights in line with the precedent set by the latter in its 2001 decision in the *Awas Tingni* v. *Nicaragua* case, which recognized indigenous peoples' collective right to territory.

Some of the limitations of the use of the law by social movements that sociolegal scholars have documented are also evident in the case. In particular, the U'wa campaign was exposed to the familiar risks of demobilization and frustration in the face of protracted suits and adverse results. During the first round of judicialization of the struggle, litigation tended to displace political mobilization. Also, the courts' decisions revolved around the procedural issue of the community's participation in the consultation process, rather than on the principled opposition of the U'wa to negotiating (even in participatory consultations) the exploration of oil in their territories. Finally, the negative effect of the long proceedings before lower and high courts and the confusion resulting from clashing court opinions was compounded by the geographic and cultural distance between the courts and the U'wa.

On balance, however, physical distance and cultural difference have worked in favor of the U'wa's legal case and political struggle. For they underlie the radical resistance of the community to oil drilling and the U'wa's uncompromising vindication of the *collective* character of their right to land. Therefore, contrary to the individualizing effect that, according to critical legal studies scholars, "rights talk" and litigation have on social movements (Kennedy 1997), in the U'wa case legal mobilization has gone hand in hand with the assertion of collective claims. The recoupling of collective action and legal mobilization through a radical redefinition of rights is thus one of the main contributions of the U'wa case (and of the indigenous rights movement writ large) to subaltern cosmopolitan legality.

10.5 CONCLUSION

In this chapter we analyzed the relation of politics and law in counter-hegemonic globalization by looking into the U'wa case, one of the most prominent instances of transnational political and legal mobilization in defense of indigenous rights. We located the roots of the struggle in the twin processes of increased resource extraction linked to neoliberal globalization and the rise of indigenous resistance and indigenous rights in Latin America over the last three decades. We followed the movement as it shifted from the local to the international scale, leading to Oxy's decision to abandon (at least for the time being) plans for oil drilling in U'wa territory. This success notwithstanding, the case is still open, as ongoing plans of Colombia's state-owned oil company for exploration, along with the increasing exposure of the U'wa to the opposite fires in the war over oil in Colombia, continue to threaten the community's survival and territory.

The considerable gains of the U'wa coalition bear witness to the powerful challenge that indigenous peoples (in alliance with indigenous rights, human rights, and environmentalist organizations) have raised to TNCs and corporate-friendly governments around the world. Also, the unique coupling of collective action and litigation for collective rights evident in indigenous struggles holds out the promise of a grassroots, multicultural redefinition of human rights. At the same time, divergences between indigenous movements and transnational supporters with regard to time frames and targets pose important obstacles to the advancement of the cause of indigenous rights. Whether or not the calls of the U'wa for renewed political and legal mobilization are heeded beyond Colombian borders will largely determine the outcome of the next battle in their long struggle for territory and culture.

References

Anaya, S. James. 1996. *Indigenous Peoples in International Law*. New York: Oxford University Press.

Anaya, S. James, and Claudio Grossman. 2002. "The Case of Awas Tingni v. Nicaragua: A New Step in the International Law of Indigenous Peoples." *Arizona Journal of International and Comparative Law* 19:1–15.

Bartra, Armando. 2005. "Añoranzas y utopías: La izquierda mexicana en el tercer milenio." Pp. 283–338 in *La Nueva Izquierda en América Latina: Orígenes y Trayectoria Futura*, edited by César A. Rodríguez-Garavito, Patrick Barret, and Daniel Chavez. Bogotá: Norma.

Brysk, Alison. 2000. *From Tribal Village to Global Village: Indian Rights and International Relations in Latin America*. Stanford: Stanford University Press.

Ceceña, Ana Esther. 1999. "La Resistencia como Espacio de Construcción del Nuevo Mundo." *Chiapas* 7:93–114.

Consejo de Estado. 1997. *Sentencia S-673*.

Corte Constitucional. 1997. *Sentencia SU-039/97*.

Dávalos, Pablo. 2005. "De Paja de Páramo Sembraremos el Mundo: Izquierda, Utopía y Movimiento Indígena en Ecuador." Pp. 359–404 in *La Nueva Izquierda en América Latina: Orígenes y Trayectoria Futura*, edited by César A. Rodríguez-Garavito, Patrick Barret, and Daniel Chavez. Bogotá: Norma.

Gedick, Al. 2003. "Resource Wars against Native People in Colombia." *Capitalism, Nature, Socialism: A Journal of Socialist Ecology* 54:85–109.

Hirschl, Ran. 2004. *Towards Juristocracy: The Origins and Consequences of the New Constitutionalism*. Cambridge, MA: Harvard University Press.

IDEADE. 1996. "Estudio Socioeconómico, Ambiental, Jurídico y de Tenencia de Tierras para la Constitución del Resguardo Unico U'wa." Bogotá.

Jimeno, Gladys. 2002. *"Possibilities and Perspectives of Indigenous Peoples with Regard to Consultations and Agreements within the Mineral Sector in Latin America and the Caribbean: Thematic Exploration."* Ottawa: The South–North Institute.

Karl, Terry. 1999. "The Perils of the Petro-State: Reflections on the Paradox of Plenty." *Journal of International Affairs* 53:31–48.

Kearney, M., and Stefano Varese. 1995. "Latin America's Indigenous Peoples: Changing Identities and Forms of Resistance." In *Capital, Power, and Inequality in Latin America*, edited by S. Halesby and Richard L. Harris. Boulder: Westview Press.

Keck, Margaret, and Kathryn Sikkink. 1998. *Activists Beyond Borders: Advocacy Networks in International Politics*. Ithaca: Cornell University Press.

Kennedy, Duncan. 1997. *A Critique of Adjudication*. Cambridge, MA: Harvard University Press.

Khagram, Sanjeev, James Riker, and Kathryn Sikkink (Eds.). 2002. *Restructuring World Politics. Transnational Social Movements, Networks and Norms*. Minneapolis: University of Minnesota Press.

Kymlicka, Will. 1999. "Theorizing Indigenous Rights." *University of Toronto Law Journal* 49:281–293.

Macdonald, Theodore. 1998. "Environment, Indians, and Oil, 'Preventative Diplomacy.'" DRCLAS News. Cambridge, MA: Harvard University.

Macdonald, Theodore, S. James Anaya, and Yadira Soto. 1998. *The Samore Case: Observations and Recommendations*. Washington, DC: OAS/ Harvard University.

Marés, Carlos Frederico. 2000. *O Renascer dos Povos Indígenas Para o Direito*. Curitiba: Juruá Editora.

Maybury-Lewis, David. 1984. "Demystifying the Second Conquest." Pp. 129–133 in *Frontier Expansion in Amazonia*, edited by Marianne Schmink and Charles Wood. Gainesville: University of Florida Press.

McCann, Michael. 1994. *Rights at Work: Pay Equity Reform and the Politics of Legal Mobilization*. Chicago: University of Chicago Press.

McMichael, Philip. 2000. *Development and Social Change: A Global Perspective*. Thousand Oaks: Pine Forge Press.

Mesa, Gregorio. 1996. "Los U'wa: Pueblo Indígena Ancestral del Norte de Boyacá." Pp. 156–175 in *Memorias Ambientales de las Provincias de Norte y Gutiérrez, Boyacá (1990–1996)*, edited by IDEADE. Bogotá: IDEADE.

ONIC. 2003. *El Desplazamiento Indígena en Colombia. Caracterización y Estrategias para su Atención y Prevención en Areas Críticas*. Bogotá: ONIC-ACNUR-Red de Solidaridad Social.

Osborn, Ann. 1985. *El Vuelo de las Tijeretas*. Bogotá: Banco de la República.

Project Underground. 1998. *Blood of Our Mother: The U'wa People, Occidental Petroleum and the Colombian Oil Industry*. Berkeley: Project Underground.

Psacharopoulos, George, and Harry Anthony Patrinos. 1994. *Indigenous Peoples and Poverty in Latin America: An Empirical Analysis*. Washington, DC: World Bank.

Reinsborough, Patrick. 2004. "How the U'wa and People's Globalization Beat Big Oil." Pp. 4–8 in *Globalize Liberation. How to Uproot the System and*

Build a Better World, edited by David Solnit. San Francisco: City Lights Books.

Rodríguez-Garavito, César A., Mauricio García, and Rodrigo Uprimny. 2003. "Justice and Society in Colombia: A Sociolegal Analysis of Colombian Courts." Pp. 134–183 in *Legal Culture in the Age of Globalization*, edited by Lawrence M. Friedman and Rogelio Pérez-Perdomo. Stanford: Stanford University Press.

Santos, Boaventura de Sousa. 2002a. "Toward a Multicultural Conception of Human Rights." *Beyond Law* 25:9–32.

———. 2002b. *Toward a New Legal Common Sense*. London: Butterworths.

Stavenhagen, Rodolfo. 2002. "The Return of the Native." *Occasional Paper* 27:1–17.

Tapia, Luis. 2005. "Izquierda y Movimiento Social en Bolivia." Pp. 339–358 in *La Nueva Izquierda en América Latina: Orígenes y Trayectoria Futura*, edited by César A. Rodríguez-Garavito, Patrick Barret, and Daniel Chavez. Bogotá: Norma.

Van Cott, Donna Lee. 2000. *The Friendly Liquidation of the Past: The Politics of Diversity in Latin America*. Pittsburgh: University of Pittsburgh Press.

———. 2003. "Institutional Changes and Ethnic Parties in South America." *Latin American Politics and Society* 45:1–39.

CHAPTER 11

DEFENSIVE AND OPPOSITIONAL COUNTER-HEGEMONIC USES OF INTERNATIONAL LAW: FROM THE INTERNATIONAL CRIMINAL COURT TO THE COMMON HERITAGE OF HUMANKIND

José Manuel Pureza

11.1 INTRODUCTION

Charles Chaumont identified two main features in classical international law – that is, "the set of legal rules and concepts that were predominant before the end of the 1914 war" (Chaumont 1970:343). The first was the "limited participation in the creative process," meaning the Euro-centric and colonial nature of international law by that time. The second feature was the formalist character of the emergence and enforcement of international legal rules, apparently indifferent to the economic, political, and social contexts within which they were produced. The convergence of these two factors determined, in Chaumont's view, a certain identity of international law: "an abstract system, a set of formal rules disconnected from their concrete contents" (Chaumont 1970:343).

International law was being shaped as a sort of "mix between cynicism and illusionism" (Chaumont 1970:345), within which the attractive force of such broad concepts as solidarity or cooperation would serve mainly as a disguise for the accumulation of violences, injustices, and exploitations that are the true contents of the so-called international society. It should be underlined that this formalist nature – law as the formalization of power relations between strong and weak – has not been abolished together with the overcoming of classical international law as an historical product. In fact, the twentieth century witnessed a progressive replacement of a liberal, decentralized, and oligocratic international order by a social, institutionalized, and democratic one

(Pastor 1996:84). There has also been a transition from an international law pointed at guaranteeing co-existence ("how to keep them peacefully apart") toward an international law aimed at being an active instrument of cooperation ("how to bring them actively together"). Notwithstanding these substantive changes, it is of the utmost importance to recognize the ambivalence of this rhetoric of innovation. Solidarity and cooperation may be either a camouflage for domination practices or horizons of a true alternative form of social relation within the international system.

It is precisely at this point that the question concerning the possibility of an emancipatory role of international law becomes extremely useful. In 1970, Chaumont had already stated that one of the basic contradictions of the international legal system of those days was one between the primacy of order – as an output of peace, security, and friendly relations among states – and the acceptance of revolution as a radical expression of self-determination. The same strategic dualism should be seen as a crucial feature of contemporary international law.

Sharing Santos' non-essentialist perspective on law, and converging with him on the belief that an alternative use of law is possible as long as it is included in a broader political mobilization strong enough to allow struggles to be politicized before they become legalized (Santos 2002; see also Santos and Rodríguez-Garavito's chapter in this volume), I intend to explore in this chapter two different senses of a counter-hegemonic use of international legality. My purpose is to use international law to test Santos' hypothesis according to which cosmopolitan legality may both be defensive of the legal status quo and be a vehicle of a radical social change. This crossroads is a crucial one for contemporary international legal policy. Based on this assumption, I will analyze two different international legal regimes – universal jurisdiction concerning crimes against humanity and common heritage of humankind – and try to catch similarities and differences between counter-hegemonic uses of international law with a defensive and an oppositional character.

There are clear differences between these two regimes. The first one, dealing with crimes against humanity and including a strong institutional dimension, the International Criminal Court, is an expression of the demo-liberal tradition and aims only at bringing the structural traits of that tradition into the global sphere. The second regime – despite having in common with the former the reference to humankind, which pushes toward a post-Westphalian understanding of the legal and political landscape – shows an ambition of radical cut with the hegemonic international legal models at both a normative and a political level. That is why I classify the first as "defensive" and the second as "oppositional."

The main objective of this chapter is to demonstrate that in international law as well, the intensity of counter-hegemonic uses of law differs according to the concrete contexts of hegemony. And that defensive uses can have an impressive meaning, mainly in times of general devaluation of the legal regulatory mechanisms. Even a minimalist use of international legal regulation assumes nowadays a counter-hegemonic nature. However, this does not mean that minimalism has become the only counter-hegemonic use of law within the neoliberal context. There is also obvious room for an oppositional counter-hegemonic use of international law in contemporary international relations.

11.2 MAINTAINING THE STATUS QUO AS A COUNTER-HEGEMONIC GOAL

The Rome Statute that creates the International Criminal Court is the final stage of a complex process of internationalization of the jurisdiction on crimes against humanity. That process is certainly the most important dimension of the affirmation of humanitarian values in international law. It is, therefore, something far from recent. Its origins date back to 1872 and the proposal then presented by the Director of the International Committee of the Red Cross, Gustave Moynier, of creating an international court for the judgment of the infringements of the 1864 Geneva Convention for the protection of soldiers wounded in combat. That idea – later recovered in the declaration of 28 May 1915 by the governments of France, Great Britain, and Russia concerning the massacres of the Armenian population in Turkey (Clark 2001:77) – was put in practice only after the end of World War II with the Statute that created the Nuremberg International Military Tribunal. Article 6 of that Statute defined crimes against humanity as "murder, extermination, enslavement, deportation or other inhumane acts committed against any civilian population, whether before or during the war, or persecution on political, racial or religious grounds in execution or in connection with a crime within the jurisdiction of the tribunal, whether or not in violation of the domestic law of the country where perpetrated."

The ad hoc International Criminal Tribunals for Rwanda and the former Yugoslavia followed that path. The intensification of this process, at the end of the 1990s, corresponds to a moment of bifurcation in the understanding of international relations and their dominant practices. In the words of Cassese (2003), never had the tension between a Grotian and a Kantian vision of international relations had such a political appeal as after the end of the Cold War. The former is based on three main assumptions: (1) states are the only relevant actors in the world scene; (2) respect for state sovereignty is the fundamental value in international relations; and (3) inter-state relations are founded upon a logic of reciprocity, within which each state aims at maximizing its own individual interests and recognizes its partners' legitimacy to behave in the same way.

Within this framework, the existence of regimes, rules, and institutions lies on the coincidence between individual states' interests. The absence of such a coincidence implies a totally de-centralized (by each individual state) way of exercising the three classical powers: legislative, executive, and judiciary. On the other hand, the Kantian perspective includes three opposite characteristics: (1) individuals also play a major role within the international sphere; (2) universally shared values (peace, self-determination, human rights respect) give rise to rights and duties of the international community as a whole; (3) alongside the logic of reciprocity, there is a logic of *ordre public* emerging (though in a very ambivalent way).

The active role played by NGOs and several other different forms of human rights activism in the creation of the International Criminal Court seems to support Cassese's point. According to Glasius (2003), NGOs and activist coalitions have privileged four strategies. First, general ideological support, namely, through the dissemination of favorable opinions to their members. Secondly, the production of specialized documentation (journal articles and reports, and the organization of meetings and conferences) to inform and influence target groups. Thirdly, a follow-up to the whole process of inter-state negotiation, thereby contributing to the transparency of the process (for instance, the Coalition for an International Criminal Court implemented a model of twelve shadow teams corresponding to the different parts of the negotiation process, whose methods included debriefing with friendly state delegations after closed meetings or keeping "virtual vote" tallies on some crucial aspects of the process). Finally, direct or indirect support to delegates and specialists from the South, for example the technical assistance program organized by the NGO, No Peace Without Justice.

This strong involvement of human rights NGOs in the creation of the International Criminal Court and the alleged Kantian perspective that it has expressed would suggest that these developments concerning crimes against humanity constitute a counter-hegemonic use of international law. There are, however, several aspects within the Rome Statute that evidence the permanence not only of a traditional theoretical construction of international governance but also of a hegemonic understanding of international legality. The former is reflected in the limits imposed to the legal standing before the Court, in the preconditions to the exercise of jurisdiction by the Court, and in the adoption of a principle of complementarity between national jurisdictions and the Court. On the one side, the struggle conducted by NGOs for the establishment of an independent prosecutor was not strong enough to avoid the invisibility of the individual claimants before the Court. Only state parties or the Security Council may refer the commission of a crime against humanity to the Prosecutor (Article 13), unless the Prosecutor himself decides to initiate an investigation. Also, in the cases initiated by the Prosecutor or by a member state, the acceptance of the jurisdiction of the Court either by the state on the territory of which the conduct in question has occurred or by the state of which the person accused of the crime is a national is required for the Court to exercise its jurisdiction (Article 12). As a whole, these procedural options reflect a rather defensive view of global governance, in which the interests that support a conservative view of state sovereignty stand opposed to the transfer of crucial state powers to supranational mechanisms.

However, a closer look into the concrete actors that voice this Grotian perspective against the Kantian one shows that the faultlines of this dispute are much more of a political than of a technical nature. In fact, what some countries such as the United States criticize in the Rome Statute is its intention of becoming a sort of planetary judiciary with effective powers, overcoming the hegemonic view of global governance as something void of political and ethical substance and whose only peculiarity is its minimal form and minimal contents (the so-called "governance without government" alluded to in Santos and Rodríguez-Garavito's chapter in this volume).

What is at stake here is therefore the debate on global governance itself. The concept of global governance is an empty one. The Commission on Global Governance refers to it as constituting "the sum of the many ways individuals and institutions, public and private, manage their common affairs," not only involving intergovernmental relations but "as also involving non-governmental organizations, citizens' movements, multinational corporations, and the global capital market" (1995:2–3). This same emphasis on a mix between formal and informal mechanisms is stressed by Rosenau (1998:29): "global governance does not refer only to the formal institutions and organizations through which the management of international affairs is or is not sustained," but includes any "systems of rule at all levels of human activity from the family to the international organization in which the pursuit of goals through the exercise of control has transnational repercussions." The alleged political neutrality of this concept of global governance and its distance from the traditional concept of government has been used to support a representation of global governance suited to minimizing regulatory obstacles to neoliberal globalization. There is a major trend in contemporary world politics to void international institutional mechanisms of their material competences and reduce them to places of formal ratification of decisions previously taken outside them. The "move to institutions" of the 1940s and 1950s has been replaced by the "move from institutions" (the establishment of transnational normative mechanisms to promote efficiency, stability, and growth, as worthy pillars of neoliberal global governance) since the 1990s. The institutional and constitutional scenario of neoliberal globalization promotes institutional disinvestment and conformity to universal deregulation regimes (Pureza 2002).

It is against this ideological and political background that the creation of the International Criminal Court assumes a counter-hegemonic meaning. And only against this background: the real reason to think this way is that the actual alternative is an absolute inexistence of ethical-normative relevance of crimes against humanity at the international level. Within this context, the affirmation of the demoliberal status quo is in itself counter-hegemonic. The symbolic references of the supporters of the International Criminal Court are mainly those of rule of law, and their strategic goal is to expand the scope of the demoliberal tradition to the global sphere. It should be underlined that the above-mentioned normative and institutional developments concerning crimes against humanity occur at a time when a tendency toward the globalization of the rule of law and the harmonization of judicial models and practices is taking place. Santos (1999:51) suggests that this tendency is an indispensable element for the practice of the three consensuses that fuel hegemonic globalization: the neoliberal economic consensus, the weak state consensus, and the demoliberal consensus. Within this framework, courts tend to be seen as crucial mechanisms of "good governance," as necessary pillars for the safeguard of security as a basic value for market-oriented economies and societies. In a certain way, the proliferation of international courts – and the International Criminal Court is only one major example of this movement – reproduces at an international scale this tendency for the judicialization of political clashes. And the ideological background is also the demoliberal one. As Santos writes, "the neoliberal legal globalization under way is replacing the highly politicized tension between social regulation and social emancipation with a depoliticized conception of social change whose sole criterion is the rule of law and judicial adjudication by an honest, independent, predictable and efficient judiciary" (2002:445). In sum, it should be said that the counter-hegemonic meaning of the International Criminal Court is a defensive one, as its scope is only to impose – in terms of global governance – minimal ethical and normative limits to the activities of states and other international actors. Defensive because the demoliberal strategy "assumed the form of the rule of law and translated itself into a vast program of liberal concessions that aimed at expanding both the ambit and the quality of the inclusion in the social contract without threatening the basic structure of the economic and political system in force – that is, of capitalism and liberal democracy" (Santos 2002:441). The judicialization of serious breaches against basic human rights follows precisely this path. The "Nuremberg paradigm" (Pureza 2001:134) adopts a deontological view of international law according to which the political climate must always be reduced to the responsibility of individuals and their deviant behavior. Therefore, this Nuremberg paradigm canonizes a model of retributive justice aimed at establishing a microscopic truth, decontextualized from the dominant genocidal culture in complex political emergencies. Instead of giving priority to a political approach to the social and political roots of the environment that favored those crimes or a contextualization effort – favored, for example, by the "truth commissions" – the International Criminal Court and the Nuremberg paradigm have a much more limited scope. They are a counter-hegemonic construction, but a defensive one at that.

11.3 EMANCIPATION THROUGH EMANCIPATORY MEANS

The common heritage of humankind regime is perhaps the most advanced expression of subaltern cosmopolitan legality at the international level.[1] The first steps toward the common heritage legal concept were taken by the Maltese representative to the United Nations, Arvid Pardo, who in 1967 raised the need for some international regimes for communal natural resources (such as the deep seabed, the moon and other celestial bodies, and certain cultural and environmental assets) to be adopted. Following closely the perspectives drawn by Pardo, contemporary international law assumes the common heritage of humankind regime in some non-consensual international treaties like the 1982 United Nations Convention on the Law of the Sea or the 1979 International Agreement on the Activities of States on the Moon and other Celestial Bodies.

The core of this legal international regime involves a clear break with the dominant regulatory scheme for those spaces and resources. The traditional international regulation of those areas was a liberal one, constructed as a tool of the Euro-centric international system of modern times. A combination between non-appropriation and free use of the commons was the most important trait of this regime of *res communis*. Having its ancient roots in Roman law, it was developed by international legal scholars during the formation of modern international law, namely, within the debate between states (Portugal and Spain) supporting the *mare clausum* doctrine and those (Holland) supporting the *mare liberum* doctrine. That crucial controversy confronted the expansion of national sovereignties of coastal states with the safeguard of the free use of the oceans. The triumph of the freedom of the seas may be viewed as a major sign of the emergence of modernity and capitalism at the international level. In fact, the balance between non-appropriation and free use is a peculiar one, the former being understood as a mere instrument of the second. Already Plautus offered a picture of this in a curious dialogue between a slave and a fisherman: the former argued that the sea was everybody's good and the fisherman agreed; but when the slave concluded that everything found in the sea was also everybody's own, the fisherman replied that the fish caught by his nets would definitely be only his . . .

This dominant understanding of *res communis* had all the crucial features of a liberal regime. Formal equality before the law and material inequality were the two sides of the same coin. Free use for all had as its reverse an obvious first-come-first-served consequence. Apart from

---

[1] On the concept of subaltern cosmopolitan legality, see Santos (2002:Chapter 9) and Santos and Rodríguez-Garavito's chapter in this volume.

that, this traditional freedom of the seas doctrine treated the oceans as a mere route for navigation and the free flow of goods, the correspondent law of the sea being only a "law of the surface" (Dupuy 1979). The growing conscience of the three-dimensional nature of the oceans – a wealth reserve and not only a route – together with the growing conscience of the limits for the exploitation of ocean resources have forced the critique of this liberal mainstream.

Third World countries have been at the forefront of this critical movement, demanding a replacement of the deregulated freedom of the seas by a regime of non-appropriation provided with a set of basic affirmative rules. The innovation claimed by those countries was therefore the need to change the priorities between the two sides of the *res communis* regime. Taking the "*communis*" aspect seriously would mean emphasizing non-appropriation as an autonomous goal and making free use effective *for all*, despite their economic or technological differences. Within this framework, equitable sharing became the leitmotiv of the new regime, bringing back the notion of *bonum commune humanitatis* to the role of an ethical and political guideline for the progressive development of international law.

The counter-hegemonic meaning of the common heritage of humankind regime and its specificity as a form of cosmopolitan law lie most of all in its ability to express in innovative terms the principle of community – as opposed to the principles of the market and of the state – at the international regulatory level. Its two main normative pillars are an undifferentiated transpatial and an undifferentiated transtemporal concept of humankind (Pureza 1998). The first involves the appointment of all humankind as owners and managers of the spaces and resources qualified as common heritage. Radically opposed to the *res communis* liberal understanding – to which "each one on its own" is the legend – this trait of identity of the common heritage regime is also opposed to the limited participation strategy practiced for example in the Antarctic context.

On the other side, this transpatial unity also includes an affirmative action strategy: the *effective* inclusion of all humankind in the management and sharing of benefits of the common heritage requires positive discrimination in favor of the poorest countries, as regards both their presence at the institutional management mechanisms and their sharing in the material benefits obtained from the exploitation of the common heritage. The transtemporal unity of all mankind as a normative concept includes two fundamental options: the reserve of those spaces and resources for peaceful purposes and the safeguard of the rights and opportunities of future generations. Humankind is therefore perceived not only as the sum of its contemporary members but also as a biological unity of different generations. By thus constructing humankind, the common heritage regime has determined an innovative approach to the intertemporal law doctrine: it is no longer a technique of relating the present to the past (very frequent in territorial claims or in conflict of law rules) but is rather a form of bringing together the present and the future in terms of communitarian rights and duties.

In her analysis of intergenerational equity, Weiss (1989) identifies two opposite models. On the one side, the preservationist model gives absolute priority to the status quo over any kind of change, since its main contents is that "the present generation does not consume anything; rather it saves all resources for future generations and preserves the same level of quality in all aspects of the environment" (1989:22). On the other side, the opulent model overlooks the long-term degradation of the resources, since it posits that the present generation should consume "all that it wants today and generate as much wealth as it can, either because there is no certainty that future generations will exist or because maximizing consumption today is the best way to maximize wealth for future generations" (1989:23). Located between these two extremes, the principle of intergenerational equity implies a demand for a restrictive management that combines preservation with change, in order to safeguard the opportunities of future generations.

With these normative contents, the common heritage of humankind regime is no doubt an advanced expression of a counter-hegemonic international legality. The campaign organized by advanced industrialized countries against its formal incorporation in international treaties is clear evidence of this subaltern nature. There is a remarkable similarity between the strategies followed by industrialized countries with regard to both the International Criminal Court and the common heritage regime. In both cases, the institutional pillar of the regime has been the main target of those countries. This reveals that their main objectives are the elimination of enforcement mechanisms and the continuation of international soft law. The recent cases of dramatic decisions concerning peace and security taken outside the UN Security Council (e.g. Kosovo and Iraq) clearly confirm this.

In the case of the common heritage of humankind regime, this anti-institutional strategy has been most visible in the refusal of the major powers to accept the real establishment of the International Seabed

Authority, created by Part XI of the 1982 United Nations Convention on the Law of the Sea, which was given unusually effective legal powers to control the activities of states and private companies in the deep seabed. First World countries had shown their preference for a sort of rubber-stamp authority, in contrast to the position of Third World states that preferred a supranational institutional model, clearly inspired by the European Coal and Steel Community. Having been defeated by Third World countries, which managed to establish a strong institutional design for the Seabed Authority, rich countries and transnational capital started an intensive campaign against it that resulted in the signing of an international agreement that prevented the entry into force of Part XI of the 1982 Convention, including a complete neutralization of the original regulatory powers of the International Seabed Authority. All the progressive policies established in the Convention – the monopoly of the International Seabed Authority over activities taking place at the seabed, mineral production limits to compensate land-based producers, technology transfer, etc. – have been hollowed out and "shall not apply." They were replaced by the enforcement of "sound commercial principles" such as the prohibition of subsidization, the elimination of discrimination between minerals derived from the seabed and from other sources, the prohibition of the use of tariff and non-tariff barriers, and the purchase of deep seabed mining technology "on fair and reasonable commercial terms and conditions on the open market." Once again, the major contradiction has been that between an interventionist and effective regulatory and solidaristic understanding of international law and a liberal market-oriented *laissez faire*.

Thus far, I have tried to show that, at the end of the day, the intensity of counter-hegemonic uses of international law is very much conditioned by the intensity of the resistance confronting hegemonic forces. When the substantive aim is intra- and intergenerational equity, such forces prefer the traditionally "soft" nature of international law over a regulatory order endowed with institutional enforcement mechanisms. Thus, it should be no surprise that the effective counter-hegemonic scope of international regimes becomes eroded by all the forms of hegemonic resistance.

Looking at the two cases referred to above – crimes against humanity and the International Criminal Court on the one side, and the common heritage of humankind and the International Seabed Authority on the other – it must be underlined that only a small part of their original transformative project has been put into practice, due to the resistance of hegemonic countries and economic elites. Within this context, oppositional counter-hegemonic uses of international law can assume a defensive status. The case of the common heritage of humankind regime illustrates quite well this downgrading dynamics of counter-hegemony.

The different constructions of a legal regime for the common heritage of humankind reveal a trajectory in which two distinct phases can be detected. To differentiate these two phases I take the intensity of the contrast with the dominant territorialist logic as a criterion. I will call these two phases the *two ages of the common heritage of humankind.*

The first age includes all the attempts to build a normative and institutional design regulating such commons as outer space and the deep seabed, which had remained outside the expansive territorial ambitions of national states. Therefore, their common feature was their location outside territories under sovereign powers or state jurisdiction. Their classification as common heritage of humankind intended to underline that they were remainders of the process of appropriation of all spaces by the states. The discrepancy between the initial Maltese project – which aimed to classify all the ocean space as the common heritage of humankind – and the actual increase of the appropriation dynamics (continental shelf, territorial sea, and, most of all, exclusive economic zones) clearly illustrates this view. In fact, only a minimal part of the ocean (the deep seabed) has been maintained as commons in Part XI of the 1982 Convention. The consistency of the normative and the institutional components of the common heritage of humankind regime makes it a landmark in the counter-hegemonic use of international law. However, its oppositional character as a counter-hegemonic regime goes hand in hand with its residual value in spatial terms (an island of resistance within an ocean of private appropriation).

The situations I include in the second age of the common heritage of humankind have in common the application of the basic principles of intra- and intergenerational equity to cultural and environmental resources and goods that are located within the spatial jurisdiction of states. Spaces and goods classified as world heritage under the 1972 UNESCO Convention on World Natural and Cultural Heritage are examples of this new generation of the common heritage of humankind. In these cases, the territorial reference – either with a dominant or a residual value – ceases to be the common background on which the struggle between hegemonic and counter-hegemonic uses of law take place. The common heritage of humankind regime now acts within the stronghold of state territorial sovereignty, and its significance lies precisely in the deep change that this entails for the general orientation of the exercise of state sovereignty.

What is at the heart of this second age of the common heritage regime is a radical transformation in the logic and limits of state action concerning these assets and resources. Territorialist logic – expressed either through the territorial sovereignty of individual states or through the common management of non-appropriated territories – ceases to be the defining element of the regime. The new focus is on the management of these spaces and assets. The crucial element of this second age of the common heritage is therefore the notion of social and ecological function of sovereignty, understood as a sort of planetary extension of the social and ecological function of individual property. The claim to a radical change of the basic pillars of the ideological and legal-political international order ceases to exist and is replaced by a much more limited goal: the general reform of the way sovereignty is exercised worldwide, with no privileged political targets and no privileged political actors. It is true that what had previously emerged as a clear oppositional form of counter-hegemonic use of international law has been diluted and turned into a defense of the political status quo. Notwithstanding this, it should be acknowledged that such a defensive strategy carries some transformative potential with it and is therefore to be considered as a counter-hegemonic element within the contemporary world system.

From its origins, international law has always been an ambivalent instrument. Its relation with international power has always been twofold: on the one side, it has been formed to express, in legal terms, the preferences of the most powerful countries; on the other, it has been formed to put limits on the international behavior of those same countries.

This dialectic of law and power has been permanent in the history of the modern inter-state system. The emergence of peoples, third world states, and transnational social movements as crucial actors on the international scene in the twentieth century has put this dialectic in a new political and ideological context. Legality and legitimacy are, more than ever, privileged instruments to be used by counter-hegemonic forces in their struggle for a more decent and balanced international community. The defensive character that the uses those instruments currently assume is strong evidence of the real scope of hegemony in the contemporary world order.

References

Cassese, A. 2003. "A Big Step for International Justice." *Crimes of War Project Magazine* (www.crimesofwar.org).

Chaumont, C. 1970 "Cours Général de Droit International Public." *Recueil des Cours de l'Académie de Droit International de La Haye* (1970-I) 129:333.

Clark, R. 2001. "Crimes against Humanity and the Rome Statute of the International Criminal Court." Pp. 75–93 in *The Rome Statute of the International Criminal Court: A Challenge to Impunity*, edited by M. Politi and G. Nesi. Aldershot: Ashgate.

Commission on Global Governance. 1995. *Our Global Neighborhood*. New York: United Nations.

Dupuy, R. J. 1979. *L'océan partagé*. Paris: Pédone.

Glasius, M. 2003. "How Activists Shaped the Court." *Crimes of War Project Magazine* (www.crimesofwar.org).

Pastor Ridruejo, J. A. 1996. *Curso de Derecho Internacional Público y Organizaciones Internacionales*. Madrid: Tecnos.

Pureza, J. M. 1998. *O património comum da humanidade: Rumo a um direito internacional da solidariedade?* Porto: Afrontamento.

———. 2001. "Da cultura da impunidade à judicialização global." *Revista Crítica de Ciências Sociais* 60:121–139.

———. 2002. "Towards a Post-Westphalian International Solidarity." *Eurozine* (www.eurozine.com), April 26.

Rosenau, J. 1998. "Governance in a Globalizing World." In *Re-Imagining Political Community: Studies in Cosmopolitan Democracy*, edited by D. Archibugi. Cambridge: Polity Press.

Santos, Boaventura de Sousa. 1999. "The GATT of Law and Democracy: (Mis)trusting the Global Reform of Courts." In *Globalization and Legal Cultures*, edited by J. Feest. Oñati: IISL.

———. 2002. *Toward a New Legal Common Sense*. London: Butterworths.

Weiss, E. B. 1989. *In Fairness to Future Generations: International Law, Common Patrimony and Intergenerational Equity*. Tokyo: UN University.

PART THREE

LAW AND PARTICIPATORY DEMOCRACY: BETWEEN THE LOCAL AND THE GLOBAL

POLITICAL AND LEGAL STRUGGLES OVER RESOURCES AND DEMOCRACY: EXPERIENCES WITH GENDER BUDGETING IN TANZANIA

Mary Rusimbi and *Marjorie Mbilinyi**

12.1 INTRODUCTION

During the struggles for independence, political and social activists such as Mwalimu Julius Nyerere and Bibi Titi Mohamed brought women's and poor people's experiences into the public debate, albeit within the limitations of their times. Now, over forty years later, many women and men in Tanzania are concerned with how gender, race, ethnic, class, and imperial differences affect and are affected by policy developments and economic changes at the local, national, and global levels. Critical feminist activists are actively struggling to analyze and influence the decisions that affect their lives at all levels.

This chapter examines feminist struggles in Tanzania over issues of ownership and control of resources which have been led by the Tanzania Gender Networking Programme (TGNP) and the Feminist Activist coalition (FemAct), as they relate to corporate-led globalization, equity, social justice, people's participation, and social transformation. The GB Initiative (GBI) is highlighted in order to illustrate efforts by activist organizations to challenge and change the structures of power which

---

* This article is based on a revision and updating of an earlier article written by Mary Rusimbi (2003) and published in *Activist Voices* (Mbilinyi, Rusimbi, Chachage and Kitunga 2003). *Activist Voices* was based on a collective process of reflection on ten years of feminist activism in Tanzania, led by the Tanzania Gender Networking Programme and the Feminist Activist Coalition. This article has also incorporated key issues raised by Kitunga (2003) and Mbilinyi (2003) in the concluding part of their respective articles in the same collection. Appreciation is expressed here for the supportive suggestions provided by Boaventura de Sousa Santos and César A. Rodríguez-Garavito.

create policy and invent law. The analysis shares the experience of feminist efforts in linking policy engagement and legal processes to social transformation, participatory democracy, and people-owned development processes. Of particular concern has been the systematic exclusion of the majority of people from direct participation in the formulation of policy and law, and their implementation and monitoring.

The TGNP and FemAct have endeavored to advance counter-hegemonic processes by openly challenging state hegemony from "outside" the corridors of power, on the one hand, and also by engagement within top-level decision-making spaces located within government institutions on the other. There is inevitable tension in balancing these two approaches. Of prime concern is the issue of retaining independence and credibility as an autonomous activist organization, given the real dangers of cooptation. The government and its donor "partners" use examples of NGO participation in policy consultative processes as evidence of growing democratization and "ownership" of policies by "civil society." To what extent is NGO involvement merely window dressing, thus contributing to the reproduction of the status quo, and not a real challenge to the system?

In response to these queries, the TGNP and FemAct have sought to ground their advocacy activities at the "local" level, by increasing the participation of grassroots outreach groups and district-level networks in all aspects of the process. Increasing priority has been given to the concerns of unemployed youth, disenfranchised peasant producers, and small traders in both urban and rural areas. Together, our analyses and actions have confronted the linkages between macroeconomic reform policies and political "liberalization" at the national and global levels and the escalating crisis of livelihoods, resources, and HIV/AIDS at the local and individual levels. Involvement in this process has also led to stronger ties with anti-globalization movements elsewhere in Africa and worldwide. In this way, the case in hand illustrates the advancement of cosmopolitan forms of legality (Santos 2002; Santos and Rodríguez-Garavito's chapter in this volume).

These struggles take place in the context of deepening struggles over neoliberalism as an ideology and the structures of power it supports. Following seven long years of refusal to "sign" with the IMF, the government of Mwalimu Julius Nyerere was forced to accept the conditionalities of Structural Adjustment policies (SAP) in the mid-1980s. Debt and donor dependence of the post-colonial state left little room for maneuver. The resulting combination of SAP, trade liberalization, and privatization has led to a radical change in the patterns of ownership and control of basic natural resources, including land, minerals, wildlife areas, and water, and productive resources including the banking and insurance sector, manufacturing industries, and the like. Transnational corporations (TNCs) have gained far more control over basic resources in the 1990s and 2000s than they ever had in the colonial era which ended in 1961. A small group of Tanzanians and non-Tanzanians benefit from macroeconomic reforms, whereas the majority in the low and middle income groups have been excluded – excluded from the labor market, from quality social services, and from participation in decision-making about policy and the law.

12.2 THE TANZANIA GENDER NETWORKING PROGRAMME AND THE FEMINIST ACTIVIST COALITION

Since 1993, the TGNP has been among the leading civil society organizations in the country in bringing gendered and pro-poor agendas to the top levels of decision-making at all levels. Since its inception, the TGNP has recognized that gender, class, imperial, and race issues are inseparable. The organizational philosophy reflects critical feminism which links the oppression and exploitation of girls and women with that of all marginalized people and the assault on national sovereignty itself. The TGNP adopted a critical feminist transformative agenda, which is reflected in its vision statement: to see a Tanzanian society in which there is gender equality and equity, equal opportunities, and access to and control over resources for all citizens, both women and men (Mbilinyi et al. 2003).

From the outset, the TGNP's founders realized that their vision could not be achieved by one organization alone, but required collective action led by a coalition of like-minded organizations so as to build a mass social movement. Partnerships began to be built with like-minded organizations from the start, within Tanzania and beyond. An important step was taken in 1994 when a meeting was called with these organizations specifically to explore the possibility of the formation of a coalition. Top organizational leaders shared experiences, agreed with the need to establish a more formal collective process, and began to outline the main objectives of the coalition. This was the beginning of FemAct, which has continued to provide leadership on key social issues to this day (Kitunga 2003; Mbilinyi 2003). FemAct consists of more than forty organizations situated mainly but not solely in Dar es Salaam, with diverse goals and perspectives. Several are separate women's and/or youth organizations, while others are com-posed of both women and men of all ages and focus on key human rights and other issues. The diversity within the coalition has helped to enrich its work and maintain a critical position vis-à-vis mainstream women-in-development positions as well as the overall neoliberal agenda.

In its pursuit of this far-reaching vision of social transformation for gender equality and development that benefits all social sectors, the TGNP and FemAct have recognized that organized pressure groups are needed at all levels to redirect mainstream policies and resource allocation patterns into a progressive people-centered direction, and to democratize the policy-making process. Given these broad goals, intermediate objec-tives have been identified that will bring clean water closer to homes, provide quality education and health care for all, and ensure employment and sustainable livelihoods for all women and men in both rural and urban areas. The TGNP has targeted all levels where decisions are made about policies and laws that affect the day-to-day lives of ordinary people.

Policies, laws, budgets, taxes, and loans are at the heart of government decisions about resource allocation. Policies describe the needs and prioritize the strategies for meeting those needs. When decision-makers make policies and laws, they are deciding who and what is most important to focus on and what kind of focus they should receive. Budgets allocate resources to meet the social and economic needs of different segments of society according to priorities outlined in policies. Taxes are collected to fund the budgets, and loans add money to the budget in the short term and take money from it in the long term by becoming debts to be repaid. All of these will have an enormous impact on the lives and work of the poor and disempowered, which may be costly or beneficial. In general, budgets, taxes, and loans are not neutral instruments; they have different results for different social groups, according to their gender, class, race, and global-imperial location. Accordingly, each of these – policies, laws, resources, budgets, taxes, and loans – needs to be analyzed and in many cases, radically shifted from a pro-rich to a pro-poor, feminist approach.

12.3 POLICIES, LAW, RESOURCE GENERATION, ALLOCATION, AND OWNERSHIP: WHY ARE THESE A CONCERN FOR FEMINISTS?

Traditionally, policies, laws, budgets, taxes, and debts have been the realm of a few economists and planning experts whose decisions have

286

profound effects on the average citizen. With the growing dominance of donor development agencies, a large number of these experts are staff and/or consultants (foreign and nationals) working for the international financial institutions (IFIs), other United Nations agencies, and bilateral institutions. The "donor community" as a whole is dominated by a few powerful and rich nation-states led by the United States. These institutions are heavily influenced by the material needs and interests of TNCs (Chachage 2003). The "free market" ideology espoused by capitalist forces, and the reforms associated with structural adjustment, liberalization, and privatization attained a dominant position not only in Africa but worldwide from the 1980s onwards.

However, there is growing resistance to neoliberal reforms and corporate-led globalization at all levels, which has coalesced into an international anti-globalization movement linking activists in the North and the South. In this context, a growing number of activist, often feminist, organizations at the local, national, and global levels insist that decisions about resources, policies, budgets, taxes, and debts have to involve grassroots communities and the poor, directly, and can no longer be left to a small elite group of people.

When the TGNP and FemAct coalition partners started working together in the early 1990s, they were convinced that unfair and unjust decisions were being made about Tanzania's development that would have a largely negative impact on most women who were poor, and on other marginalized groups. Moreover, the founders were concerned that these policies and the laws to implement them were taking Tanzanian citizens down the road of increasing class, ethnic, and gender inequality – the opposite direction to "development." A strong critique of neoliberal pro-market reforms was adopted from the start, and is reflected in the first major publication of the TGNP, namely, the *Gender Profile of Tanzania*, published in 1993.

At this time, SAPs and the mechanisms of cost sharing in basic social services and retrenchment in the public sector had led to a dramatic reduction in access by the poor, both women and men, to social services (health care and education). Liberalization and privatization policies resulted in massive lay-offs of government workers as well as those employed in the private sector. The incomes of the majority declined as a result of hard fiscal and economic policies and a political shift which gave increasing prominence to the needs and interests of big capitalist investors, especially TNCs. The majority of men and women felt overwhelmed by these changes and completely left out of the structures of decision-making responsible for these policies and strategies (Chachage 2003).

In 1994, the TGNP organized an open public symposium to critically examine SAPs and the economic rules and regulations prescribed by the World Bank and the IMF in terms of their impact on women and the poor. This event marked the TGNP's first major effort to raise a public debate about macroeconomic policies. A prominent woman politician opened the symposium with a critical statement on macro-reforms. A high level of participation resulted from the combination of methods used to provoke discussion, including the presentation of an analytical paper, a drama, and small group discussions (TGNP 1994). The media were involved and ensured that the key issues raised were publicized nationwide. There were two concrete results from this symposium. First, the issue of SAPs was raised to a higher level of public debate. Secondly, the TGNP recognized more clearly its mandate to address macro-level policy issues and achieved a greater understanding of how to move forward.

In subsequent years, the TGNP, working closely with several FemAct partners, built on early efforts such as this symposium to understand macro-level policy and, more specifically, its manifestations in national policies, budgets, taxes, and debts, and their impact on women and other marginalized groups and on gender class relations. In 1995, for example, the TGNP undertook systematic field research associated with its voter education drive in order to find out what the priority issues were from the point of view of the poor and disempowered at the grassroots level in villages and towns. People, both women and men and young people, denounced the dramatic decline in access to social services (especially education and health care) as a result of cost-sharing and reduction of public support for social services. They testified on how much poorer they had become during the years associated with macroeconomic reforms. At a FemAct feedback session in 1996, member organizations initially agreed to campaign together for gender equity in primary education and health. However, further analysis brought the realization that equity was meaningless in a situation where the majority of all children, both girls and boys, were denied access to education. FemAct agreed to lobby for a major increase of government resources to basic social services in the public sector, thereby challenging macroeconomic reform processes. This process of reflection led the coalition to discover "GB" as a means for analysis and advocacy to achieve these goals.

12.4 WHAT IS GB?

"GB" (gender budgeting) is not about demanding a separate budget for women. Rather, it is about using a "gender lens" to analyze national policies and associated public expenditures and revenues. GB is a conceptual tool for critical feminist activists to use in analyzing policies and budgets, including taxes and debts, so as to promote a more equitable allocation of resources. For example, through a GB analysis, feminists can understand and critique how resources are raised and allocated. Which taxes create an unfair burden on the poor and women? How are revenues allocated? Which social groups benefit more, which least? Are the funds collected reaching the people in ways that improve their lives? What proportion of budget allocations from the center actually reach the district? The community? The health facility, school or demonstration farm? What concrete improvements have occurred in women's, men's, and children's lives as a result of a given policy and its budget?

Furthermore, a gender budget analysis can critique the ways in which policies, laws, and budgets are developed. Who was involved in the process? Did women, youth, and poor people participate? A GB initiative takes the analysis further by actively promoting equality for women and youth, a more equitable use of public resources for all marginalized people, greater accountability of public leaders at all levels, and more direct participation in decision-making and the production of law.

GB started in Australia, followed by South Africa, and has been used by several different countries and regions in the world to achieve a broader policy focus on gender issues as well as to refocus the government's commitment on gender and pro-poor needs. The TGNP was among the first organizations in Africa to promote GB, and has since participated in several forums at regional and national level to share its experiences and learn from others. The amount of attention given to GB carries within it opportunities and threats, a point which will be explored at the end of this chapter. Suffice it to say here that the TGNP has had to remain continually vigilant against the dangers of cooptation resulting from gender mainstreaming, and complacency which could result from claiming "easy victories."

The Gender Budget Initiative (GBI) in Tanzania began in 1997 when some twenty NGOs then comprising FemAct decided to make it a priority campaign issue, with the TGNP in the lead. The broad aim was to change political and economic governance processes (policies, budgets, taxes, and debts), to make them more democratic and responsive to the needs and demands of the poor, women, and other disempowered groups. The analysis would be carried out from a pro-poor, feminist, anti-imperial perspective. The TGNP and its key FemAct partners devoted considerable time to learning more about the budget-making process in Tanzania, collectively, before deciding together on effective strategies to be used to investigate policy and budgets, to disseminate the information as widely as possible, and to influence the budget-making process during the first years of research and advocacy.

Gradually, it became clear that the GBI objectives were about democratizing governance and law-making processes in the political and economic arena by empowering poor men and women to challenge macroeconomic policies and policy processes at different levels. One result was intended to be more concrete public support for basic social and economic services which were of special priority to the poor and disempowered, including women and youth. Furthermore, the GBI discouraged government's unusually high dependence on external loans and grants, and instead lobbied for increased mobilization of local resources for a more sustainable development plan. As the initiative shifted its focus from advocacy and research during the first phase, to an activist campaign in the second phase, it has sought to activate the potential of grassroots communities (particularly, poor women, men, and youth) to challenge IMF/World Bank policy frameworks, such as policies on user fees in health and education.

The GBI lobbying initiative has developed into a two-phase program. The first phase took place between 1997 and 2000 and involved coalition building among NGOs; opening doors to decision-makers at the national level; initiating strategies for public participation at the local level; linking with regional allies; and engaging with international advocacy actions. The second phase of the campaign started in 2001, and is aimed at building a broader public campaign on the key issues identified during the first phase. GBI activities are too numerous to be analyzed in detail here; only a few key landmarks are highlighted.

12.4.1 Phase I: opening the doors
In the early years of both the TGNP and FemAct, it was still unusual for feminists to organize themselves collectively and carry out lobbying and advocacy activities concerning macroeconomic policies vis-à-vis high-ranking members of the government and parliament on a regular

basis. The decision-makers' doors were closed, and access to basic information about key policies, laws, budgets, taxes, and debt issues was highly constrained. Furthermore, most of the important decision-making negotiations between the government and IFIs and other donor agencies were held outside Tanzania with no involvement by civil society. This included the annual discussions in Washington DC with the World Bank and the IMF, and the annual consultations involving all donors which were traditionally held in Paris (the "Paris Club" talks).

At this stage, feminists were just beginning to network and form coalitions around macroeconomic issues, develop regional allies, and gather grassroots support. Therefore, the first phase of the GBI campaign involved opening the doors at several levels: nationally, internationally, regionally, and locally. Phase I established the foundation for a broader national campaign that is currently being implemented under Phase II.

12.4.1.1 Coalition building among civil society organizations
One of the primary objectives of the GBI's first phase was to strengthen understanding, consensus, and collective action among civil society organizations. GB is a powerful tool for transforming resource allocation decisions and processes so as to meet the needs of poor men and women. But it is just a tool. The only way that it can make a real difference and lead to radical social transformation is when it is employed by a broad social movement which is well grounded at all levels.

As a first step, a series of capacity building and organizing activities were planned to develop and strengthen FemAct members. Due to the diversity of coalition members' backgrounds and experiences, capacity building was seen as a necessary step toward creating and maintaining a successful coalition. Members with expertise and outside persons from the government and academia were invited to organize training sessions and public seminars. With much energy and excitement, the coalition spent months collecting and sharing as much information as possible about GB issues and activities around the world; learning about gendered economics, law, policy processes, lobbying, and advocacy strategies. In the process, they identified and supported organizational strengths and weaknesses and conducted numerous reflection and planning sessions. After this intensive capacity building exercise, the TGNP and FemAct partners had gelled into a well-consolidated team, informed with information, specific tasks, and a group of implementers who were conceptually prepared for the program ahead of us.

At the same time as the coalition was enhancing its capacity, it was also actively developing the GBI's conceptual and organizational strategic plan. The coalition was fortunate to have time and resources to carry out extensive planning and organizing activities, thanks to the support of a sympathetic bilateral donor who at that time was taking what other donors considered to be a big risk. For over six months, the coalition engaged in operational and conceptual strategic planning, debate, and reflection. Given the complexity of the issues, there was a need to attain conceptual clarity and some level of equal understanding. One of the most interesting aspects of this strategic planning was a debate that centered around what the proposed action was about – a "women's budget" or a "gender budget."? The TGNP and FemAct members agreed that the concept of a "gender budget" was the only one consistent with the original conceptual framework and ideological position which linked gender and class (and imperial/race/ethnic) issues. Moreover, in practical terms, a program which focused solely on *women's* access to resources would be marginalized, and lose a popular following. The coalition decided that, in Tanzania's context, a gender-budget approach that included the needs and interests of poor men and youths would be more appropriate, considering that the majority of the population was disempowered and lacked equal access to resources and decision-making power.

This early period of learning, reflection, and investigation laid an important foundation of capacity, ownership, legitimacy, and momentum upon which GBI objectives could be pursued. The energy of more than thirty NGOs working together collectively as a coalition lent legitimacy to the process, and won more attention from government and the public. Once the coalition had this recognition, it was able to continue building upon the interest and commitment it was generating. Not only did this foundational work enhance the capacities of the member organizations and feminist activists involved to carry out the GBI campaign, it also strengthened the coalition's capacity to work together on other important issues such as sexual offenses and the abuse of women and children.

12.4.1.2 Grounding with the grassroots at the district and community levels
Another aspect of coalition building was forming strong partnerships with local level civil society actors. As noted earlier, the TGNP adopted a two-pronged strategic approach which combined policy

engagement with contentious activism at all levels. In other words, it involved legal mobilization as well as direct action. The building of strong links and networks at the local level was seen as an important step because (1) the local initiatives could inform the ongoing policy advocacy activities at national and international levels, (2) the knowledge and information derived from policy engagement at the national and international levels could be shared with those organizing at the local level, and (3) grounding at the grassroots level could ensure that a sound social base was provided for the GBI, as steps towards the creation of a popular social movement.

Specific districts and actions were identified for involvement during the planning processes. These were partly determined by the location of Intermediary Gender Networks (IGNs) at the district and/or regional and zonal levels (Mbilinyi 2003). Consisting of local community-based organizations, NGOs, and other civic associations, local IGNs participated in the early formulation processes of the GBI. Other participants included outreach groups of the TGNP and local partners of other FemAct members in the districts such as those of TAMWA. The coalition focused their attention on elected district councilors, the whole district leadership (planners, budget officers, and others), and the communities (both men and women). Councilors and district technical personnel were important as a point of entry, so as to be able to engage directly in district level planning and governance processes.

The first GBI activities undertaken at the district level were carried out through participatory action research. Kondoa Rural District in Dodoma Region and Kinondoni District in Dar es Salaam were chosen to bring out the diversity in local situations, Kondoa being among the poorest districts, and Kinondoni one of the most developed and fragmented in social class terms. The findings documented the shocking effects of policies and economic reforms on social services. For example, in Kondoa, our local partners, together with the TGNP animator facilitators, were able to expose the completely run-down situation in local hospitals and dispensaries. Many lacked even one doctor; professional personnel had to leave their posts to look for needed drugs; and night guards were injecting patients with medicine. Pregnant women were being turned away at hospital doors because they could not afford to buy gloves and other equipment for the childbirth, as called for by cost-sharing measures. The results of the research were shared locally at feedback workshops involving local activists, members of parliament, district authorities and councilors, and the media. Inflamed by the enormity of the problems in the health sector, the Kondoa MP raised a storm in Parliament by describing how drugs were now being administered by unskilled nightwatchmen. The people in Kondoa have continued to lobby their own district local councils using the advocacy skills developed during the early phase of GBI.

These are some of the activities that contributed to the growth and institutionalization of IGNs. In some cases, IGNs have been able to change the budgets in their districts. For example, in Kisarawe (Coast Region), Kinondoni and Songea (Ruvuma Region), an intensive program of supporting local civil society organizations and district councilors was undertaken to build their capacities of policy analysis and GB and to raise awareness of the links to broader constituency interests (HIV/AIDS, poverty, etc.). The Kinondoni IGN was able to successfully lobby their local council to adopt issues such as youth employment, student transportation, and violence. The Kisarawe IGN chose to focus on HIV/AIDS and its relationship to poverty. They have initiated weekly seminars and an outreach program which works with poor women and men in the community. These were important processes for building local capacity, informing the national level with grassroots concerns, and broadening the movement.

12.4.1.3 National government sectors, parliamentarians, and processes

In the early years, much of the GBI effort at the national level was necessarily focused on opening the doors for dialogue and building space for consultation within government circles (and in the parliament). For this to happen, the campaign needed several layers of access within the government in terms of people, information, time, and participation. This access was essential because GB requires analysis of resource allocation structures, information that only the government can provide. Furthermore, activists needed to be able to identify potential allies, sympathizers and opponents within government; and to develop with allies a mechanism for gender budget training and internalization which could be sustained by relevant actors.

One of the campaign's first steps at the national level was to conduct a large national level research effort, on specific sectors and policies. The sectors examined were those corresponding to the concerns raised by grassroots partners: health, education, agriculture, and later trade and industry. A team comprising of NGOs, independent researchers, economists, and government officials embarked on an in-depth analysis of budgetary policies and processes surrounding gender and class issues

within each of the selected sectors. The research findings were packaged as reports to the sectors and popular reports for the public. Then
the publications were disseminated and publicized widely to create an
environment for public debate on issues of policy, budgets, and democracy. Once the issues were defined and had gained the attention of the
government and the public, a series of formal activities were organized
to discuss the research and to take the next steps toward identifying
entry points for change.

For example, in November 2000, the TGNP and FemAct issued a
public statement to the World Bank which refuted the continuation of
user fees in health and education. Cost-sharing and privatization, along
with budget cuts, had led to a drastic reduction in social service
delivery, and contributed to impoverishment of the majority. Therefore,
according to the statement, "international donor policies that intend to
support the processes of development in Tanzania should support these
sectors rather than targeting them for budget cuts and privatization."

Building on the avenues expanded within the government, the
TGNP and FemAct organized informal and formal meetings with key
actors within the government, parliament, and other selected institutions in order to reinforce the initial gains made from the research
process. The strategy for these follow-up meetings was to take an
awareness-raising approach, hoping to strengthen the conceptual capacity and knowledge base of key government actors about the link
between gender and economics, with the assumption that pro-poor
decisions and policies would follow. Hence, part of the agenda of
such meetings concerned how the policy-making, planning, and budgeting processes could potentially support progressive processes for the
majority of women, youth, and poor men in the country. This information was presented through sensitization workshops, as a conscious
tactic for non-aggressive lobbying.

During and after these training/working sessions, the TGNP and
FemAct partners engaged in lobbying specific government actors in
the selected sectors on several key issues. One of the major issues
lobbied for at the national (and local) levels was on having more
open, participatory, and responsive systems of governance and law-
making. This was based on one of the major research findings, that
policy and budget processes in the country were non-participatory,
exclusive, and often took positions against the interests of poor groups
in the country including women and girls. The TGNP and FemAct
lobbied for the government to provide more space for direct

participation of the poor and women in policy and planning processes of the country, and for greater transparency and accountability in the allocation of public resources (both expenditures and revenues).

Other key issues lobbied for included the removal of user fees in health and education, the elimination of corruption, and participatory democracy in general. The coalition picked up the demands of peasant producers for the reintroduction of producer subsidies to support their access to farm inputs, fair prices, and government regulation of the market. When the government introduced new legislation to liberalize land law, thus jeopardizing the land rights of peasant producers and all Tanzanians, the coalition became part of a broad campaign led by one of its members, HakiArdhi (Chachage and Mbilinyi 2003).

At the same time, the coalition continued to reiterate the problems associated with the constraints generated by the macroeconomic and fiscal policy frameworks and processes adopted by government with pressure from the donor community. The research had shown that, with the adoption of the World Bank/IMF-led structural adjustment and macroeconomic stabilization programs, the role of the state in the economy had been reduced. Privatization, deregulation, and deficit reduction associated with cutting expenditures on social services meant that the state was less able to guide the development process and to respond to the needs of poor men and women. The TGNP and FemAct sought to make national decision-makers aware of the negative impact of macro policies and processes on women and poor people, and called for a review of the whole SAP/liberalization/privatization package.

Thus the short-term emphasis of the GBI was on reforming the policy and budget frameworks so as to provide quality public social and economic services for poor groups and women, to eliminate user fees and to bring back subsidies for small-scale farmers. The long-term emphasis was on advocating for a reduced role of IFIs and other donors in policy and financial management of the nation's economy, and the greater participation of the poor and disempowered. Ultimately, both strategies advocated for national resources to be put back in the hands of the people.

The TGNP and its partners have also realized that lobbying and awareness raising are not one-time activities but require ongoing engagement and support. For example, new MPs joined the parliament in 2000 and needed new skills and information. Many other parliamentarians still need to be supported and informed on gender and technical issues relating to budgets, policies, debts, poverty, and participatory democracy, including the role of civil society organizations. A major challenge is how to make elected representatives at all levels, including MPs, district councilors, and village government leaders, more accountable to the people. Training and awareness-raising alone will not lead parliamentarians and cabinet ministers to adopt critical feminist progressive agendas. Strong public pressure is needed on many fronts, which requires the growth of a popular social movement.

The parliament itself is facing growing challenges relating to its role, especially in holding the government accountable in its policy/budget implementation processes. Multi-party political reforms and the hegemonic position of neoliberal pro-market ideology have led to two different outcomes which seem to be vying with each other. On the one hand, many argue that the level of debate and social critique within parliament has dramatically reduced, with the executive branch of government asserting much more power than before through mechanisms of party discipline attached to the ruling party. So-called opposition parties have failed to provide a powerful alternative voice. During the last two years, however, a growing number of MPs in the ruling party, CCM, along with other parties, have begun to mobilize themselves through parliamentary sub-committees to challenge specific aspects of macroeconomic reform. A recent example is parliament's rejection of the government's strategies for privatization of the National Micro-Finance Bank in 2002/2003, led by members of the Finance and Economics Sub-Committee.

Within this kind of environment, it has remained a challenge to critical feminist activists and their partners to identify and support progressive MPs, to encourage them to raise gender class issues, and to challenge the entire structure of decision-making. That final step is unlikely under present conditions, as it would mean committing "class suicide", i.e. undermining the privileges and power which MPs and other government officials now have.

12.4.1.4 *Regional and international networking to impact IFI frameworks*

In subsequent years, the lobbying emphasis has expanded to include other policy processes which influence national and sectoral budgets. These other processes include the Poverty Reduction Strategy (PRS), the Public Expenditure Review (PER), the Consultative Group (CG), Local Government Reform, and others. The PRS is a key process that seeks to shift more national resources to poverty reduction goals.

However, from our point of view, this process is controlled and influenced by IFI policy frameworks, and its very nomenclature (reduction of poverty) attracts attention away from the real issue of participatory development and the eradication of exploitation and oppression. The PER process is responsible for ensuring increasing financial transparency, coordination, and accountability within the government machinery. This process, from our view, is also far too directed by donors. The CG process is supposed to be a consultative avenue between government and donors on issues related to financing the development budget. The participation of civil society organizations is highly limited in both the PER and CG processes, with very little room to involve community-based organizations.

Each of the processes noted above has been imposed on the Tanzanian government as conditionalities for loans, just as SAPs were in the early 1990s. Also, like SAPs, these processes direct the government's development priorities and resource allocation decisions. At the same time, they also create potential opportunities to engage in processes having profound gender and class effects. Each has been opened up to participation by civil society organizations. Therefore, the coalition decided to get involved with the macroeconomic frameworks and processes that constrain the national government's autonomy. However, it also recognizes the danger that donor-led consultative processes may actually undermine democratization processes internal to national politics. Limited participation in a management exercise is not the ultimate goal, and government officials can correctly dismiss it as neocolonial politics. Ultimately, civil society organizations need to engage with, and democratize, the government itself through a popular democratic struggle.

For all IFIs' and donors' talk about economic liberalization going hand in hand with democracy, none of the IFIs' processes came along with democratic structures. The doors of the World Bank, the IMF, and the WTO have been the hardest ones to open, and this is still the most challenging area in which to see tangible results. Moreover, they continue to struggle to dominate decision-making processes at the national level. These spaces have to be created, just as they were within the national government, but, in this case, the barriers are even greater. After much protest and many consultative meetings, we have yet to see any real change in macroeconomic policy. The IFI-led processes are too big, too far away, and too strong for one country-level feminist network to influence – and win. Participation in larger networks within the country, regionally, and internationally needs to be increased and improved strategically so as to build up enough public pressure power for real change.

At the regional level, the TGNP and FemAct have joined active coalitions, and have been engaged in collective action around key issues. For example, the TGNP is an active member of the Southern Regional Civil Society Network on trade issues. Through this network, it has organized lobbying activities on issues of trade and SAPs and the impacts they have on women and poor groups. At the international level, the TGNP has been active in building strategic partnerships with like-minded organizations and networks around the world, including the "50 Years is Enough" engagement with World Bank issues and organizing with respect to the WTO.

The major contribution of such partnerships has occurred at two levels. First, these coalitions have greater access to the targeted institutions than a country-level coalition. Therefore, we have sent our critiques of IFI power and policies through these international coalitions. A second important contribution was reciprocal in nature: international coalitions have invited and supported members of the TGNP and FemAct to participate and contribute to international events. In this way, GBI issues have become more visible at the national as well as the international levels, and our presence has strengthened the international movement.

12.4.2 Phase II: consolidating and strengthening our voices and collective action

The major work of the second phase of the GBI in Tanzania started in 2000/2001 with a deepened focus on activist actions and organizing through a broad-based campaign. This phase continued to employ the same analytical tools and advocacy strategies of GB with an added component of increased collective action at both the national and the local levels. Back in 1994, when planning the GBI campaign, we had already thought that, after building bridges, we would turn the GB work into a focused nationwide campaign. At the beginning of Phase II, we incorporated the strategies and lessons learned from Phase I into our new focus. One of the main lessons gained from Phase I was a heightened recognition of the need to ground the movement at the grassroots level. The policy and legal issues and processes being challenged were much larger than our networks. These issues required the weight of a *broad social movement*, with the people's perspectives and experiences in the lead.

The process of collective reflection on achievements and challenges that had arisen during the first phase of GBI was an extremely important part of the overall campaign process. Involving grassroots partners, district networks (IGNs), FemAct partner organizations, and TGNP members and staff, participatory processes which we call animation were used to assess the situation, and to analyze and plan appropriate action to move the campaign forward. Always underlying this reflection process was the ultimate aim of real, substantive social change at local and national levels.

The TGNP and FemAct have continually emphasized the significance of participatory and collective ways of organizing and decision-making in their work. Animation enables people coming from oppressed and exploited positions to recognize the knowledge which they have and to use it to organize themselves and to act for real structural change. It also provides a space within which people coming from different locations and different perspectives can communicate with each other while breaking down social barriers. The combination of logic and artistry, theory and practice, analysis and emotion, leads to an amazing effervescence of joy, anger, and anguish, combined with reflection, and a growing clarity of purpose and commitment to act, indeed, the desire to act, and to act *now*. Strong bonds result from this brew, along with self-esteem, mutual respect, and fun (Mbilinyi 2003).

The planning and implementation of the Phase II campaign on GB was enriched by the Phase I GBI experiences. The TGNP and its partners' engagement with the government, parliament, and the local authorities generated a rich base of data, information, and experiences pertinent for enhancing the Phase II campaign objectives. For example, the knowledge of how government operates, and of policy environments, legal procedures, and strategies for responding to the needs of the majority of its population, was particularly useful in sharpening the strategies and processes of the Phase II campaign. Also, through the earlier efforts on coalition building and networking with other like-minded civil society organizations, a database of progressive civil society actors had been created. The database was regarded as a key ingredient for building the social movement. In this way, the information and database links assisted in providing different avenues for the expansion and nourishment of partnership building and mobilization strategies at both the national and local level, with a broader-based ownership and participation of civil society organizations in the campaign processes.

12.4.2.1 The "Return Resources to the People" campaign

The coalition's overall transformation goals remain the same as in Phase I: the democratization of political and economic governance institutions and processes, including the development of a participatory development process, with gender equity and justice at all levels.

The TGNP and FemAct decided to focus the campaign on a single entry point where all the issues of interest converged. This was important because the GB issues of policy, resource allocation, and democratic governance were considered too abstract to attract broad-based interest. Therefore, the coalition decided upon the entry point of HIV/AIDS, because it affected every social group and most families, and was connected to broader policy and democracy issues. The campaign would challenge the way in which HIV/AIDS has been reduced to an individual problem concerning sexuality and culture, which can be solved through changes in individual behavior alone. The higher vulnerability to infection resulting from chronic ill health, malnutrition, and prevalent sexual disease, the lack of adequate employment and incomes to ensure access to food security and good health care, the high exposure to contaminated blood, syringes, and other factors, and the low access to drugs and health care associated with structural adjustment in health care – all of these were being ignored by researchers and policy-makers.

Under the banner of "Return Resources to the People: Break the Silence on the Linkages between Gender, Resources and HIV/AIDS," the two main assumptions of the campaign are that HIV and AIDS are a problem of unequal ownership and control over resources as well as a gender issue. The campaign is aimed at (1) contributing to and strengthening informed public debates and discussions that generate alternative thinking around issues of democracy, economics, poverty, resources, policy, budgets, gender, and HIV/AIDS, (2) linking with ongoing feminist and other progressive initiatives at the national, regional, and global levels to challenge and pressure international governments and IFIs to adopt more equitable political, economic, and social policies with respect to poor countries so as to reduce the marginalization of the people, especially poor women, men, and youths, (3) strengthening strategies for ensuring that the Tanzanian government and its key donor partners direct resources to the majority of the people, so that women and men can manage their own lives in a sustainable way, and (4) organizing collectively and building stronger linkages between feminist activists and other civil society organizations in order to ensure that national resources are distributed according to the priorities and needs of the majority, and that there is deeper participatory democracy and governance, especially at the local level, to allow for enhanced collective decision-making and a more fair distribution of resources.

At the operational level, the targeted focus of the campaign has been planned at three levels. At the international level, the coalition is joining hands with other progressive social movements to tackle the question of globalization and unfair trading systems in the world, particularly those perpetuated through the WTO and commercially driven pharmaceutical companies (e.g. drugs for HIV/AIDS; see Klug's chapter in this volume). At the national level, the TGNP and the FemAct coalition are activating a broader grassroots-based movement for challenging and transforming the undemocratic top-down decision-making processes of government and resource management, in order to promote equity and social justice at all levels. At the public and community levels, the campaign is generating an empowering debate around critical issues of concern to the majority. These include income and food security for all; quality health, water, and education for all; grassroots control over key resources, including land, forests, and water; increased revenue from large-scale investments to communities and local/central government apparatuses; and the right to a sustainable livelihood in rural and urban areas.

12.4.2.2 Highlights of the campaign
The "Return Resources to the People" campaign was formally launched by a march and rally on International Women's Day (March 8, 2003), which involved more than 2,500 women and men from all sectors of society. More than 120 people directly participated in the planning and preparation for the march and the rally which followed, including representatives from nearly all the member organizations of FemAct. Youth groups took on responsibility for making hand-painted posters proclaiming the main messages, such as "Break the silence – HIV/AIDS is about resources and gender!" and "The problem of the world today is not poverty, it is exploitation!" and "HIV/AIDS is a structural problem!" and "The resources of Africa should remain in Africa!" and "Women are especially vulnerable to HIV/AIDS – stop sexual abuse!"

Later in the year, policy-makers and other government authorities were invited to participate in a panel discussion with activists on the issue of policy, resources, and HIV/AIDS, focusing on macro policies

such as the Poverty Reduction Strategy. Hundreds of actors participated, including representatives from the IGNs who took the lead in
raising grassroots issues and in challenging government endorsement of
neoliberal policies.

In September 2003, the biannual Gender Festival provided an international forum at which to seek wide support for the campaign.
FemAct and other partners participated in planning and implementing
the festival, which is held at the TGNP's Gender Resource Center in
Dar es Salaam. More than 1,000 participants attended from all over
Tanzania and from neighboring countries in Africa and worldwide. Key
campaign publications were launched, there was a special celebration
of "ten years of feminist activism," and the GBI campaign song,
"Return Resources to the People" (in Kiswahili) was launched with
enthusiastic dancing during the formal opening.

A second march and rally was organized on April 24, 2004 in
solidarity with actions all over the world to protest the World Bank
and IMF, on the occasion of the sixtieth anniversary of their founding.
More than 500 women and men took part in the march, and more than
800 people participated in the rally. The guest of honor, a notable
national figure, endorsed the main position taken by the campaign,
arguing that post-colonial governments in Africa can say no to external
"donors" and remain accountable to their people, not the big investors.

One of the major developments from 2003 to 2004 was the increasingly significant role of youth networks and grassroots outreach groups
in helping to define the main issues to be addressed, preparing for
the march/rally and making presentations. The weekly Gender and
Development Seminar Series has become an important space within
which grassroots people interact with activists operating at local and
national level to discuss and consider strategies of action and plan their
implementation. The involvement of FemAct partners, district networks, and local outreach groups has also been enhanced by systematic
programs to develop capacity in terms of conceptual analysis – in this
case, of the connections between macro policies, global capitalism,
resources, gender, and HIV/AIDS – through a process of dialogue.

The march and rally on April 24 was the culmination of a full week
of action, that involved TV and radio talk shows and interviews, a press
conference, and a book launch and panel discussion on global capitalism and the IFIs. Of special importance in terms of the future of the
campaign was the circulation of a petition denouncing the World Bank
and the IMF and calling for their radical transformation or abolition.

More than 2,900 signatures were collected, mainly by local groups carrying out door-to-door canvassing – or in many cases, from hawker to hawker, food stall to food stall. The process of explaining the purpose of the petition and the act of signing were far more significant than anticipated. Many people were frightened, and wanted to know, "is it legal to sign a petition?" "what does the ruling party say on this?" We also realized just how valuable the march and rally have become as ways to strengthen contentious organizing and contentious discourse.

The campaign has also generated an amazing diversity and number of publications in a short time. The majority are popular materials written in accessible Kiswahili with graphic illustrations. They include *Utandawazi na Wewe* (Globalization and You), *Rasilimali, Jinsia na Ukimwi* (Resources, Gender and HIV/AIDS), and *Mwongozo wa Kuibua Mdahalo wa Kitaifa Juu ya Sera za Uchumi na Mahusiano ya Ukimwi, Rasilimali na Jinsia* (Guidelines on Facilitating Public Discussions on Economic Policy and the Linkages between HIV/ AIDS, Resources and Gender). Campaign posters were produced in Kiswahili in 2003, capturing key messages of the campaign – including some mentioned above in relation to the 2003 march and rally.

During 2003, several activists engaged collectively in a reflection on ten years of feminist activism associated with the TGNP and FemAct, which led to the publication of two full-length books, *Activist Voices* (Mbilinyi et al. 2003) and *Against Neo-Liberalism* (Chachage et al. 2003). An analytical report of the first phase of the campaign was published in 2004, along with a short critique of so-called debt relief as controlled by the World Bank and the IMF.

Side by side with printed media has been the production of videos and an assortment of dramas and songs created and performed by youth partners at the local level. Caps and T-shirts helped to mobilize participation in the 2003 launching of the campaign. Strong links with the media have helped to publicize the campaign at the national and international levels.

12.5 REFLECTIONS FOR FUTURE ACTIVISM[1]

Ongoing reflection on the progress of the campaign has highlighted several issues which are presented below. Although based on experiences in Tanzania, we believe that these issues are relevant to the

[1] This section is based on Kitunga (2003), Mbilinyi (2003), and Rusimbi (2003).

experiences of activists engaged in the building of social movements and transformative legal practices elsewhere – especially in Africa where, in most countries, there is still a weak development of popular organizations and movements.

From the foregoing, it is clear that the TGNP and FemAct have injected something new into the women's movement and the democratization movement in civil society as a whole in Tanzania. It has reclaimed the political content which was lost when the women's movement was coopted into the gender and development mainstream safety zone. Gender, a concept born out of critical feminist discourse and meant to clarify the social construction of women's subordination in conjunction with class, ethnicity, and imperial relations, has been rehabilitated to serve the emancipatory purposes for which it was coined. State and development bureaucracies, in contrast, justified tokenism as a strategy for women's advancement. These bureaucracies have used gender analysis to initiate "gender and development" projects, which are safe and non-threatening to the status quo. The discourse adopted reduces gender to a management project, and gender training to the transmission of a bundle of techniques and tools of analysis.

Critical feminism challenges the status quo; and within FemAct, gender analysis is used to identify which elements in the patriarchal and imperial social structure should be targeted and dismantled. The coalition has put into practice an approach which challenges the interlocking features of patriarchy and global capitalism and other forms of oppression in our present context in Tanzania.

The TGNP and FemAct have also marked a turning point in the democratization movement in civil society by showing that, instead of working in isolation and competing with each other, joint action actually works. Before its inception, activist NGOs worked pretty much in isolation, duplicating efforts, and, given the different approaches and outlooks, sometimes undoing each other's successes. This created psychological vulnerability and invited divisive tendencies and manipulation by state and donor agents whose actions (deliberately or not) pitted one NGO against another. Since the consolidation of FemAct, there is more sharing of methodologies, approaches, and information; but, more importantly, a collective commitment to activist lobbying and advocacy as a necessary political component of NGO work. This has stimulated some of the participating NGOs which started as service organizations to add an advocacy component to their strategies.

FemAct stands as a role model for civil society organizing where activism is not sporadic and dependent on a single charismatic visionary leader or organization but is group-centerd and collective. It has shown by example that networking at national, regional, and international levels is useful and effective if there is a strong organizational base which links grassroots struggles and perspectives and those of activists located at other levels of society into a single activist movement. The organizing principles need to be open and flexible enough to enable different grooves and strands to consolidate themselves within it and to draw strength and support from others. All the members of the coalition are in networks with grassroots and intermediary level organizations through which concerns are shared and action mobilized. Though not yet fully consolidated throughout the country, these are signs that a grassroots-based movement is in the making. The challenge is for FemAct to increase its capacity for learning and interacting. It also needs to consciously support the networking and organizing capacities of grassroots and intermediary organizations which function as its focal points; and through them recruit more organizations and individuals at the grassroots level into the movement.

The TGNP and FemAct partners have deliberately adopted a two-pronged strategy for opening up lobbying space within the government (i.e. legal mobilization) and challenging them from the outside at the same time (i.e. direct action). The inevitable tensions inherent in doing both collaboration and contention vis-à-vis government (and donors) present a continual challenge that requires continual reflection and strategy modification.

The process of "gender mainstreaming" inherent to policy engagement of this nature has been criticized for associating otherwise activist organizations, including the TGNP, too closely with the government. Participants in the process, i.e. members of the TGNP and FemAct, have raised these concerns as part of the continuing reflection process (Kitunga 2003). The danger is that GB may provide legitimacy to processes that are being challenged, thus coopting the activist agenda. As some have argued, we might win the battle for gender mainstreaming, but lose the war for transformative change. For example, messages about gender and poverty may be accepted and key "gender-sensitive" phrases sprinkled into policies, but the real goals and vision run the risk of being diverted. Moreover, by opposing the power of IFIs and the conditionalities that constrain government, the campaign may provide government with an excuse for its failure to take significant steps on behalf of its own citizens, and women, poor men, and youths in particular.

At the same time, there is no denying the fact that the overall policy framework is determined by the IMF, the World Bank, the WTO, and the donor community as a whole. Within this policy framework, policy advocacy and lobbying have a limited impact in affecting fundamental changes. Achievements through this strategy cannot have a lasting effect unless an alternative development paradigm is adopted. The coalition faces the urgent challenge of working with others to develop a new development vision, and of mobilizing a social force to push for its actualization.

Because global political and economic forces have a great impact locally, especially in relation to the state–citizen relationship, local level action needs to be supported by international advocacy. For example, gains made through international lobbying have to be followed up at the local level by putting pressure on the government after accession or ratification of an international treaty to make appropriate changes in the domestic legal and institutional frameworks. This implies that FemAct efforts to strengthen grassroots level networks and activism have to be matched with an equally rigorous effort to forge and consolidate mutually supportive linkages at national, regional, and global levels. Grassroots perspectives will in this way be brought to the attention of national, regional, and international action agendas and strategies. Given the limited autonomy of the nation-state within the context of imperial globalization, a strategy is needed for proactive activism which is tightly linked to other Third World global actions.

12.6 CONCLUSION: THE WAY FORWARD

At the end of Phase II, the TGNP and FemAct partners would like to see a broad-based movement that is engaged effectively in organizing, acts collectively, and has increased space in which people can play a more effective role in local and national decision-making processes and outcomes. Deliberate steps need to be taken to strengthen contentious organizing and contentious discourse at all levels, involving all social groups.

Within this context, the need for critical reflection on the campaign's agenda, issues, and strategies at different levels cannot be over-emphasized. Faced with the power of neoliberal economic models of development, it can be very easy for a campaign like this to adopt mainstream discourse about "good governance," "poverty reduction," and "gender and development" which has lost the original people-centered political content.

The campaign coalition needs to foster new ways of thinking, acting, and doing politics. A major challenge is to strengthen capacities in both contentious actions and rigorous social analysis. Policy analysis is one aspect, but democratization of society and governance will call for far more, moving beyond the constraints of existing government structures and policies to imagine and create a different world and a different form of governance. Participatory processes of animation will contribute to this "search for alternatives."

What is sharply noticeable in the experiences of the TGNP, FemAct, and the GBI campaign is group-centered leadership and participatory approaches in the production and reproduction of knowledge, and in organizing itself. This is especially evident in the case of the TGNP, where animation guides the way in which key decisions are made within the organization itself, as well as in its social relations with other organizations at local and national levels. The process is as important as the output or results of a given activity.

In the short term, the campaign will continue to advocate for popular control of national resources in order to ensure that the benefits reach the majority of the citizens of this country. Within these parameters, the campaign will reject economic policy contexts that constrain and marginalize the majority of the population, with specific attention to poor women, men, and youths.

One of the major challenges ahead is to become even more conscious of the link between social base and social movements, and to concentrate on the facilitation of self-organizing among the poor and disempowered themselves. Being grounded in a mass movement of grassroots level groups and organizations will provide the necessary foundation for a mass social movement at the national and Pan-African levels. In this regard, strategies are being developed to "decentralize" the campaign and to strengthen the involvement of neighborhood groups.

The documentation of these struggles from a critical feminist perspective will be essential so that activists and critical scholars learn from progress, contributions, and challenges, and develop strategies to take the struggle forward. The campaign also recognizes the need to document its struggles for future generations of activists. Where would we be now without the contributions made – and documented – by early women activists such as Bibi Titi Mohamed, a major leader of the anti-colonial movement in the 1950s? The stories about this campaign will provide lessons for future generations as they struggle for equity and justice.

References

Chachage, Seithy L. 2002. *Reflections on Civil Society in Tanzania: The Case of TGNP and AJM*. Dar es Salaam: Development Policy Management Forum.

2003 "Gender Impoverishment and Class Reproduction." In Mbilinyi *et al.* (2003)

Chachage, Seithy L., and Marjorie Mbilinyi (Eds.). 2003. *Against Neo-Liberalism*. Dar es Salaam: TGNP and E&D Limited.

Geiger, Susan. 1997. *TANU Women*. Oxford: James Currey.

KIHACHA. 2002. *Food is Politics*. Dar es Salaam: IDS, University of Dar es Salaam.

Kitunga, Demere. 2003. "Policy Advocacy and Lobbying in Feminist Activism." In Mbilinyi *et al.* (2003).

Mbilinyi, Marjorie. 2001. *Budgets, Debt Relief and Globalization*. Accra: Gender and Economic Reforms in Africa Programme.

2003. "Animation and the Feminist Social Movement." In Mbilinyi *et al.* (2003).

Mbilinyi, Marjorie, Mary Rusimbi, S. L., and Demere Kitunga (Eds.). 2003. *Activist Voices: Feminist Struggles for an Alternative World*. Dar es Salaam: TGNP and E&D Limited.

Rusimbi, Mary. 2003. "Struggles over Resources and Democracy: TGNP's Experience with GB." In Mbilinyi *et al.* (2003).

Santos, Boaventura de Sousa. 2002. *Toward a New Legal Common Sense*. London: Butterworths.

TGNP. 1993. *Gender Profile*. Dar es Salaam: E&D

1994. *Structural Adjustment: Exploitation or Oppression*. Dar es Salaam: TGNP, mimeo.

2004. *Gender Budget Analysis in Tanzania: 1997–2000*. Dar es Salaam: E&D Limited.

Tsikata, Dzodzi, and Joanna Kerr (Eds.). 2000. *Demanding Dignity*. Accra: Third World Network-Africa.

Wignaraja, Poona. 1993. "Rethinking Development and Democracy." In *New Social Movements in the South*, edited by Poona Wignaraja. London: Zed Books.

CHAPTER 13

TWO DEMOCRACIES, TWO LEGALITIES: PARTICIPATORY BUDGETING IN PORTO ALEGRE, BRAZIL

Boaventura de Sousa Santos

Today, two forms of globalization confront each other: the hegemonic neoliberal globalization driven by the interests of global capitalism, and the counter-hegemonic globalization, or globalization from below, driven by the transnationally networked resistance of subaltern classes and social groups against the exclusions, dispossessions, and discriminations caused or aggravated by neoliberal globalization (Santos 2002). I focus on the political and legal nature of the initiatives and struggles constituting counter-hegemonic globalization, which I refer to as subaltern cosmopolitan politics and legality. In this vast social field of confrontational politics and law, I distinguish two basic processes of globalization: global collective action through transnational networking through local/national/global linkages, on one side, and local or national struggles whose success prompts reproduction in other locales or networking with parallel struggles elsewhere. In chapter 2 above, I dealt with the first process, illustrating it with the analysis of the World Social Forum. In this chapter, I deal with the second process. I illustrate it with the analysis of participatory budgeting (PB) in Porto Alegre, a local initiative of social redistribution through participatory democracy considered by the United Nations as one of the most successful experiments of urban management and which has been adopted in 194 cities in Brazil and also in Latin America and Europe.

The chapter is organized as follows. In the first section, I provide the analytical framework. In the second and third sections, I present the main traits of PB conceived of as a form of participatory redistributive democracy. In the fourth section, I analyze the confrontational legal plurality involved in PB.

13.1 THE STATE AND DEMOCRACY AS CONTESTED TERRAINS

In the last twenty or thirty years, the state underwent a profound transformation which can be summarized in the following way: from being the solution to social problems, the state becomes *the* problem, the solution of which is a necessary (if not also a sufficient) condition for the solution of all the other social problems. While under both demo-liberalism and demo-socialism[1] a strong democratic state was a necessary (if not a sufficient) condition for a strong civil society, under the conditions of neoliberalism a weak democratic state is a necessary (if not a sufficient) condition for a strong civil society. While the modern capitalist state gained legitimacy among the popular classes by creating non-mercantile interactions among citizens through an ever expansive conception of public goods, the neoliberal state must withdraw as much as possible from social regulation (not to mention economic regulation), and promote the multiplication of market interactions among citizens through the provision of predictable legal rules. While up until now the state grounded its privileged political role in its sovereign prerogative and its power of coercion, the neoliberal state must become whenever feasible (virtually in all issues except those of internal or external security) a partner among others in broad contexts of social governance in which state and non-state actors participate in a tendentially equal footing.[2]

These transformations have been so massive (though much more in discourse than in practice) that much progressive political thinking has declared the state as a relatively obsolete entity, struggling to survive more for the sake of its own interests than for the sake of society's interest. I have claimed that this is the wrong conclusion to draw from the profound transformation that the state has undergone in recent decades (see Santos 2002). Rather than an erosion of the state's sovereignty or of its regulatory capacities, what is occurring is a transformation of sovereignty and the emergence of a new mode of regulation, in which the public goods up until now produced by the state (legitimacy,

---

[1] On these concepts see Santos (2002:Chapter 9).
[2] On the question of governance, see chapter 2.

social and economic welfare, security, and cultural identity) are the object of permanent contention and painstaking negotiation among different social actors under state coordination. Having lost the monopoly of regulation, the state still keeps the monopoly of meta-regulation, that is to say, the monopoly of articulation and coordination among subcontracted private regulators. This means that, today, notwithstanding appearances to the contrary, the state is more than ever involved in the politics of social redistribution – and hence in the determination of the criteria of inclusion and exclusion. In this new political organization the state is a partial institution, but a crucial one since it has become a social field open to competition among agents of political subcontracting and franchising carrying alternative conceptions of the public goods to be delivered. The struggle for the public control of the state and for the democratic reform of the state – and, more broadly, of the political society, in Gramsci's terms – have never been so important for the protection of the social interests and rights of the subaltern classes. PB in Porto Alegre originates from this political understanding and shows that a successful struggle must involve both political and legal resources and that state legality must be resorted to in tandem with non-state legality.

While the state has become a highly contested institution, democracy has known in the same period an unprecedented recognition, reaching out into the whole globe and being transformed into a political conditionality of funding by the international financial institutions. Here also the transformations are massive: from a political privilege of a few countries in the North Atlantic to a political regime available to all countries; from a general name for different types of democracy to just one type, liberal or representative democracy; from a political regime in some tension with capitalism, to the political face of capitalism; from a regime with some potential for social redistribution, to a non-distributive regime; from a regime whose legitimacy is both the cause and the consequence of the social contract, to a regime legitimated by the autonomy of the individual, free to enter individual (not social) contracts.

These transformations have not occurred without contradictions, grounded not so much on new forms of democratic theory (which have not proliferated) but rather on grassroots political practices, particularly in the global South where democracy apparently had no deep roots. Such practices have been, in general, characterized by the following features: refusal of the idea of representative democracy as the only form of democracy and reliance on an alternative form, defined as participatory or deliberative democracy or, more generally, as grassroots democracy; pragmatic conception of the relations between representative democracy and participatory democracy which may include confrontation as well as complementarity; focus on social redistribution based on a new equation between participation and social benefit, an equation that, contrary to the modern idea of the social contract, reenacts the aspiration and the demand for social justice in repeated, transparent, and only minimally mediated acts of political participation (see Santos, forthcoming). Porto Alegre's PB is probably one of the most successful practices of participatory democracy. The relationship with representative democracy is mostly of complementarity but, as legal controversies surrounding PB show, may also involve moments of confrontation.

13.2 PARTICIPATORY BUDGETING IN ACTION[3]

13.2.1. Antecedents

Brazil is a society with a long tradition of authoritarian politics. The predominance of an oligarchic, patrimonialist, and bureaucratic model of domination has resulted in a state formation, a political system, and a culture characterized by the following: political and social marginalization of the popular classes, or their integration by means of populism and clientelism; elitism of the democratic game and liberal ideology resulting in a huge discrepancy between the "legal country" and the "real country;" enormous obstacles against the construction of citizenship, the exercise of rights, and popular autonomous participation.

Brazil is also a society characterized by outrageous social inequalities. In 1964, a military *coup d'etat* against the democratically elected leftist government led to a military dictatorship that lasted until the early 1980s. With the democratic transition, the political debate centered on the democratization of Brazilian political life and the actual construction of citizenship. The emphasis on rights of citizenship, political decentralization, and strengthening of local power led to the 1988 Constitution. This new political context created the conditions for political forces on the left to set up innovative experiments in popular

---

[3] I present here a summary of the results of my empirical research on PB in Porto Alegre conducted between 1995 and 2002. The most intensive fieldwork was carried out between 1995 and 1997, but I followed the evolution of the participatory budget until January 2002. For a more detailed analysis, see Santos (1998; forthcoming).

participation in municipal government. This political opportunity was facilitated by the fact that the political forces in question were closely related to the popular movements that in the 1960s and 1970s had struggled for the establishment and recognition of collective subjects among the subaltern classes.

Among such political forces the *Partido dos Trabalhadores* (Workers' Party, henceforth, PT) is to be singled out. The PT was founded in the early 1980s out of the labor movement, which was particularly strong in the state of São Paulo and one of the most important forces in the struggle against the military dictatorship. The electoral gains of PT have been dazzling. In the early 1990s, the PT was already the major opposition party. In 2003, one of its founders – Lula da Silva – became President of the Republic. In the late 1980s, the PT, in coalition with other leftist political forces, won the local elections in several important cities – such as São Paulo, Porto Alegre, Santos, Belo Horizonte, Campinas, Vitória, and Goiania – and introduced in all of them institutional innovations encouraging popular participation in municipal government.[4] Of all these experiments and innovations, those implemented in Porto Alegre have been by far the most successful, with wide recognition both inside and outside Brazil.[5]

Porto Alegre, with a population of 1.3 million, is the capital of the state of Rio Grande do Sul. When, in January 1989, the PT took over the administration of Porto Alegre, a new modality of municipal government was installed, known as "popular administration." It was based on an institutional innovation aimed at guaranteeing popular participation in preparing and carrying out the municipal budget, hence, in the distribution of resources and the definition of investment priorities. This new measure, which became known as "participatory budgeting" and celebrated its fifteenth anniversary in 2004, has been the key to the success of the PT municipal government.

Porto Alegre is a city of ample democratic traditions and a highly organized civil society. During the dictatorship, the city's grassroots organizations focused their activity on strengthening the labor unions and on such community movements as neighborhood and street associations, soccer clubs, cooperatives, mothers' clubs, cultural groups, etc.

[4] See Villas-Bôas (1999), Carvalho and Felgueiras (2000), Avritzer (2002), Carvalho *et al.* (2002).
[5] For a comparison with the application of PB in Barcelona, see Moura (1997). Echevarría (1999) compares PB in Porto Alegre and Córdoba (Argentina). For instances of the application of PB principles in the Americas and Europe, see Becker (2000).

These movements and organizations were either of a general nature or concerned with specific demands, such as the struggle for bus lines, the struggle for sewers or street paving, the struggle for housing or health centers, and so on. A powerful, diversified popular movement thus emerged, one that in the early 1980s became deeply involved in local government.

In 1988, the startling political ascent of the PT began. Without precedent in the city, in 1992 and again in 1996 the party in government managed to elect its successor: Tarso Genro, vice-mayor in the first PT mandate, became mayor in the second, and Raul Pont, vice-mayor in the second mandate, became mayor in the third. In 2000, Tarso Genro was reelected mayor. The mayoralty was taken over by his vice-mayor in 2002 when Tarso Genro became the PT candidate in state elections. He lost the elections and, in early 2003, became a minister in the Lula Government.

13.2.2. The institutions and the process of PB

Municipal power in Brazil lies in two separately elected bodies: the mayor (*Prefeito*), the executive body, and the Chamber of Deputies (*Câmara de Vereadores*, or CV), the legislative body. According to the 1988 Constitution, the competence to approve the budget is vested in the CV. Since 1989, the Workers' Party and the Popular Front have controlled the *Prefeitura* but have not had the majority in the CV.

One hardly needs to stress the importance of PB for the political and administrative relations between the state and the citizens. In Brazil, the public budget includes three levels: federal, state, and municipal. Municipalities have relative autonomy in determining revenue and expenditure. Revenue is either local (taxes and tariffs of various kinds) or the result of federal or state transferences. Expenditure is classified into three large groups: (1) personnel; (2) public services; and (3) investment in works and equipment. The relative autonomy of municipalities relates mainly to the third type of expenditure. Since the budget does not have to identify the works and services to be carried out – the mere establishment of an expenditure ceiling is sufficient – the executive has ample leeway for budgetary implementation. However, the budget must be approved by the legislative body.

The PB promoted by the *Prefeitura* is a form of public government that tries to break away from the authoritarian and clientelist tradition of public policies, resorting to the direct participation of the population in the different phases of budget preparation and implementation, with special concern for the definition of priorities for the distribution of investment resources. PB and its institutional framework have no formal legal recognition.[6] In political and legal terms, it is a hybrid entity politically sanctioned by the executive branch of the local government but illegal and politically illegitimate from the point of view of the legislative branch. The legal recognition of PB could only be provided by the CV, albeit within the limits of federal and state legislation. As we will see below, the issue of the legalization of PB is a major topic in an ongoing conflict between the executive and the legislative in Porto Alegre politics.

As things stand now, since the definition and approval of the budget is a legal prerogative of the CV, the *Prefeitura*, in strict legal terms, limits itself to submitting to the CV a budget proposal that the latter is free to approve, to change or to reject. In political terms, however, because the executive's proposal is sanctioned by the institutions of PB and thus by the citizens and community organizations and associations that participate in them, the executive's proposal becomes a *fait accompli* for the legislative body in view of the political risks for the deputies in voting against the "will of the citizens and the communities." The majority of the CV thus claims that, by institutionalizing the participatory budget without involving the legislative body, the executive has in real terms emptied out the latter's jurisdiction over budgetary matters. Hence the political conflict that will be dealt with below.

13.2.2.1 The institutions

PB is a structure and a process of community participation based on three major principles and on a set of institutions that function as mechanisms or channels of sustained popular participation in the decision-making process of the municipal government. The three principles are: (1) all citizens are entitled to participate, community organizations having no special status or prerogative in this regard; (2) participation is governed by a combination of direct and representative democracy rules, and takes place through regularly functioning institutions whose internal rules are decided upon by the participants; and (3) investment resources are allocated according to an objective method based on a combination of "general criteria" (substantive criteria

---

[6] The Organic Law of Porto Alegre states that the budget must be discussed with the population. Recently, the Mayoralty successfully fought a case against a plaintiff that had asked the courts to declare the PB unconstitutional (Sérgio Baierle, personnal communication).

established by the participatory institutions to define priorities) and "technical criteria" (criteria of technical or economic viability as determined by the executive in accordance with federal, state, or city legal norms).

The basic institutional setup of PB consists of three kinds of organs. First, the administrative units of the municipal executive are responsible for managing the budgetary debate with the citizens, mainly the *Gabinete de Planejamento* (the Planning Office, or GAPLAN) and the *Coordenação de Relações com as Comunidades* (the Coordination of Relations with the Communities, or CRC). Secondly, the community organizations – which are autonomous vis-à-vis the municipal government and constituted mainly by regionally based organizations – mediate between citizen participation and the choice of priorities for city regions. Since they are autonomous structures and hence depend on the organizing potential of each region, they do not exist in every region concerning PB. They bear different kinds of organization and participation according to the local traditions of the regions: popular councils, township unions, and regional articulations. Thirdly, mediating institutions of community participation link the first two kinds of institutions. They are the Council of the Government Plan and Budget (also known as the Participatory Budget Council, or COP), Regional Plenary Assemblies, the Regional Budget Forum, Thematic Plenary Assemblies, and the Thematic Budget Forum.

13.2.2.2 *The participatory process*

The main goal of PB is to encourage a dynamic and to establish a sustained mechanism for joint management of public resources through shared decisions on the allocation of budgetary funds and for government accountability concerning the effective implementation of such decisions. In a brief summary, PB centers around the regional and thematic plenary assemblies, the Forum of Delegates,[7] and the COP.[8]

The city is divided into sixteen regions and six thematic areas. The latter were established in 1994. Today they are: (1) transportation and circulation; (2) education and leisure; (3) culture; (4) health and social

---

[7] The Forum is composed of delegates elected according to a criterion based on the number of participants in each of the Regional and Thematic Assemblies.

[8] The COP is composed of councilors elected in Regional and Thematic Assemblies. It also includes one representative of UAMPA and another of SIMPA (the Union of Municipal Workers), as well as two representatives of the Mayoralty who have no right to vote.

welfare; (5) economic development and taxation; and (6) city organization, urban, and environmental development.

Until 2002, there were two rounds (*rodadas*) of plenary assemblies in each of the regions and on each of the thematic areas.[9] Today there is only one round. The assemblies have a triple goal: to define and rank regional or thematic demands and priorities; to elect the delegates to the Fora of Delegates and the councilors of the COP; and to evaluate the executive's performance. The delegates function as intermediaries between the COP and the citizens, individually or as participants in community or thematic organizations. They also supervise the implementation of the budget. The councilors define the general criteria that guide the ranking of demands and the allocation of funds, and vote on the proposal of the Investment Plan presented by the executive.

The evolution of the criterion to determine the number of delegates to the regional and thematic fora bears witness to the increasing involvement of the citizens in PB. Initially, the criterion was one delegate for every five people attending the assembly. In the early 1990s, this changed to one delegate for every ten people and later to one delegate for every twenty people. After several revisions, in 1999, a fixed number was adopted (one delegate per each group of ten participants), which was implemented in 2000–2001. This option reflects the *Prefeitura*'s concern with getting more people involved in PB. The delegates elected in the plenary assemblies are usually indicated by the leaders of the associations present at the meetings. Thus, a citizen not integrated in a collective structure does not have much chance of being elected delegate.

Before the *rodada* or plenary assembly, intermediate preparatory meetings take place. They are organized by the community or thematic organizations and associations. At such meetings the demands approved by each association or organization (e.g. neighborhood associations, mothers' clubs, sports or cultural centers, housing cooperatives, unions, non-governmental organizations, etc.) are ranked by the participants according to priorities and general criteria. In the intermediate meetings there is much discussion and voting, but the real negotiations leading to proposals to be voted on tend to take place behind the scenes at informal meetings of the community leaders. The

---

[9] As I shall stress below, over the years there have been many changes in the way the PB functions, a fact that highlights the dynamism of the democratic learning process embodied by the PB.

levels of conflict depend on the level of community organization and on the level of political polarization among the leaderships.

At these intermediate meetings each region or theme rank-orders sectoral priorities. Until 1997, the regions rank-ordered four priorities among the following eight sectors or themes: sewerage, housing, street paving, education, social assistance, health, transportation and circulation, and city organization. In 1997, the COP introduced some changes in this regard. From 1998 onwards, the regions rank-ordered four priorities among twelve themes or, starting in 2001, thirteen themes: sewerage, housing, street paving, public transportation and circulation, health, social work, education, leisure, sports, public lighting, economic development, culture, and environment. These changes reflect the discussions in the COP in recent years, in which the majority of councilors had claimed the expansion of themes covered by PB. Each sector or theme is divided into sub-themes. For instance, housing includes land legalization (regularization of landed property), land and house registration, urbanization, and social housing projects.

The elected priorities are given grades according to their ranking: the first priority is grade 4; the fourth priority is grade 1. Likewise, the specific works proposed by the citizens in every theme or sector are rank-ordered as well (e.g. street paving: the first priority is street A; the second priority is street B, etc.). Sectoral priorities and ranks of works in every sector are forwarded to the executive. On the basis of these priorities and rankings, adding up the grades of the different priorities in all the regions, the executive establishes the first three priorities for the budget in preparation. Over the years, housing, sewerage, street paving, and land regularization have been the most common themes of the first three priorities, the order of priority changing from year to year. For instance, for the 2001 budget, the three priorities were: street paving (34 points), housing (32 points), and sewerage (27 points). In more recent years, education and health care have emerged as priorities.

In the plenary (regional and thematic) assemblies, two councilors and two substitutes in every region and theme are elected for the COP. The councilors are elected for a one-year mandate and can only be reelected once. Their mandate can be revoked by the Regional or Thematic Forum of Delegates in a meeting called especially for that purpose with at least two weeks' notice. Once the quorum is established (50 percent + 1 of the delegates), the mandate can be revoked by a two-thirds majority vote.

319

The institutional organs of community participation are then constituted: the Fora of Delegates (sixteen regional and six thematic delegates) and the COP. The Fora of Delegates are collegiate organs with consulting, controlling, and mobilizing functions. The Fora meet once a month and the two major tasks of the delegates are to supervise the works and to act as intermediaries between the COP and the regions or thematic areas.

The COP is the main participatory institution. It plans, proposes, supervises, and deliberates on the budget's revenue and expenditure (Budgetary Proposal). Here the elected citizens become acquainted with the municipal finances, discuss and establish the general criteria for resource allocation, and defend the priorities of regions and themes. Once inaugurated in July/August, the COP meets once a week on a set day, usually from 6.00pm to 8.00pm.

During August, the detailed preparation of the budget begins. While the executive conciliates the citizens' demands with the so-called "institutional demands" (the proposals of the municipal secretariats) and prepares the budgetary proposal on revenue and expenditure, the COP engages in the internal process of training the newly elected councilors to familiarize them with the internal rules and the criteria for resource distribution.

The tasks of the COP are carried out in two phases. In August and September, the COP discusses the budget matrix. On the basis of revenue and expenditure forecasts made by the executive during the *rodada*, the major sets of investment are allocated according to the thematic priorities established in the regional discussions. In this phase, on the basis of the government's proposal, the councilors take a vote, for example, on how many roads will be paved, or how much money will be allocated to health, housing, and so on. Major or structural public works, whether proposed by the thematic assemblies or by the government itself, are also discussed. Once approved by the COP, this matrix is turned into a draft of the Budget Law to be handed out to the CV by September 30. From September to December the COP prepares the Investment Plan, which includes a detailed list of the works and activities prioritized by the COP, and thus the specific allocation of resources programmed for every region and thematic area. The debate concerning investments is limited by the estimated general revenue and expenditure with personnel and other expenses estimated by the executive, including fixed expenditures enforced by federal legislation, such as the percentages constitutionally ascribed to education and health.

At the same time, the COP follows the debates on the budget proposal in the CV and puts pressure on the legislators by meeting with individual members of the CV, mobilizing the communities and thematic areas to attend the debates or to organize rallies outside the building.

13.2.2.3 The distribution of investment resources: methodology and criteria of decision-making

The distribution of investment resources follows a method of participatory planning that begins when priorities are indicated at the regional and thematic plenaries and at the intermediate meetings and reaches its climax when the COP approves the Investment Plan with detailed works and activities discriminated by investment sector, region, and the whole city.

As we saw above, the regions and thematic areas begin by defining the sectoral priorities that are to guide the drafting of the budget proposal concerning the global distribution of investment resources. The regions also determine and rank-order the specific demands within each priority. Once the priorities of the different regions are established, the distribution of investments is carried out according to the general criteria defined by the COP and the technical criteria defined by the executive. Concerning the regional assemblies, the general criteria are: lack of urban infrastructures and/or services; total population of the region; and the priority given by the region to specific sector or theme. To each criterion is ascribed a weight in a scale that has varied through the years (from 1 to 4 or from 1 to 5) in proportion to the importance attributed to it by the COP. Each region is given a grade concerning each of the criteria and the type of investment as related to the second and third criteria. The grades are determined in the following way: (1) according to the region's total population as provided by the executive's official statistical data; the larger the region's total population, the higher the grade; (2) according to the region's need vis-à-vis the investment item in question; the higher the need, the higher the grade; and (3) according to the priority ascribed to the items of investment chosen by the region; the higher the priority of the sectoral demand presented by the regions, the higher their grade in the investment sector in question.

An example helps to illustrate how the general criteria are translated into a quantified allocation of resources. In 1997, the relative priority given by the sixteen regions to street paving determined the inclusion in the Investment Plan of a global expenditure item for street paving corresponding to 20 km of streets to be paved. The distribution of this amount by the different regions was the result of the application of the criteria, their weight, and the grade of the region in each criterion. The grade received by each region in each criterion is multiplied by the general criterion's weight. The sum of the partial points (grades x weight) amounts to the total grade of the region in that specific sectoral demand. This total grade determines the percentage of the investment resources that will be allocated to the region in that sector. Let us analyze the case of two contrasting regions. Extremo Sul, a region with 80.21 percent need for street paving, and Centro with 0.14 percent. Concerning the need criterion, which at the time carried a general weight of 3, Extremo Sul had the highest grade (4)[10] and accordingly got 12 points (3 x 4), while Centro, with the lowest grade (1), got 3 points (3 x 1). Concerning the criterion of total population, which at the time carried the general weight of 2, Extremo Sul, with a population of 20,647, had the lowest grade (1) and hence got 2 points (2 x 1), while Centro, with a much larger population (293,193), had the highest grade (4) and hence got 8 points (2 x 4). Finally, concerning the criterion of the priority given by the region, which at the time carried a general weight of 3, Extremo Sul gave the highest priority to paving and, accordingly, had the highest grade (4) and thus got 12 points (3 x 4), while Centro gave a very low priority to paving and thus had the lowest grade (0) and consequently got no points (3 x 0). As a result, the sum total of points for Extremo Sul in the item of street paving was 26 points (12 + 2 + 12) while Centro's total was 11 points (3 + 8 + 0). Since the global number of points for all regions was 262 points, Extremo Sul received 9.9 percent of the investment, that is, 1,985 meters of street paving, while Centro received only 4.2 percent of the investment, or 840 meters of paving.

When the first PT executive took office in 1989, the administration's three major objectives were: reversal of priorities, administrative transparency, and popular participation in the city's governance (Genro and Ubiratan 1997). The first objective (reversal of priorities) was reached in the three criteria and their respective weights proposed by the executive and accepted by the regions. For several years, the need criterion (services or infrastructure need) was ascribed the highest weight, whereas the population criterion was ascribed a lesser weight.

[10] In the 1998 budget, the grades in this criterion ranged from 1 to 5.

This discrepancy was justified by the need to transfer resources from the region with the most population, the Center, which was also the richest one, to the poorest and less well equipped regions.

13.3 PARTICIPATORY BUDGETING: TOWARD A REDISTRIBUTIVE DEMOCRACY

In this section I analyze some of the most salient political features of PB. I also identify the major challenges facing PB as well as the problems and even dilemmas lying ahead.

13.3.1. Participation, negotiation, and redistribution

PB is a process of decision-making based upon general rules and criteria of distributive justice discussed and approved by regular, institutional organs of participation in which the popular classes have majority representation. The communities in which they live and organize are recognized as having urban collective rights that legitimate both their claims and demands and their participation in the decisions taken to meet them.

The selection of priorities and works included in the Investment Plan is reached by means of objective criteria, defined through a complex process of negotiation that takes place at the intermediate meetings, regional assemblies, thematic plenaries, and the COP. It is today generally recognized that PB changed the political culture of community organizations, from a culture of protest and confrontation to a culture of conflict and negotiation. Indeed, conflict and negotiation do not occur among the regions alone but within each region as well, and it is equally complex and tense at the intraregional as it is at the interregional level.

The objectivity and transparency of the criteria are expressed in the points earned by each region and the percentage of investment resources into which they are converted. The points system was the methodology conceived to rank-order priorities and to turn those priorities into resource and investment quantities determined by general criteria. The points system aims at converting the political decisions reached through complex negotiations into the detailed distribution of resources included in the Investment Plan and ensuring that such conversion is as faithful and objective as possible.

The latter concern implied successive refinements of the distributive methodology that endowed PB with great operational and functional complexity. The increase and diversity of participation, together with the increasing intensity and differentiation of demands, has also contributed decisively to making calculating methodologies even more complex and sophisticated. The complexity of the points system results from the fact that it seeks to articulate measures of participation, on the one hand, with measures of priority and recognized necessity, on the other. The participation measure guarantees the democratic legitimacy of political decisions, while the priority and necessity measure guarantees the fidelity, objectivity, and transparency of the conversion of political decisions into distributed resources.

Because of its major concern with the democratic nature of the distribution, PB may be considered the embryo of a redistributive democracy. As I have indicated, the democratic nature of the distribution is guaranteed by a calculating methodology that has become increasingly sophisticated. It can be said that, when it does entail an increase of bureaucracy, democracy evolves together with an increase of decisional complexity. The following working hypothesis could indeed be formulated: in internally differentiated societies, the stronger the bond between democracy and distributive justice, the more complex the methodology that guarantees such a bond tends to be. The decrease of complexity that bureaucracy allows for cannot but bring about the loosening of the bond between democracy and distributive justice.

The redistributive efficiency of PB has been fully confirmed. Suffice it to mention that in PB the poorest region of the city, Ilhas (nowadays a micro-region of Humaitá/Navegantes/Ilhas), with a population of about 5,000 (almost all of whom are classified as needy people), has the same decisional weight as the wealthiest region, Centro, with 271,294 inhabitants, of whom less then 3 percent are considered needy (Larangeira 1996:4).

By reversing the priorities that traditionally determined resource distribution by the municipal government, PB brought striking material results. As regards basic sanitation (water and sewerage), in 1989 only 49 percent of the population was covered. By the end of 1996, 98 percent of households had water and 85 percent were served by the sewerage system. According to *O Estado de São Paulo*, an influential newspaper, while all the previous municipal governments of Porto Alegre had built some 1,100 kms of sewerage systems, the two PT administrations alone built 900 kms between 1989 and 1996. Concerning street paving, 215 kms were built at the rate of 30 kms per year. Even so, only one-half of the street paving deficit (approximately 500 kms) was eliminated.

The granting of legal titles to land holders, which, as we have seen, is a high priority in many regions where the popular classes live, is an issue on which the power relations of the city have eloquent expression, since 25 percent of the available urban land is owned by fourteen people or entities. Nonetheless, in the past seven years it was possible to urbanize the slums and build many houses for the marginal populations. Concerning education, the number of students enrolled in the elementary and mid-level public schools has steadily risen since 1989, and in 2004 a full 37.5 percent of the funds distributed through PB was allocated to education.

13.3.2. Autonomy and co-government

For its founders and activists, PB is the manifestation of an emergent, non-state public sphere where citizens and community organizations, on the one hand, and the municipal government, on the other, converge with relative autonomy from each other through a political contract. The experience of PB configures, therefore, a model of co-government, i.e. a model for sharing political power by means of a network of democratic institutions geared to reaching decisions by deliberation, consensus, and compromise.

The problems facing a system of power sharing are well expressed in the relationship between the COP and the executive. Such a relationship has been polemical all along. In the beginning, while the community leaders wanted the COP to have unconditional deliberative power, the executive searched for a formula capable of reconciling the decisions of the COP and the political representativity of the mayor inscribed in the Brazilian Constitution. The formula is as follows: the COP's decisions are made by simple majority. The decisions are forwarded to the executive. In the case of veto by the mayor, they return to the COP for a new evaluation. Rejecting the mayor's veto requires a qualified majority of two-thirds of the vote. If rejection occurs, the matter goes back to the mayor for evaluation and final decision. Since, according to the Constitution, the power to approve the budget is vested in the legislative body, this formula accommodates the constitutional requisite: formally, the budget proposal submitted to the CV is the mayor's proposal.

The mayor's veto must be substantiated and can only be exercised for technical reasons and financial evaluation. To date, however, the veto has not been exercised, since, whenever the executive had reservations concerning a work, its position was explained to the community by its technical staff and the community ended up agreeing.

The consensus-building process is complex because the problems under discussion as well as the decisions taken often have, besides the political dimension, a strong technical dimension. Moreover, "technical criteria" constitute one of the limits of participation and are themselves sometimes the object of debate and conflict. The internal rules of PB include the technical criteria established by the various departments of the executive. Some of the technical criteria currently in force are: all community claims and demands found technically nonviable by the city's administration are cancelled; preference is given to works-in-progress; and the pluvial network will not be installed in streets without pavements because the network, being open to allow for the collection of rain water, might be blocked by sand and rubbish.

In such a system of co-government, the executive does have a very active role, if only because it controls technical knowledge and also because it either generates the relevant information or has privileged access to it. Its presence in PB is quite strong by reason of its coordinating functions both in the COP through its two representatives, even though they do not have the right to vote, and in the regional assemblies through the CRC delegate in the region. Furthermore, the executive itself forwards autonomous investment proposals to the COP, the so-called "institutional demands," which have their origin in executive departments and which usually concern the maintenance or improvement of urban infrastructures.

In addition to technical limits, there are financial limits, which are not always duly considered by the assemblies. Suffice it to mention that, for financial reasons, only 30 percent of the demands originally formulated by the community can be taken care of. Sometimes, the way the demands and priorities are formulated does not take into account certain technical conditions that increase the cost beyond what the communities themselves consider reasonable. For example, the fact that street paving must include street lighting increases its cost by a large amount. Nowadays, the percentage of investments included in the budget varies between 15 and 20 percent, which is high by Brazilian standards.

The credibility of the political contract that constitutes PB resides in the effectiveness of the decisions and in the accountability both of the executive and of the representatives of the civil society in the COP (see Abers 1998, 2000). The fact that only 30 percent of the demands may be considered is less important than the effective satisfaction of the demands selected for inclusion in the Investment Plan. Several mechanisms guarantee effectiveness and accountability. First, the political will of the executive must be mentioned. The basic principle of the municipal government is to fulfill as rigorously as possible the Investment Plan and to justify what is left unfulfilled. Secondly, there are committees – created within the Fora of Delegates – whose function is to supervise the works. In the case of delays or alterations, the delegates have direct access to the Mayor's Office to ask for explanations. Thirdly, the very structures of PB strongly encourage accountability. The two institutions of regular functioning – the COP and the Forum of Delegates – are bound to the grassroots institutions: the Regional Assemblies and the Thematic Plenaries. The latter two organs, because they are open to the individual and collective participation of all citizens, exercise a double popular control, upon the performance of the executive and upon community representation itself. In practice, the exercise of control is sometimes problematic, as witness the debates about the quality of representation and about transparency and accountability.

As I have indicated, the close linkage of participation to resource distribution and to the effectiveness of decisions is one of the core features of PB. This alone explains why, for five months, PB councilors meet at least once a week, often twice or thrice a week, with no remuneration, even travel expenses. This linking of participation to distribution is, no doubt, one of the virtues of PB, but perhaps also a limitation. According to Tarso Genro, it is common for a region or micro-region to stop participating in the meetings and assemblies after their demands have been met. They usually begin participating again, once they realize that in the year in which they did not participate there was no investment made in their region or micro-region.

The close binding articulation of participation, distribution, and the effectiveness of decisions may eventually provoke some additional tension in the already tense field of co-government that constitutes the political contract between the executive and the organized communities, for two main reasons: the limits to investment; and the major works that transcend the interests both of specific regions and of specific thematic areas.

Is the political contract of co-government that sustains PB a contract among equal partners? This question raises the issue of the autonomy of the institutions and processes of the participatory budget. I argued that this political contract is based on the premise that the autonomy of both the elected mayor and the popular movement becomes a mutually relative autonomy. The question is: whose autonomy is more relativized by entering the contract? PB is an initiative of the PT popular administration of Porto Alegre, and its basic institutional outline has been designed over the years by the executive. It is part of a political program of redistribution of public resources and democratization of the state. This political program is also the meeting ground for a demand with a similar political orientation advanced by the popular movement and sustained over the years by much struggle. The issue is, then, how this convergence of political will has been carried out, on whose terms and timetables, and with what outcomes.

Without any doubt popular participation in PB is very active. Is it also autonomous? What does it mean to be autonomous? Autonomy cannot be conceived as popular spontaneity, as a native capacity to organize poor people in degraded communities without the support or influence of external, organized political forces. Autonomy rather must be conceived as the popular capacity to channel external support and put it at the service of objectives, demands, and agendas generated in the communities. In the Brazilian context, autonomy is measured by the capacity to develop organizational strength and effectiveness by maneuvering among competing external political influences, using such competition to impose demands that, however important for the community, do not represent a priority for any of the political forces in competition.

Since PB is not a popular movement but an institutional constellation designed to operate as a sustained, regularly functioning meeting place for the popular movement and the municipal government, the question of the autonomy of PB must be formulated as the real capacity of the popular representatives in such institutions to shape agendas, timetables, debates, and decisions. In this sense, autonomy, rather than a stable characteristic of a given political process, is the ever-provisional outcome of an ongoing struggle. Thus conceived, PB's autonomy must be discussed at the level of the operational functioning of PB institutions, including coordination, agendas, and timetables.

The coordination of PB institutions is in the hands of the executive's representatives, and the agenda and the timetable are proposed by them. But the executive's role in this regard has been increasingly questioned and challenged by the councilors and delegates. The observation of the COP meetings in particular shows that the councilors have become more assertive and aggressive, and that the procedural rules of the meetings have often been disrupted by heated debates. One of the most widely violated rules is the prohibition of direct dialogue among the councilors. This rule states that interventions must have been previously notified and must take place in the order in which they have been registered.

Concerning the agenda, the conflict between some councilors and the executive is often quite open. Councilors have consistently fought for an expansion of municipal activities to be submitted to the PB institutions, but in general such proposals have met resistance from government representatives. The basic argument of the government is that there are matters that engage the city as a whole and which for that reason cannot be submitted to a debate that tends to promote particularistic solutions, be they relative to the regions or to themes. The councilors counterargue that they represent the whole city and that the real issue is a different one: the opposition of the executive to the further decentralization of municipal services (culture, health, sports, recreation, etc.). The councilors have been more and more openly critical of the executive coordination and agenda setting. In an interview, one councilor, who is very active in the popular movement, told me: "Sometimes I feel that I am being manipulated, that I am here to legitimate the popular administration and nothing else. PB is the best thing that could happen in this city but it has to operate our way."[11]

Concerning timetables, deadlines, and times for debate, the discussions in the COP have also become more conflictual. On one side, the councilors claim that they need more time to process information, to ask for clarification and to consult with their constituencies. On the other side, the executive representatives claim that the deadlines are not an invention or whim of the executive but rather are established in laws promulgated by the CV. They also claim that to debate is fine but that it is very frustrating to verify that after heated, long discussions there is no quorum to vote because in the meantime some less interested or more pressed councilors have left the meeting.

13.3.3. From technobureaucracy to technodemocracy
Conflict and mediation between technical and political issues, between knowledge and power, is one of the main features of PB. If it is true that technical criteria limit the field of participation and deliberation, it is likewise true that the PB process has radically changed the professional culture of the technical staff of the executive. The technical staff has

[11] Interview, Porto Alegre, April 10, 1997.

329

increasingly been submitted to a profound learning process concerning communication and argumentation with lay populations. Their technical recommendations must be conveyed in accessible language to people who do not master technical knowledge; their reasonability must be demonstrated in a persuasive way, rather than imposed in an authoritarian fashion; no alternative hypothesis or solution may be excluded without showing its unviability. Where earlier a technobureaucratic culture prevailed, gradually a technodemocratic culture has emerged.

This transformation has not been easy. According to Tarso Genro, during the period between 1992 and 1996, there was more progress in changing the language and discourse of the engineers when addressing the people in the communities than in changing their dismissive attitudes vis-à-vis what people had to say. In other words, the capacity to make him or herself understood has improved more than the capacity to listen. When Raul Pont initiated his mandate (1996–2000), he became particularly sensitive to the fact that the structure and process of PB were very little known among the municipal workers and staff. In view of this, in 1997 the mayor launched a program targeted at the municipal staff, which he called "Program for Internalization of Participatory Budgeting." This program was announced as part of a much broader program of an overall internal democratization of the state. In an interview, the official in charge of coordinating this program told me that, "in order to be fully consolidated the PB must be part of the everyday work of a municipal worker."[12] A working group was set up to organize workshops with the workers and staff about the cycle, rules, criteria, and methodology of the PB. The targets of the workshops were to be addressed sequentially: staff that deal directly with PB; staff that mediate between the executive and the community; and finally the supervisors and directors.

In light of the complex details of the operation of PB, it is not surprising to find situations that, no matter how apparently trivial, may be a source of tension between PB participants and municipal staff, even when the latter are supportive of PB. An example of this is the accreditation procedure. This is the process by which the people, the delegates, and the councilors identify themselves as they enter the room where the meeting is to be held. They must show their ID card and fill out a form. The accreditation is entrusted to a group of

[12] Interview, Porto Alegre, April 6, 1997.

municipal personnel designated by the mayor. Even if we only take into account the regional and thematic plenaries, the staff must verify the credentials of hundreds of people in twenty-two meetings per month (sixteen regional and six thematic). Because it resulted from a personal appointment by the mayor, the verification of credentials was understood for a while as a political job to be performed by volunteers. As time went on, however, some of the people refused to perform this job, invoking the many evenings they could not spend with their families. As a result, the executive considered paying overtime pay to the staff who checked the credentials.[13] As a consequence, the COP now has an executive secretary paid for by the municipal administration through the CRC.

The road from technobureaucracy to technodemocracy is a bumpy one. In the course of time, as the delegates and councilors have become more assertive, disputing more openly the technical criteria and solutions presented by the professional staff, the latter have become more defensive, yet the conflict between competing knowledges has all but faded away. In my field observations, I witnessed many lively debates between residents and engineers about street paving, the location of sewer pipes, and so on, and was impressed by the argumentative capacity of the community leaders.

13.4 COMPETING LEGALITIES AND LEGITIMACIES: PB AND THE CÂMARA DE VEREADORES

As a political and legal hybrid, PB has an element of "dual power," indeed of double dual power. On one side, there is a complementary (if often conflictual) dual power between the *Prefeitura* and the organized citizenship, a political hybrid which I have called co-government. On the other side, there is a confrontational dual power between this form of co-government and the municipal legislative body. The latter consists in the fact that the co-government of the democratically elected *Prefeitura* and the organized citizenship leaves out another democratically elected institution, the municipal legislative body (the CV), indeed the institution entrusted by the Constitution with the discussion and approval of the budget.

---

[13] The system that was adopted does not in fact pay overtime. Rather, the work of the PB officers gains them extra points for future promotion.

In addition to a form of dual power, this situation also comprises a form of confrontational legal plurality at the city level: on one side, the official legality, on the other, the unofficial legality, which, to make things even more complex, has been developed with the active participation of one of the official institutions of local government, the *Prefeitura*. The confrontation is political and is often defined as a confrontation between representative democracy and participatory democracy. To be sure, such confrontation exists, but it is more complex than the contrast expressed by this duality. On the one hand, the *Prefeitura*, though politically on the side of participatory democracy, is an institution elected by the mechanisms of representative democracy. On the other hand, PB, though an expression of participatory democracy, contains in it mechanisms of representative democracy, the elected councilors and delegates. In fact, in complex political processes, participatory democracy always presupposes the creation of instances of delegation and representation. Thus, the basic structures of PB are involved in a double institutional articulation with the institutions of representative democracy at the urban level (the mayor and his or her executive) and with the representative institutions derived from participatory democracy at the community level. This articulation between participation/representation at the community level calls for careful reflection that cannot be undertaken here.

The political contract that exists between the executive and the communities has thus far not been extended to the legislature. On the contrary, the relation between PB and the legislature has been one of constant conflict (sometimes involving physical confrontation). If, according to the Constitution, it behooves the legislature to approve the municipal budget, PB has utterly preempted this function. To be sure, as we have seen, according to the PB cycle the proposal of the budget law, after it has been prepared in the COP, is forwarded to the legislature for debate and approval. Theoretically, the legislature could reject the proposal, but the fact that it has already been legitimated by the participation of citizens mobilized by PB compels the legislature always to approve the budget presented. It ends up, therefore, being a formality.

According to some, however, given the budgeting technique traditionally adopted in Brazil, the legislature has never actually deliberated substantially on the budget. The truth is that, given the fact that the indication in the budget of the concrete works to be carried out is not required, the executive has always had ample leeway in budget execution. But the fact of the matter is that such a system also created the opportunity for the legislature to influence the execution by the traditional populist and clientelist methods. The legislators had their electoral folds in the different regions and the votes they gathered from them were directly related to the works they managed to include in the budget. Now, this was precisely the clientelist system that PB intended to put an end to, and herein for the most part resides the hostility with which the legislators not linked to the PT regard PB. While the duality of power between PB and the executive (notwithstanding the problems and tensions identified here) has been dominated by a logic of complementarity and cooperation, the duality of power between PB and the CV has been dominated by a logic of open or latent conflict. It is both a duality of power and a duality of legality and legitimacy. As one legislator told me in an interview: "The PT has coopted and demoralized the popular movement. The participatory budget is a diabolic invention of the PT to stay in power forever. Look, how many people participated in the participatory budget last year? A little more than 10,000. Well, I was elected by a larger number. Why am I less representative than the councilors of the COP?"[14] Another legislator less hostile to PB said in an interview: "I think the participatory budget is an excellent idea but I don't see – except for political reasons of the PT – why the *Câmara de Vereadores* is not involved. We don't want to absorb participatory budgeting. We would like to have a part in it. For instance, a percentage of the investment fund should be left to the *Câmara* to allocate."[15] As yet another legislator put it: "The budget arrives at the *Câmara* in a cast. We're tied up. It is not fair because after all we are the legislators."[16]

One of the sources of the tension between representative and participatory democracy has been the debate of the last few years on the official legal codification of PB, which illustrates the interplay between politics and law that is central to counter-hegemonic initiatives. As it stands today, PB is based on a political contract with the executive and is ruled only by its unofficial internal rules and the organic law of the *Prefeitura*. The crucial question is whether the future safeguard of PB should not include its juridical consolidation, that is, its conversion into municipal law through an act of the legislative body. This is conceivable, since, given the popularity of PB, most members of the

---

[14] Interview, Porto Alegre, April 10, 1997.   [15] Interview, Porto Alegre, April 10, 1997.
[16] Interview, Porto Alegre, April 12, 1997.

CV would be, in principle, in favor of it – provided, of course, that the CV retained some measure of control over PB.

There are different positions on this, even inside the PT and the executive. While some believe that legal, formal recognition of PB will help to defend its existence if in the future an executive hostile to citizen participation is elected, others argue that such codification would be a submission of participatory democracy to representative democracy, do away with the political autonomy of PB, and subject it in the future to legislative manipulation according to the majorities obtainable in the CV. In an interview, one PT legislator said: "I participate in the plenaries of the participatory budget and even have a vote as a citizen who happens to be also a legislator. The legislators should integrate themselves in the participatory budget and not seek separate and privileged participation and decision-making."[17] Other PT legislators and leaders think that the tension between PB and the CV is not a "healthy one" and may be risky in the future. According to them, it is not in the interest of the PT to demoralize the legislative body and contribute to removing its prerogatives. Some of them have even presented proposals concerning the legalization of PB. One of them said in an interview: "I'm in favor of a type of legalization that does not plaster the participatory budget, and that contributes to consolidating it as an official component of our political system, a mark of our specificity."[18]

The issue of legal codification is one among many dimensions of the conflict between the executive and the CV where the PT does not hold the majority. The COP councilors have a clear understanding of this, and the divisions inside the COP on this issue reflect broader cleavages in city politics and the community movement. In spite of the political restrictions on the budgetary prerogatives of the CV, the latter makes many amendments every year. These amendments are discussed in the COP. In the meeting of August 7, 1997, the GAPLAN representative read the most important amendments and commented on their negative impact, emphasizing that through them the legislators were trying to limit the autonomy of PB. He exhorted the councilors and delegates to mobilize quickly and strongly in order to try to defeat these amendments in the CV. He concluded: "They want to embarrass the PB. This is war and when you are at war you don't stop the war to prepare and debate." Some councilors were displeased by this

---

[17] Interview, Porto Alegre, April 11, 1997.   [18] Interview, Porto Alegre, April 10, 1997.

comment and asked for more time to analyze the amendments, because after all it is in the interest of PB to cut some of the executive expenditures. One of them said: "I don't agree with [the GAPLAN representative]. This is not a war. We are democratically debating and discussing with the *Câmara de Vereadores* ... I don't disagree with the proposal of the coordinators, but the proposal is also a way of appropriating the issue. If we are going to discuss what the autonomy of the COP is, then there is much more to be discussed." Implied in this comment is, of course, the fact that the issue of the autonomy of the COP must be raised not only vis-à-vis the CV but also vis-à-vis the executive.

The issue of official codification of PB has been discussed on and off in the COP. Some councilors have favored some kind of legal institutionalization. Others have opposed it in the name of PB's autonomy, an autonomy that should be expressed in a form of legal plurality. According to them, it amounts to a kind of legal fetishism, and therefore to political alienation, not to accept as fully legal the bottom-up informal and unofficial legality that has emerged from the struggle for participatory democracy. In this debate, the international recognition and praise of PB is often mentioned. One of the councilors commented in the COP meeting of March 3, 1997: "The way the PB has been operating in the last eight years without any official regulation by the government is what makes it possible for us to go ahead and be internationally recognized."

The issue of codification will probably remain as an unresolved tension in the Porto Alegre's PB for some time. PB has, indeed, destabilized the old ways of doing politics in the city, and the CV is trying to reconstitute its political space in the new political conditions created by PB. This reconstitution may, nonetheless, reveal some unexpected continuities with the "old ways."

13.5 CONCLUSION

Since PB is a very dynamic social and political process, it is difficult to draw many conclusions or projections from it. Up until now, PB has been a remarkable means of promoting citizen participation in decisions concerning distributive justice, the effectiveness of decisions, and the accountability of the executive and of the delegates elected by the communities to the COP and the Forum of Delegates. The success of PB has been widely recognized, not only in the city of Porto Alegre and in Brazil, but also internationally. Many cities in Brazil, throughout Latin America, and also in Europe have been adopting the PB system under various forms.

To my mind, the future of PB depends, to a large extent, on how its principles and practices of democratic participation are strengthened and extended to areas or issues that have not yet been included in PB. It also depends on how its autonomy is improved and consolidated so that the break with the old clientelist politics becomes irreversible.

The assessment of PB shows that these are very demanding conditions and may even involve some dilemmas. For instance, the consolidation of PB makes political sense only if it breaks with the old patrimonialist-clientelist system. But is such consolidation possible without some form of continuity with the old system? As an emergent political reality, PB tends to have a destabilizing effect, not only in political terms, but also in ideological and cultural terms. However, a destabilizing idea that succeeds in becoming a sustainable practice is always in danger of losing its destabilizing potential as its success increases. The routine of mobilization leads to routine mobilization. Participation remains high but common citizens are gradually replaced by specialized participatory citizens. The dilemma here rests in the fact that, although the radicalization of the experiment is the only weapon against routinization, there is an undeterminable threshold beyond which radicalization will irreversibly compromise the success of the experiment. There is no way out of this dilemma. Yet the tension it creates may itself be sustainable (thus contributing to the continuing, if always problematic, success of the experiment) provided that the participants engage in a reflexive self-subversion: by this I mean the constant radicalization of political consciousness centered on the limits of the radicalization of political practice.

PB is today part of counter-hegemonic globalization, not just because it is being replicated in other cities around the world, but above all because its emancipatory aspiration for social justice carried out through a political strategy based on innovative conceptions of democracy and legality and on new articulations between political parties and social movements has become one of the most credible guiding ideas mobilizing countless social movements and progressive NGOs around the world in their struggles against exclusion, dispossession, and discrimination produced or intensified by neoliberal globalization. PB is today a crucial piece of the new redistributive democracy at the local level. Its political logic is the creation of public, nonstate spheres in which the state is the key agency of articulation and coordination. The creation of these public spheres is, in the present conditions, the only democratic alternative to the proliferation of fascist private spheres sanctioned by the state (see Santos 2002). PB epitomizes the emergence of new political constellations of democratic struggles allowing for more and ampler democratic deliberations on greater and more differentiated aspects of sociability. It points to forms of high-intensity democracy emerging in different ways in different parts of the world as a progressive and creative response to the transformations undergone by the state in the last two or three decades. This subaltern cosmopolitan politics and legality is not just taking the state seriously, it is rather converting it into what I have called the newest social movement (Santos 2002:Chapter 9).

As PB illustrates, the state as the newest social movement carries with it a major transformation of state law as we know it. Cosmopolitan law is here the legal component of struggles for democratic participation and experimentation in state policies and regulations. It involves both state official law and non-state (or quasi-non-state), unofficial (or quasi-unofficial) law played out in forms of confrontational or complementary legal pluralities and interlegalities.

References

Abers, Rebecca. 1998. "From Clientelism to Cooperation: Local Government, Participatory Policy, and Civic Organizing in Porto Alegre, Brazil." *Politics & Society* 26:511–537.

2000. *Inventing Local Democracy: Grassroots Politics in Brazil.* Boulder: Lynne Rienner.

Avritzer, Leonardo. 2002. "Modelos de Deliberação Democrática: Uma análise do orçamento participativo no Brasil." Pp. 561–597 in *Democratizar a Democracia: Os Caminhos da Democracia Participativa*, edited by Boaventura de Sousa Santos. Rio de Janeiro: Record.

Baierle, Sérgio. 1998. "Experiência do Orçamento Participativo: um oásis no deserto neoliberal?" (www.portoweb.com.br).

2001. "OP ao Termidor?" Paper presented at the workshop *O Orçamento Participativo visto pelos seus investigadores*, Porto Alegre, May 31–June 2.

Becker, A. J. (Ed.). 2000. *A Cidade Reinventa a Democracia: As Contribuições do Seminário Internacional sobre Democracia Participativa.* Porto Alegre: Prefeitura de Porto Alegre.

Carvalho, Maria do Carmo, and Débora Felgueiras. 2000. *Orçamento Participativo no ABC: Mauá, RibeirãoPires e Santo André.* São Paulo: Pólis.

Carvalho, Maria do Carmo Albuquerque, Ana Cláudia C. Teixeira, Luciana Antonini, and Inês Magalhães. 2002. *Orçamento Participativo nos Municípios Paulistas: Gestão 1997–2000*. São Paulo: Pólis.

Echevarría, Corina. 1999. *Democratización del Espacio Público Municipal mediante la Implementación de Instituciones de Géstion Participativa: Estudio Comparado de los casos de la Municipalidad de la Ciudad de Córdoba (Argentina) y la Prefectura de Porto Alegre (Brasil)*. MA Thesis, Universidad Nacional de Córdoba.

Genro, Tarso, and Ubiratán Souza. 1997. *O Orçamento Participativo: a experiência de Porto Alegre*. São Paulo: Fundação Perseu Abramo.

Larangeira, Sónia. 1996. "Gestão Pública e Participação: A Experiência do Orçamento Participativo em Porto Alegre (1989–1995)." Paper presented at the 48° *Encontro Anual da Sociedade Brasileira para o progresso da Ciência*, São Paulo, July.

Moura, Maria Suzana. 1997. *Cidades Empreendedoras, Cidades Democráticas e Redes Públicas: Tendências à Renovação na Gestão Local. Salvador*. PhD Dissertation, Universidade Federal da Bahia.

Santos, Boaventura de Sousa. 1998. "Participatory Budgeting in Porto Alegre: Toward a Redistributive Democracy." *Politics & Society* 26:461–510.

2002. *Toward a New Legal Common Sense*. London: Butterworths.

(Ed.)., forthcoming. *Democratizing Democracy: Beyond the Liberal Democratic Canon*. London: Verso.

Villas-Boâs, Renata (Ed.). 1999. *Balanço das Experiências de Orçamento Participativo nos Governos Locais*. São Paulo: Instituto Pólis.

CHAPTER 14

LIFE, LIFE WORLD, AND LIFE CHANCES:
VULNERABILITY AND SURVIVAL
IN INDIAN CONSTITUTIONAL LAW

Shiv Visvanathan and *Chandrika Parmar*

14.1 INTRODUCTION

This chapter is a series of observations on a thought experiment. It is
written by two authors, neither of whom is an authority on law but both
of whom recognize that law is a kind of environment, a second skin in
which many of us swim. As one wag put it, "when you don't like law,
one calls it bureaucracy but when one admires and judges it as creative
or exotic, it becomes jurisprudence."

The constitution of India falls under the second category. Popular
films like *Dev*, *Garv*, and *Khakee*, endow it with an almost canonical
status. However, during the last few years, the National Democratic
Alliance (NDA), the coalition party which was in power until May
2004, was keen to institute a review of the constitution. There was a
sense that the constitution, despite a coral reef of amendments, was
anachronistic. But the debate over the review was seen in parochial
terms and not much came of it.

The authors were requested to write a monograph on the Directive
Principles of State Policy (DPSP). India is one of the three countries,
along with Ireland and Russia, whose constitutions have a chapter on
DPSP. Part IV of the Indian constitution (Articles 36–51) contains the
DPSP. As rights, these are not enforceable, yet they constitute part of the
frame within which rights are articulated. The DPSP add a vision of
economic democracy to the idea of fundamental rights. Included among
them are requirements that the state has to provide free and compulsory
education to children, the prohibition of the consumption of alcoholic

drinks, the prohibition of the slaughter of cows, calves, and other milch and draught cattle, and the protection of the environment (see Basu 2001). As a legal text, the chapter on the DPSP is seen as an anomalous and ambiguous entity. The DPSP are not justiciable and yet are supposed to be crucial for judicial interpretations. They lack the universality and the applicability of the constitution's section on fundamental rights. In fact, many lawyers we interviewed consider the chapter as "not law." As one leading professional bluntly stated, "anything that cannot stand up in a court of law should not be in the constitution." Yet the DPSP as a framework for future laws – a wish list, heuristic, utopia – continues to fascinate.

The constitiutional review committee had requested a straightforward report on the progress of various items listed in the chapter. We decided to pursue a different question. We decided to ask how futuristic were the DPSP, and we unraveled the question by creating an encounter between the constitution and the social philosophy of grassroots movements and NGOs. The question we asked was: if the Review Committee, with its professional galaxy of lawyers, had a seminar with the grassroots groups fighting over land, roads, caste, soil, and health, how would the DPSP be re-read?

This chapter is divided into sections. The second section raises the problematic of the DPSP and examines how one should read them. The third section examines the whole issue of state responsibility for the environment, focusing on the relation between the idea of the commons and the legal notion of eminent domains. The fourth section examines the Land Acquisition Act and its implications for the large-scale displacement of people in India. The fifth section explores the possible approach to technology and obsolescence by considering the fishing struggle in Kerala as an example. The sixth section examines the relation between community and livelihood, and studies the role of the local community or *Panchayat* system. The seventh section explores the issues of diversity and heritage. The eighth and final section then locates the DPSP within the debate on democracy, observing that a new vision of the DPSP could play a role in creating frameworks, heuristics for encountering globalization.

14.2 INDIVIDUAL RIGHTS VERSUS THE DIRECTIVE PRINCIPLES OF STATE POLICY: BETWEEN THE JUSTICIABLE AND THE NON-JUSTICIABLE

The preamble to the constitution and the DPSP are the two most dialogic parts of the constitution. The preamble is virtually an invitation to the constitution, asking the citizen to walk through and around the constitutional edifice. The DPSP are an amphibious entity. If rights are justiciable, the DPSP are not. They are directives to the state and are seen as instruments for governance. What fascinates one most about these directives was that they were hints of utopia, borrowed as fragments from competing utopias. They appear like a jigsaw puzzle built from bits of other jigsaw puzzles. Thus, you had frames or bytes from Gandhi, Hinduism, nationalism, communism, and socialism. One can understand the formal embarrassment of lawyers dealing with this array of anomalies.

Two things intrigue one about the DPSP – the problem of language and the concept of time. Explicitly there is only one time bar. The state was expected to provide free and compulsory education to all children up to the age of fourteen within the first ten years of independence. This was not fulfilled but it raises an important question. Should one attach *time bars* to the DPSP? Should questions of health, nutrition, and education be time tagged? Do we say that after ten or twenty years, the directive principles, rather than being wishful thinking, should become an enforceable right? Do we treat them as rights in waiting? Or are we otherwise forced to accept the observation in the Constitutional Assembly (1949) that it was a blank check drawn on a penurious bank? The question of a time bar might be the only marker of sincerity.

There is a second notion of time, which the idea of rights needs. A citizen exists almost as a timeless entity. The DPSP would provide him with a sense of a life cycle. It would see him not only as marginal but as old and discarded. Old age as well as childhood then become grounds for action. The DPSP also need to link the biological cycle to the innovation chains of technology. Possibly one cannot have human rights against obsolescence, but surely obsolescence is a criteria for the DPSP. The obsolescence of the worker and the craftsman needs some recognition in a manifesto of caring. Is the obsolescence of tribes, craftsmen, and farmers inevitable in the face of technology or is it a process that can be challenged within an idea of justice? The question before us is do we embrace the progress and innovation of the corporation and create laws to guarantee it or do we also create a model of caring for a defeated people? Or do we just let them disappear from our census, de-list them from those included in a revenue village?

How do we approach the DPSP? One can do it *systemically* or *systematically*. If one were systematic, one would consider each item in the shopping list and provide an assessment of its current status. It would be a bit like the human development indicators produced by the United Nations Development Program (UNDP). If one were systemic, one would not see them as discrete indicators but as relational notions. The DPSP are a set of connections. At one level, they look like a random set of dots or talking points. Which other constitution links cow slaughter, alcoholism, environment, and employment in one frame? We could read the dots like the points in a *Kollam* or *rangoli*. They are the points around which we draw a picture of governance. What looks like chaos is actually an idea of a future social order. In fact, the DPSP are visions of a future *social* order.

There are different ways of seeing them. The first is the often-repeated justiciability axis. Justice Chinnappa Reddy unfolds a second distinction. In his ruling in the case of *Akhil Bharatiya Soshit Karamchari Sangh* v. *Union of India* (1981), he claims that the fundamental rights are basically political and deal with freedom and protection against excessive state action. The DPSP guarantee not *political* freedom but *social* and *economic* freedom *through* state action. The distinction between political and socioeconomic is clear. The DPSP are the future duties of the state, but they are presently not binding. If we deal with the directive principle dualistically, we get an impoverished picture of them. The DPSP should be treated as cybernetic loops. They provide (1) frameworks of guidance and feedback for the state and (2) a wider environment for rights to prevent them from becoming arid. They provide a variety of contexts to the formal text of rights. One confronts a scenario of connections. Thus, instead of saying there is a right to life abstractly, we link *life* to *livelihood*, *life style*, *life chances*, and *life world*. If right to life has a formal dictionary meaning, the DPSP provide the contexts in which the right acquires new meanings and connections and even a new dynamic. In fact, the DPSP behave like linguistic shifters providing new forms of social and political meaning and thus enhancing the creativity of the fundamental rights.

Rights, rather than being a formal language, become a wide-ranging ordinary language. Rights, instead of being formally correct, acquire a sense of dialect, pidgin, Esperanto, translatability. They acquire the richness of a language, not only the exactitude of grammar. There was a sense of this in the Constituent Assembly. Just consider the fact that the DPSP use terms like *vocation, job, work,* and *livelihood* to discuss the idea of employment. Was it carelessness or a sense that each word caught a different meaning of work in society?

These are not just the fluidities of context. The DPSP get their original contexts from the variety of ideologies that underpin them.

342

Today, many of these ideologies are dead or passive. Socialism as an imagination has lost its eloquence. How does one sustain the search for justice in this context? There are two frames, which provide the notion of justice in a wider sense today. There is first the idea of entitlements, which is incorporated in many development discourses including the UNDP reports (see Sen 1999). There is then the collective voice of grassroots groups, which seek not just entitlements, but an idea of the *commons* not just as a resource pool, a grazing land, but also as a gene pool of skills, ideas, and knowledges. Entitlement has as its epicenter, the individual of liberal theory while the idea of the commons celebrates civil society's attempts to increase the number of choices in a social frame. One can explore this by examining the DPSP on environment.

14.3 EQUITY, ECOLOGY, AND LIFE CHANCES: FUNDAMENTAL RIGHTS AND THE COMMONS

The constitution of India is the first constitution that formally recognized a specific responsibility for the environment. This recognition, however, was a gradual one. Initially, as Diwan and Rosencraz (2001) point out, there was little to differentiate an environmental law from other laws. The sequence was a standard one of the establishment of a statute and the creation of an administrative body with policing power. No new principles were established, and the body of case law was unimpressive.

The Constituent Assembly did not systematically consider whether the question of environment should be dealt with by parliament or state legislatures. In fact, environment as an issue blurred into the wider struggle between the centre and various states about who should wield these powers. At a meeting of the drafting committee in July 1949 to discuss the division of legislative powers, the Ministry of Agriculture proposed that forest and fisheries be transferred from the state list to the concurrent list (the joint list of responsibility between states and centre) but this was strongly opposed by state representatives. It was only in 1976 that environmental protection was formally incorporated into the constitution through the forty-second amendment. Article 48(A) was added to the DPSP and stated: "The State shall endeavour to protect and improve the environment and to safeguard the forests and wildlife of the country." More interestingly, Article 51A(g) included among the fundamental duties of the citizen, "the responsibility to protect and improve the natural environment including forests, lakes, rivers and wild life and to have compassion for living creatures." One notices that protection of flora as opposed to forests does not figure in the constitution.

If formal statements were an index, India would be among the most progressive environmental nations in the world. However, the Indian constitution suffers not only from a formal gap between law and application but also from a deeper schizophrenia where the structure and philosophy of the law itself vitiates the nature of rights. This is most visible in the nature of the Forest Act.

One must begin by asking what is the philosophy of the Forest Act? How does it relate to the problems of the environment in India? And finally what is it about the Forest Act that makes it the epicenter of the environmental crisis in India threatening life, livelihood, and life chances?

The question of environment in India deals with survival. India is not just an affluent country with an affinity for a clean environment. Environment in India is about economics. India's forest movements are not fighting to protect the forests because they love "nature" but also because it means survival. Environmental struggles in India are about economics and about justice. Two points must be remembered. As Tom Kocherry put it, "two thirds of India depends on nature for survival" (s/d:6). The forest is not wilderness but a home of the people who have a relationship with it. We have to also remember that the environmental challenge in India is not about creating fresh frameworks for law but undoing the impact of colonial law and its current imitations.

Indian forest law was a combination of Oriental and Anglo-Saxon law. To understand this, one must understand the notions of property, possession, use, and control endemic to the colonial model of law. Originally, the forest was a commons. The forest dwellers in India did not recognize the forest as property. Such an idea did not exist within their worldview. Forest dwellers merely possessed it. It was the rulers who claimed ownership of forests. But in the traditional system, they did not claim revenue nor did they generally interfere with the forest dwellers.

The British destroyed this reciprocity by appropriating the Oriental idea that the king owned the land. They used this to subvert the idea of the commons. The sovereign now had absolute rights over the commons. Colonial law obtained control of forest land through two concepts – the idea of the "eminent domain" and the idea of "public purpose." If concepts could kill, the above two are definitely ecocidal.

The principle of eminent domain guaranteed the colonial sovereign total control or sovereignty over the forests. It also granted the sovereign the right to appropriate the property of individual citizens of the forest. According to the Indian Forest Act of 1927, "no person can claim a right to private property in forest land merely because he is domiciled there, or even if his forefathers have lived there for centuries. Nor do such people have any rights over forest produce." The British employed the principle of eminent domain in the Land Acquisition Act of 1894 and the Forest Act. After independence, the government of India replicated the principle of eminent domain in the Forest Conservation Act 1980, and the Wildlife Protection Act 1972. What forest law destroyed was the notion of the commons and the tribals' right to occupancy and use of the forest or even in conceptualizing it. Its idea of criminal liability created a conflict model of forestry, a perpetual battle between tribals, peasants, and the state over the use of the forest. The overall impact was devastating. Distress migration by tribals began with the colonial demand for revenue.

The destruction of the forest as a commons has been one of the overlooked aspects of development. In fact, the post-Independence era paid little attention to the commons. The government enacted numerous proposals for land reform but such plans were concerned with *private property* in mind (Singh 1986). The government has attempted to increase the purchasing power of the poor through land reform and agricultural inputs, but it has failed to consider the decline of the commons. The privatization of the commons destroyed people's access to land, to raw materials, to minor forest produce, medicines, and firewood. What is worse, it turned what was free into a market economy. The destruction of the commons might be the greatest source of the poverty of the countryside. Not only did it monetize the forest, it created a further injustice in the very manner it classified the forest for use (see Jodha 1994).

Forest produce was classified into major and minor forest produce. According to the forest department, only timber and fuel wood, which the industrialist needed for raw material and the state for revenue, are considered major forest produce. The rest, which the tribals use and are dependent on, is "minor forest produce." Fernandes, Menon, and Veigas (1998), in their study of Orissa, show that the tribals depend for 50 percent of their needs for food, cattle fodder, and other needs on minor forest produce. They add that, in a country in which "modern" allopathic medicine based health care is not accessible to the rural inhabitants, the tribals have to depend on wild medicinal shrubs, herbs, roots, and fruits from the forest.

Chatrapati Singh (1986), one of the most brilliant exponents on common property resources, argued that the socialism of the constitution was a misdirected one, particularly in the way it privatized the commons. He remarked that it is normal to think of a socialism that disempowers the maharajahs (kings) and the zamindars (landlords). But such a simplistic view overlooks the fact that the same laws of acquisition and denial of compensation apply to forest dwellers and tribals who are at the bottom of the poverty line. Evidently, the jurisprudence concerning the state's power under eminent domain in India must work out a much more complex solution for compensation so that it does justice to the poor (or those who have been made poor) and is not merely preoccupied with the appropriation of the wealth of the rich.

Jodha (1994), in his classic essay on common property resources, adds a devastating set of data based on his studies on six states. Jodha concluded that: (1) the rural poor receive the bulk of their fuel supplies and fodder from common property resources (CPRs) (CPR income accounts for a conservative estimate of 14 to 23 percent of household income); and (2) for the rural poor, employment days generated by CPR-based activities were higher than the days of employment on their own farm or public works under the anti-poverty programs (Jodha 1994:170–172). One must also consider benefits to the village as a whole rather than to individual households. Those villages where CPRs were managed well had, according to Jodha's survey, better nutrition, no drinking water problem, and lesser dependence on government grants and relief.

The overall studies of the Forest Act reveal that it created only an ironic socialism that impoverished the poor. The state, rather than being an agency for welfare, becomes ecologically destructive. Its ecological management was violative of justice. We are thus faced with two stark questions. Should the DPSP affirm the validity of the commons? Secondly, should the Forest Act be completely transformed so that it is in line with the rudiments of justice guaranteed by the constitution? What other ways exist to bridge the gap between legislative safeguards and ecological lawlessness? There is finally not just schizophrenia of law but also a failure of legal innovation. Singh notes that common law legislation elsewhere has invoked new legal principles. He notes that occupancy rights of tribals over common land have now been established in Canada, New Zealand, Australia, and Nigeria (1986:24). It is such a lacuna that the review commission and grass roots groups must consider, especially as common law issues go beyond questions of the left and the right.

14.4 RETROGRADE LAWS: THE LAND ACQUISITION ACT

If the destruction of the commons is one of the great challenges for developing the notion of rights today, the Land Acquisition Act (LAA) of 1894, which allows the state to acquire any land for "national purpose" without the promise of resettlement, the depredations of development offer a second crisis of opportunity. In both, the question of poverty is the vexatious issue. In the first, it was a question of common property. In the second, it is a question of private property appropriated for development. To most marginals in India, the LAA constitutes a tragedy as big as the dispossession of the commons, particularly the struggle of tribals and peasants against large development projects.

Large development projects demand large tracts of land, which are acquired under the LAA. The LAA allows the state to assert its right over a piece of land provided it is acquired for the public good. For grassroots struggles, the words "public good" and "national purpose" have been devastating threats to livelihoods. Let us begin with a litany of facts. According to the *Indian Disasters Report* (Parasuraman and Unnikrishnan 2000), development projects like dams, roads, and canals have displaced 500,000 people each year as a direct consequence of land acquisition. The report adds that hydroelectric and irrigation projects are the largest source of displacement, followed by mines, power stations, industrial complexes, and military installations, and finally sanctuaries and parks and technical interventions.

Each mode of acquisition has triggered an emblematic grassroots struggle like Koel-Karo, Balliapal, Rajaji National Park, Rawat Bhata, and the fishing struggle in Kerala. The demographics of displacements are also revealing. The 29th Report of the Commissioner for Scheduled Castes and Tribes notes that, even though tribal people are roughly 7.5 percent of the population, over 40 percent of the displaced until 1990 came from these communities (see Fernandes 1995:50). The official Working Group on Development and Welfare of Scheduled Tribes concluded on the basis of a comprehensive study of 110 projects that 1.6 million people were displaced by these projects. The report also focused attention on "multiple displacements." Many communities, which underwent resettlement, were displaced a second time without any consideration of the trauma it entailed. The examples of Singrauli, the New Mangalore Port, the Konkan railways, and the Kalnai dam come immediately to mind. The question one is forced to ask is: are current Indian models of development genuinely constitutional?

Secondly, is the Land Acquisition Act violative of the DPSP and their promise of livelihood? Thirdly, should we define more strictly what "public purpose" or "national purpose" mean? Should the DPSP constitutionally demand social impact assessments of large-scale projects? Should we consider these audits merely technical devices or instruments of justice guaranteeing some protection to the most vulnerable sections of our society? Movements against displacement constitute one of the key struggles against injustice. How do the DPSP respond to this issue?

The LAA was a colonial invention created to acquire possession of land for roads, canals, salt manufacture, railways, and public projects. The acquisition was legitimated in terms of the principle of eminent domain and justified on grounds of "national or public purpose." What an ordinary citizen wandering through the maze of law is stunned by is the complete lack of definition of what public purpose means. There is no legislation defining public purpose. Whatever leads one has, come from case law. The court rulings in *Petit v. Secretary of State for India, Kameshwar Singh*, etc. reveal that there is no attempt to define the concept. In fact, the courts have veered away from such a task, pleading for an Alice-in-Wonderland-like elasticity. The Mulla Committee (1979) attempted to list the uses of the word "public," stating that this list of synonyms defined the limits of universe (Singh 1986:37). Oddly, the court and the committees seem fascinated by "purpose," but seem wary of defining "public." The realistic cynicism of Singh (1986) attributes it to the fact that it is tacitly understood that the word "public" refers to the rich. It is they who benefit from these legislations, and it is they who can afford to go to the courts. The demand for a definition of "public purpose" has been one of the consistent demands of grassroots groups. Who the "public" is needs to be determined. Are victims of development a part of the public (see Ramanathan 1995:45–49)?

It is in this context that grassroots groups have sought to comment systematically on the new additions to the LAA. One of the pleas resonating through this group is that development follows the DPSP and that the latter include the right to rehabilitation.

The first thing that grassroots groups recognize is that the amended Act does not define public purpose either. They recognize that development and resettlement are relative strangers to the law. While the empowerment of the state to acquire control over land, forests, and other natural resources has been enabled by the law, the umbrella of "public purpose" has provided it shelter from judicial challenge. The challenge of the grassroots is simple. The glossary of development, public purpose, and national interest necessarily entails the displacement of a people.

These groups (see Ramanathan 1995) have proposed a tripartite modification of the LAA. They demand: (1) the definition of the concept of public purpose; (2) the right to information sensitive to the fact that we operate in a society which is generally illiterate and even more illiterate about the law; and (3) a wider understanding of the notions of compensation and rehabilitation, which understands livelihood and community in its widest sense.

What the grassroots reflections on development projects do is to provide a commentary on justice and socialism of the constitution. One is tempted in fact to redefine socialism not in the "industrial" sense but on behalf of tribals, peasants, and other marginals. Here, socialism is not defined in terms of the opposition of public to private, but is socialism based on the rediscovery of the commons and the recovery of the community and of a notion of justice beyond compensation.

The National Working Group on Displacement, which included a spectrum of activists like Achyut Yagnik, Pradip Prabhu, Girish Patel, Medha Patkar, and Bittu Sahghal, captures this logic and spirit in its suggestions. The report's writers can merely highlight their arguments. "The group proposes that all projects must be planned and executed within the framework of constitutional limitations and in furtherance of constitutional goals and values" (Ramanathan 1995:48).

The activists opposed to the LAA then note that, "as people and communities are involuntarily displaced by a project, their right to reside and settle in any part of India under Article 19(1c) of the Constitution, subject to reasonable restrictions in the interests of the general public is compromised. The special interests of tribes are also compromised. By displacing and uprooting the community and depriving it of its livelihood and resource base, the projects deprive them of their right to life." The group also demands that the principles of justice embodied in various directive principles should animate the projects.

In a constitutional sense, we have to ask whether the notion of sustainability could be enshrined into the constitution as part of the DPSP. Sustainability incorporates and connects justice, renewability, and equity. Maybe sustainability is not an enforceable right, but, as part of the DPSP, could it be an animating element of the constitution?

One could agree with the working group that "the concept of public interest raises important constitutional questions particularly in the light of the Socialist State as declared in the Preamble and equitable distribution of national resources as enunciated in Article 39(b) and (c) of the Constitution" (Singh 1986:45). The group adds that the Supreme Court and the High Court have taken an enlightened view of constitutional provisions as relating to development projects. But some economic and philosophical issues remain:

(1) a redefinition of the concept of public purpose and a public debate on it;
(2) a complete listing of persons affected by the project. The ownership and title of land should not be the only criteria. Whoever is dependent on land for livelihood should either directly or indirectly be included, such as landless laborers, traditionally unauthorized cultivators, encroachers, grazers, fisher folk, nomads, and forest produce gatherers (see Ramanathan 1994:45–50).
(3) The idea of compensation as an index of justice needs to be rethought. "Cash compensation is the only mode of compensation known to law," but cash compensation is a reductive portfolio of the law and it cannot be adequate to understand a lived concept such as loss of livelihood. What are missing here are the non-tangibles, which are not monetizable, the sense of community and the possibility of survival and competence after the trauma of displacement (Ramanathan 1995:48).

There is finally a philosophical issue we must confront. Indian law is basically utilitarian in its understanding of development. It accepts the dispensability of marginal people. In fact, cost–benefit analysis becomes a scientific guise for eliminating marginals from the process of development. We need to consider the following questions: (1) What should be the ideological or philosophical basis of the DPSP as applied to development projects? (2) How do we incorporate ideas of sustainability, vulnerability, and renewability into the constitution? (3) Can the DPSP incorporate non-monetized ideas of compensation? (4) Does a right to rehabilitation belong to the fundamental rights or the DPSP?

14.5 TRANSFER OF TECHNOLOGY: RENEWABILITY, OBSOLESCENCE, AND LIFE WORLD

Between the violent appropriation created by the Forest Act and the violence of displacement created by development projects lies a third form of violence, the violence of obsolescence created by technical interventions. What one wishes to emphasize is that *livelihood is a function not only of access to natural resources but also of access to technology.* It also raises the question of justice as a niching of technologies. This question has been raised in a series of debates around shifting cultivation, the struggle between trawlers and traditional boats, and the future of craft traditions centering around materials like the bamboo. It once again emphasizes the relation between the implicit idea of the commons present in the DPSP and the demands of justice. It raises in particular the issue of how the constitution and the DPSP in particular confront the issue of the transfer of technology.

Unfortunately, technology per se receives little systematic attention in the DPSP. The question of livelihood and the right to work need to focus systematically on the notion of "obsolescence." The constitution has focused on natural resources and on assistance to workers, but it has little to say about technology and technological interventions as a constitutional problem. What can the DPSP, which uphold the right to work, say about technology? Can sustainability work without sensitivity to renewability and obsolescence? How does the constitution mediate between the dynamics of subsistence and the dynamics of industrial innovation? One is not getting embroiled in any romantic idea of technology. One is only asking how a constitution confronts issues of technological change within the framework of justice and choice. Should a certain sensibility to the social and ethical problems of the transfer of technology be articulated in some form in the DPSP? Is choice of technology only an issue in steel, electronics, and plastics, or is it as relevant at subsistence levels?

The socialistic framework of the DPSP focuses on property. It focuses on land reform and nationalization, but not on the relation of technology to property. Obsolescence usually refers to a zero sum game between two technological competitors where one produces an innovation, which outstrips the technological competence of the other. If justice is only market driven and determined, such a notion might be adequate. But often obsolescence might be artificially maintained or be ecologically indifferent. It might not realize that different ecologies need different kinds of technologies. The notion of equity demands adjudication between the different forms of technology. One need not place them on a linear gradient where one points to the past and is doomed and the other looks hopefully to the future. The state was expected to be an adjudicator of technologies in India. The question one must ask is how successful has it been, and, secondly, whether the DPSP can address the issues within the framework of governance.

Three events in recent times have raised the issue between technological intervention, obsolescence, and justice in an urgent way. They are the debate over shifting cultivation, the great struggle between trawlers and traditional boats, and the issue of craftsmen using bamboo as a raw material. We shall consider the first as a paradigmatic example.

Tom Kochery, general coordinator of the World Forum of Fish Harvesters and Fish Workers, observes that India, with its 6,000-km coastline and its innumerable rivers, lakes, and lagoons, has 12 million fisher people who have accumulated a vast fund of knowledge about resources in their locality and developed an array of technologies each suited to a particular ecological niche. Such an immense diversity of fishing techniques tended to maximize ecological sophistication rather than techno-economic efficiency. The introduction of modernization beginning with the Indo-Norwegian project of 1953 spurred market forces and industrialized fishing in parts. More critically, it polarized the industry between trawlers and the traditional fishing boats.

Technological change also produced a conflict-ridden situation (which escalated in the 1960s and 1970s) between trawler crews and Catamaran fishermen. Since they exploit identical fishing grounds and target similar species, the trawlers with their superior catching capacity affected the catches of the traditional fishermen (see Kurien and Achari 1994:219). The question of productivity needs to be related to the wider one of equity, ecology, and justice.

The large trawlers were a threat to the livelihood of the traditional fishermen, who began organizing to fight this menace. Through an accumulation of sit-ins, hunger strikes, and picketing, the Fishers Forum has been able to obtain marine fishing regulations covering most of coastal India.

In 1993, the Kerala government imposed a ban on trawling in the monsoon season in order to protect certain species during their breeding season. The trawlers went to court challenging the ban, and, in June 1994, the Supreme Court delivered a judgment in support of the ban on bottom trawling. In his judgment Justice Reddy declared that the public interest cannot be determined only by looking at the quantum of fish caught in a year. The government is under an obligation to protect the economic interest of the traditional fishermen and to ensure they are not deprived of their slender means of livelihood.

The Supreme Court was an enlightened one. But one must note that it overturned earlier high court judgments in favor of the trawler owners and also that it took over two decades of protest to get some semblance of justice. The question is whether we need to work out links between equity, technology, and justice. How do we guarantee that traditional fishermen are not deskilled in such a process of obsolescence? Do we allow market forces to operate and hope the politics of civil society can blunt it? Or do we create a semblance of sensitivity to such issues constitutionally? Obsolescence is an issue of governance. It raises problems of concentration of wealth, unemployment, and deskilling. Should the DPSP address only monopolies of wealth or should it also look at the social problems of technological regimes? Obsolescence creates marginal groups whose fate as a community becomes problematic, as they can no longer follow their traditional choices of occupation.

14.6 COMMUNITY AND LIVELIHOOD: DECENTRALIZATION AND SELF-GOVERNANCE

The link between *community* and *livelihood* is one of the life-giving affirmations implicit in the DPSP. A sense of community needs a sense of decentralization. Only local self-government can provide for local control and use of resources. The idea of self-governing villages has always been an integral part of the rural tradition. The *Panchayat* system was active both in the medieval and Mughal periods, but it fell into disuse during British colonial rule.

It was one of the ironies of the Constituent Assembly that the first draft of the Indian constitution did not contain provision for the *Panchayats*. Partly, it might have been impelled by Dr. Ambedkar's critique of the Indian village. Ambedkar, as leader of the lower castes, saw the Indian village as a sink and unredeemable in terms of its institutions. Mahatma Gandhi noted this omission, and observed that the absence of *Panchayats* might reflect the absence of the voice of the people. The idea of *Panchayats* was thus ambivalently inserted into Article 40 of the constitution, which provided that "the state shall take steps to organize village *Panchayats* and endow them with such powers and authority as may be necessary to enable them to function as units of self-government."

India's development programs operated without a full sense of the importance of *Panchayats* for governance. It is true that up to the 1960s there was some sense of the importance of Panchayats. The community development projects launched in 1952 realized that they would reach a dead end without effective instruments of local participation. The

Balwant Mehta committee appointed to study community development programs concluded that development could not succeed without local initiatives. The Mehta committee recommended the establishment of a "Panchayati Raj" system but left it to each state to work out the modalities.

By 1959, all states had a Panchayati Act and by the mid-1960s more than 217,300 villages covering 92 percent of India had formal *Panchayat* systems. Yet within the next decade *Panchayats* were on the decline. In fact, the government itself was responsible for downgrading *Panchayats* through an implicit process of double-think.

The development agendas of the 1960s tended to bypass community development programmes. There was little or no effort to improve *Panchayats* as an institution. The state not only ignored the *Panchayat* in development programs but also failed to fund regular elections. In many states *Panchayat* elections were not held for twenty years. What was most ironic was the confusion of cause and effect. The *Panchayats* were corrupt and ineffective but it was they rather than the bureaucracy that was blamed for the situation. It was a typical social analysis in which the victim was blamed for the situation.

Yet, if the official failed, the traditional and the customary showed that *Panchayats* could work. One has to examine the fascinating institution of *Van Panchayats* (forest *Panchayats*) to understand how *local communities* could be active and effective despite constraints in managing local resources.

Consider the case of *Van Panchayats* in Uttar Pradesh (now Uttarakhand). Present since 1931, there are now over 4,000 of these institutions in Uttar Pradesh. They are a direct consequence of the Forest Act, which deprived local people of access to common lands. This created a conflict-ridden situation, which led to the establishment of forest *Panchayats* for the management of non-commercial Class I forests. The members were elected informally but not secretly, and served for five years. The *Van Panchayats* helped manage these forests as a commons, providing villagers with grazing space, fodder, leaves for composting, and wood for construction. They also assured that these forests were not subject to over-extraction (Ballabh 1993).

A generation of superb environmentalists has observed that *Van Panchayats* have worked creditably under severe constraints. They are captive to the official rituals of harassment and permission. For instance, they can now appoint forest guards only with the permission of the Deputy Commissioner, even though the guards are paid from members' contributions. The *Van Panchayats* have often been allocated degraded land. Yet, if renewability is a criterion, they have often functioned better than the forest department. The work of Anil Aggarwal, N. C. Saxena, Robert Chambers, and Jayanto Bandhopadhyaya have all shown the effectiveness of community management of resources.

And yet, what was common and even academic wisdom was neglected constitutionally. It took another decade of efforts and the work of enlightened technocrats like Nirmal Mukherjee and Malcolm Adesheshiah for the government to realize that *Panchayats* must constitute the effective and life-giving third tier of government.

14.7 RIGHT TO INFORMATION: TRANSPARENCY AND ACCOUNTABILITY

To operate successfully, this principle of governance needs the affirmation of the right to information. Information is central to governance, and we have to ask whether the right to information must be a part of the DPSP. Information establishes a link to transparency and accountability without which a social audit of the government would be impossible.

The recent campaigns to establish the right to information capture and sustain the spirit of the DPSP as frameworks for empowerment. Central to this has been the campaigns of the Mazdoor Kisan Shakti Sangathan (MKSS), a coalition of workers and peasants active especially in the state of Rajasthan.

In its campaign in Rajasthan the MKSS established the link between development and survival and they amplified this understanding through the idea of public hearings or *Jan Sunwaii*. These public hearings on development expenditure revealed that in some districts up to 85 percent of development project budgets were not spent on development. The MKSS helped establish the four key principles of development as an act of governance: transparency of development spending, accountability, sanctity of social audit, and redress.

The hearings revealed a great chain of corruption, which led to the suspension of some officials. It led to the strike of *Grama Sevaks* (village officials) who asserted that they were answerable only to the senior officials and subject only to governmental and not social audits. *Panchayat* representatives, block development officers and *Grama Sevaks* organized a protest against the pressures of transparency. The MKSS replied with a *dharna* (an agitation) that attracted tremendous public support not only from women, trade unions, and ordinary citizens, but also from creative Indian Administrative Service (IAS) officers who applied the right to information innovatively. The MKSS battle was not just an assertion of transparency but also a statement of the necessity of people's knowledge, which challenged governmental secrecy and the lack of accountability. It emphasized that participation is something to be affirmed not only in the workplace but across the entire framework of governance.

14.8 BETWEEN PROPERTY AND HERITAGE: ISSUES OF BIODIVERSITY

A concern for information and the right to information were not present in the original DPSP. The closest synonyms were those of access, participation, and heritage or history. The right to information provided a crucial link between community, governance, and justice. It provides for a notion of memory through the idea of heritage. Article 49 of the constitution affirms the obligation of the state to "protect every monument or place or object of artistic and historical interest ... from spoliation, disfigurement, destruction, and removal." The DPSP are matter of fact about monuments. They restrict them to built-up artifacts of a certain kind and force us to face up to the implicit tensions of conservation in India.

We must remember, however, that built-up heritage constitutes only one aspect of heritage. Should the DPSP include ideas of cultural and biological heritage? Should they articulate a right to diversity not only because it sustains livelihoods but also because it is a manifestation of cultural and biological heritage? Heritage is a precious form of lived information. Should one allow corporations to patent it? Does our cultural heritage allow for the patenting of life forms? This problem has been raised repeatedly in the recent debates about diversity, biopiracy, and community patenting systems, and farmers' rights both among grassroots groups and among professionals in the debate about intellectual property rights.

One has to begin by understanding that there are two paradigmatic approaches to diversity. The first centers around subsistence communities where survival is a creative bond to local biodiversity and conservation. The emphasis here is on the integrity of ecosystems and species. Vandana Shiva (1999) observes that biodiversity in these societies has an intrinsic value, while for industrial and commercial systems biodiversity is reductively seen as "raw material" for the production of commodities and the maximization of profits. The immediate example that comes to mind is the coconut, which has over 123 listed uses. In a monoculture industrial system, the coconut would be seen as a source of oil.

Diversity in India is a celebration of nature and culture. Ashis Kothari notes that there are over 1,000 species of mango (1997:50) But even the varieties of mangoes pale before the 40,000 varieties of rice. Kothari reflects that one often fails to see the biodiversity of subsistence agriculture as an innovative one. A single species of rice collected from the wild some time in the distant past has diversified into 40,000 varieties as a result of the ingenuity and innovative skills of farming communities. In his observations on rice, Kothari (1997:50) adds that tribals in the hills of Nagaland grow as many as twenty varieties of rice within a single year in their terraced fields. There is nothing monocultural about rice. Some varieties of rice are grown for use during festivals and marriages; several others are grown for their taste, color, or smell, and others for their pesticidal and soil fertilization characteristics. If rice is one testimony, medicine offers another bouquet of examples. India has over 7,500 species of medicinal plants, whose lore and use are kept alive by 360,000 traditional medical specialists. This process of biodiversity is threatened in many ways. The monoculture pursuit of profits cuts down variety. For instance, in the state of Andhra Pradesh, the use of high-yielding varieties (HYV) eliminated 95 percent of the rice varieties in the Godavari district.

Even more destabilizing is the extension of patents and intellectual property rights to biodiversity. Shiva (1999) points out that currently India has no coherent framework of biodiversity legislation. Different ministries pursue different projects and operate at cross-purposes. What we need is legislation protecting agricultural diversity and farmers' rights and our current heritage of medicinal plants. There is a necessity to understand the biodiversity convention. Shiva insists that (1) biological diversity should be treated as the sovereign property of its country of origin; (2) the sovereign property rights embodying this biological and intellectual heritage should be seen as prior to the regime of intellectual property rights; and (3) biodiversity property rights should be vested not only in the state but also in the local communities and the traditional practitioners. Finally, she argues that no Patent Act should function before the overall framework of biodiversity is in place (Shiva 1999).

The real threat to biodiversity emerges from the new patent laws and the possibilities of biopiracy. Shiva argues that the lack of intellectual property protection for India's biological and cultural heritage makes them vulnerable to the "biopiracy" present in the Western patenting system.

The standard criteria for recognizing intellectual property rights (IPRs) generally tend to ignore indigenous knowledge and innovations. In fact, knowledge often flows as a gift from Third World countries and returns as a patent. Today, local farmers and even the UN's Food and Agriculture Organization recognize the need to protect farmers' rights.

The classic case of this in recent times has centered around Neem, a local plant whose leaves were used as a germicide and insecticide, and around Basmati rice. For centuries, the West ignored Neem. In fact, it did not consider the practices of farmers and doctors in India as worthy of attention. The growing opposition to chemical products led to a search for natural pesticides and to the Neem. By 1985, US and Japanese firms had taken out a dozen patents on Neem pesticides and Neem toothpaste. The question one has to ask is whether Neem patents constitute novel forms of knowledge or do we state that such forms of novelty are only based on the ignorance of a 2,000-year-old tradition of biopesticides in India?

The question of Basmati rice raises similar issues. In 1997, a patent was granted to Rice Tech Inc., a US company, on Basmati lines and grains. The Basmati variety was derived from the Indian Basmati, and crossed with semi-dwarf varieties. The question is whether Rice Tech Basmati is the Indian Basmati and novel at the same time. If Basmati patents were recognized in India, Indian farmers would ironically be forced to pay royalties to Rice Tech.

The examples of Neem and rice have triggered a countrywide debate over the equitable nature of IPRs. It raises three sets of questions. Should India accept IPRs before we state our commitment to farmers' rights at least in the DPSP? Should the DPSP develop a concept of heritage that works against biopiracy? Should we work for an alternative patenting system that transcends the ethnocentric limitations of Western patenting systems by recognizing knowledge beyond the realm of Western scientific journals and redefining the notions of innovation present in genetic engineering? The recent struggles of the *Beej Bachao Abhiyan* (Save the Seed) in the Himalayas and the Appiko movement in Karnataka demand that we reflect on how the socialism of the preamble and the DPSP should be reworked to provide a more equitable framework for IPRs as they relate to ownership, equity, and the right to livelihood.

The discussion on IPRs raises the question of the centrality of food to the entire social order. Food as a process, a product, and a symbol becomes one of the features uniting citizen, state, and corporation. In fact, there is pressure to recognize the right to food as a fundamental right. The centrality of food as a marker is central to issues of globalization. Through genetic engineering and the patent system, corporations are seeking to redefine the civilizational nature of food. Yet, food and the right to food are missing in the DPSP. In fact, the DPSP's emphasis on health and nutrition is incomplete in the absence of a right to food. Should there be some provision to guarantee food security? Should we define food as merely calorific intake, or link the need to guarantee food to the right to the diversities of food both as agriculture and as cuisine. The right to food should be the hub around which the right of farmers to seed and the right of consumers to a variety of food can also be located dynamically. If the DPSP reflect the search for non-violent social order, the right to food and the right to prevent violence to food may become one of the key DPSP principles in the age of globalization.

14.9 COGNITIVE JUSTICE: VULNERABILITY, KNOWLEDGE, AND LIVELIHOOD

The voice of the grassroots movements and the search for justice through a critique of livelihood and knowledge provided one bundle of concepts on how to cope with marginality and vulnerability in society. Notions like cognitive justice, the celebration of knowledge as a commons, the links between knowledge and livelihood, and the argument for the ecological embeddedness of the constitution, provided a new heuristic for the constitution. In a professional sense, such a theory is available in the writings of Alvares (1992), Shiva (1988), Singh (1986), and Visvanathan (1997). It anchors the search for a constitution based on the citizen as a marginal coping with the new enclosure movements of industry and capital. But an acceptance of such concepts would demand a paradigmatic change both in the constitution and in the construction of the democratic imagination.

The crisis of development and the globalization of markets and democracy transformed many of the institutions (like the nation-state) that could have effected such changes. The explosion of social movements created a widening circle of democracy but with an ironic twist. Democracy had acquired epidemic proportions over Asia, Africa, and Eastern Europe, but the democracy one was celebrating was not the democratic imagination of the movements but the good boy theory of liberal democracy.

The good boy theory of democracy valorizes democracy but narrows it in terms of formalist legal terms. The good boy theory of democracy does not look at the complexities of democracy or its contradictions. An invention of market-friendly liberals and World Bank agencies, it operates through a set of indicators. If you echo the right words, you can get away with murder.

The most celebrated word is *elections*. Electoral politics has become a substitute for democratic politics. There is little acknowledgment of the variety of issues that fail to emerge. India is the world's biggest democracy but issues like pollution and floods cannot be raised.

The good boy theory of democracy merely creates a minimum skeletal frame to make democracy market-friendly. Since there is virtually no Indian imagination around this process, corporations, foundations and the World Bank have stepped in to fill the gap.

There is then the emphasis on *rights*. One needs a universal notion of rights, but there is a twisted quality to the process. The classic case is child labor. The enthusiasm of many NGOs for campaigns against child labor is not unexpected. But what is at one level a pathology, also sustains crafts, is a way of generating income, and is a learning process. We have to distinguish between forms of child labor and tackle it in a nuanced way. But once the international bandwagon begins, can one's NGO be far behind?

The idea of rights is connected to the notion of *contracts*. The globalization regime is a regime of contracts and patents. The patenting of life, the patenting of seeds and household remedies that have long been a part of the local commons violates the ethical and aesthetic codes of these societies because these societies refuse to patent life forms. In fact, they see the seed as the gift which they have to preserve as an act of trusteeship.

Finally, there is the idea of official *sustainability* or eco-friendliness stemming from an ecocratic idea of society. A whole baggage of new categories from risk, to green technologies, to ecological audits flood our policy worlds turning even good ideas into a part of a nexus of cynicism and corruption.

This imitative, superficial style of environmentalism complements an equally superficial but glossy attitude to rights, elections, and so on. Not only does it not add to the question of values, it blunts the dissenting imagination of our society, subverting radical critique, creating ambivalence over environmentalism, which in the long run might benefit middle class consumerism and conscience but damage the real possibilities of democracy.

The negotiation between dissenting grassroots imaginations and formal policy produces, as it were, a halfway house centering more on the works of the economist Amartya Sen (1984), the scientist M. S. Swaminathan (1999), and part of the feminist imagination that can be absorbed into World Bank policy. The central words are entitlements and social capital. There is a shift in the sites from movements to institutions. The emphasis is not on survival, marginality and livelihood but on child labor, nutrition, and education, especially of the female child. The poetics of policy seem easier with a world more amenable to human development indicators. The new emphasis is on illiteracy and employment, not on vulnerability, livelihood, and survival. The political theory of movements would have demanded a paradigmatic change. The work of Sen or Swaminathan draws only a few epicycles around the reigning theories of market and democracy. In that very moment, the DPSP become a text more amenable to incremental indicators rather than a real leap toward alternative cosmologies and an alternate vision of the good society. The lesson we learned in the conversation with law is that each master narrative creates its own models of permissible dissent, that even in thought experiments in constitutional law some experiments are more equal than others. Yet the DPSP as a legal framework provide one of the best heuristics for confronting globalization. Globalization as a model of change seeks to embed itself by creating new laws around nature, technology, property, life, and innovation. One needs a fluid framework, a collection of heuristics which can translate the demands of movements into methodologies for the constitution. The DPSP provide the framework to link the local and the singular with the global. Only such fluid frameworks can help assess the trends and counter-trends of globalization. One hopes the global forum would prioritize this in its agenda for the future.

References

Alvares, Claude. 1992. *Science, Development and Violence*. Delhi: Oxford University Press.

Ballabh, Vishwa. 1993. "Van Panchayats." *Seminar* 406:33–35.

Basu, Durga. 2001. *Introduction to the Constitution of India*. Delhi: Wadhwa.

Diwan, Shyam, and Armin Rosencranz. 2001. *Environmental Law and Policy in India*. Delhi: Oxford University Press.

Fernandes, Walter. 1995. "Tribal Displacement: Struggles and Implications for Resettlement." *Lokayan Bulletin* 11(4):50–56.

Fernandes, Walter, Geeta Menon, and Philip Viegas. 1988. *Forests, Environment and Tribal Economy: Deforestation, Impoverishment Marginalisation in Orissa.* Delhi: Indian Social Institute.

Guha, Ramchandra (Ed.). 1994. *Social Ecology.* Delhi: Oxford University Press.

Jodha, N. S. 1994. "Common Property Resources and the Rural Poor." Pp. 150–189 in Guha (1994).

Kocherry, Thomas (s/d). "Indian Fisheries over 50 Years." Unpublished manuscript.

Kothari, Ashis. 1997. *Understanding Biodiversity Orient.* Hyderabad: Longman.

Kurien, John, and Thankappan Achari. 1994. "Overfishing the Coastal Commons: Causes and Consequences." Pp. 190–217 in Guha (1994).

Nandy, Ashis (Ed.). 1988. *Science, Hegemony and Violence.* Delhi: Oxford University Press.

Ramanathan, Usha. 1995. "Displacement and Rehabilitation." *Lokayan Bulletin* 11(5): 41–56.

Sen, Amartya. 1984. *Resources, Values and Development.* Delhi: Oxford University Press.

Shiva, Vandana. 1988. *Staying Alive: Women, Ecology and Development.* Delhi: Kali for Women.

1999. "Biotechnological Development and the Conservation of Biodiversity." Pp. 193–213 in Shiva and Moser (1999).

Shiva, Vandana, and I. Moser (Eds.). 1999. *Biopolitics.* Hyderabad: Orient Longman.

Singh, Chatrapati. 1986. *Common Property and Common Poverty: India's Forests, Forest Dwellers, and the Law.* Delhi: Oxford University Press.

Swaminathan, M. S. 1999. *A Century of Hope: Harmony with Nature and Freedom from Hunger.* Channai: East West Books.

Visvanathan, Shiv. 1997. *A Carnival for Science.* Delhi: Oxford University Press.

Watal, Jayashree. 2001. *Intellectual Property Rights in the WTO and Developing Countries.* Delhi: Oxford University Press.

CHAPTER 15

BOTTOM-UP ENVIRONMENTAL LAW AND DEMOCRACY IN THE RISK SOCIETY: PORTUGUESE EXPERIENCES IN THE EUROPEAN CONTEXT

João Arriscado Nunes, Marisa Matias and *Susana Costa**

15.1 INTRODUCTION

The problems faced by so-called "risk societies" (Beck 1992),[1] including environmental problems, are best understood within the context of what Santos (2002:72–75) has called the collapse or crisis of the model of "normal" social change and, in particular, the crisis of the strategies of hegemony and trust used by the state and based on two key institutions, law and science. Responses to this crisis have bred some innovative experiences in citizen action and democratic participation.

This chapter takes up these issues through the presentation and discussion of struggles over environmental law and policies in Portugal, a semiperipheral country within a core regional space of the

* This chapter is partially based on research for the projects "Analyzing Public Accountability Procedures in Contemporary European Contexts" (PubAcc-HPSE-CT2001-00076) and "Science, Technology and Governance in Europe" (STAGE-HPSE-CT2001-50003), both funded by the 5th Framework Program for Research of the European Commission; "Reinventing Social Emancipation: Towards New Manifestos", funded by the MacArthur (Grant Award # 98-52316-GSS) and Gulbenkian Foundations; and on Marisa Matias' MA thesis (SFRH/BM/361/2000) in Sociology, submitted to the School of Economics at the University of Coimbra. This was completed by additional research and a re-analysis of the materials produced for these projects. We are grateful to the members of the teams of PubAcc and STAGE for their comments on our Portuguese materials. Boaventura de Sousa Santos inspired many of the ideas we tried to explore and suggested new ways our materials could be used. The Center for Social Studies of the University of Coimbra provided the conditions that made this work possible.
[1] On the new forms of "technical," "scientific," or "green" citizenship in Europe and criticisms of Beck's theses, see Irwin (1995); Irwin and Michael (2003); Callon, Lascoumes, and Barthe (2001); Barry (2001); Jamison (2001); and Fischer (2000).

world-system, the European Union. Our aim is threefold: to describe and discuss the interplay of the national and the European and global scales in the making of domestic environmental regulation and legality; to characterize the tensions and conflicts arising in the attempts to enact environmental policies invoking state legality in local settings; and, finally, to examine the emergence and the dynamics of collective actors in their struggles over the environment, as they articulate scales and modes of intervention and of legality while opposing national environmental policies and hegemonic appropriations of European and international environmental regulations. A case of conflict over waste disposal and management will be examined in detail. The final section discusses the case in the light of the set of issues raised by Santos (2002) on the conditions for counter-hegemonic appropriations of law.

15.2 LAW, ENVIRONMENT AND THE DILEMMAS OF "ECOLOGICAL MODERNIZATION"

Starting in the 1970s, influential accounts of the existence of a global environmental crisis circulated and were widely discussed in international fora, from the 1972 UN Conference on the Human Environment, held in Stockholm, to the 1992 Earth Summit, in Rio de Janeiro. Response to that crisis would allegedly require integrated and comprehensive policies based on scientific management and drawing on new developments in systems analysis, within existing social and institutional arrangements. Several versions of this approach were commissioned in the 1970s and 1980s by international institutions (like the United Nations and the OECD) or by think tanks, and environmentalists often endorsed much of the diagnosis, even if they came up with alternative solutions. Viewed from the South, however, the notion of a global crisis was often regarded as a distraction from the situated problems that were affecting a majority of the world population. The mapping of this debate is an important indicator of the emerging North/South division in the diagnosis of and response to environmental problems.[2]

---

[2] Several reports published in the 1970s and 1980s (such as the 1972 *Limits to Growth* report to the Club of Rome and the 1987 *Our Common Future* report to the United Nations, known as the Brundtland Report) share many common assumptions, such as the existence of a global ecological crisis and the role of experts and scientists and of scientific management in responding to the crisis. But they pointed towards different political implications. See Hajer (1995), for a fuller discussion. On the implications of the "global crisis" thesis for the definition of

A second line of change arose from transformations in the strategy and modes of intervention of many environmental organizations. After the relative decline of the campaigning approach (namely, against nuclear power) which had its peak in the late 1970s and early 1980s, environmental organizations reoriented their action toward an increasing concern with devising feasible responses to well-identified environmental problems as part of a strategy for environmentally sound development, giving rise to so-called "green" expertise as an asset to gain a place in the emerging arena of ecological modernization.[3]

The notion of ecological modernization emerged as a rationale for the reconciliation of economic growth within a capitalist order with the concern for environmental protection and the depletion of resources. It approached environmental regulation as a win–win or positive-sum game; pollution was redefined as a problem of inefficiency to be "fixed" through more efficient (i.e., "green" or "cleaner") technologies; the "balance of nature" was to be respected; "remedial" approaches to the environment were to be replaced with "anticipatory" approaches; and sustainable growth became the alternative to prevailing models of growth (Hajer 1995:65). Ecological modernization, however, is a heterogeneous program. It may be conceived in a "techno-corporatist" or in a "reflexive" mode. The first mode relies upon techno-institutional fixes to problems and the leading role of science and technological development in providing "green" solutions to environmental problems; the second recognizes the centrality of politics and of the need to mobilize citizens to provide solutions that are both environmentally and socially sustainable and just (Hajer 1995:281).

Despite the different and often contradictory definitions of sustainable development by diverse actors, the outright rejection of the concept by some and, in recent years, the aggressive moves by neoconservative governments in several European countries and in the United States toward anti-regulatory policies, sustainable development is a central tenet of European Union policy statements and underlies many of the policy initiatives of international organizations and national governments.[4]

---

environmental problems and policies and of the scales at which these problems are identified and acted upon, see Taylor (1997), and Buttel and Taylor (1992). As we shall see, this is a central issue in place-based conflicts over waste management.

[3] On this, see Hajer (1995) and Jamison (2001).

[4] For discussions, see Redclift (1987, 1999); Sachs (1999); Jamison (2001), and the contributions to Kenny and Meadowcroft (1999), Jamison and Rohracher (2002), and Jamison (1998). An alternative approach, based on experiences from the South (Colombia) can be found in Escobar (2000).

Dissenting voices and forces have emerged, nonetheless, from different countries and regions of the world. They draw on a broad range of forms of knowledge and experience, including the same scientific disciplines and forms of expertise claimed by the hegemonic promoters of sustainable development. They, too, assert the need for environmental regulation and for adequate legal frameworks. But they start from very different premises and are often committed to radical changes in the dominant models of economic growth, technological development, and consumption. Their conception of sustainability is at odds with the attempt at promoting a virtuous circle between a capitalist economy based on the current model of accumulation and the misplaced confidence in the adequacy of techno-institutional "fixes."[5]

Conflicts over waste disposal and management bring a new meaning to the contested notion of "sustainability." They appear at the crossroads of struggles against the exclusion, marginalization, or silencing of groups of people or local populations who are particularly affected by the "externalities" of the dominant mode of economic and social organization associated with neoliberal globalization, on the one hand, and environmental degradation and health hazards, on the other.[6] Like other kinds of struggles, these may originate at the local or national scale and often articulate themselves transnationally, giving rise to initiatives explicitly aimed both at the confrontation with neoliberal globalization and its economic, social, political, and environmental consequences and at the active search for alternatives to it. Taken together, these initiatives, "focused on the struggle against social exclusion, a struggle which in the broadest terms encompasses not only excluded populations but also nature," constitute counter-hegemonic globalization (Santos 2002:459). Both hegemonic and counter-hegemonic forces play with the discrepancies between scales of legality and of regulation in complex, multiscale, regulatory architectures such as the one prevailing within the space of the European Union, and with the well-known discrepancies between law in books and law in action and the effects of the non-enactment or partial enactment of laws. Law (in this case, environmental law) and the

---

[5] On these movements and initiatives, see Santos (2002:Chapter 9). For useful discussions of the diversity of environmental movements across the world with clear counter-hegemonic orientations, see Martinez-Alier and Guha (1997) and Peet and Watts (1996).

[6] On toxic waste management, the health effects of environmental pollutants, and alternative policy proposals for waste disposal and management, see Hofrichter (2000), Gottlieb (2001), Thornton (2000), Kroll-Smith, Brown, and Gunter (2000), and McCally (2002).

regulatory frameworks associated with it are not (nor can they ever be) just ways of disciplining a given field of social practices. The environment appears as a space of intersection of heterogeneous processes (biological, geological, technological, cognitive, social, cultural, legal, and political) giving rise to an "unruly complexity" (Taylor 2001, 2003) which legal or regulatory frameworks fail to contain.

It is often the case that local environmental struggles are dismissed by hegemonic forces as "emotional" displays based on ignorance and irrational fears, as the outcome of manipulations by hidden (or not so hidden) interests, or as instances of the "NIMBY (Not In My Back Yard) syndrome", of selfish refusals to contribute to the response to collective problems. "Scaling up" the struggle, forging alliances with other struggles and with other national and transnational actors are crucial moves for escaping the disqualification of citizen actions and struggles that goes with making the label "local" stick to them.

The case study discussed in the fourth section of this chapter analyzes the different uses of law as a resource in an environmental struggle over waste disposal and management, and how the very object of the struggle was constructed as a heterogeneous assemblage of the scientific/technical, the legal, the political, the economic, and the sociocultural (Irwin and Michael 2003), mobilizing a range of actors across the local, national, and transnational scales. But, first, let us have a brief look at the European and Portuguese legal and institutional frameworks from which this struggle emerged.

15.3 LAW AND ENVIRONMENTAL STRUGGLES IN THE EUROPEAN AND PORTUGUESE CONTEXTS

15.3.1 The European context

The European Union and, in particular, its executive body, the European Commission, is a huge machine of normative production, in the form of directives and regulations, which are binding on member states. These directives and regulations cover nearly every area of public life, including the environment. Delays or failure to transpose directives into the domestic law of member states gives rise to situations where citizens or stakeholders in a given sector may invoke European legality in order to advance their claims, but the tools for making those claims effective within the territory covered by the jurisdiction of the nation state are lacking (though they can be brought to European courts). Within national spaces, counter-hegemonic struggles may take the form of demands for the transposition into domestic law and/ or of the actual application of directives or regulations. In countries where the regulation of fields like the environment or consumer protection was implemented, for all practical purposes, as a consequence of that country's joining the supranational space of the European Communities (now the European Union), this is a common feature of the way law is used in contested fields within the European space.[7]

European regulation of the environmental field has given normative shape to the approach of ecological modernization.[8] The aim is to make a model of development based on a capitalist economy, technological innovation, and a reformed welfare state (the so-called "European social model") compatible with environmental protection and the renewability of resources, through strategies of sustainable development.

15.3.2 The Portuguese context

Beyond the similarities with other countries within the EU, some of the peculiarities of Portugal as a semiperipheral society are particularly interesting from the point of view of the subject of this chapter (Santos, 1990, 1993). These include the absence of a strong, organized civil society based on social movements and citizen organizations and associations; a weak and incomplete welfare state, coupled with a strong welfare society; and a gap between the formal definition of citizens' rights and the actual access to these rights and between advanced legislation and conservative social practices. Differences with other EU countries are not just of a quantitative kind, but they involve structural features and social dynamics which are the outcome of specific historical pathways. In 1974, Portugal emerged from a forty-eight-year-long dictatorship, overthrown by a military coup which opened up a revolutionary period that lasted until November 1975, and saw the end of the Portuguese colonial empire. The 1976 Constitution and, in that same year, the first elections for parliament, the presidency, and local government, marked the beginning of a period of "normalization" of the democratic regime, leading to accession to the European Communities in 1986.

---

[7] Where national legislation existed before the country joined the EU (as in Scandinavia), struggles may have as their object the protection against attempts at "downgrading" the legislation through compliance with European standards, seen as less advanced.

[8] Successive Environment Action Plans, starting in the 1970s, provided the political framing of this regulation. The current plan, from 2002, is the Sixth. For detailed information on these plans, see http://europa.eu.int/comm/environment/.

The extent and pervasiveness of the gap between legal frameworks and social practices, between "law in books" and "law in action," despite constitutional revisions, changes in government policies, and European integration, underline the structural character of this highly visible feature of both politically stable periods and periods of change. Its most obvious expressions are the lack of enforcement of legislation due to the absence of a complementary regulatory framework, the partial or selective enactment of the laws, or the need for exceptional measures for the enforcement of laws.

In Portugal, the market as a regulatory principle has never become as central as it is in other countries, such as the core countries of the EU. The state, in contrast, has appeared as a sort of tutorial entity over Portuguese society. Far from being strong, however, the state is intertwined with many organized interests and corporatist pressure groups. Over the last two decades, there were initiatives by the state itself to reduce the ubiquitous presence of the state in Portuguese society by creating and promoting "secondary civil society" – the outcome of intitiatives of "top-down" creation of civil society, without the underlying dynamics of grass-roots movements or intitiatives – thus giving rise to what Santos (2002:457) has called "strange civil society" – those sectors of society granted civic and political rights but which are denied actual access to social, economic, and cultural rights, including environmental rights.

The 1976 Constitution explicitly recognized environmental rights as basic citizenship rights. But the first move toward a comprehensive environmental politics had to wait until Portugal joined the European Communities in 1986 – as was the case with other areas of social and political life. The new field of environmental politics was mostly the outcome of changes in domestic law in compliance with European directives and regulations, and it opened up a space and new instances of legitimation and appeal for citizen action to make the state, the administration, and the political system more accountable (Gonçalves 2001).

Landmarks in environmental policy in Portugal were the first general environmental law (Lei de Bases do Ambiente, 1987), drafted in compliance with EC requirements, and the creation of the Ministry of the Environment in 1990, regarded as a formal recognition of the environment as a crucial sector of government policies. The actual definition and enactment of a comprehensive legal and regulatory framework in the environmental field, however, was still to come, and the discrepancy between legal frameworks and political and administrative practice persisted, even if under new forms.

The 1980s also witnessed the emergence of new collective actors in the environmental arena. Local and national environmental organizations were created, often as a response to place-based problems. Although their relative weakness – in comparison with movements in other European countries – is often stressed (Rodrigues 1995), some of these organizations have a high public profile. One of them, Quercus, was to become a key actor in the field, drawing on a combination of high-quality scientific expertise and public intervention. Over the years, Quercus strengthened its activist stance. The role of local associations, known as ADAs (Associações de Defesa do Ambiente), in dealing with issues such as the local impacts of household and hazardous industrial waste management was also a prominent one.

Waste management was defined as a priority when a socialist minority government came to power in 1995, though the first measures for dealing with this issue date from 1985. This was followed, the following year, by the creation of the Institute for Waste (Instituto dos Resíduos, or IR) and, in 1997, by a general law on waste management and the definition of Strategic Plans for Solid Household Waste (PERSU), Hospital Waste (PERH), Industrial Waste (PESGRI), and Agricultural Waste (PERAGRI).[9]

The period from 1975 to 1978 had witnessed the first significant mobilizations over environmental issues in Portugal, including large-scale protests with participants from several European countries, such as the one in Ferrel (in central Portugal) against a proposed nuclear plant. But the real boost to environmental activism came in the 1990s, with protests all over the country directed at government policies in relation to the construction of sites for the incineration or co-incineration of industrial hazardous waste and of landfills for household waste. This turned waste management into a central, contested field of Portuguese social and political life over the last decade and an object of broad media coverage. Which specific policy decisions triggered these protests? What were the claims of the protesters and their repertoires of collective mobilization? Who were the new collective actors emerging from these conflicts? How were different forms of legality mobilized by the various actors in these conflicts?

The case presented below provides a convenient point of entry into an exploration of these issues.

---

[9] For details of these plans, see Nunes *et al.* (2002, 2003) and Matias (2002).

15.4 ENVIRONMENTAL STRUGGLES AND COUNTER-HEGEMONIC USES OF LEGALITY: A CASE STUDY[10]

In 1996, Scoreco, a consortium including two Portuguese cement companies (Cimpor and Secil) and a French company (Suez Lyonnaise des Eaux), was created to promote co-incineration as a new technology offering a viable means for the disposal and management of hazardous industrial waste, as well as for generating energy from waste for cement kilns. In December 1998, Souselas[11] was selected as one of four possible sites for the co-incineration facilities, together with Maceira, in the Leiria district. The ensuing public controversy and the first protests against this decision became a major issue in national and local political debate. In January 1999, a Committee for Struggle Against Co-Incineration (CLCC) was created.[12] The local population framed this process as another episode in the twenty-five-year-old history of the difficult co-existence with a cement plant and its impacts on health and the environment. The lack of information on the operation of the cement plant and the consequent distrust of the population were crucial to the emergence of alternative framings of co-incineration and of its impacts.[13]

The controversy and the protest lasted for a period of almost four years. Initiatives taken by local citizens and other actors involved in, or allied to, the protest movement included two petitions to Parliament, delivered in January 1999, which gathered about 65,000 signatures (50,000 from Coimbra and 11,000 from Leiria), calling for the government's decision to be revoked, and several initiatives by local citizen movements and organizations to discuss the drafting of legislative initiatives with members of Parliament. These were accompanied by mass demonstrations, sit-ins and concentrations in front of the cement kiln in Souselas, experiments in "popular epidemiology" (see below), and the organization, in April and June 2000, of an International Forum on Co-Incineration. The first session of the Forum focused on

[10] This section draws upon research by Matias (2002) and by Nunes and Matias (2003).
[11] A small parish in the municipality of Coimbra, located about 5 km from the city centre, which had 3,144 inhabitants in 2001. Maceira was later replaced by Outão, sited in a natural park, near Setúbal.
[12] On the composition of the Committee, see Matias (2002). It included, among others, citizen organizations such as the civic association Pro Urbe, trade unions and local business organizations, local and national environmental associations, and the parish council of Souselas.
[13] These processes are related to the ways in which the actors frame "their claims, their opponents and their identities" (McAdam, Tarrow, and Tilly 2001:16).

alternatives to co-incineration, with the participation of a specialist in cement kilns, an expert in clean production, an official of the European Commission (with expertise in strategies for waste management) and a representative of the Portuguese Ministry of the Environment. The second session, on public participation, gathered activists, counter-experts, and social scientists who discussed the political and social dimensions of industrial waste management and citizen participation. The role of counter-expertise was crucial to a debate in which scientific and technical controversy soon became a central aspect.

From very early on, all the opposition parties represented in Parliament supported a proposal for the suspension of co-incineration until a scientific commission could determine whether it was the safest available method (as their defenders claimed) for the treatment of hazardous industrial waste. This had been one of the demands of the protest movement, and the drafting of the law to be submitted to Parliament was the outcome of intense exchanges between representatives of the movement and members of Parliament. In April 1999, two laws, in fact, had been drafted, one by the Parliament – creating the "Independent Scientific Committee for the Treatment of Dangerous Industrial Waste" – and another by the government – creating the "Independent Scientific Committee for the Environmental Control and Supervision of Co-Incineration." The "dual" regulation of the Comissão Científica Independente (CCI) was "solved" by another law, issued on the same day by the government, stating that the two Committees should be considered one and the same, the (narrower) government's definition of the scope of the task of the committee prevailing and excluding the evaluation of alternative methods. The Committee excluded those experts who had publicly stated their criticism of co-incineration, and the work of the Committee members was largely based on literature reviews, mostly of documents produced by the cement industry. The results of the work by the CCI were (strategically) announced the day before the International Forum organized by the opponents to co-incineration started. In an interview to a national newspaper, the Minister of the Environment declared: "Four scientists are in full agreement. It is now time for a political decision on the matter based on science and objective knowledge and not on prejudice, ignorance or demagogy" (Público, May 20, 2000). Science thus became the ultimate source of legitimacy for government policy. But the report met with the criticisms of counter-experts, particularly of the environmental association Quercus.

In July/August 2000, the process was halted again by a parliamentary initiative of the Green Party. A second committee of experts – the Medical Working Group (GTM) – was formed as part of the CCI to assess the health effects of co-incineration. The group was chaired by one of the members of CCI, and its findings were released in December 2000: co-incineration had no harmful effects on the health of local populations, and the control of emissions would ensure that the risks were "socially acceptable." One of the members of the GTM, however, voted against the report, invoking the uncertainties concerning the consequences of exposure to emissions generated by co-incineration. During the sixty days the medical report was open to public discussion, 11,650 written comments were sent to the Ministry of the Environment contesting the results, but not a single one was considered relevant to the final decision on whether the process should advance or not. Thus, the Minister decided to proceed with the tests of co-incineration. An epidemiological study of the population of Souselas, which had been scheduled to start at the same time, had to be delayed because of a generalized boycott. The publication of the GTM report was accompanied by a "new version" of the CCI report, with the deletion of some of the contents that had been the target of the strongest criticisms by those opposing co-incineration. As a response to the GTM report, in January 2001, several associations joined the Institute of Hygiene and Social Medicine of the University of Coimbra to produce a preliminary analysis of the health situation in Souselas, based on data from the Regional Health Office, suggesting a high prevalence of some types of pathologies associated with environmental factors, such as respiratory pathologies and breast cancer.[14]

By the end of the year, the CCI presented the result of the tests held in Souselas. Once again, these results were contested by a counter-report elaborated by the CLCC, based on the same data, showing that for almost every single parameter measured the level of emissions was higher with co-incineration. Shortly afterwards, after a defeat in the local elections in December 2001, the Prime Minister resigned and national elections were held. The victory of the Social Democratic Party (SPD, liberal) brought the process to a halt, with the decision to drop co-incineration as a method for treating hazardous industrial waste and resuming the task of both completing an inventory of hazardous waste in Portugal and defining a comprehensive strategy for its management.

---

[14] This initiative may be described as a form of what Phil Brown has called popular epidemiology (Kroll-Smith, Brown, and Gunter 2000).

The controversy over co-incineration brought the debates on environmental strategies, citizen participation, scientific expertise, democracy and science, and state–society relations to the public scene. But the scope and depth of the debate were limited by the fact that not just citizen action but scientific controversies as well were dismissed by the government. In fact, the only scientists whose opinions were taken into account in the decision-making processes were the members of the scientific committees who offered the two reports mentioned above. The Portuguese state had little experience with issues of risk management, and these, therefore, were subjected to conventional political strategies, revealing a complete lack of trust and belief in any form of citizen participation, to the point of transforming public consultations into mere formalities. A report by the National Committee for the Environment and Sustainable Development (CNADS), an independent advisory body, though admitting that co-incineration could be a viable response to the problem of hazardous industrial waste, was clear in recommending the opening up of a process of information, dialogue, and consultation with the local population, due to the potential for conflict involved.

Science was not the only source of authority drawn upon by the parties in this struggle. Law played a very central role, both through its use by the protest movement against the government and by the latter and its allies as a weapon against the protesters. Environmental and consumer associations such as Quercus and the National Association for Consumer Protection appealed to the Supreme Administrative Court to suspend or reverse decisions made by the government. Quercus, for instance, invoked lack of access to the document by the state agency (Instituto dos Resíduos) that authorized the start of the tests of co-incineration in Souselas in March 2002 to request the suspension of the tests in the other site. The Court should have decided on the request within ten days, but it took until September 2003 – in a display of the well-known slow pace of the judicial system in Portugal – for a decision to be issued, declaring any action useless, since the process of co-incineration had already been suspended following a vote in Parliament.

The CCI, in turn, in an unprecedented move, sued three scientists who had criticized in public the reports issued by the Committee. The court dismissed the cases against all of them. In this instance, courts of law were used by scientists supporting "official" policies against counter-experts. Fifteen citizens of Souselas were sued as well for the local boycott of the presidential elections of 2000. In December 2001, however, the Attorney's Office suspended the process.

The movement opposing co-incineration combined direct and collective action with a number of initiatives aimed at the revocation or modification of existing legislation or the production of new legislation related to co-incineration and to hazardous waste management in general. Both local government and the Parliament were targeted. On several occasions, between January 1999 and February 2001, representatives of the protest movement met with members of parliamentary opposition parties, with the Parliamentary Committee for Territorial Administration, Local Government, Social Equipment and the Environment, and with representatives from all parties. These meetings led to several parliamentary debates on co-incineration and a number of legislative initiatives by the Green Party with a view to the suspension of the process and to initiating the design of a national strategy for industrial waste based on procedures such as reduction, reuse, and recycling. The largest opposition party, the PSD (liberal), supported the first aim, but insisted on replacing co-incineration with the construction of a specialized incinerator. Some of these initiatives led to a partial convergence among opposition parties and some MPs from the Socialist Party (which supported the government) to suspend the process until more was known on the possible consequences of co-incineration for the environment and human health.

The alliance between the movements against co-incineration, on the one hand, and the institutions and actors of representative democracy, on the other, was crucial for overcoming the attempts at confining the struggle to the local and making it vulnerable to the charge of "NIMBYism." The charge did appear, but the intervention of political parties and the parliamentary debates helped turn the debate over co-incineration into a discussion of options for hazardous industrial waste management and, thus, into a subject of national interest, rather than a parochial struggle over the siting of the waste management units. This articulation was also the condition for turning claims against co-incineration voiced by the movement into legally binding decisions, legitimated by a vote in Parliament.

This case is exemplary as well from the point of view of the way different actors took advantage of the tensions and discrepancies between national, European, and international legality on environmental matters. As a party to the Stockholm Convention (2001), the Portuguese government declared its opposition to any process involving the production of persistent organic pollutants (POPs). The Convention confirmed the preference of member-states for non-thermal alternatives for the treatment of toxic waste, since incineration and co-incineration contribute significantly to the production of POPs. Thus, the government used a double standard, promoting thermal alternatives in Portugal and opposing them in intenational fora. The protest movement took advantage of this duality of discourses to reinforce opposition to co-incineration. In March 2001, the Director of the Scientific Unit of Greenpeace declared that the co-incineration of hazardous industrial waste in the neighborhood of populated areas or of a natural park (the other site that had been proposed by the CCI to replace Maceira) was an "irresponsible" decision by the Portuguese authorities, and as such should be condemned.

European directives on waste management and environmental strategies were put to good use by the protest movement. An instance of this was Directive 2000/76/EC regarding waste incineration, which defines the limits of emissions from cement plants producing hazardous waste. In fact, this Directive was used by the opponents of co-incineration as "proof" that there was a difference between the levels of emissions resulting from cement plants burning hazardous waste and those plants employing other methods of disposal, thus refuting the government's and the CCI's claims that no such difference existed. More generally, frequent reference was made by the movement against co-incineration to European directives and regulations and to international conventions as arguments against government policies and options in the field of waste management. Indeed, under the circumstances, EU law was mobilized as a crucial resource for counter-hegemonic action.

Finally, the conspicuous absence of forms of deliberative democracy or the "hollowing out" of forms of consultation (such as public audiences for the discussion of environmental impact assessments) are closely associated with an exclusionary and authoritarian version of representative democracy, based on the denial of the legitimacy of citizens to make elected political actors or state officials accountable for their actions in any way other than through other representatives or through courts of law. The slow pace of the latter and the costs of sustaining long struggles in the judiciary discourage citizens from resorting to them. As a result, citizen response to secrecy and authoritarian modes of governing (at the national, municipal, and local levels) tends to go through local forms of collective action, falling within the purview of radical democracy (Mouffe, 2000), which, however, search for alliances with opposition forces within representative bodies, such as the national Parliament and municipal assemblies.

15.5 DISCUSSION

Under what conditions do struggles over waste disposal and management qualify as emerging instances of "subaltern cosmopolitanism" (Santos, 2002; Santos and Rodríguez-Garavito's chapter in this volume)? The answer to this question requires careful and detailed analyses of cases that are exemplary in the way they concentrate and display "the potential that lies implicit or hidden" in these struggles, allowing the identification of "emergent qualities and entities at a moment and in a context in which they can be easily discarded as having no future-bearing quality, as being insignificant or indeed as being past oriented" (Santos 2002:465). The play of different legal and regulatory frameworks at different scales offers opportunities for the irruption of counter-hegemonic uses of law. Santos (2002:465–471) discussed the conditions in which translocal and transnational articulations of struggles may give shape to embryonic forms of an alternative, emergent cosmopolitan legality. To what extent does the case analyzed here fulfill these conditions?

1. The case displays a range of practices involving hegemonic legal resources, including the use of courts for access to documents denied by the administration or for contesting decisions or actions taken by hegemonic forces in the name of law, democratic legitimacy, or scientific-technical soundness. Transnational legal or normative resources were also mobilized to counteract the action of the national government. These included European Union directives and regulations as well as international protocols and conventions. The counter-hegemonic character of the mobilization of these resources depends on their integrating heterogeneous configurations of forms of action deployed at different scales and articulating official state legality, EU and international legality, and local, non-official conceptions of legality. These configurations allow uses of hegemonic legal and normative tools which are counter-hegemonic in their effects.
2. Being part of configurations of forms of action, law and rights were combined with a broad repertoire of resources for collective action, including some which were denounced by hegemonic actors (the state, local government, industry, and some scientists and experts) as illegal (blocking the entrance of waste into waste management sites), illegitimate (claiming a voice in debate and decision-making

or making demands on hegemonic actors for accountability to citizens), or irrational (such as claims for the inclusion of citizens in the debate and decision-making and denying legitimacy to scientists, experts, and elected officials to make decisions without a due process of consultation and hearings with the local populations). The references to legality and the claims on hegemonic actors drew on the references to constitutional rights, to existing domestic law, to European directives and regulations, and to international conventions and protocols, and on counter-expertise. Their effectiveness was conditional on the "demonstration effect" (Barry 2001) achieved through broad political mobilizations, including demonstrations, public fora, direct action, petitions to parliament, and legal action.

3. The episode discussed here suggests that the definition of who the subaltern are is dependent on the specific struggles and on the particular forms of power that can be identified in these settings and situations. The struggle does point to the emergence of spaces and situations where heterogeneous actors are denied voice and the right to participate in decision-making processes which may have serious consequences for their health, well-being, and the environment. Citizens who are involved in these processes are thus pushed toward the boundaries of what Santos has called the strange civil society, of conditions that define the subaltern in Portuguese society.
This subaltern condition can provide a ground for mobilizations and forms of collective action pointing toward subaltern cosmopolitanism. It is still an open question, however, whether these will lead to the constitution of coalitions and citizen initiatives which would endow them with some persistence beyond the particular situations that triggered struggles like the one discussed here. The very heterogeneity of the coalitions emerging as new collective actors make it difficult for the latter to persist in the absence of interscalar articulations taking the issue beyond the local context and in the absence of a common, localized focus for continuing struggles. In the two cases, this would involve broadening the struggle against the siting of waste management technologies to an active demand for a strategy for the problem as part of a broader strategy of sustainable development, and creating fora promoting the participation of citizens and the monitoring of environmental policies and actions for local development.

4. Although contested issues were identified first at the local level, citizens and their allies tried to articulate local demands, based on

claims for being treated with justice, with demands for a national solution to the problem of waste disposal and waste management through an alliance with parliamentary forces, and drawing as well on European directives and international conventions to strengthen their case against government policies. The building of interscalar coalitions was a crucial step in the eventual success of this strategy. The outcome of a struggle may depend precisely on the extent to which actors manage to successfully build these interscalar coalitions. This may be achieved through the articulation of forms of participatory and radical democracy, which provide the means for making the problem visible, and the resources of representative democracy, particularly the capacity of parliamentary parties and their members to take legislative initiatives based on collaborations with citizen movements and organizations or with environmental NGOs. This, in turn, requires an active policy of alliances enabling (partial) convergences and collaborations which may be more or less durable, but are certainly indispensable for granting legitimacy and, eventually, binding power to legislative initiatives directed against the government and other hegemonic actors.

5. Populations in small villages or townships are extremely vulnerable to discretionary action by hegemonic actors in matters related to the environment. The selection of sites for landfills and incinerators or co-incinerators usually falls upon those who have neither the numbers nor the political influence to oppose these decisions. These choices are made in the name of a higher national interest in solving a pressing national problem. Any opposition is dismissed or denounced as an instance of the NIMBY syndrome and citizens are thus excluded from having any say in these decisions. Consultation processes, even when they are mandatory, are most often exercises in presenting decisions which either have already been made or will be made without any regard for the arguments of local populations. The way protest is treated – by describing protesters as irrational, manipulated, selfish, or opportunistic – adds to this disqualification of citizens, who are thus pushed to the boundaries of the strange civil society.

6. The principle of the community took shape through collective mobilizations which, even if anchored in the common belonging to a locality and organized for the defense of the local environment and the health of the population, struggled to articulate their local action with broader definitions of appropriate action and

appropriate technologies for waste management. As for the market, citizens and other counter-hegemonic actors opposed hegemonic coalitions which included business interests, but they were active supporters of "green," more environmentally friendly technologies of waste management offered by private companies. Within these specific contexts, both community and market had to be articulated in ways that prevented charges of NIMBYism or of lack of economically and technologically viable alternatives to "end-of-pipe" solutions. Whether the resulting forms of community and market may be labeled as subaltern depends on the context.

7. The gap between the excess of meaning and the deficit of task is one of the main sources of potential weakness of counter-hegemonic movements. On some occasions, expectations that the use of hegemonic legality will allow subaltern actors to have their way may prove excessive, and lead to defeat. On other occasions, expectations that mobilization would allow the subaltern agenda to be pushed forward yielded limited though important results, in so far as they led to an interruption of the process citizens struggled against, but did not extend into the definition and enactment of a comprehensive, anticipatory, or precautionary approach to waste management. The struggle against co-incineration rested upon a definition of its objectives as enacting an agenda akin to "reflexive" ecological modernization, against the hegemonic agenda based on a (formal) "techno-institutional" understanding of environmental policy coupled with a "remedial" approach to waste management. But the outcome of the struggle was conditioned by the difficulty of turning collective mobilization into the emergence of new public spheres allowing citizens and other actors in the process to come together in deliberative fora.

8. The combination of demoliberal legality and "bottom-up" legality under the conditions of a semiperipheral society which is part of a core region of the world-system may be an unavoidable path for collective action, allowing a productive exploitation of the tensions and gaps between legality at different scales in order to promote non-hegemonic responses to the authoritarian enforcement of hegemonic programs. In this instance, the mobilization of EU law, of European directives and regulations, and of more general definitions of EU environmental policies proved to be an important tool for granting legitimacy to the local protest movement in its struggle against the national government and its policies. A more

general point can be made on the need for a *situational* characterization of transnational legality as a resource for counter-hegemony or as a tool for reinforcing hegemony. In other situations, EU legality may be used as a tool for lowering standards of environmental protection that previously existed in a given country, where environmental legislation was more advanced than EU legislation, as in some Scandinavian countries. In these cases, the alleged loss of economic competitiveness may be invoked by businesses, industries, and governments to adopt the less strict standards of the EU. In acceding countries (such as those which were part of the former Soviet bloc), "Europe" and EU directives are often invoked by the state and by governments to promote extensive transformations of national law in different fields, thus foreclosing public debate.

References

Barry, Andrew. 2001. *Political Machines: Governing a Technological Society*. London: Athlone Press.

Beck, Ulrich. 1992. *Risk Society*. London: Routledge.

Buttel, Frederick H., and Peter J. Taylor. 1992. "Environmental Sociology and Global Environmental Change: A Critical Assessment." *Society and Natural Resources* 5:211–230.

Callon, Michel, Pierre Lascoumes, and Yannick Barthe. 2001. *Agir dans un monde incertain: essai sur la démocratie technique*. Paris: Seuil.

Escobar, Arturo. 2000. "El lugar de la naturaleza y la naturaleza del lugar: globalización o postdesarrollo?" Pp. 113–143 in *La Colonialidad del Saber: Eurocentrismo y Ciencias Sociales. Perspectivas Latinoamericanas*, edited by Edgardo Lander. Buenos Aires: CLACSO/UNESCO.

Fischer, Frank. 2000. *Citizens, Experts, and the Environment: The Politics of Local Knowledge*. Durham, NC: Duke University Press.

Gonçalves, Maria Eduarda. 2001. "Europeização e direitos dos cidadãos." Pp. 339–366 in *Globalização: Fatalidade ou Utopia?*, edited by Boaventura de Sousa Santos. Porto: Afrontamento.

Gottlieb, Robert. 2001. *Environmentalism Unbound: Exploring New Pathways to Change*. Cambridge, MA: MIT Press.

Hajer, Maarten. 1995. *The Politics of Environmental Discourse: Ecological Modernization and the Policy Process*. Oxford: Oxford University Press.

Hofrichter, Richard (Ed.). 2000. *Reclaiming the Environmental Debate: The Politics of Health in a Toxic Culture*. Cambridge, MA.: MIT Press.

Irwin, Alan. 1995. *Citizen Science: A Study of People, Expertise and Sustainable Development*. London: Routledge.

Irwin, Alan, and Mike Michael. 2003. *Science, Social Theory and Public Knowledge*. Maidenhead: Open University Press.

Jamison, Andrew (Ed.). 1998. *Technology Policy Meets the Public. PESTO Papers 2*. Aalborg: Aalborg University Press.

2001. *The Making of Green Knowledge: Environmental Politics and Cultural Transformation*. Cambridge: Cambridge University Press.

Jamison, Andrew, and Harald Rohracher (Eds.). 2002. *Technology Studies and Sustainable Development*. Munich: PROFIL.

Kenny, Michael, and James Meadowcroft (Eds.). 1999. *Planning Sustainability*. London: Routledge.

Kroll-Smith, Steve, Phil Brown, and Valerie J. Gunter (Eds.). 2000. *Illness and the Environment: A Reader in Contested Medicine*. New York: New York University Press.

Martinez-Alier, Juan, and Ramachandra Guha. 1997. *Varieties of Environmentalism: Essays North and South*. London: Earthscan.

Matias, Marisa. 2002. *Conhecimento(s), ambiente e participação: A contestação à co-incineradora em Souselas*. Coimbra: Faculty of Economics, University of Coimbra.

McAdam, Douglas, Sidney Tarrow, and Charles Tilly., 2001. *Dynamics of Contention*. Cambridge: Cambridge University Press.

McCally, Michael (Ed.). 2002. *Life Support: The Environment and Human Health*. Cambridge, MA: MIT Press.

Mouffe, Chantal. 2000. *The Democratic Paradox*. London: Verso.

Nunes, João Arriscado, and Marisa Matias. 2003. "Agonistic Spaces, Contentious Politics and the Trials of Governance: Environmental Policies and Conflict in Portugal." Discussion Paper, Science, Technology and Governance in Europe Network.

Nunes, João Arriscado, Jorge Correia Jesuíno, Carmen Diego, Sandra Carvalho, Susana Costa, and Marisa Matias. 2002. "Portuguese National Profile." Discussion Paper, Analysing Public Accountability Procedures in Contemporary European Contexts Project.

Nunes, João Arriscado, Marisa Matias, and Susana Costa. 2003. "Household Waste Management and Public Accountability in Portugal: The Case of the Taveiro Landfill." Discussion Paper, Analysing Public Accountability Procedures in Contemporary European Contexts Project.

Peet, Richard, and Michael Watts, (Eds.). 1996. *Liberation Ecologies*. New York: Routledge.

Redclift, Michael. 1999. "Pathways to Sustainability: Issues, Policies and Theories." Pp. 66–77 in *Planning Sustainability*, edited by Michael Kenny and James Meadowcroft. London: Routledge.

1987. *Sustainable Development: Exploring the Contradictions*. London: Methuen.

Rodrigues, Maria Eugénia. 1995. *Os novos movimentos sociais*. Coimbra: Centro de Estudos Sociais.

Sachs, Wolfgang. 1999. "Sustainable Development and the Crisis of Nature: On the Political Anatomy of an Oxymoron." Pp. 23–41 in *Living with Nature: Environmental Politics as Cultural Discourse*, edited by Frank Fischer and Maarten Hajer. Oxford: Oxford University Press.

Santos, Boaventura de Sousa. 1990. *O Estado e a Sociedade em Portugal (1974–1988)*. Porto: Afrontamento.

1993. "O Estado, as relações salariais e o bem-estar na semiperiferia: O caso português." Pp. 15–56 in *Portugal: Um retrato singular*, edited by Boaventura de Sousa Santos. Porto: Afrontamento.

2002. *Toward a New Legal Common Sense*. London: Butterworths.

Taylor, Peter. 1997. "How Do We Know We Have Global Environmental Problems? Undifferentiated Science – Politics and Its Potential Reconstruction." Pp. 149–174 in *Changing Life: Genomes, Ecologies, Bodies, Commodities*, edited by Peter J. Taylor, Saul E. Halfon, and Paul N. Edwards. Minneapolis: University of Minnesota Press.

2001. "Distributed Agency Within Intersecting Ecological, Social, and Scientific Processes." pp. 313–332 in *Cycles of Contingency: Developmental Systems and Evolution*, edited by S. Oyama, P. Griffiths, and R. Gray. Cambridge, MA: MIT Press.

2003. "A Reconstrução da Complexidade Ecológica Sem Regras: Ciência, Interpretação e Prática Reflexiva Crítica." Pp. 529–551 in *Conhecimento Prudente para uma Vida Decente: 'Um Discurso Sobre as Ciências' Revisitado*, edited by Boaventura de Sousa Santos. Porto: Afrontamento.

Thornton, Joe. 2000. *Pandora's Poison: Chlorine, Health, and a New Environmental Strategy*. Cambridge, MA: MIT Press.

Index